Violence in
Intimate Relationships

CRIMINAL JUSTICE TITLES AVAILABLE FROM BUTTERWORTH–HEINEMANN

African American Perspectives on Crime Causation, Criminal Justice Administration, and Crime Prevention
Anne T. Sulton, 0-7506-9813-6

American Jails: Looking to the Future
Kenneth E. Kerle, 0-7506-9846-2

The Art of Investigative Interviewing
Charles L. Yeschke, 0-7506-9808-X

The Changing Career of the Correctional Officer
Don A. Josi and Dale K. Sechrest, 0-7506-9962-0

Comparative and International Criminal Justice Systems
Obi N. I. Ebbe, 0-7506-9688-5

Contemporary Criminal Law
David T. Skelton, 0-7506-9811-X

Contemporary Policing: Personnel, Issues, and Trends
M. L. Dantzker, 0-7506-9736-9

Crime and Justice in America: A Human Perspective, Fifth Edition
Territo, Halsted, and Bromley, 0-7506-7011-8

Criminal Investigation: Law and Practice
Michael F. Brown, 0-7506-9665-6

Criminal Justice: An Introduction
Philip P. Purpura, 0-7506-9630-3

Criminal Justice Statistics: A Practical Approach
Lurigio, Dantzker, Seng, and Sinacore, 0-7506-9672-9

Criminology and Criminal Justice: Comparing, Contrasting, and Intertwining Disciplines
M. L. Dantzker, 0-7506-9731-8

Death Penalty Cases: Leading U.S. Supreme Court Cases on Capital Punishment
Barry Latzer, 0-7506-9939-6

Explaining Crime, Fourth Edition
Paul S. Maxim and Paul C. Whitehead, 0-7506-9784-9

Introduction to Law Enforcement: An Insider's View
William G. Doerner, 0-7506-9812-8

The Juvenile Justice System: Law and Process
Mary Clement, 0-7506-9810-1

Violence in Intimate Relationships
Nicky Ali Jackson and Giselé Casanova Oates, 0-7506-9874-8

Violence in Intimate Relationships
Examining Sociological and Psychological Issues

Nicky Ali Jackson, Ph.D.
Giselé Casanova Oates, Ph.D.
Purdue University Calumet

Butterworth–Heinemann
Boston Oxford Johannesburg Melbourne New Delhi Singapore

Recognizing the importance of preserving what has been written, Butterworth–Heinemann
prints its books on acid-free paper whenever possible.

 Butterworth–Heinemann supports the efforts of American Forests and the Global
ReLeaf program in its campaign for the betterment of trees, forests, and our
environment.

Library of Congress Cataloging-in-Publication Data
Violence in intimate relationships : examining sociological and
  psychological issues / [edited by] Nicky Ali Jackson, Giselé
Casanova Oates.
     p.   c.m.
  Includes bibliographical references and index.
  ISBN 0-7506-9874-8 (alk. paper)
    1. Family violence. 2. Dating violence. 3. Gays—Abuse of.
4. Aged—Abuse of. I. Jackson, Nicky Ali. II. Oates, Giselé
Casanova.
HV6626V555   1998
362.82'92—dc21   97-45881
                                          CIP

British Library Cataloguing-in-Publication Data
A catalogue record for this book is available from the British Library.

The publisher offers special discounts on bulk orders of this book.

For information, please contact:
  Manager of Special Sales
  Butterworth–Heinemann
  225 Wildwood Avenue
  Woburn, MA 01801-2041
  Tel: 781-904-2500
  Fax: 781-904-2620

For information on all Butterworth–Heinemann books available, contact our World Wide Web
home page at: http://www.bh.com

10 9 8 7 6 5 4 3 2 1

Printed in the United States of America

Contents

About the Editors		**ix**
Contributors		**xi**
Preface		**xiii**
Acknowledgments		**xv**

1   Child Physical Abuse   **1**

Randi M. Tolliver, Linda A. Valle, Cynthia A. Dopke, Laura Dolz Serra, and Joel S. Milner

Definitional and Theoretical Issues	2
Models of Child Physical Abuse	4
Characteristics of Offenders and Victims	6
Prevention and Treatment	12
Conclusion	15
Editorial Summary	15
References	16

2   Child Sexual Abuse   **25**

Judy N. Lam

Historical Recognition of Child Sexual Abuse	27
Legal and Operational Definitions of Child Sexual Abuse	29
Prevalence and Incidence of Child Sexual Abuse	33
Overview of Other Research in the Field	34
Correlates of Child Sexual Abuse	36
Characteristics of Offenders and Victims	40
Prevention and Treatment	43
Legal Issues and Future Trends	46
Conclusion	50
Editorial Summary	50
References	51

3 Child Neglect   57
Shaffdeen A. Amuwo and Jacqueline B. Hill

Historical Recognition of Neglect   57
Organized Efforts Against the Neglect of Children   58
Medical Community's Recognition
    of Child Abuse and Neglect   60
Legal Definitions of Child Neglect   61
Child Abuse Prevention and Treatment Act   62
Overview of Other Research in the Field   64
Correlates of Child Neglect   65
Integrated Model of Child Neglect   67
Characteristics of Offenders and Victims   71
Prevention and Treatment   73
Legal Issues and Future Trends   74
Conclusion   75
Editorial Summary   75
References   76

4 Dating Violence as a Social Phenomenon   83
Carroy U. Ferguson

Historical Recognition of Dating Violence   84
The Emergence of Date Rape as a Special
    Case of Dating Violence   87
What Is Dating Violence? Does It Have Legal Status
    as a Social Phenomenon?   90
Overview of Other Research in the Field   94
Correlates of Abuse for Dating Violence   98
Characteristics of Offenders and Victims   102
Prevention and Treatment   105
Legal Issues and Future Trends   107
Conclusion   109
Editorial Summary   109
References   109

5 Wife Abuse   119
Michael P. Brown and James E. Hendricks

History of Wife Abuse   120
Legal Definition of Wife Abuse   122
The Nature and Extent of Wife Abuse   123
Correlates of Wife Abuse   124
Characteristics of Offenders and Victims   126

Prevention and Treatment   128
Legal Issues and Future Trends   130
Conclusion   131
Editorial Summary   131
References   132

6

Husband Battering: A Review of the Debate over a Controversial Social Phenomenon   **137**

Sylvia I. Mignon

Historical Recognition of Husband Battering   138
Definitions of Husband Battering   141
Overview of Other Research in the Field   143
Correlates of Abuse   147
Characteristics of Offenders and Victims   150
Prevention and Treatment   152
Conclusion   153
Editorial Summary   154
References   154

7

Male-to-Male Gay Domestic Violence: The Dark Closet   **161**

Tod W. Burke

Brief History of Same-Sex Domestic Violence   162
Definition of Domestic Violence   163
Special Concerns   165
Characteristics of Offenders and Victims   167
Cycle of Violence   170
Prevention and Treatment   171
Future Trends and Recommendations   174
Conclusion   175
Editorial Summary   176
References   176

8

Lesbian Battering: The Other Closet   **181**

Nicky Ali Jackson

Historical Recognition of Lesbian Battering   182
Definitions of Abuse   183
Overview of the Research in the Field   184
Correlates of Abuse   185
Characteristics of Offenders and Victims   188
Prevention and Treatment   190

Legal Issues and Future Trends   192
Conclusion   192
Editorial Summary   193
References   193

9 Understanding Elder Abuse and Neglect   195
Jacqueline B. Hill and Shaffdeen A. Amuwo
Historical Recognition of Elder Abuse   196
Legal Definitions of Elder Abuse   197
Definitions of Abuse and Neglect   198
Indicators of Physical Abuse   200
Indicators of Emotional Abuse   201
Overview of Other Research in the Field   201
Characteristics of Offenders and Victims   202
Correlates of Elder Maltreatment   205
Prevention and Treatment   207
Case Example of Financial Exploitation   209
Older Americans Act of 1965   210
Legal Issues and Future Trends   210
Conclusion   211
Editorial Summary   211
References   212
Appendix   217

10 Cultural Perspectives on Intimate Violence   225
Giselé Casanova Oates
Research on Ethnic Minorities and Intimate Violence   227
Cultural Considerations   231
Influence of Culture on Intimate Violence   236
Implications for Prevention and Treatment   237
Conclusion   238
Editorial Summary   238
References   239

Index   245

About the Editors

NICKY ALI JACKSON, Ph.D., is an associate professor of criminal justice at Purdue University Calumet. She has presented numerous papers at conferences on domestic violence, faculty victimization, and law enforcement. She has been an invited speaker, discussing dating violence and harassment, at high schools and universities. Dr. Jackson has been published in several texts as well as in the *Journal of Family Violence*. Her recent publication, *Contemporary Issues in Criminal Justice: Shaping Tomorrow's System*, is being used at several universities. She earned her master's degree in criminal justice from the University of Illinois at Chicago, where she also obtained her doctorate in sociology. Currently, she teaches sociology and criminal justice courses, including Social Problems, Juvenile Delinquency, and Introduction to the Criminal Justice System, and runs the field experience course.

GISELÉ CASANOVA OATES, Ph.D., a clinical psychologist, is an associate professor of psychology and the acting coordinator of the Ethnic Studies Program at Purdue University Calumet. She earned both her master's and doctoral degrees in clinical psychology from Northern Illinois University, DeKalb, Illinois. In her clinical practice, Dr. Oates has worked with victims and perpetrators of physical and sexual abuse. Academically, she has instructed courses on family violence, child abuse, and neglect. She has published and presented articles in the area of physical child abuse, and her research interests include family violence and multicultural issues in psychology.

Contributors

SHAFFDEEN A. AMUWO, Ph.D., is an assistant professor of community health sciences and Assistant Dean for Student Affairs at the School of Public Health, University of Illinois at Chicago. His research interests are domestic and community violence prevention, school and community intervention needs assessment, and international health.

MICHAEL P. BROWN, Ph.D., is an associate professor of criminal justice and criminology at Ball State University. His research interests include criminal justice education, ethical decision making, intermediate sanctions, institutional corrections, and juvenile justice.

TOD W. BURKE, Ph.D., is an associate professor for the Department of Criminal Justice at Radford University, Radford, Virginia. Dr. Burke has published numerous articles in adademic and professional journals and texts on topics including profiling serial killers, Asian gangs, multiple personality as a legal defense, police custody death syndrome, occupational violence, dispatcher stress, privacy on the Internet, home drug testing, education of officers, and use of pepper spray. He has served as an expert on television programs, including *Eye to Eye with Connie Chung*, and he is a former Maryland police officer.

CYNTHIA A. DOPKE, M.A., is a doctoral candidate in clinical psychology at Northern Illinois University. She is currently working on an intervention program for high-risk mothers that is supported by a grant from the Illinois Department of Children and Family Services. Her research interests include the relationship between child physical abuse, social information processing, and stress.

CARROY U. FERGUSON, Ph.D., is a professor at the College of Public and Community Service, University of Massachusetts at Boston and the director of the college's Peer Advising and Service Internship program. Dr. Ferguson is the author of several books in the field. His research and professional work involves looking at the phenomenon of consciousness and its relationship to the quality of personal and societal life.

JAMES E. HENDRICKS, Ph.D., is a professor of criminal justice and criminology at Ball State University. Dr. Hendricks has field experience in the positions of police officer, chief deputy sheriff, deputy coroner, director of a victim advocate program, correctional counselor, and mental health worker. His research interests include crisis intervention, law enforcement, and victim advocacy.

JACQUELINE B. HILL, M.S.W., M.P.H., A.C.S.W., is an assistant professor of social work in the Department of Behavioral Sciences at Purdue University Calumet. Her research interests are child abuse and neglect among drug-abusing women, violence prevention, and education.

JUDY N. LAM, Ph.D., is an assistant professor and Stress Institute faculty member in the School of Psychology at Roosevelt University in Chicago. Her research interests include resiliency in women with histories of child sexual abuse, trauma and resiliency, obsessive-compulsive disorder and anxiety disorders, and cross-cultural manifestations of anxiety disorders.

SYLVIA I. MIGNON, Ph.D., is an assistant professor of criminal justice at the University of Massachusetts at Boston. Dr. Mignon is also on the faculty of the Alcohol and Substance Abuse Studies program there. Her research and publications have included police response to domestic violence, police attitudes toward the death penalty, elderly alcoholism, and physicians' perceptions of alcoholics.

JOEL S. MILNER, Ph.D., is a professor of psychology, distinguished research professor, and director of the Family Violence and Sexual Assault Research program at Northern Illinois University. His current research interests include the description and prediction of intrafamilial child sexual abuse and the testing of a social information processing model of child physical abuse.

LAURA DOLZ SERRA, Ph.D., is a researcher in the Departamento de Psicologia Bascia at the Universidad de Valencia, Valencia, Spain. Her dissertation project and published research use observational techniques to examine the in-home parent-child interactional patterns in physically abusive, high-risk, and nonabused parents.

RANDI M. TOLLIVER, B.A., is a doctoral candidate in clinical psychology at Northern Illinois University. Currently, she is the recipient of a National Institute of Mental Health Research Training Fellowship in the areas of family violence and sexual assault. Her research interests include the effects of social support on child physical abuse sequelae and social information processing styles of aggressive and physically abused adolescents.

LINDA A. VALLE, M.A., is a doctoral candidate in clinical psychology at Northern Illinois University. She is currently project director for a longitudinal study being conducted by the U.S. Navy. Her research interests are in the areas of child maltreatment and interpersonal violence and include cognitive and affective characteristics of perpetrators, victim effects, and the buffering effects of social support.

Preface

Intimate violence issues have become a national concern for Americans. Contrary to popular belief, individuals are more vulnerable to violence by acquaintances than by strangers. Consequently, citizens and policy makers have recognized that problems within the home must not always remain there; at times, it is necessary for the government to intervene. Statutes have been created that specifically address certain types of relationship violence. As a result, police are now being trained on how to handle these cases. Guidelines proposed for detecting abuse have been distributed to schools, churches, hospitals, and social service agencies. In addition, shelters have been developed in the hope of providing immediate assistance to individuals in need.

Researchers initially studied child maltreatment and later examined wife abuse. Subsequently, other populations were recognized as legitimate victims, such as dating couples, husbands, and gay partners. In addition, scholars have explored racial and cultural factors impacting intimate violence. Although public awareness of violence in intimate relationships has increased, it still remains a major social problem. Abolishing violence may be too idealistic: a more realistic goal is to minimize aggressive behavior among intimate partners. Continued research and education will lead to the development of innovative prevention and treatment strategies.

The purpose of *Violence in Intimate Relationships* is to acknowledge various forms of intimate violence, ranging across a person's life span. Each chapter aims to synthesize the extant literature on these topics by addressing the following:

- Historical recognition of the problem
- Definitions of abuse
- Correlates of abuse
- Characteristics of offenders and victims
- Prevention and treatment

The first three chapters are devoted to child maltreatment (physical abuse, sexual abuse, and neglect); there is no possible way to cover this material adequately in one chapter. Chapter 4 examines dating violence. It is important to understand aggression at this level, particularly since Americans are delaying marriage and remaining in dating relationships longer than in the past. Clearly, no intimate violence book would be complete without an examination of spouse abuse. Chapter 5 focuses on wife abuse, and Chapter 6 explores the more controversial topic of husband battering. A population that has typically been ignored in domestic violence literature is homosexuals.

Two chapters are devoted to this topic. Chapter 7 addresses gay male-to-male aggression, and Chapter 8 concentrates on lesbian battering. Chapter 9 examines one of the most neglected areas of intimate violence, elder abuse. Finally, to better serve a society composed of diverse populations, Chapter 10 addresses cultural variations in violent partnerships.

EDITORS' NOTE

The approach of this book is drawn from a family violence perspective. Chapters allow the reader to analyze the material presented critically rather than provide the editors' analysis. It is hoped that the contents of this book will provide useful information and challenge the reader to develop a framework for evaluating theoretical perspectives on intimate violence.

Acknowledgments

We would like to thank Laurel DeWolf of Butterworth–Heinemann for providing guidance and allowing us the freedom to be creative in pulling this project together. Her assistance was invaluable, and it was a pleasure working with her. The editors would also like to acknowledge Argosy for their hard work and support in meeting all deadlines. They are an exceptionally bright and talented group who were invaluable in shaping such a wonderful book. In addition, this book could not have been completed without the contributions of our colleagues. We extend our deep gratitude to them all, who were put under a time constraint, particularly during the holiday season.

Dr. Jackson would specifically like to thank her parents, Dr. Mir Masoom and Firoza Ali, for their love and support in all her endeavors. She also thanks her sisters and brother, Nancy, Mimi, and Ishti, for always helping her remember her familial roots. She has been very fortunate to have such a wonderful family. Last, but most importantly, she must thank her husband, Dr. Ralph F. Jackson, for buying her the computer she long desired. She thanks him for always being there for her and for giving support in her career choices. Without his constant pushing, it would take her forever to complete any task.

Dr. Oates would like to acknowledge her parents, Marguerite Boudreaux Casanova and Isidro Casanova, for their unconditional love and support. She also thanks her siblings, Michele, David, and Nanette, for their encouragement. Finally, she extends her gratitude to her husband, Roger (Vin) Oates, for his patience on those long evenings that she spent with this manuscript instead of with him.

The editors would like to dedicate this book to their children, Rhys Jackson and Tatiyana Oates, who were both born during the preparation of the manuscript. Thanks to both of you for putting up with little sleep and hectic scheduling. They are a joyous addition to the Jackson and Oates families. The contents of the book, along with continued research on intimate violence, will help create safer homes, schools, and neighborhoods for each of you and for future generations.

Child Physical Abuse

**Randi M. Tolliver, B.A., Linda A. Valle, M.A.,
Cynthia A. Dopke, M.A., Laura Dolz Serra, Ph.D.,
and Joel S. Milner, Ph.D.**
Family Violence and Sexual Assault Research Program
Department of Psychology
Northern Illinois University

Recognition of child physical abuse as a social problem has primarily occurred during the twentieth century. The 1874 case of Mary Ellen Wilson, who was beaten almost daily by her stepmother, is frequently regarded as the catalyst for modern child protection efforts (Giovannoni and Becerra, 1979; Oates, 1996; Wiehe, 1992). In 1874, no legal definition of child physical abuse or means of intervening in Mary Ellen's situation existed. Therefore, her case was presented to the New York chapter of the American Society for the Prevention of Cruelty to Animals on the basis that Mary Ellen was a member of the animal kingdom and thus merited the same consideration as animals. Primarily due to Mary Ellen's case, the New York Society for the Prevention of Cruelty to Children was founded in 1875.

Widespread public recognition of child physical abuse, however, did not emerge until the middle of the twentieth century. Between 1946 and 1960, several studies published by American and English physicians described children with conditions such as subdural hematomas and multiple long-bone fractures that appeared to be the results of trauma (see Oates, 1996, for a review). Although some physicians suggested that maltreatment by parents was the cause of the injuries, society overall appeared unwilling to accept the notion that parents intentionally injured their children. In 1962, however, an American physician and his colleagues (Kempe, Silverman, Steele, Droegemueller, and Silver, 1962) published an article that identified

302 children who had received injuries as a result of being "battered" by their care-takers. This article on the battered child syndrome profoundly influenced society's response to the maltreatment of children. By 1966, for example, all fifty states had passed laws requiring physicians to report suspected cases of child physical abuse. State statutes were later expanded to mandate all professionals working with children to report any suspicion of child physical, sexual, and emotional abuse or child neglect (Lindsey, 1994; Wiehe, 1992).

Since mandated reporting legislation was enacted, the number of official reports of abuse and neglect has increased substantially. In 1962, when the "battered child syndrome" (Kempe et al., 1962) first received national attention, 10,000 reports of child maltreatment were made (Lindsey, 1994). In 1994, 2.9 million reports were made (U.S. Department of Health and Human Services, National Center on Child Abuse and Neglect, 1996). Of the suspected maltreatment cases reported in 1994, 1,011,628 reports were confirmed. Approximately 26%, or 255,907, of these children were victims of physical abuse. Thus, 4 out of every 1,000 children younger than eighteen years of age were confirmed victims of physical abuse during 1994. Initial analyses of reports made in 1995 (Daro, 1996) indicated comparable numbers of children were reported and substantiated as victims of child physical abuse and other forms of maltreatment. The number of confirmed reports of child physical abuse probably underestimates the actual incidence rate, however, because most incidents of child maltreatment occur in the privacy of the home and may never be reported (Oates, 1996).

The movement sparked by the publication of the battered child syndrome article included the development of various explanatory models of child physical abuse. In addition, efforts increased to discover the characteristics of child physical abuse perpetrators and victims so that treatment programs could be developed. This chapter discusses definitional and theoretical issues and explanatory models of child physical abuse, then reviews the extant research on child physical abuse perpetrator characteristics and victim effects. The chapter concludes with a discussion of current prevention and treatment efforts.

DEFINITIONAL AND THEORETICAL ISSUES

Definitions specify the core criteria for inclusion in a category. In the case of child physical abuse, the definition determines what incidents are and are not considered to be abusive (Giovannoni and Becerra, 1979). Although the majority of existing definitions emphasize the "nonaccidental physical injury of a child" (Myers, 1992, p. 102), to date no universally accepted definition for child physical abuse has been developed. The use of multiple definitions affects official estimates of the incidence of abuse because incidents defined as abusive in one state may not be defined as abusive in another. The use of multiple definitions of abuse also hinders the integration and comparison of research studies, because researchers may consider very dissimilar actions as physically abusive.

Broad definitions of child physical abuse tend to use general and sometimes vague terms, such as "intent to harm" and "nonaccidental physical injury," which must then be interpreted (Giovannoni and Becerra, 1979; Rubin, 1992; Zuravin, 1991). Because numerous, subjective interpretations of terms such as "nonaccidental" and "intent to harm" are possible, broad definitions tend to encompass a wide range of behaviors. For example, social service agencies, who are charged with investigating reports of abuse, preventing continued abuse, and providing treatment, may broadly define child physical abuse as "endangerment" (i.e., the prediction that the parents' actions will result in harm to the child).

The use of broad definitions facilitates intervening in families considered at risk for child physical abuse and allows for consideration of community and cultural factors related to each individual case (Giovannoni and Becerra, 1979). Subjective interpretation of a term such as "endangerment," however, may result in child welfare workers evaluating cases on the basis of a worker's own value system and personal biases, to the detriment of ethnic minority group parents who may differ from mainstream American society in their child-rearing practices. Evidence suggests that ethnic minority groups are frequently overrepresented among reported cases of child physical abuse (Peled and Kurtz, 1994; Rubin, 1992). Whether this overrepresentation results from evaluation bias, from a greater proportion of minority group members being found in socioeconomically disadvantaged conditions frequently associated with child physical abuse, or from other factors remains an empirical question.

In contrast, narrow definitions of abuse use specific terms and encompass fewer behaviors (Giovannoni and Becerra, 1979; Rubin, 1992; Zuravin, 1991). Narrow definitions tend to be limited to the most severe incidents of physical abuse (Peled and Kurtz, 1994). For example, definitions of child physical abuse used in criminal courts tend to focus narrowly on demonstrable harm, or the consequences of the act (e.g., bruises, broken bones) due to the need for objectivity and unequivocal physical evidence in legal proceedings (Giovannoni and Becerra, 1979).

Two additional issues to consider are the heterogeneous nature of child physical abuse as reported in the literature and the overlap between physical abuse and other forms of child maltreatment. First, incidents defined as child physical abuse under the same definition may still be heterogeneous, differing in chronicity, frequency, and severity (Zuravin, 1991). The majority of abusive incidents tend to fall somewhere between behaviors clearly identifiable as abuse and normal parental disciplinary practices (Rubin, 1992; Straus, 1994). Second, child physical abuse can co-occur with child neglect, child sexual abuse, and child emotional abuse. Determining what characteristics are unique to child physical abuse with respect to etiological factors and victim effects is thus difficult, hindering attempts to design effective prevention and treatment programs. In addition to the lack of agreement on definitional issues, a lack of agreement on theoretical issues characterizes legal, research, and clinical approaches to child abuse (for more detailed discussions, see Ammerman, 1990; Azar, 1991). As the next section illustrates, theoretical explanations or models of child physical abuse differ in their assumptions about the etiology of abuse and emphasize factors from different levels of analysis, including individual, family, community, and cultural factors (e.g., child defects or parental skill deficits, environmental stressors). Theories also vary with respect to the attention given to the factors purported to precipitate abuse (i.e., *what* factors contribute to abuse) versus the processes through which these factors supposedly operate to precipitate abuse (i.e., *how* identified factors contribute to abuse; Ammerman, 1990). Finally, various explanatory models of child physical abuse contain various forms of antecedent-consequent relationships (e.g., single cause, single effect; multiple cause, multiple effect).

MODELS OF CHILD PHYSICAL ABUSE

Historical Overview

Early explanations of abuse focused on factors from single levels of analysis (perpetrator and contextual models) and simple antecedent-consequent relationships. The earliest model, a psychiatric model (Kempe et al., 1962), described perpetrators of child abuse as having pathological personality characteristics that predispose them to behave violently toward their children. Another early model, a sociological model (Gil, 1970), invoked cultural factors such as societal values and economic conditions as the primary explanation for child abuse. The fundamental problem with the early models has been their inability to explain why some parents with an identified "causal" factor (e.g., pathological personality, insufficient financial resources) become abusive, whereas other parents with the same identified "causal" factor do not. For example, data suggest that only 10% of physically abusive parents have mental disorders (Kelly, 1983).

To address some shortcomings of these early models, more complex models began to emerge beginning in the 1970s. In particular, models began to include more than one level of analysis, more complex antecedent-consequent relationships, and attention to both potential causal factors and processes by which these factors might operate. Current explanations can be broadly categorized as interactional and organizational models, which include the following model types: cognitive-behavioral, family systems, learning and situational, parent-child interactions, parent-environment interactions, and sociobiological (for a review, see Tzeng, Jackson, and Karlson, 1991). More detailed descriptions of models are available elsewhere (e.g., Ammerman, 1990; Azar, 1991; Tzeng et al., 1991). Because recent trends have largely focused on cognitive-behavioral and organizational models, further discussion is limited to these types of models.

Organizational Models

Organizational models attempt to delineate the factors important in abuse. Two of the best-known organizational models are the ecological (Belsky, 1980, 1993) and transactional (Cicchetti and Rizley, 1981) models.

The ecological model incorporates the interaction of factors from the individual, family, community, and cultural domains in explaining child physical abuse. Examples of some factors within these domains purported to precipitate abuse include a predisposition to abuse, the presence of intra- and extrafamilial stressors, and cultural values that espouse violence and corporal punishment (Belsky, 1980, 1993).

The transactional model (Cicchetti and Rizley, 1981) suggests that various factors may either increase or decrease the likelihood of child abuse. In this model, factors that increase the likelihood of abuse are considered *potentiating* factors (e.g., poor parental frustration tolerance, abuse-fostering societal values), whereas factors that decrease the likelihood of abuse are called *compensatory* factors (e.g., marital harmony). For both potentiating and compensatory factors, conditions of short duration are considered *transient*, whereas conditions of long duration are called *enduring*. Combinations of these factors and conditions yield four possible components. Transient potentiating factors are termed *challengers,* enduring potentiating factors are called *vulnerability* components, transient compensatory factors are considered *buffers*, and enduring compensatory factors are called *protective* components. Cicchetti and Rizley (1981) posited that the four components are bidirectionally and interactively influential in producing abusive and nonabusive behavior. When potentiating factors outweigh compensatory factors, abusive behavior is predicted.

Taken together, the ecological and transactional models define the complete range of domains and components that may contribute to abuse. That is, potentiating or compensatory factors and transcient or enduring conditions may work at the individual, family, community, and cultural levels to impact abusive and nonabusive behavior. Thus, the ecological and transactional models together provide a useful framework in which to conceptualize factors associated with child physical abuse.

Cognitive-Behavioral Models

Whereas organizational models strive to provide an overview of the factors important in child physical abuse, or *what* domains of factors contribute to abuse, cognitive-behavioral models have been developed in attempts to explicate the processes by which relevant factors operate to precipitate abuse, or *how* identified factors contribute to abuse. Several cognitive-behavioral models have been advanced. For example, one cognitive developmental model focuses on the growth of parental thinking about themselves and their child (Newberger and Cook, 1983). Inadequate cognitive development with respect to the parent role, conventional child norms, child's perspective, and parent-child interactions is purported to contribute to abuse. A second cognitive-behavioral model emphasizes parental expectations, attributions, and overreactions to children's noncompliance (Larrance and Twentyman, 1983; Twentyman, Rohrbeck, and Amish, 1984). As an extension of this model, one proposed social cognitive-behavioral model (Azar, 1986, 1989) suggests that parents' deficient cognitive skills, poor impulse control, and negative interactions with their children precipitate abuse, particularly when combined with high stress or low social support. A transitional model whereby increasingly coercive parent-child interactions are thought to lead to abuse has also been proposed (Wolfe, 1987).

More recently, a social information processing model that integrates the various cognitive processes discussed in the child abuse literature has been advanced (Milner, 1993). Three cognitive processing stages and a fourth cognitive-behavioral response stage are considered. Abusers, compared with nonabusers, are hypothesized to differ in their perceptions of their child's behavior (stage 1); expectations, interpretations, and evaluations that assign meaning to the child's behavior (stage 2); information integration and response selection (stage 3); and response implementation and monitoring (stage 4). Activities at the first three cognitive stages are believed to mediate the final parental behavior response implementation and monitoring stage. The existence of preexisting information structures (e.g., beliefs about the appropriateness of corporal punishment) are proposed to impact processing at the cognitive stages. In addition, factors from other ecological levels (e.g., environmental stressors) are thought to impact information processing and thus parenting behavior.

CHARACTERISTICS OF OFFENDERS AND VICTIMS

Characteristics of Offenders

Research has found many common characteristics among perpetrators of child physical abuse that can be grouped into several overlapping domains: demographic and social, biological, cognitive and affective, and behavioral (e.g., Milner and Chilamkurti, 1991). Table 1–1 provides an outline of offender characteristics supported to varying degrees by research. Before discussing the research, however, note that

Table 1–1 Child Physical Abuse: Characteristics of Offenders.

Demographic and social factors
  Nonbiological, single, or young parent
  Large number of children
  Lower socioeconomic status
  Childhood history of receiving or observing maltreatment
  Current family conflict
Biological factors
  Neuropsychological deficits
  Psychophysiological hyperreactivity
  Physical health problems
Cognitive and affective factors
  Alcohol and drug disorders
  Emotional problems and negative affectivity
  Loneliness and social isolation
  Low self-esteem, low ego strength, external locus of control
  Stress and distress
  Differences in processing of child behavior
  Hostility toward children and empathy deficits
Behavioral factors
  Problem-solving skill deficits
  Problematic parent-child interactions
  Attachment problems

factors found to be associated with child physical abuse do not necessarily cause abuse. Associated factors may simply be markers for other, underlying causal influences. For example, lower socioeconomic status, which is associated with abuse, does not itself cause abuse. Lower socioeconomic status, however, is associated with lower levels of parental affection, poor communication, and negative parent-child interactions, which may all contribute to abusive behavior.

Demographic and Social Factors Approximately 80% of all perpetrators of child physical abuse are parents or other caretakers (National Center on Child Abuse and Neglect, 1996). Stepparenthood is associated with child physical abuse and has been hypothesized to reflect a lesser emotional commitment to the child (Daly and Wilson, 1996). When the outcome is severe injury, however, the relationship between stepparenthood and abuse appears to hold only for male perpetrators (Hegar, Zuravin, and Orme, 1994). Other demographic and social factors associated with abusive behavior appear to reflect lower levels of parental resources. For example, being a single parent or a young parent, having a large number of children, and having lower socioeconomic status are associated with physical abuse (Cappelleri, Eckenrode, and Powers, 1993; Creighton, 1985). A childhood history of receiving or observing maltreatment is also a risk factor (see Kaufman and Zigler, 1987). Similarly, evidence suggests that current family conflict (e.g., marital disharmony and violence) is associated with child physical abuse (see Wolfe, 1985).

Biological Factors The role of offender neuropsychological deficits in abuse remains unclear. Elliott (1988) suggested that some disorders (e.g., episodic dyscontrol, antisocial personality, and attention deficit disorder) associated with neuropsychological deficits present risks for child abuse. Elliott also suggested that specific cognitive deficits, such as problems in verbal processing, reduce parents' ability to cope with family problems and increase the risk for child physical abuse. One study (Nayak and Milner, 1995) reported inferior performance by individuals at high risk, compared with low risk, for child physical abuse on measures that assess conceptual ability, cognitive flexibility, and problem-solving ability.

Knutson (1978) proposed that child physical abusers possess a hyperreactive trait. Psychophysiological studies generally support the view that abusers and at-risk parents are more physiologically reactive to child-related and stressful non–child-related stimuli (for reviews, see Milner and Chilamkurti, 1991; Wolfe, 1985). Although the manner in which physiological reactivity contributes to child physical abuse has yet to be demonstrated, autonomic lability is thought to increase the likelihood that parents will react to children's behavior with verbal and physical aggression.

Compared with nonabusers, child physical abusers report more physical handicaps and health problems (e.g., Conger, Burgess, and Barrett, 1979) and have more psychosomatic illnesses (Steele and Pollock, 1968). Although it is unclear if abusive parents have more physical health problems or if they simply report more physical problems, parental reports of frequent physical health problems appear to be associated with an increased risk for parenting problems.

Cognitive and Affective Factors   Research has not supported the early conceptualization that child abuse is precipitated by pathological personality characteristics in the abuser (Kempe et al., 1962). As mentioned previously, less than 10% of abusers have been found to have mental disorders (Kelly, 1983). Although most child physical abusers are not mentally ill, psychopathology does appear to increase the risk for parenting problems and may be related to severe abuse (e.g., death). An association also appears to exist between child physical abuse and alcohol and drug disorders (Kelleher, Chaffin, Hollenberg, and Fischer, 1994). In addition, abusive parents are more likely than comparison parents to report emotional problems and negative affectivity, especially depression, anxiety, and hostility (for a review, see Milner and Chilamkurti, 1991). Abusive parents report more feelings of loneliness, which may reflect reduced levels of social support, a potential compensatory factor for child abuse, than nonabusive parents. Personality factors associated with offenders of child abuse include poor ego strength, low self-esteem, and an external locus of control, which includes blaming others for one's problems (see Milner and Chilamkurti, 1991).

Research generally supports the notion that abusive, compared with nonabusive, individuals report more stress in their lives (e.g., life event changes, daily hassles, and parenting stressors; see Milner and Chilamkurti, 1991). Whether or not abusers are actually exposed to more stressors or merely report more exposure is unclear, yet abusers appear to perceive stressors as more aversive (see Wolfe, 1985). In addition, evidence suggests that abusers, compared with nonabusers, do not use social supports, which may serve to buffer the negative effects of environmental stressors (see Wolfe, 1985). Not only are environmental stressors associated with child abuse, but they appear to be related to the level of perceived justification by abusers for their violent behavior (Dietrich, Berkowitz, Kadushin, and McGloin, 1990).

Several cognitive and affective differences between abusers and nonabusers specifically related to children have been reported (for reviews, see Milner and Chilamkurti, 1991; Wolfe, 1985). For example, abusers appear to have an inadequate knowledge of child development. Compared with nonabusers, abusers also report more problematic behavior in their children, which is most evident in specific circumstances (i.e., everyday living situations, ambiguous situations, and mildly aversive situations), and evaluate child behaviors more negatively. In some contexts, abusive mothers make different attributions for children's behavior, most often attributing more blame and hostile intent to their child when judging the child's negative behaviors. Abusers are likely to have inappropriate expectations regarding their children's abilities in situations that involve complex child behaviors. In addition, abusers experience higher levels of hostility in response to a distressed child and concomitantly report less empathy for children than nonabusers. The combination of the last two factors may increase the likelihood of child assault.

Behavioral Factors   A number of behavioral differences between abusers and nonabusers appear to reflect general problem-solving and specific parenting skill deficits (see Cerezo, 1997; Milner, 1993; Wolfe, 1985). Overall, compared with nonabusive parents, abusive parents appear to have poorer problem-solving skills (e.g., Hansen, Pallotta, Tishelman, Conaway, and MacMillan, 1989). In terms of parent-child interactions, physically abusive parents, relative to nonabusive parents, appear to use ineffective and excessively negative parenting methods that may serve to maintain problematic parent-child relations (for reviews, see Milner and Chilamkurti, 1991; Wolfe, 1985). Compared with nonabusers, abusers engage in fewer interactions and communicate less with their children. When interactions occur, abusive parents are more intrusive, rigid, and inconsistent than nonabusive parents and also use more harsh disciplinary techniques and fewer positive parenting behaviors to manage their children's behavior. For example, abusive parents more often use verbal and physical assertion and less reasoning and explaining as well as less praise and rewards than do nonabusive parents. Parent-child attachment problems have also been reported among abusing parents and their children.

Characteristics of Victims

Although much of the research in the field of family violence has focused on the behavior and treatment of the abusive parent, significant attention has been directed toward determining the consequences of abuse (e.g., Conaway and Hansen, 1989; Hansen, Conaway, and Christopher, 1990; Lamphear, 1985; Malinosky-Rummell and Hansen, 1993). Table 1–2 provides an outline of victim characteristics supported by research. Although there are numerous ways of conceptualizing the damaging effects of child physical abuse on its victims, a developmental perspective is taken here. A developmental perspective asserts that the developing individual is embedded in and dynamically interactive with his or her social context and that changes in either the individual or context thus may alter the course of development (Lerner, 1988). An individual's early patterns of adaptation may be incorporated into later adaptive patterns, and likewise an individual's early disturbances in functioning are likely to contribute to the emergence of later deviant behaviors (Houck and King, 1989). Therefore, infants and children who are physically abused appear to be at greater risk for adaptive failure during early development, which may continue throughout their lives.

Although information about victim effects has been arranged according to broad developmental stages, extant data are insufficient to make a direct link between the emergence and persistence of particular consequences of child physical abuse and specific life stages (Milner and Crouch, 1993). The developmental framework presented here is used only to indicate the importance of recognizing the impact of abuse from a developmental perspective.

Infancy and Early Childhood   As mentioned earlier, physical and neurological damage (e.g., subdural hematoma, fracture of long bones, multiple soft tissue injuries) are potential consequences of physical abuse during development (Kempe et al., 1962; Kolko, Moser, and Weldy, 1990). For example, Dykes (1986) conducted a follow-up study of Caffey's (1974) "shaken baby syndrome." Caffey reported that shaking an infant by the trunk or extremities produces acceleration-deceleration of the head, leading to shearing and stress on attachments between outer surfaces of the brain and inner surfaces of the skull, resulting in subdural hematomas. The most severe and irreversible consequence of child physical abuse is death. At least 1,111

Table 1-2   Child Physical Abuse: Characteristics of Victims.

Infancy and early childhood
  Physical and neurological damage
  Insecure attachments
  Avoidance of peers
  Negative social interactions
Middle and late childhood
  Aggressiveness, hyperactivity, conduct problems (externalizing behaviors)
  Social detachment and withdrawal (internalizing behaviors)
  Sleep disturbances
  Intellectual deficits
Adolescence
  Conduct problems
  Aggressiveness
  Juvenile delinquency
  Depression
Adulthood
  Aggressiveness
  Low self-esteem
  Social isolation
  Increased incidence of abuse toward own children

children in the United States died as a result of being abused or neglected in 1994 (U.S. Department of Health and Human Services, 1996).

During infancy and early childhood, physically abused children, when compared with nonabused children, demonstrate a greater degree of insecure attachments to caretakers (Crittenden and Ainsworth, 1989; Egeland and Sroufe, 1981). For example, Egeland and Sroufe (1981) found that one-year-old physically abused infants, after being left alone in a strange situation and then reunited with their parent, tended to avoid contact and maintain distance from their parent. In contrast, securely attached children directly approached and sought proximity with their parent. Physically abused children also have been observed to avoid peers more often (George and Main, 1979; Haskett and Kistner, 1991) and to engage in more negative social interactions (Haskett and Kistner, 1991; Howes and Eldredge, 1985; Klimes-Dougan and Kistner, 1990; Main and George, 1985) than nonabused children.

Middle and Late Childhood   One of the most frequently cited behavioral consequences of child physical abuse during middle and late childhood is the predominance of externalizing behavior problems, such as excessive aggressiveness, hyperactivity, and conduct problems (Dodge, Bates, and Pettit, 1990; Jaffe, Wolfe, Wilson, and Zak, 1986; Kinard, 1980; Widom, 1989; Wolfe and Mosk, 1983). Kaufman and Cicchetti (1989) reported that children who were physically abused, compared with victims of other forms of child maltreatment, were rated by their peers as significantly more aggressive.

Even though a history of child physical abuse is often associated with an array of externalizing behaviors, abused children, compared with nonabused children, also have been reported to demonstrate higher levels of internalizing behaviors, including social detachment, withdrawal, acute anxiety, sleep disturbance, and self-destructiveness (Green, 1978; Kaufman and Cicchetti, 1989). Physically abused children also tend to exhibit lower self-esteem (Green, 1978; Kazdin, Moser, Colbus, and Bell, 1985), depression (Kazdin et al., 1985), and more frequent suicidal ideation (Green, 1978) than nonabused children. Kaufman and Cicchetti (1989) reported the tendency for abused children to exhibit both externalizing and internalizing behavioral tendencies, whereas other children display one or the other behaviors. Therefore, the relationship between the use of aggression and withdrawal as a coping mechanism for physically abused children is often unclear.

In addition, compared with nonabused children, physically abused children have been reported to earn lower scores on standardized measures of intelligence (Barahal, Waterman, and Martin, 1981; Hoffman-Plotkin and Twentyman, 1984) and psycholinguistic abilities (Morgan, 1979; Vondra, Barnett, and Cicchetti, 1990) and to demonstrate more academic deficits (Morgan, 1979; Wodarski, Kurtz, Gaudin, and Howing, 1990). Physically abused children have been reported to have delayed reading skills and language development (Oates, Peacock, and Forrest, 1984). Environmental variables (e.g., neglect, impoverishment) that often coexist with physical abuse, however, may contribute to the intellectual deficits observed in physically abused children (Bee et al., 1982; Vondra, Barnett, and Cicchetti, 1990).

Adolescence   The receipt of child physical abuse in adolescence appears to have consequences similar to those reported in earlier developmental stages. For example, the receipt of child physical abuse in adolescence has been associated with conduct problems (Carlson, 1991; Williamson, Bourduin, and Howe, 1991), aggressive behavior (Zimrin, 1986), and juvenile delinquency (Famularo, Kinscherff, Fenton, and Bolduc, 1990; McCord, 1983; Wodarski et al., 1990). Compared with nonabused adolescents, adolescents who have been physically abused also tend to exhibit depression (Becker, Kaplan, Tenke, and Tartaglini, 1991; Farber and Joseph, 1985), anxiety (Farber and Joseph, 1985), difficulty in establishing interpersonal relationships (Zimrin, 1986), and suicidal ideation (Farber and Joseph, 1985).

Whether physical abuse of adolescents is a continuation of abuse that began during childhood or whether it results from changes in parent-child interactions as the child reaches adolescence and the family faces different developmental challenges remains an important issue (Lourie, 1979). Garbarino (1989) suggested that family interactions in which physical abuse emerges only as the child moves into adolescence appear to differ from interactions in families in which the abuse begins during childhood (Garbarino, 1989). For example, parents who physically abused their adolescents, compared with parents who abused preadolescents, are less likely to have been abused themselves during childhood.

Adulthood   Research indicates that, compared with adults without a childhood history of abuse adults with childhood histories of physical abuse exhibit higher incidences of aggressiveness (Briere and Runtz, 1990; Kroll, Stock, and James, 1985), more problems related to alcohol use (Brown and Anderson, 1991; Kroll et al., 1985; Martin and Elmer, 1992), lower self-esteem, and increased social isolation (Altemeier, O'Connor, Sherrod, and Tucker, 1986). For example, in a forty-year prospective study, McCord (1983) investigated the quality of interaction between 232 males and their respective parents. Results suggested that men who had been physically abused, neglected, or rejected as children, compared with men who had at least one parent who seemed to be pleased with the behavior of and concerned about the welfare of the child, were at higher risk for becoming alcoholic, mentally ill, or involved in criminal activity.

Researchers also have reported that parents who were abused as children tend to display an increased incidence of abuse toward their own children (e.g., Kempe et al., 1962). Between 7% and 68% of physically abusive parents have reported the receipt of physical abuse during childhood (e.g., Farber and Joseph, 1985; Gil, 1970; Herrenkohl, Herrenkohl, and Toedter, 1983). This relationship is known as the intergenerational transmission of aggression and suggests that patterns of violent behavior are passed from one generation to the next (see reviews by Kaufman and Zigler, 1987; Widom, 1989). It is necessary to note, however, that not all adults who were physically abused children abuse their own children.

PREVENTION AND TREATMENT

As mentioned previously, potentiating and compensatory factors present at the level of the individual, family, community, and societal levels may interact to increase or decrease episodes of child maltreatment (Cicchetti and Rizley, 1981). Parental practices, poverty, neighborhood environment, cultural background, social isolation, and multiple stressors are several necessary factors that should be considered in effective child abuse prevention (Belsky, 1980). Therefore, physical abuse prevention programs attempt to reduce the likelihood of physical maltreatment by improving functional factors (e.g., parental skills and knowledge regarding the child's development and behavior) and by mitigating structural factors (e.g., poverty, poor neighborhood conditions).

Types of Prevention and Treatment

Treatment efforts may be directed at families with a documented history of maltreatment (tertiary prevention), directed at selected populations deemed to be at risk for child physical abuse (secondary prevention), or aimed at social problems such as reducing the incidence of abuse and identifying concern in the general population (primary prevention) (for reviews, see Wekerle and Wolfe, 1993; Wolfe, Reppucci, and Hart, 1995).

Tertiary prevention emphasizes preventing the recurrence of child physical abuse. Interventions with abusive parents typically involve skills training in child management, anger control, stress management, or a combination of the three (Azar and Wolfe, 1989), and such behavioral and cognitive approaches and social network interventions appear promising (Wolfe and Wekerle, 1993). Intervention also often includes providing educational resources; cognitive restructuring; decreasing parents' use of power-assertive discipline and aversive parent-child interactions; increasing appropriate parent-child interactions; and improving parents' problem-solving abilities, social skills and social support system, self-control, and stress-management skills (Cerezo, 1992). The effectiveness of these interventions at preventing abuse may be diminished, however, because identified abusers are often defensive and resistant to entering therapy (Morton, Twentyman, and Azar, 1988).

Secondary prevention is directed toward families seriously at risk for child maltreatment. Secondary prevention uses some form of screening criteria, testing, or risk assessment to identify groups at risk for child physical abuse (Milner, 1986). For example, secondary prevention programs (e.g., Healthy Families America, Opening Doors) select participants according to sociodemographic variables associated with maltreatment in the literature (i.e., risk factors) or use a cutoff score on a scale of abuse potential (Wekerle and Wolfe, 1993). Treatment may be offered to the child, the parents, or the entire family. Interventions at the secondary level include educational programs for pregnant and parenting teenagers, assisting new parents in strengthening parent-infant attachment (Wekerle and Wolfe, 1993), and improving parents' sensitivity and responsiveness to their children. In addition, programs seek to increase parents' overall ability to care for their infants, thereby reducing the probability of child illness as a stressor and decreasing false attributions of a child's aversive behavior as well as increasing parental self-efficacy (Azar and Siegel, 1990).

Primary prevention assumes that all families are more or less at risk for child physical abuse and is not concerned with screening or diagnosis (Milner, 1986). Primary prevention consists of programs directed at different age levels and developmental phases of family life within a given community. The programs begin during the prenatal period and furnish prospective parents with information and skills related to infant care and development. Many programs also provide education and support for parents with infants and preschool-aged children, with continuing child services after the child reaches school age. The programs may be directed toward several areas, including increasing community knowledge about child physical abuse and its prevention, providing education in life skills, providing parent education and support groups, and increasing the number of child abuse prevention agencies in the community (National Committee to Prevent Child Abuse, 1990).

Focus of Prevention

Although the preceding review suggests that a broad range of prevention programs exist, professionals working with physically abusive families tend to direct their efforts more specifically toward three areas: increasing parental competence (Wekerle and Wolfe, 1993; Wolfe and Wekerle, 1993; Azar and Siegel, 1990), increasing economic self-sufficiency of families, and discouraging societal values that condone the use of corporal punishment and other forms of violence (Hay and Jones, 1994). To date, however, programs focused on increasing parental competence have received the most attention.

"Competence" is a general evaluative term referring to the quality or adequacy of a person's overall performance in a particular task. A competent performance need not be exceptional, but merely adequate (McFall, 1982). Parental competence has been defined as sensitivity to the child's developing abilities and communication (Wolfe and Wekerle, 1993). Competent parents possess an adequate repertoire of child-rearing strategies and problem-solving skills that allow them to adapt their responses appropriately to any given situation and to the skill level of their child (Azar and Siegel, 1990). Parental competence is influenced by parental factors (e.g., parents' level of education, child-rearing attitudes, background experiences), child characteristics (e.g., child temperament, health, developmental level), and the family context (e.g., marital relationship, quality of social networks and support, community resources; Belsky, 1984). Professionals seek to increase parental competence in five areas that are reportedly problematic for physically abusive parents: altering maladaptive interpretive processes (e.g., unrealistic expectations of children, poor problem-solving skills, negative evaluations of child behavior), improving parenting skills, improving impulse control, improving the ability to cope with stress, and increasing social skills (Azar and Siegel, 1990).

With respect to economic self-sufficiency, one of the most frequently cited structural factors contributing to elevated risk of maltreatment is poverty (Gelles, 1983, 1992; Gil, 1970; Kempe et al., 1962; Pelton, 1978; Steele and Pollack, 1968). Poverty may have indirect effects that increase the likelihood of problems considered to be related to maltreatment or poor outcomes (Hay and Jones, 1994). For example, poor families tend to have higher levels of stress, to begin parenting at earlier ages, and to have limited knowledge about child care compared with more economically self-sufficient families. Although structural risk factors in general and in the role of poverty have received less attention from child maltreatment prevention specialists than programs focusing on increasing parental competence, prevention programs for at-risk families should include training that combines improving the parent's educational level, vocational skills, and employment status with child-related services, such as preventive health care, parenting education, day care, and early childhood education (Quint, Fink, and Rowser, 1991).

At the societal level, education may be the crucial component for reducing acceptance of violence. As mentioned, recognition of child abuse as a social problem has occurred primarily during the twentieth century. The use of corporal punishment and other forms of violence by parents may continue because these behaviors have historical foundations in many cultures, as evidenced by policies for dealing with children in schools and other institutions, religious teachings, the media, and oral and written history (Hay and Jones, 1994; Hay and Volpe, 1992). Educating families in family relations, parenting skills, and child development may help prepare future generations to fulfill parental roles without violence (Hay and Jones, 1994).

In addition, mass media (e.g., television, radio, video games) have the potential to contribute greatly to the promotion or prevention of child physical abuse. The media can increase risks for child abuse by glorifying violence and by unrealistically portraying families and children. A clear link exists between violent and antisocial entertainment and the abuse of children and other vulnerable persons (Hay and

Jones, 1994), and evidence suggests that exposure to television violence encourages aggressive behavior by both children and adults (Heath, Bresolin, and Rinaldi, 1989). The media can also serve as an agent for prevention (Hay and Jones, 1994; Olsen and Spatz, 1993) by providing positive and entertaining materials at a low economic and environmental cost. Educational programs for adults (e.g., parent education, child development, child care) and children (e.g., problem solving without violence, communication with peers) are available for home use and facilitate learning. Unfortunately, such programs are limited in availability.

CONCLUSION

Although research in the areas of child physical abuse offender characteristics and victim effects and outcome research on prevention programs has been accumulating, additional research is needed. A number of factors have been associated with child physical abuse. Which etiological factor or combination of factors are necessary and sufficient to cause physical abuse, however, remains to be determined. Similarly, a direct link has not been established between the receipt of abuse at various developmental stages and its detrimental effects on subsequent physical, affective, behavioral, and cognitive development. Finally, additional research is needed to determine the effectiveness of existing prevention and treatment programs as well as to facilitate the development of new programs.

EDITORIAL SUMMARY

Child physical abuse has been a longstanding problem, yet its recognition as a social problem did not occur until the twentieth century. The 1874 case of Mary Ellen Wilson is often regarded as the catalyst for current child protection efforts and the founding of the Society for the Prevention of Cruelty to Children. In 1962, an article identifying and describing the battered child syndrome added impetus to the child protection movement.

No universally accepted definition for child physical abuse has been developed. The use of multiple definitions affects official estimates of incidence of abuse and hinders the integration and comparison of research studies. Broader definitions of child physical abuse use general terms, such as "intent to harm" and "nonaccidental physical injury," which are left to subjective interpretation. Narrow definitions use specific terms, encompass fewer behaviors than the broad definitions, and tend to be limited to the most severe incidents of physical abuse. A variety of models have been proposed to explain the causes of child physical abuse. Each model emphasizes factors from different levels of analysis, including individual, family, community, and cultural factors.

Common characteristics among perpetrators of child physical abuse have been identified and can be grouped into several overlapping domains: demographic and social, biological, cognitive and affective, and behavioral factors. Child physical abuse may alter the course of development for its victims. Physical abuse that occurs during early developmental stages (i.e., infancy and childhood) may contribute to the emergence of later deviant behaviors.

Prevention programs tend to direct their efforts toward three areas: increasing the competency of parents, increasing the economic self-sufficiency of families, and discouraging the tolerance that society has for violence and the use of corporal punishment. The physical abuse of children is a serious societal problem, and continued research is needed to determine the effectiveness of existing prevention programs and to give further insight into offender characteristics and victim effects.

REFERENCES

Altemeier, W. A., O'Connor, S., Sherrod, K. B., and Tucker, D. (1986). Outcome of abuse during childhood among pregnant low-income women. *Child Abuse and Neglect, 10,* 319–330.

Ammerman, R. T. (1990). Etiological models of child maltreatment: A behavioral perspective. *Behavior Modification, 14,* 230–254.

Azar, S. T. (1986). A framework for understanding child maltreatment: An integration of cognitive behavioural and developmental perspectives. *Canadian Journal of Behavioural Science, 18,* 340–355.

Azar, S. T. (1989). Training parents of abused children. In C. E. Schaefer and J. M. Briesmeister (Eds.), *Handbook of Parent Training* (pp. 414–441). New York: Wiley.

Azar, S. T. (1991). Models of child abuse: A metatheoretical analysis. *Criminal Justice and Behavior, 18,* 30–46.

Azar, S. T., and Siegel, B. R. (1990). Behavioral treatment of child abuse: A developmental perspective. *Behavior Modification, 14,* 279–300.

Azar, S. T., and Wolfe, D. A. (1989). Child abuse and neglect. In E. J. Mash and R. A. Barkley (Eds.), *Treatment of Childhood Disorders* (pp. 451–493). New York: Guilford Press.

Barahal, R. M., Waterman, J., and Martin, H. P. (1981). The social cognitive development of abused children. *Journal of Consulting and Clinical Psychology, 49,* 508–516.

Becker, J. V., Kaplan, M. S., Tenke, C. E., and Tartaglini, A. (1991). The incidence of depressive symptomology in juvenile sex offenders with a history of abuse. *Child Abuse and Neglect, 15,* 531–536.

Bee, H. L., Barnard, K. E., Eyres, S. J., Gray, C. A., Hammond, M. A., Spietz, A. L., Snyder, C., and Clark, B. (1982). Prediction of IQ and language skills from perinatal status, child performance, family characteristics, and mother-infant interaction. *Child Development, 53,* 1134–1156.

Belsky, J. (1980). Child maltreatment: An ecological integration. *American Psychologist, 35,* 320–335.

Belsky, J. (1984). The determinants of parenting: A process model. *Child Development, 55,* 335–343.

Belsky, J. (1993). Etiology of child maltreatment: A developmental-ecological analysis. *Psychological Bulletin, 114,* 413–434.

Briere, J., and Runtz, M. (1990). Differential adult symptomatology associated with three types of child abuse histories. *Child Abuse and Neglect, 14,* 357–364.

Brown, G. R., and Anderson, B. (1991). Psychiatric morbidity in adult inpatients with childhood histories. *Child Abuse and Neglect, 14,* 357–364.

Caffey, J. (1974). The whiplash shaken infant syndrome: Manual shaking by the extremities with whiplash-induced intracranial and intraocular bleedings, linked with residual permanent brain damage and mental retardation. *Pediatrics, 54,* 396–403.

Cappelleri, J. C., Eckenrode, J., and Powers, J. L. (1993). The epidemiology of child abuse: Findings from the Second National Incidence and Prevalence Study of Child Abuse and Neglect. *American Journal of Public Health, 83,* 1622–1624.

Carlson, B. E. (1991). Outcomes of physical abuse and observation of marital violence among adolescents in placement. *Journal of Interpersonal Violence, 6,* 526–534.

Cerezo, M. A. (1992). *Programa de asistencia psicologica a familias con problemas de relacion y de abuso infantil* (The psychological program for families with relational problems and child abuse). Valencia, Spain: Generalitat Valenciana. IVSS.

Cerezo, M. A. (1997). Abusive family interaction: A review. *Aggression and Violent Behavior, 2,* 215–240.

Cicchetti, D., and Rizley, R. (1981). Developmental perspectives on the etiology, intergenerational transmission, and sequelae of child maltreatment. *New Directions for Child Development, 11,* 31–55.

Conaway, L. P., and Hansen, D. J. (1989). Social behavior of physically abused and neglected children: A critical review. *Clinical Psychology Review, 9,* 627–652.

Conger, R. D., Burgess, R. L., and Barrett, C. (1979). Child abuse related to life change and perceptions of illness: Some preliminary findings. *Family Coordinator, 28,* 73–78.

Creighton, S. J. (1985). An epidemiological study of abused children and their families in the United Kingdom between 1977 and 1982. *Child Abuse and Neglect, 9,* 441–448.

Crittenden, P. M., and Ainsworth, M. D. S. (1989). Child maltreatment and attachment theory. In D. Cicchetti and V. Carlson (Eds.), *Child Maltreatment: Theory and Research on the Causes and Consequences of Child Abuse and Neglect* (pp. 432–463). New York: Cambridge University Press.

Daly, M., and Wilson, M. I. (1996). Violence against stepchildren. *Current Directions in Psychological Science, 5,* 77–81.

Daro, D. (1996). Current trends in child abuse reporting and fatalities: NCPCA's 1995 annual fifty-state survey. *The APSAC Advisor, 9*(2), 21–24.

Dietrich, D., Berkowitz, L., Kadushin, A., and McGloin, J. (1990). Some factors influencing abusers' justification of their child abuse. *Child Abuse and Neglect, 14,* 337–345.

Dodge, K. A., Bates, J. E., and Pettit, G. S. (1990). Mechanisms in the cycle of violence. *Science, 250,* 1678–1683.

Dykes, L. J. (1986). The whiplash shaken infant syndrome: What has been learned? *Child Abuse and Neglect, 10,* 211–221.

Elliot, F. A. (1988). Neurological factors. In V. B. Van Hasselt, R. L. Morrison, A. S. Bellack, and M. Hersen (Eds.), *Handbook of Family Violence* (pp. 359–382). New York: Plenum Press.

Egeland, B., and Sroufe, L. A. (1981). Attachment and early maltreatment. *Child Development, 52,* 44–52.

Famularo, R., Kinscherff, R., Fenton, T., and Bolduc, S. M. (1990). Child maltreatment histories among runaway and delinquent children. *Clinical Pediatrics, 29,* 713–718.

Farber, E. D., and Joseph, J. A. (1985). The maltreated adolescent: Patterns of physical abuse. *Child Abuse and Neglect, 9,* 201–206.

Garbarino, J. (1989). Troubled youth, troubled families: The dynamics of adolescent maltreatment. In D. Cicchetti and V. Carlson (Eds.), *Child Maltreatment: Theory and Research on the Causes and Consequences of Child Abuse and Neglect* (pp. 685–706). New York: Cambridge University Press.

Gelles, R. J. (1983). International perspectives on child abuse and neglect. *Child Abuse and Neglect, 7,* 375–386.

Gelles, R. J. (1992). Poverty and violence toward children. *American Behavioral Scientist, 35,* 258–274.

George, C., and Main, M. (1979). Social interactions of young abused children: Approach, avoidance, and aggression. *Child Development, 50,* 306–318.

Gil, D. G. (1970). *Violence Against Children.* Cambridge, MA: Harvard University Press.

Giovannoni, J. M., and Becerra, R. M. (1979). *Defining Child Abuse.* New York: Free Press.

Green, A. H. (1978). Psychopathology of abused children. *Journal of the American Academy of Child Psychiatry, 17,* 92–103.

Hansen, D. J., Conaway, L. P., and Christopher, J. S. (1990). Victims of child physical abuse. In R. T. Ammerman and M. Hersen (Eds.), *Treatment of Family Violence* (pp. 17–49). New York: Wiley-Interscience.

Hansen, D. J., Pallotta, G. M., Tishelman, A. C., Conaway, L. P., and MacMillan, V. M. (1989). Parental problem-solving skills and child behavior problems: A comparison of physically abusive, neglectful, clinic, and community families. *Journal of Family Violence, 4,* 353–368.

Haskett, M. E., and Kistner, J. A. (1991). Social interactions and peer perceptions of young physically abused children. *Child Development, 62,* 979–990.

Hay, T., and Jones, L. (1994). Societal interventions to prevent child abuse and neglect. *Child Welfare, 73,* 379–403.

Hay, T., and Volpe, R. (1992). *Discouraging Corporal Punishment of Children through Legislation and Education.* Paper presented at International Society for the Prevention of Child Abuse and Neglect, Ninth International Congress, Chicago.

Heath, L., Bresolin, L. B., and Rinaldi, R. C. (1989). Effects of media violence on children. *Archives of General Psychiatry, 46,* 376–379.

Hegar, R. L., Zuravin, S. J., and Orme, J. G. (1994). Factors predicting severity of physical child abuse injury: A review of the literature. *Journal of Interpersonal Violence, 9,* 170–183.

Herrenkohl, E. C., Herrenkohl, R. C., and Toedter, L. J. (1983). Perspectives on the intergenerational transmission of abuse. In D. Finkelhor, R. J. Gelles, G. T. Hotaling, and M. A. Straus (Eds.), *The Dark Side of Families: Current Family Violence Research* (pp. 305–316). Beverly Hills, CA: Sage.

Hoffman-Plotkin, D., and Twentyman, C. T. (1984). A multimodal assessment of behavioral and cognitive deficits in abused and neglected preschoolers. *Child Development, 55,* 794–802.

Houck, G. M., and King, M. C. (1989). Child maltreatment: Family characteristics and development consequences. *Issues in Mental Health Nursing, 10,* 193–208.

Howes, C., and Eldredge, R. (1985). Responses of abused, neglected, and non-maltreated children to the behaviors of their peers. *Journal of Applied Developmental Psychology, 6,* 261–270.

Jaffe, P., Wolfe, D., Wilson, S., and Zak, L. (1986). Similarities in behavioral and social maladjustment among child victims and witnesses to family violence. *American Journal of Orthopsychiatry, 56,* 142–146.

Kaufman, J., and Cicchetti, D. (1989). Effects of maltreatment on school-age children's socioemotional development: Assessments in a day-camp setting. *Developmental Psychology, 25,* 516–524.

Kaufman, J., and Zigler, E. (1987). Do abused children become abusive parents? *American Journal of Orthopsychiatry, 57,* 186–192.

Kazdin, A. E., Moser, J., Colbus, D., and Bell, R. (1985). Depression symptoms among physically abused and psychiatrically disturbed children. *Journal of Abnormal Psychology, 94,* 298–307.

Kelleher, K., Chaffin, M., Hollenberg, J., and Fischer, E. (1994). Alcohol and drug disorders among physically abusive and neglectful parents in a community-based sample. *American Journal of Public Health, 84,* 1586–1590.

Kelly, J. A. (1983). *Treating Child-Abusive Families: Intervention Based on Skills-Training Principles.* New York: Plenum Press.

Kempe, C. H., Silverman, F. N., Steele, B. F., Droegemueller, W., and Silver, H. K. (1962). The battered-child syndrome. *Journal of the American Medical Association, 181,* 14–17.

Kinard, E. M. (1980). Emotional development in physically abused children. *American Journal of Orthopsychiatry, 50,* 686–696.

Klimes-Dougan, B., and Kistner, J. (1990). Physically abused preschoolers' responses to peers' distress. *Developmental Psychology, 26,* 599–602.

Knutson, J. F. (1978). Child abuse as an area of aggression research. *Journal of Pediatric Psychology, 3,* 20–27.

Kolko, D. J., Moser, J. T., and Weldy, S. R. (1990). Medical/health histories and physical evaluation of physically and sexually abused child psychiatric patients: A controlled study. *Journal of Family Violence, 5,* 249–267.

Kroll, P. D., Stock, D. F., and James, M. E. (1985). The behavior of adult alcoholic men abused as children. *Journal of Nervous and Mental Disease, 173,* 689–693.

Lamphear, V. S. (1985). The impact of maltreatment on children's psychosocial adjustment: A review of the research. *Child Abuse and Neglect, 9,* 251–263.

Larrance, D. T., and Twentyman, C. T. (1983). Maternal attributions and child abuse. *Journal of Abnormal Psychology, 92,* 449–457.

Lerner, R. M. (1988). Personality development: A life-span perspective. In E. M. Hetherington, R. M. Lerner, and E. M. Perimutter (Eds.), *Child Development in Life-Span Perspective* (pp. 21–46). Hillsdale, NJ: Lawrence Erlbaum.

Lourie, I. S. (1979). Family dynamics and the abuse of adolescents: A case for a developmental phase specific model of child abuse. *Child Abuse and Neglect, 3,* 967–974.

Lindsey, D. (1994). Mandated reporting and child abuse fatalities: Requirements for a system to protect children. *Social Work Research, 18,* 41–54.

Main, M., and George, C. (1985). Responses of abused and disadvantaged toddlers to distress in agemates: A study in the day care setting. *Developmental Psychology, 21,* 407–412.

Malinosky-Rummell, R., and Hansen, D. J. (1993). Long-term consequences of childhood physical abuse. *Psychological Bulletin, 114,* 68–79.

Martin, J. A., and Elmer, E. (1992). Battered children grown up: A follow-up study of individuals severely maltreated as children. *Child Abuse and Neglect, 16,* 75–87.

McCord, J. (1983). A forty-year perspective on effects of child abuse and neglect. *Child Abuse and Neglect, 7,* 265–270.

McFall, R. M. (1982). A review and reformulation of the concept of social skills. *Behavioral Assessment, 4,* 1–33.

Milner, J. S. (1986). *The Child Abuse Potential Inventory: Manual* (2nd ed.). Webster, NC: Psytec Corporation.

Milner, J. S. (1993). Social information processing and physical child abuse. *Clinical Psychology Review, 13,* 275–294.

Milner, J. S., and Chilamkurti, C. (1991). Physical child abuse perpetrator characteristics: A review of the literature. *Journal of Interpersonal Violence, 6,* 345–366.

Milner, J. S., and Crouch, J. L. (1993). Physical child abuse. In R. L. Hampton, T. P. Gullotta, G. R. Adams, E. H. Potter, and R. P. Weissberg (Eds.), *Family Violence: Prevention and Treatment* (pp. 25–55). Newbury Park, CA: Sage.

Morgan, S. R. (1979). Psycho-educational profile of emotionally disturbed abused children. *Journal of Clinical Child Psychology, 8,* 3–6.

Morton, T. L., Twentyman, C. T., and Azar, S. T. (1988). Cognitive-behavioral assessment and treatment of child abuse. In N. Epstein, S. E. Schlesinger, and W. Dryden (Eds.), *Cognitive-Behavioral Therapy with Families* (pp. 87–117). New York: Brunner/Mazel.

Myers, J. E. B. (1992). *Legal Issues in Child Abuse and Neglect.* Newbury Park, CA: Sage.

National Center on Child Abuse and Neglect. (1996). *Child Maltreatment 1994: Reports from the States to the National Center on Child Abuse and Neglect.* Washington, DC: U.S. Department of Health and Human Services.

National Committee to Prevent Child Abuse. (1990). *Adolescent Parents Services Evaluation Final Report.* Report prepared by L. Barbera-Stein, M. Breen-Upsal, E. Jones, J. Kraft, K. McCurdy, L. Mitchel, C. Moelis, D. Sherman, and D. Daro. New York: William T. Grant Foundation.

Nayak, M. B., and Milner, J. S. (1995). *Neuropsychological Functioning: Comparison of Mothers at High- and Low-Risk for Child Physical Abuse.* Manuscript submitted for publication.

Newberger, C. M., and Cook, S. J. (1983). Parental awareness and child abuse: A cognitive-developmental analysis of urban and rural samples. *American Journal of Orthopsychiatry, 53,* 512–524.

Oates, R. K. (1996). *The Spectrum of Child Abuse: Assessment, Treatment, and Prevention.* New York: Brunner/Mazel.

Oates, R. K., Peacock, A., and Forrest, D. (1984). The development of abused children. *Developmental Medicine and Child Neurology, 26,* 649–656.

Olsen, J. L., and Spatz, C. (1993). Prevention of child abuse and neglect. *Applied and Preventive Psychology, 2,* 217–229.

Peled, T., and Kurtz, L. (1994). Child maltreatment: The relationship between developmental research and public policy. *The American Journal of Family Therapy, 22,* 247–262.

Pelton, L. H. (1978). Child abuse and neglect: The myth of classlessness. *American Journal of Orthopsychiatry, 48,* 608–617.

Quint, J. C., Fink, B. L., and Rowser, S. L. (1991). *New Chance: Implementing a Comprehensive Program for Disadvantaged Young Members and Their Children.* New York: Manpower Demonstration Research Corporation.

Rubin, G. B. (1992). Multicultural considerations in the application of child protection laws. *Journal of Social Distress and the Homeless, 1,* 249–271.

Steele, B. F., and Pollock, C. B. (1968). A psychiatric study of parents who abuse infants and small children. In R. E. Helfer and C. H. Kempe (Eds.), *The Battered Child* (pp. 103–147). Chicago: University of Chicago Press.

Straus, M. A. (1994). *Beating the Devil Out of Them: Corporal Punishment in American Families.* New York: Lexington Books.

Twentyman, C. T., Rohrbeck, C. A., and Amish, P. L. (1984). A cognitive-behavioral model of child abuse. In S. Saunders, A. M. Anderson, C. A. Hart, and G. M. Rubenstein (Eds.), *Violent Individuals and Families: A Handbook for Practitioners* (pp. 87–111). Springfield, IL: Charles C. Thomas.

Tzeng, O. C., Jackson, J. W., and Karlson, H. C. (1991). *Theories of Child Abuse and Neglect.* New York: Praeger.

U.S. Department of Health and Human Services, National Center on Child Abuse and Neglect. (1996). *Child Maltreatment 1994: Reports from the States to the National Center on Child Abuse and Neglect.* Washington, DC: U.S. Government Printing Office.

Vondra, J. I., Barnett, D., and Cicchetti, D. (1990). Self-concept, motivation, and competence among preschoolers from maltreating and comparison families. *Child Abuse and Neglect, 14,* 525–540.

Wekerle, C., and Wolfe, D. A. (1993). Prevention of child physical abuse and neglect: Promising new directions. *Clinical Psychology Review, 13,* 501–540.

Widom, C. S. (1989). Does violence beget violence? A critical examination of the literature. *Psychological Bulletin, 106,* 3–28.

Wiehe, V. R. (1992). *Working with Child Abuse and Neglect.* Itasca, IL: F. E. Peacock.

Williamsom, J. M., Bourduin, C. M., and Howe, B. A. (1991). The ecology of adolescent maltreatment: A multilevel examination of adolescent physical abuse, sexual abuse, and neglect. *Journal of Consulting and Clinical Psychology, 59,* 449–457.

Wodarski, J. S., Kurtz, P. D., Gaudin, J. M., Jr., and Howing, B. A. (1990). Maltreatment and the school-age child: Major academic, socioemotional, and adaptive outcomes. *Social Work, 35,* 506–513.

Wolfe, D. A. (1985). Child-abusive parents: An empirical review and analysis. *Psychological Bulletin, 97,* 462–482.

Wolfe, D. A. (1987). *Child Abuse: Implications for Child Development and Psychopathology.* Newbury Park, CA: Sage.

Wolfe, D. A., and Mosk, M. D. (1983). Behavioral comparisons of children from abusive and distressed families. *Journal of Consulting and Clinical Psychology, 51,* 702–708.

Wolfe, D. A., Reppucci, N. D., and Hart, S. (1995). Child abuse prevention: Knowledge and priorities. *Journal of Clinical Child Psychology, 24,* 5–22.

Wolfe, D. A., and Wekerle, C. (1993). Treatment strategies for child physical abuse and neglect: A critical progress report. *Clinical Psychology Review, 13,* 473–500.

Zimrin, H. (1986). A profile of survival. *Child Abuse and Neglect, 10,* 339–349.

Zuravin, S. J. (1991). Research definitions of child physical abuse and neglect: Current problems. In R. H. Starr, Jr., and D. A. Wolfe (Eds.), *The Effects of Child Abuse and Neglect: Issues and Research* (pp. 100–128). New York: Guilford Press.

2

Child Sexual Abuse

Judy N. Lam, Ph.D.
School of Psychology
Roosevelt University

Child sexual abuse (CSA) has been documented in numerous research studies and clinical investigations as a prevalent phenomenon. Many professionals consider a history of CSA to be a precursor of significant emotional and behavioral disturbances in adulthood. The findings cut across disciplines, and the literature of the medical, psychiatric, psychological, social work, nursing, and legal communities reflects a continuing and growing concern about CSA and its aftereffects. This chapter provides an overview of the research on CSA, specifically in the areas of (1) historical recognition of CSA, (2) definitions of CSA, (3) causes of CSA, (4) consequences of CSA, (5) profiles of offenders and victims, (6) prevention strategies, and (7) legal issues and future trends.

First, though, consider two challenges in any examination of CSA. Three pervasive forms of denial have to be recognized and removed. As a person at the individual level, as a person at the professional level, and as a citizen at the societal level, one may engage in denial, not wanting to believe that CSA is a prevalent occurrence. In addition, terms have to be carefully selected. Each term, such as "offender" or "victim," used to label the people who are involved in CSA may have a meaning that is specifically associated with that term.

CSA is a form of abuse that is also known as incest when it occurs in the family context. Given this cultural preconditioning, it is not surprising that citizens and professionals often respond with a sense of revulsion and disbelief accompanied by a wish to discredit reports of CSA as a result of a need to deny a universally unpleasant fact (Ganzarain and Buchele, 1988). It has been widely acknowledged that Sigmund Freud, the originator of psychoanalysis, was one of the first professionals in the early

1900s to uncover and then repudiate the reality of incest, or intrafamilial CSA, in the lives of his patients. More recently, Kluft (1990) shared his own process of discovery, from ignorance to eventual understanding, about his personal experiences with CSA: "I recalled how my ignorance did not become awareness, understanding, and knowledge without going through prolonged and recurrent phases of skepticism, disbelief, and denial" (p. 11). Kluft (1990), however, undertook self-analysis and uncovered that he, during his childhood, had known several girls and women who were victims of incest. The somewhat affluent and sheltered nature of his neighborhood had not been able to protect its members from CSA. Thus, Kluft (1990) concluded that to maintain his sense of security and comfort he had succumbed to a universal need to suppress knowledge about incest. Kluft (1990) reasoned: "It is emotionally easier for us to believe that such occurrences are infrequent or apocryphal or occur only to individuals who are very different from us" (p. 34).

Thus, we must be aware of our own attitudes and beliefs toward CSA as well as to monitor any emerging knowledge of our personal experiences with this phenomenon. Confronting CSA may be difficult because this type of abuse can challenge our sense of self and our assumptions about the innocence of children. Should we uncover no personal experiences with CSA, we could turn to one of the many excellent books that have been published since the 1970s to understand the subjective experience of a CSA survivor (Bass and Thornton, 1983; Blume, 1990). Prior to the media's unflinching attention and the public's gradual acceptance of CSA, Armstrong (1978) compiled a volume of moving narratives from twenty-six women who had survived incest. The power of these survivors' voices may help us to set aside our own need to engage in denial to protect ourselves from the shock and horror of CSA. The complexity of the thoughts and feelings that these survivors experienced as children during their abusive encounters and as adults during their healing processes have been powerfully documented. CSA activities tend to be chronic occurrences of fast and brutal events, but as children, these survivors often did not recognize any feelings of anger or hate. Instead, these survivors recounted feelings of being persuaded, cajoled, threatened, deceived, seduced, coerced, or betrayed by the offenders. We may feel a sense of gratitude about these survivors' courageous revelations, because we know that their testimonials have contributed to dramatic changes in the society's attitudes toward CSA.

Next, let us look at the meanings commonly associated with the use of the specific terms—victim, survivor, resilient adult, offender, aggressor, abuser, and perpetrator—to label individuals. It has been argued that we run the risk of labeling people and placing them in rigid categories by the designations that we choose to use. The terms "victim" and "perpetrator" may imply that a crime had been substantiated when, in fact, the CSA activities were merely alleged, not corroborated, or never referred to the criminal justice system. Professionals active in the area of CSA often disagree about which of these terms to use, but they have been careful about providing clear rationales for the terms they do choose to use.

For example, Blume (1990) considered the term "victim" to be an accurate description of the captive child, who is truly passive and helpless. This term points out that the child was not the wrongdoer but instead the unfortunate subject of a sexual crime. On the flip side, the term overlooks the power the child might have been given over other members in his or her family, or in other situations, because of the "specialness" of his or her role as the CSA victim (Ganzarain and Buchele, 1988). The next term, "survivor," is the most appropriate to describe a person who has, in some ways, triumphed against incredible odds: "On one level, that term can be applied simply because she is still here. . . . On a deeper level, she is a 'survivor' because a 'victim' is characterized by passive helplessness and is seen with pity . . . there is strength, dignity, resilience, and entitlement to respect" (Blume, 1990, p. 20). Higgins (1994) agreed with the emphasis on a person's strength and proposed that the term "resilient adults" be used instead because it captures the spirit of these characteristics better than the term "survivor." Higgins (1994) reasoned: "Unlike the term survivor, resilient emphasizes that people do more than merely get through difficult emotional experiences, hanging on to inner equilibrium by a thread" (p. 1). More importantly, "Resilience captures the active process of self-righting and growth that characterizes some people so essentially" (Higgins, 1994, p. 1).

Here, the terms "victims" when discussing children and "survivors" or "resilient adults" when discussing adults with histories of CSA are used. Finally, the terms "offenders," "aggressors," "abusers," and "perpetrators" refer to the individuals who had been alleged to have perpetrated CSA activities on children. These terms do not mean that the allegations of CSA had actually been substantiated in a court of law.

HISTORICAL RECOGNITION OF CHILD SEXUAL ABUSE

The historical recognition of CSA was, in essence, society's fight against denial and how this struggle progressed. In the twentieth century, the struggle to overcome denial has evolved through four phases, characterized as follows: (1) CSA happened, but it really did not happen; (2) CSA happened, but it really was not so harmful; (3) CSA happened, but it is really harmful and we should do something about it; and (4) CSA happened, and I can tell you how really harmful it is because it happened to me.

During the first phase, psychoanalysts were among the first to acknowledge CSA and among the first to rescind the existence of CSA. Freud shed light on the negative consequences of incest in his paper, entitled the *Aetiology of Hysteria,* published in 1896 (Westerlund, 1986). He presented his groundbreaking theory and findings to his colleagues at the Vienna Society for Psychiatry and Neurology. In investigating the psychic links underlying his adult patients' hysterical symptoms, Freud accumulated evidence that, as children, many of the women were sexually abused by their fathers or by individuals trusted by their families. During the presentation, however, Freud tried to make his findings more acceptable by citing that random strangers or untrustworthy governesses were the typical perpetrators of CSA.

Freud's colleagues, embedded in the conservative culture of the day, expressed vigorous doubts that CSA actually took place. Freud quickly rescinded his original findings and reformulated his theory to regain professional credibility and to lessen the impact of his socially unacceptable findings. According to Westerlund (1986), Freud chose to repudiate his patients' recollections and to hypothesize that the CSA activities did not actually take place. Instead, he interpreted his patients' accounts as mere flights of fancy and expressions of unconscious desires (Westerlund, 1986). In this reformulation, Freud denied the basic experience reported by his patients: their subjective reactions to the reality of their CSA experiences. As a result, for several decades psychoanalysis concerned itself with the more culturally acceptable theory of psychosexual development rather than confronting the reality of powerful adults violating the trust of dependent children through unwanted sexual assault.

During the second phase, researchers overcame the recognition problem, but they still did not recognize the negative effects of CSA. Nearly half a century went by before Ferenczi (1949), another psychoanalyst, took the term "incest" literally and further documented its negative aftereffects in his child patients. Despite this early contribution, other authors that followed did not condemn CSA as being globally harmful. A few investigators concluded that CSA experiences had relatively minor effects on adult adjustment (Gagnon, 1965). For example, Bender and Blau (1937), who were among the first to document the effects of sexually abusive activities on children, did not find any negative aftereffects. Instead, they found that some of the children had initiated, maintained, and concealed the sexual encounters. This finding led the authors to conclude that these children were deriving benefits from the sexual relationships with adults. Another example involves researchers who conducted the first national survey of sexual habits and patterns. Kinsey, Pomeroy, Martin, and Gebhard (1948) found that as many as one in four women and one in ten men were sexually assaulted, before age eighteen, by someone they knew. Instead of condemning CSA, however, these researchers speculated that the child victims probably would not be disturbed by such sexual contact had they not been culturally conditioned to respond negatively to being sexually assaulted.

During the third phase, other historical factors set the stage for a wider recognition of CSA and its aftereffects (Bagley and King, 1990). First, children finally emerged as a special class worthy of protection. Legislative actions were pursued following the publication of an article focused on the negative effects of child abuse, entitled "The battered-child syndrome," by Kempe, Silverman, Steele, Droegemueller, and Silver (1962). By 1966, despite the sparse literature, all fifty states in the United States had passed legislation that "allowed for a diagnosis of CSA with corroborating medical evidence of trauma" (Pfohl, 1977, as cited in Bagley and King, 1990, p. 32). Second, the civil rights movement of the 1950s and 1960s raised women's consciousness. As a result, many people began to question and to attack prevailing social and political forces. Issues relevant to women's lives such as abortion, rape, and assault and violence within relationships were reframed as widespread social injustices rather than individuals' personal pathologies. Third, the breakthrough in the research community came with full force in the 1970s and 1980s. As clinical and empirical research proliferated, landmark studies on the effects of CSA on the psychosocial and sexual functioning of CSA victims and survivors were published (see Browne and Finkelhor, 1986; Herman, 1981; Russell, 1983).

During the fourth phase, numerous survivors broke through their own denial and invited societal confrontation by speaking out about their CSA experiences. CSA survivors' sources of anguish and triumphs were told. The survivors' testimonials, in conjunction with the growing body of professional literature, brought about society's unprecedented attention to the reality of CSA. Finally, CSA was recognized as a widespread social problem with far-reaching effects that merit serious examination so that it can be treated effectively and, perhaps eventually, be prevented. Currently, the collective knowledge base is a joint venture being cocreated by CSA survivors and professionals. Accounts written by CSA survivors or narrated to professionals document rich descriptions of painful childhood experiences and subsequent healing processes. Blume (1990) observed that much of what is known about CSA came, appropriately, from the survivors: "Professionals are letting go of the tendency to tell incest survivors about themselves, and are letting the survivors have their own voice. In this regard, I, like my colleagues, am a conduit, not an originator" (p. xvii). This statement resounds with integrity because it acknowledges the centrality of CSA survivors' knowledge gained through experience. In giving voice to their experiences, resilient adults who survived CSA symbolically rejected the domination intrinsic to the experience of CSA and countered the objectification inherent to a professional investigation of CSA.

CSA survivors, in conjunction with professionals and concerned citizens, had collectively forced society to confront the reality of CSA. Therefore, it is disturbing that the unprecedented societal attention of individuals and communities within our society has not yet deterred new occurrences of CSA. Given that the prevalence of CSA had remained constant, the public is somehow reassured by publicized accounts of how people had "survived and triumphed over" CSA to be productive and resilient individuals. The ranks of these resilient adults include celebrities whose personal trials and tribulations are known to millions of people around the world. In addition to their triumphs, celebrities such as Oprah Winfrey, Rosanne Barr, and many others help to demystify the notion that CSA is something that happens to them, not to us. Their accounts serve to reinforce the collective responsibility of individuals within this society to hear and respond to CSA survivors' voices in an empathic and humane manner. CSA occurs in all groups regardless of ethnicity or socioeconomic status. When CSA happens in one family, the reverberations of its consequences impact each and every one of us, no matter how far removed from that particular family. CSA does not just injure one person or individuals within one family; CSA affects everyone within our society.

LEGAL AND OPERATIONAL DEFINITIONS OF CHILD SEXUAL ABUSE

There are major challenges associated with legally and operationally defining CSA. These two major categories of definitions serve different purposes. The purpose of a legal definition of CSA is essentially to allow the prosecution of CSA perpetrators to proceed. The purpose of an operational definition, on the other hand, is to allow the accumulation of knowledge about CSA and its aftereffects to continue.

The Child Abuse Prevention and Treatment Act of 1974, Public Law (P.L.) 93-247, provided a legislated and specific definition of sexual abuse:

> The term "sexual abuse" includes—(i) the employment, use, persuasion, inducement, enticement, or coercion of any child to engage in, or having a child assist any other person to engage in, any sexually explicit conduct (or any simulation of such conduct) for the purpose of producing any visual depiction of such conduct, or (ii) the rape, molestation, prostitution, or other such form of sexual exploitation of children, or incest with children, under circumstances which indicate that the child's health or welfare is harmed or threatened thereby, as determined in accordance with regulations prescribed by the Secretary. (Department of Health and Human Services, 1986, p. 50)

The 1978 amendments, Title I of P.L. 95-266, for the first time explicitly defined sexual exploitation and failure to provide necessary medical care as forms of child abuse. The Child Abuse Amendments of 1984, P.L. 98-457, defined a child as any person under the age of eighteen. This law also expanded the definition of a person who is responsible for the child's welfare to include employees of a residential facility or out-of-home care agency. Thus, Goldstein (1987) stated that, from the perspective of the penal code, "A child molester will be defined as a significantly older individual who engages in any type of sexual activity with individuals defined as children" (p. 19).

The fourth edition of the American Psychiatric Association's (1994) *Diagnostic and Statistical Manual of Mental Disorders (DSM-IV)*, the handbook of all psychiatric diagnoses, is a resource that provides extensive information and diagnostic criteria concerning syndromes related to mental conditions. Its definition of pedophilia, a synonym of child molester, includes three distinct but related criteria: (1) the sexual activity or the fantasy of this activity with, (2) children who are prepubertal, and (3) is the person's preferred or exclusive method of achieving sexual excitement (American Psychiatric Association, 1994).

There is a need to define CSA operationally in any investigation. At present, there is a lack of agreement among researchers and clinicians regarding the operational definitions of CSA, indicating the degree of complexity associated with this phenomenon. To arrive at an operational definition of CSA, researchers have to make decisions along dimensions that are specific to CSA. Blume (1990) provided a useful framework to organize the most important dimensions requiring careful considerations:

1. Age of victim and perpetrator. Younger age may be associated with more severe and long-term effects.

2. Relationship to perpetrator. Intrafamilial versus extrafamilial CSA may be associated with different effects.

3. Emotional violation. The betrayal of trust by a primary caregiver may be even more destructive than the sexual activities.

4. Extent of contact. There is a relationship between the actual act and degree of damage.

5. Use of force or coercion. Any concomitant emotional or physical abuse can multiply the already violent effects of CSA.

6. The number of abusers. This factor interacts with the perpetrators' relationship to the victim in its effects.

7. Duration of the abuse. Single events can be as traumatic as chronic abuses.

8. Disclosure. Appropriate reactions by the authorities to the child's disclosure of CSA could be helpful.

9. Outside resources. Other adults, children, places, pets, or emotional outlets could provide support.

10. Internal resources such as the child's history, attitudes, areas of deficits, and inner strengths. Strengths are composed of the child's capacity to rationalize, understand and assess, not to blame herself or himself, hope for change, and use humor.

Using this set of dimensions as an organizing framework, several of these dimensions are more crucial than others in determining the operational definitions of CSA. In particular, most clinicians and researchers are careful to exercise their professional judgment and to state explicitly the decisions they made along the more critical dimensions (such as relationship, emotional violation, age, and type of sexual acts) to arrive at the operational definition they used in their theoretical paper or empirical study.

First, the relationship of the perpetrator to the victim is an important dimension because it allows researchers to categorize the CSA as intrafamilial or extrafamilial. If the perpetrator is a family member or extended family member, then the CSA is classified as incest or intrafamilial CSA. Thus, intrafamilial CSA is specifically defined as sexual activities occurring in a preexisting relationship between a sexually mature adult and a dependent child (Gelinas, 1983) who are related by blood and legally prohibited to marry (Faller, 1988). Most professionals would also agree that *forbidden by taboo* is a defining attribute of this type of CSA. Given the intimate nature of a family and the chronic nature of intrafamilial CSA, the CSA becomes an integral part of the child victim's formative psychosocial experiences. Extrafamilial CSA is operationally defined as sexual activities occurring between a child and someone who is outside the child's family, who may be known (such as a friend or neighbor), or who may be a complete stranger. Ritual abuse or cult abuse, perpetrated on a child or children by one or more individuals or by groups, has been gaining attention. Extrafamilial CSA may involve significantly more physical violence, perhaps even an act of rape.

These two broad categories of CSA may be somewhat similar in their fundamental nature, yet they have very different effects on the child victims because of their specific contexts. Bagley and King (1990) discussed the important characteristics of incest and its impact. They proposed that incest typically involves sexual acts that are subjected to society's incest taboo. Incest involves acts that are usually repeated over a long period, that may not necessarily involve intercourse, and that may include less physical force and violence. Finally, incest may be psychologically and emotionally loaded for all the members in the family before and after the discovery of the CSA activities. For the child victims, the likelihood that the incest activities could cause physical and psychological trauma is greater than a one-time act of rape.

Regarding incest, a lack of agreement exists on whether the preexisting relationship should be restricted to relatives related by blood, be expanded to include those related by marriage or adoption, or be broadly defined to include all relatives. A broad definition of incest was provided by Blume (1990): "The imposition of sexually inappropriate acts, or acts with sexual overtones, by—or any use of a minor child to meet the sexual or sexual/emotional needs of—one or more persons who derive authority through ongoing emotional bonding with that child" (p. 4). This definition has far-reaching implications because it reframes CSA from the perspective of the victim.

Second, the emotional violation dimension has considerable importance. Butler's definition (1985) included the conditions of "unwanted" and "harmful": "Any sexual activity or experience imposed on a child which results in emotional, physical, or sexual trauma" (p. 5). Trauma is considered to be the result of an event that is typically outside the range of usual human experience (American Psychiatric Association, 1994) and that is experienced by a person as sudden, overwhelming, and disruptive. Bagley and King (1990) observed that children are not capable of informed consent. Therefore, it is likely that any intrusion imposed on a child victim could be experienced by the victim as sexually, physically, or emotionally traumatic and injurious. In considering trauma a critical dimension, the operational definition of CSA is unavoidably restricted.

Third, regarding the dimension of age, defining the relationship as between an adult and a child implies that an age difference or gap should exist for a sexual act to be considered abusive. Most professionals would agree on a difference of at least five years as being a significant factor in judging whether or not CSA took place.

Finally, another dimension requiring professional judgment involves choosing the specific sexual acts. Wyatt and Peters (1986) stated that some researchers restricted their operational definitions to sexual touch (e.g., fondling, genital contact, attempted or completed vaginal intercourse, oral sex, and anal sex), whereas other researchers broadened their definitions to include noncontact activities (i.e., exposure, sexualized comments, and verbal propositions). In considering these two dimensions, Russell (1983) observed that professionals have not yet agreed on what specific sexual acts inflicted at what age constitute CSA.

There is little agreement among professionals about the decisions that have to be made along each of the dimensions. Despite the difficulties, however, many professionals believe in the importance of operationally defining CSA as a prerequisite to examining it. Most do agree that CSA is a violation that is intrinsically devastating and damaging to the victim's sense of self (Herman, 1981). There is a current need to arrive at a more agreed upon operational definition. Without such an agreement within the research community, comparing findings across studies can be difficult because the results are dependent, in part, on the operational definitions being used.

PREVALENCE AND INCIDENCE OF CHILD SEXUAL ABUSE

As a result of the numerous operational definitions of CSA used, it is not surprising that estimates of CSA incidences vary widely (Wyatt and Peters, 1986). Specifically, the studies using narrowly or conservatively defined operational definitions of CSA usually found lower rates of CSA in the studies' samples. Conversely, the use of broader and less restrictive operational definitions of CSA found higher rates. Also, the true rate is an unknown quantity because it is likely that the rate of actual occurrence exceeds the rate of detected occurrence.

Early estimates of the incidence of incest were relatively low. In 1955, Weinberg estimated the incidence of incest to be approximately one case per million persons per year. This figure is consistent with the estimate, one to two cases per million persons per year, provided by two other researchers, Kinsey et al. (1948) and Gagnon (1965). Gebhard, Gagnon, Pomeroy, and Christenson (1965), however, increased the estimate to 5,000 cases per million persons per year. In 1979, Finkelhor further increased the estimate to one case per 100 persons per year. More recently, the estimates of the prevalence of CSA were increased to a range of 11% to 62%. (It is important to note that the estimates of incidence rates appear deceptively lower than prevalence rates because incidence rates take into account the added dimension of time.)

In an attempt to narrow the range of reported prevalence rates to a more useful number, Feldman et al. (1991) reviewed the literature to find the studies that provided the "best evidence" as a result of the rigor of their research designs. They concluded that only three studies focusing on CSA scored highly on several strict criteria, indicating that those studies had used sound methodological designs. These studies (1) used a general population, (2) used a restricted definition of the relationship and considered sexual abuse to have occurred only between a person who is five years older than a child who is under the age of fourteen, (3) had high or very high response rates to preserve the representativeness of the original sample population, and (4) used reliable or valid survey instruments. When these studies' findings were considered, Feldman et al. argued that the underlying prevalence rate appears to have remained stable at approximately 12% since the 1950s. More specifically, these studies provided estimates of prevalence rates of 12% in the 1940s, 10% in 1983, and 12% in 1983.

In sum, if early findings are compared with the numbers cited today, one might prematurely conclude that cases of CSA are cn the rise. Feldman et al. (1991), however, argued that the true prevalence of CSA remained relatively stable. In essence, the numbers of people reporting their histories of CSA may reflect society's gradual capacity to overcome its denial about the reality of CSA. Hence, societal changes have generated heightened awareness of CSA and its aftermath, and cases that otherwise might have gone undetected are more likely to be disclosed.

OVERVIEW OF OTHER RESEARCH IN THE FIELD

The weight of the evidence suggests that there is a substantial relationship between CSA and adaptation. Findings from the clinical and empirical literature (Browne and Finkelhor, 1986; Herman, 1981) consistently documented an association between CSA and pervasive negative effects in the victim's immediate and adult functioning. For example, a broad range of long-term aftereffects such as depression, self-destructive behavior, anxiety, isolating and stigmatized feelings, low self-esteem and self-concept, repeated victimization, and substance abuse were documented. There is also evidence of difficult interpersonal relationships and sexual maladjustment. Some individuals may also engage in prostitution, promiscuity, or sexual deviancy. These long-term consequences of CSA can be organized into six general areas: post-traumatic stress, cognitive distortions, altered emotionality, disturbed relatedness, avoidance, and impaired self-reference (Briere and Runtz, 1993). Several excellent reviews are available (Beitchman et al., 1992; Browne and Finkelhor, 1986; Kendall-Tackett, Williams, and Finkelhor, 1993; Mey and Neff, 1982). The implications of these findings, in conjunction with the prevalence of CSA, are staggering: "Given our 'minimum estimate' of a rate of child sexual abuse of 20 percent in women, and an estimate that a quarter of victims have long-term problems . . . , we estimate that about 5 percent of all women . . . have chronically impaired adult adjustment" (Bagley and King, 1990, p. 127).

In any discussion of the consequences of CSA, there are four interrelated issues to consider: (1) defining the time frame of the consequences (short-term and medium-term versus long-term aftereffects), (2) specific and differential effects of CSA and child physical abuse, (3) methodological considerations, and (4) future research needs. In considering the time frame of the consequences, researchers typically define short-term or immediate effects as the behaviors, feelings, or attitudes that the child victim experiences during the CSA or shortly after its disclosure. Medium-term effects include those psychosocial and emotional qualities that the victim experiences six months after the CSA, as either its direct or indirect consequences, whereas long-term effects may be those qualities still being experienced several years later (Mey and Neff, 1982).

This issue is important because the two earlier reviews were based primarily on studies that were published. For the most part, those studies that were available were retrospective studies of adults, and this unbalanced focus had led to the short-term effects of CSA being underestimated and underdocumented. For example, Browne and Finkelhor (1986) reviewed four studies of children and reported that a large portion of the child victims displayed reactions of fear, anxiety, depression, anger and hostility, and inappropriate sexual behavior. Later studies that focused on children, however, revealed other categories of severe reactions. These reactions included posttraumatic stress disorder, aggression, behavior problems, depression, and poor self-esteem in addition to the reactions documented in the first review (Kendall-Tackett et al., 1993).

Second, several of the dimensions that make an agreed-upon operational definition of CSA difficult to achieve are the same factors that shape a victim's reactions. The factors of CSA that are critical in determining the nature of the aftereffects are (Goldstein, 1987; Groth, 1978):

1. The nature and duration of the relationship of the victim to the offender

2. The duration of the CSA activities

3. The type of CSA activities imposed upon the victim

4. The degree of aggression or severity of force used

5. The victim's developmental state or maturity at age of the onset of CSA

6. The age difference between the victim and the offender

7. The sophistication of the child about CSA

8. The environment or context of the CSA

9. The degree of the victim's participation

10. The gender of the victim and the offender

11. The degree of support from the family and professionals upon disclosure of the CSA

Beitchman et al. (1992) suggested that these CSA specific factors help to determine the nature of the aftereffects. Specifically, greater harm is associated with abuse involving a father or 'epfather, penetration, longer duration, and the use of force or threat of force. 'ue experience of force or threat of force seems to be a necessary concomitant of anxiety, fear, and suicidal ideas and behavior. The association between age of onset of CSA (i.e., pre- or postpubertally) and adult outcome is equivocal and is confounded by other abuse specific variables such as degree of invasiveness, duration of the abuse, and age at which the CSA terminated. Even though most of the studies of CSA focus on women, there is some evidence to support the notion that men with histories of CSA may experience long-term difficulties in the domains of sexual dysfunction, gender identity conflict, homosexuality, and increased risk of becoming sex abuse perpetrators.

Many researchers argued that there is a need to examine the specific and differential effects of CSA (Beitchman et al., 1992). Wind and Silvern (1992) suggested that sexual, physical, or combined abuse each may have specific and differential correlates in adult functioning. CSA was specifically associated with posttraumatic stress disorder (Kendall-Tackett et al., 1993), sexual dysfunction and sexualized behavior (Beitchman et al., 1992; Briere and Runtz, 1990; Kendall-Tackett et al., 1993), and homosexual experiences and depression (Beitchman et al., 1992), whereas physical abuse was associated with aggression (Briere and Runtz, 1990). Beitchman et al. found that both sexual and physical abuse have common long-term correlates (e.g., internalizing symptoms and adult victimization) and that the combined abuse was associated with more unfavorable outcomes than either type of abuse alone. In light of sparse evidence, Beitchman et al. cautioned that a specific relationship between CSA and a specific post–sexual abuse syndrome and multiple or borderline personality disorder remains to be established.

Third, these issues have broad methodological implications. As Wind and Silvern (1992) contended: "Findings from research examining only sexual abuse can be misleading, for they cannot determine which adult characteristics are actually attributable to the sexual abuse, rather than to physical abuse that is concomitant but unidentified" (p. 262). Beitchman et al. (1992) also suggested that the specific effects of CSA, independent of other variables such as parental pathology, still need to be investigated in hypothesis-driven research designs. In addition, the documented aftereffects are characteristics of individuals who also happen to have a history of CSA. Given the correlational and retrospective nature of most research designs used, it does not necessarily follow that the CSA had definitively caused these aftereffects.

Regarding other methodological considerations, the research strategies used in most empirical studies limit the generalizability of most findings. Investigators tend to focus on the first or second levels of the systems model. Clearly, the questions and variables on these levels are the easiest to ask and operationalize. More difficult to conceptualize and operationalize are the hypotheses on the other levels, particularly the levels related to the family and its interactions with the community and cultural factors.

Finally, the adoption of the theory-building systems model is proposed for the meaningful interpretation of the correlates of CSA and its aftereffects (Faller, 1988). Epidemiological research such as a national database of CSA prevalence rates and prevailing attitudes is needed (Bagley and King, 1990; Mey and Neff, 1982). Small-scale empirical studies would benefit from more rigorous designs and methods such as the use of comparison or matched peer groups; large and representative samples; standardized, reliable, and valid outcome instruments specific to CSA (Briere and Runtz, 1993); standardized research designs and operational definitions of sexual abuse; and better record keeping (Browne and Finkelhor, 1986).

CORRELATES OF CHILD SEXUAL ABUSE

Researchers have used several conceptual models, largely centered on the correlates of intrafamilial CSA, that help to organize the growing body of research. The research is significant because it aims to provide some ways of thinking about why some adults act on their inclinations to sexually abuse children. For example, Finkelhor and Browne (1985) proposed a model suggesting the existence of four traumagenic dynamics that accounts for a particular set of psychological and behavioral aftereffects in sexually abused individuals. In this section, two of the earlier models are introduced, and the research in the context of the systems model is discussed.

Two conceptual models have been frequently used in correlates of child abuse and neglect (physically, sexually, or emotionally) research (Wolfe, 1985). The first conceptual model, the one most frequently used, assumes that the personality attributes of the individuals within the family are the primary variables of interest during the course of a clinical or research investigation. Thus, psychological characteristics such as self-esteem, depression, anxiety, impulse control, childhood events, coping, and defense mechanisms were examined. CSA is often conceptualized to take place within an individual family's pathologies. The other frequently used conceptualization is the social interactional model. This model proposes that the pattern of interaction among individuals within a family is a reciprocal one, that antecedent events may be the precipitants of abuse, and that consequences may serve to maintain the abuse (Wolfe, 1985). This model also takes into account the social context such as stressful life events that may interact with the parents' ability to provide competent care. Theoretical formulations and contributions using the second model, mostly qualitative research such as clinical case studies, helped to shift the locus of blame gradually from the mother to the society.

A third conceptual model, rooted in systems theory (P. D. Alexander, 1985; Faller, 1988; Lam, 1989), has been proposed. This conceptual model takes the family and social factors into account and proposes that family relations and social dynamics may independently contribute to the outcomes of the CSA survivor (P. D. Alexander, 1985; Edwards and Alexander, 1992; Faller, 1988). Several studies had investigated the differential effects of CSA and family characteristics to adult functioning (Fromuth, 1986). Edwards and Alexander (1992) proposed that the theoretical integration of family systems theory and sexual abuse research should be considered because the social context is a significant contributing factor to the process and outcomes of CSA. Faller (1988) also suggested that a systems model with four interacting factors or levels—cultural, environmental, family, and individual—is necessary to an in-depth understanding of the correlates of CSA.

Within a systems model, individuals and families each represent just one level (or factor) of an interrelated model. Each level acts on its own and interacts with each other to produce both main and interaction effects. A systems model of CSA that takes into account the interrelatedness influences of the four levels must be adopted because a narrow focus on personal characteristics or pathology unfairly locates most of the blame on the individual. Instead, a major portion of the responsibility of CSA should be placed on the family and its interactions with the community (or environment) and the society (or culture). The systems model of CSA is heuristically useful because it considers the role of contributing factors.

At the first level, or cultural factor, of a systems model, professionals have speculated that a traditionally patriarchal culture implicitly gives permission for men to exert power over women and children. Herman (1981) had observed:

> Whereas male supremacy creates the social conditions that favor the development of father-daughter incest, the sexual division of labor creates the psychological conditions that lead to the same result. Male supremacy invests fathers with immense power over their children, especially their daughters. The sexual division of labor, in which women nurture children and men do not, produces fathers who are predisposed to use their powers exploitatively. The rearing of children by subordinate women insures the reproduction

in each generation of the psychology of male supremacy. . . . The greater the domination of the father, and the more caretaking is relegated to the mother, the greater the likelihood of father-daughter incest." (pp. 62–63)

Given this argument, it is not surprising that any child would be helpless in the face of a father who looms larger than life with the combined authority of parent, man, and adult. Other authors also call for the problem of CSA to be located squarely on the unequal power balance and the fathers in our society (Garbarino 1980; Wattenberg, 1985). Faller (1988), however, cautioned against overgeneralizing on the basis of the male dominance argument. Clearly, not all men are rapists and child abusers. It is more likely that some of the CSA perpetrators might have incorporated the male dominance beliefs to a greater extent than the general population, which then allowed them to act on their sexual attraction to children.

The other cultural values of a society that permit child abuse include (1) tolerance of increasing levels of all types of violence, such as high rates of homicide; (2) attribution of publicly disturbing actions to defective parenting; (3) acceptance of inadequate social supports that could inhibit the abuse of children; and (4) allowance of physical punishment of children in family and schools and violence toward children in general (Garbarino, 1980). Bagley and King (1990) argued that the cycle of child abuse is perpetuated through generations to come when violence trickles down from the society to the family and individuals. The violence in society is generalized in families as a method of social control. Thus, children may be maltreated or exploited as they are being subjected to a systematic process of socialization and control, which is tolerated under the powerful influence of society's values.

From the perspective of family characteristics, the scope of the inquiry includes the study of CSA as a symptom of an overall and more pervasive family dysfunction (Lustig, Dresser, Spellman, and Murray, 1966). As part of their seminal work, Lustig et al. (1966) attempted a consideration of the third level of the systems framework, the family and community interactions. The dysfunctional family does not seem to have an integrated structure with clearly delineated roles organized along sexual and generational lines. Instead, it tends to rely heavily on noninstitutionalized role relations. Since it is culturally isolated from the community, its members seemingly have to fulfill their instinctual desires within the family.

The second level, or environmental factor, includes socioeconomic factors and social isolation. First, at least three studies published between 1926 and 1951 found that economic factors played a causal role in CSA and asserted that low socioeconomic status was associated with the occurrence of CSA (Faller, 1988). More recent authors disputed this assertion and cited the methodological limitations of the earlier studies as grounds for skepticism. For example, the studies' sampling biases and referral sources might have led to a skewed sample along the dimension of economic and poverty status, limiting the studies' samples to participants who were already successfully criminally prosecuted, psychiatrically hospitalized, or involved in child protective service (Faller, 1988). Furthermore, Faller (1988) wondered whether or not "poverty is associated with other factors that contribute to the risk of sexual abuse" (p. 96) such as physical overcrowding or unemployment conditions that might expose the offender to sexually arousing and accessible situations.

Social isolation is the second component of the environmental factor investigated by researchers. P. D. Alexander (1985) asserted that families in which CSA occurs are socially isolated as a result of their geographical isolation in rural areas. Approximately 25% to 30% of child protection cases in rural areas are sexual abuse, compared with 13% nationwide (Faller, 1988). Using the explanatory power of the systems model, P. D. Alexander (1985) proposed that the relationship of the family to its environment can be classified as being open or closed, and other variables in the family and its community deemed to be the cause and the effect of CSA activity can be identified. First, the degree of closedness of the family as social system places them at greater risk for CSA. The family that is vulnerable to CSA is typically more socially isolated and is less likely to engage in information exchange with its environment than other families (P. D. Alexander, 1985). Social isolation may be a causal factor of CSA because the family lacks access to appropriate sexual partners, the family lacks normative pressure from the socially upheld incest taboo, or the community avoids the family due to some unusual behavior (Faller, 1988). Moreover, it is likely that the family's initial social isolation was imposed by a father who intended to limit his family's access to the outside world (Faller, 1988). Alternatively, it is likely that this family's social isolation is the direct result of the community members' avoidance of the family because they know about the CSA. Thus, social isolation is also an effect of CSA (Faller, 1988).

The third level, or familial factor, includes the conceptualization of incest as a symptom of a family's dysfunction and a mechanism in its preservation (Lustig et al., 1966). The dysfunctional family is socially isolated and avoids any natural growth or change, tending to safeguard and maintain an inappropriate homeostasis (P. D. Alexander, 1985). It may be more rigid and inflexible in its communication patterns than other families and may lack structural integration and role differentiation among its members. Predispositions include the daughter assuming the maternal role, an impaired sexual relationship between the parents, the father's unwillingness to have an extramarital affair, and the unconscious participation of the mother. The incest preserves the parents' dependency needs, sexual adequacy, and role competence and also serves the child's needs for revenge on his or her nonnurturant mother and for a reduction of separation anxiety.

The fourth level, or individual factor, includes descriptions of the personal pathologies of family members. A child who had been sexually abused tends to introject the aggressor and the guilt feelings of the perpetrator to cope with the abuse. The child victim usually feels physically and morally helpless, and his or her personality has not yet grown strong enough to resist the overpowering authority of the father (Ferenczi, 1949). An integrated system of maternal introjects is often lacking in the daughter due to her mother's nonnurturant care, resulting in pseudomaturity and ego fusion with her mother. The daughter has a lack of tolerance of being abandoned and likely engages in incest to reduce separation anxiety (Lustig et al., 1966). The daughter typically does not disclose the incest because she depends on her family or is overly fearful of her father's threats of parental divorce and societal punishment (Herman, 1981).

The father was found to be pathologically disturbed in his ability to maintain self-control, to be impulsive or reckless due to alcohol abuse (Ferenczi, 1949), or to be in a regressed ego state and to be sexually acting out (Lustig et al., 1966). Due to an early emotional deprivation or abandonment, the father typically lacked a direct psychological connection with his own father. Thus, he harbored uncertainty about his own masculinity and a need to maintain a facade of being a competent patriarch. The father typically had convinced himself that he cared about the child and did no harm to the child (Lustig et al., 1966).

The mother was found to be not intimate enough for the child victim to turn to for help (Ferenczi, 1949). She also experienced physical or psychological abandonment as a child and thus feels ambivalent about her daughter, perhaps to the point of unconsciously putting her daughter in the maternal and spousal role so as to maintain her dependency on the marriage (Lustig et al., 1966). This assertion of the mother as the "cornerstone in the pathological family system" (Lustig et al., 1966, p. 39) was rejected by Herman (1981), who argued that the father should be held most accountable because of his intrinsically powerful position.

CHARACTERISTICS OF OFFENDERS AND VICTIMS

The characteristics of fathers, mothers, and victims have been documented by numerous investigations. Despite inconsistent findings, the weight of the evidence suggests that CSA cuts across age, gender, socioeconomic status, ethnicity, and psychological characteristics (Blume, 1990). Individual offenders' characteristics can include intrafamilial versus extrafamilial abuse, a harsh or depriving childhood experience, difficulties in adult relationships, a history of traumatic sexual experience, and substance abuse (Faller, 1988). The characteristics of a nonoffending parent can include a history of traumatic sexual experience and some form of physical or emotional incapacity (Faller, 1988). The characteristics of the victim can include an acceptance of the sexual role and a CSA accommodation syndrome (Summit, 1983).

A defining characteristic of the offenders is that most of them (about 90%) are men (Blume, 1990; Herman, 1981). Male offenders are more likely to commit overt and direct sexual acts and to victimize any accessible child, regardless of gender. They are also more likely to go from child to child within the family or from victim to victim outside the family. Women are seldom reported as being the offender, but it is likely that there are many more cases than have been documented. When women are perpetrators, the acts most often reported are ones that are emotional, focused on relationship and bonding, or directed to the care of the child's body. Goldstein (1987) observed that when offenders are adolescents, they were typically assumed to be either good boys experimenting or evil boys deserving of imprisonment. It is more likely, however, that the adolescent offender perpetrated because he was a CSA victim. Sex rings, cult abuse, or satanic abuse may involve child molesters who may or may not be pedophiles who are passive and nonaggressive.

The type of CSA, intrafamilial versus extrafamilial abuse, interacts with gender and age to characterize offenders. Mental health professionals have used these factors to develop a framework to categorize offenders. These categorical descriptions are conceptualized as not being mutually exclusive and along a continuum of perceived severity (Summit and Kryso, 1978):

1. Incidental: accidental or unplanned

2. Ideological: adult sincerely believes that the child benefits

3. Psychotic intrusion: adult suffers reality confusion

4. Subcultural environment: few cultural contradictions within adult's subculture

5. True endogamous incest: parent chooses to eroticize a child

6. Misogynous incest: parent motivated by hatred or fear

7. Imperious act out of authority: adult uses inherent power

8. Pedophiliac: adult is erotically fascinated by child

9. Child rape: adult feels powerful and is violent

10. Perverse abuse: bizarre, destructive, ritual, or multiple partners

On the basis of this mental health framework, a law enforcement typology of offenders emerged to guide arrests and convictions instead of treatment interventions (Goldstein, 1987). In general, child molesters can be divided into two broad categories: situational and preferential. The situational child molester category consists of four major patterns of behavior: regressed, morally indiscriminate, sexually indiscriminate, and inadequate. Typically, individuals falling within these categories perpetrate sex offenses as a result of situational factors such as mood, intoxication, social stressors, and mental states. The preferential child molester category consists of three major patterns of behavior: seduction, introverted, and sadistic. The four major characteristics typical of preferential child molesters include:

1. A chronic pattern of behavior: was a sexual abuse victim, has limited dating experiences, was dishonorably discharged from the armed services, has sudden moves and changing jobs, has prior arrests, has multiple victims, and makes bold and repeated attempts

2. Using children as sexual objects: is over age twenty-five and has never married, lives alone or with parents, has limited intimate and peer relationships, has a "cover" relationship if married, has an excessive interest in children, has age and gender preference, and has an idealized view of children

3. Using strategies to obtain victims: is skilled at selecting vulnerable children, identifies with children, has access to children, is involved in activities with children that exclude other adults, seduces and manipulates children, has interests appealing to children, and shows sexually explicit material to children

4. Having sexual fantasies about children: has a home decorated as a child would, photographs children and uses them in fantasies, and collects child pornography or erotica

Under the category of intrafamilial CSA, researchers were interested in the characteristics of the mother and the family. The earlier descriptions of the mothers' characteristics were unfavorable: dependent, needy, weak, cold, or abandoning (Blume, 1990; Faller, 1988; Lustig et al., 1966). Thus, due to incapacity and characterological problems, mothers were often described as being inadequate in their roles as the family's homemaker, children's caregiver, and husband's sexual partner (Faller, 1988). Blume (1990), however, argued that many mothers do not have these negative characteristics. For example, there are mothers who had attempted to seek protection for their daughters from the court system. They were often frustrated because the system tended to award full custody to the perpetrating fathers. Herman (1981) also pointed out that the justice system has been known to protect the men who committed crimes against women and children.

The defining characteristic of the families is that most of them are likely to be high in marital conflict or to be headed by a single parent (Faller, 1988; Herman, 1981). In general, these families are likely to have members who have difficulties with depression, substance abuse, and violence (Beitchman et al., 1992). The phenomenon of the intergenerational transmission of abuse has been well documented. Blume (1990) stated: "Incest is not the consequence of one sole family member gone renegade. It often passes through generations from victimizer to victim-become-victimizer to victim-become-mother-of-victim" (p. 9).

The factors that are characteristic of the families and their social contexts during cases of intrafamilial CSA may include (Faller, 1988; Goldstein, 1987):

1. Extreme overprotectiveness of the child because of jealousy and fear of discovery
2. Extreme paternal dominance to coerce victim's acceptance of sexual role
3. Marked role reversal between mother and victim
4. Overreaction to victim's learning in sex education classes
5. Marked social isolation from the social community
6. Multiple exposures to several men involved with the mother
7. No supervision or controls for the child
8. Marital relationship unstable or breaking up
9. Lack of sexual satisfaction in the marriage
10. Strict or fundamental religious background
11. Physically abusive
12. Suppression of any issue related to sex

Finally, a defining characteristic of the victims is that most of them (about 85%) are girls (Herman, 1981). Age interacts with gender differentially (young girls and older boys), according to Browne and Finkelhor (1986); one in four girls and one in ten boys are at risk of being victimized prior to adolescence (Herman, 1981). Girls are victimized about ten times more often than boys. Blume (1990) cited a few statistics to exemplify this assertion:

1. Girls under age six comprised 35% of all reported child sexual abuse cases in 1985.

2. Most rape victims are between the ages of ten and nineteen, one-fourth of them are under age twelve.

3. Two-year-olds and then three- and four-year-olds were overrepresented in reported cases of sexual abuse to the Los Angeles Department of Health Services in 1984.

4. A large number of babies and preschool children were treated at the Columbia Presbyterian Medical Center's Family Center for syphilis, venereal warts, genital injuries, and gonorrheal infections of the throat in 1985.

Additionally, at least 1 in 100 girls is abused by her father, and one-third of the perpetrators are relatives of the victim (Finkelhor, 1979).

Goldstein (1987) proposed that children are vulnerable to CSA because of their unsatisfied needs, regardless of their family circumstances. Children, however, from poverty-stricken, unstable, or broken homes, might be even more vulnerable to victimization because of a greater degree of psychosocial needs. Most likely, children become and remain compliant victims as a result of many characteristics inherent to their developmental stages: (1) did not know that they can say no to authority figures; (2) felt guilty about participating and fear of hurting the offender; (3) received psychosocial or monetary compensation; (4) received peer group pressure, brainwashing, or threats of physical force to comply with CSA; and (5) survived by developing the child sexual abuse accommodation syndrome to learn to live with the CSA (Goldstein, 1987). Typical manifestations of this syndrome include feelings of secrecy, helplessness, and entrapment about the abuse; accommodation and tolerance of the abuse; delayed and unconvincing disclosure of the abuse; and retraction of the allegations of the abuse (Summit, 1983).

PREVENTION AND TREATMENT

Bagley and King (1990) discussed factors needed for the healing of society. It seems clear that CSA will continue as long as society's attention is myopically focused on the plight of children and pathology of perpetrators rather than on the societal context. Through the lens of community psychology, however, the focus can gradually be shifted from the individual to the society. Rather than merely treating the individuals' reactions to the occurrence of CSA, prevention can try to reeducate society and communities so that incidences of CSA would not be frequent, albeit, secretive occurrences.

The issues involved in the conceptualization of preventive strategies and more specific strategies in the area of CSA can be determined. Defining preventive interventions has been a key challenge in the relatively new field of prevention science. Therefore, it is not surprising that the subfield of applying prevention science in the area of CSA has not yet been fully formed. Many suggestions have been made, but a sustained body of research in this subfield has not yet emerged. Recently, an Institute of Medicine report (Mrazek and Haggerty, 1994) recommended that the term "prevention" be placed on a mental health intervention spectrum for mental disorders: (1) prevention, which aims to intervene before the initial onset of a clinically diagnosable disorder to reduce the occurrence of new cases of disorders; (2) treatment, which aims to deliver mental health services and to provide effective treatments; and (3) maintenance, which aims to reduce relapse and recurrence and to provide rehabilitative services to ameliorate long-term consequences. Prevention itself can be subcategorized into universal, selective, and indicated preventive interventions. Universal preventive strategies target the low-risk public, selective preventive strategies target an identifiable risk group, and indicated preventive strategies target high-risk persons.

Yet, the recent definitions are different from the ones in the traditional public health classification system. Three levels of prevention were identified. Specifically, primary, secondary, and tertiary levels are arranged in increasing order of preventiveness, with the primary level being most preventive in nature (Caplan, 1964). Bagley and Thurston (1988) used this prevention framework as the organizing principle around which preventive strategies in the area of CSA can be systematically addressed. Primary prevention, being conceptually the furthest away from the event and therefore the most preventive in nature, aims to address directly the mediating structures such as the root causes and cultural values that foster the development of CSA. Primary prevention adopts a broader political stance to achieve its aims. It challenges the conventional foundations of values and behaviors and encourages society to "look back as a collective entity at its own development in a self-critical manner, acknowledging its own liabilities, and determine new directions to incorporate chosen values" (Bagley and King, 1990, p. 207).

Thus, critically examining and changing key socialization processes is an example of primary prevention. Specifically, these areas are global and include the critique of the historical powerlessness of women and children, the rigid social roles and sexual objectification of people, the violence and compulsive repetition of attempts to exercise power, the stigmatization and rejection by society of deviant individuals, and the healing from the harm and the learning of new attitudes and behaviors (Bagley and King, 1990). Child advocacy is another example of primary prevention, and it could take the form of lobbying for adequate services for all children as well as their families within the general public that has not been identified as being at any increased risk for CSA. These critical services are good for everyone and should provide all children with appropriate nutrition, health care, intellectual stimulation, and emotional and physical security and their families with day care, educational facilities, playgrounds, street safety, recreational opportunities, and basic emotional and financial securities.

Secondary prevention intends to detect, intervene, or treat a problem before CSA occurs. In the intervention or treatment of a developing case of CSA, every effort should be made to minimize the harm that can be caused by the use of individual or community-based therapeutic models. Preventive education programs are also directed toward increasing parents' understanding of the nature of stressors and awareness of how their own levels of distress could contribute to child abuse. Within the context of CSA, the strengthening and empowerment of children through educational exercises are important components of primary and secondary prevention. These strategies typically include educating and training professionals, school personnel, and parents on educational methods that have been shown to work well with children. What these methods have in common is their goal of educating children through presentations, books, or videos to identify and resist uncomfortable touches. The sensitivity of the professionals or parents to the children's reactions to the stimulating nature of the material during educational sessions is central to the effectiveness of these methods.

Tertiary prevention, the closest level to the event because the intervention takes place after the fact, tries to prevent the recurrence of CSA and minimize its long-term consequences. Bagley and King (1990) encouraged professionals to adopt a humane and empathic attitude toward survivors and offenders. Instead of ignoring or minimizing the effects of CSA, the victims should be treated, survivors and families empowered, offenders rehabilitated, and the effectiveness of these treatments and interventions evaluated. Therefore, the education of professionals is a critical component that standardizes the quality and effectiveness of intervention services being provided. Upon the disclosure of CSA, stigmatization of the survivors, the perpetrators, or their families as a universal reaction to the injured so as to dissociate from the possibility of a similar fate is often an unfortunate result. Professionals are not immune to these feelings and need to be educated about their culturally conditioned responses to CSA as well.

Being members of society, professionals as well as citizens may engage in denial and reject the survivors, the offenders, or their families to maintain their own level of comfort. For example, they may want to preserve a sense of righteousness by focusing on the perceived defectiveness of the identified individuals and ask, "Why should we or society change if the locus of the evil is only within a few misfits?" Pathologizing and labeling these individuals as deviant may be an attempt to keep from thinking about the need for radical societal changes. Bagley and King (1990) are advocates of the need to engage in the collective healing of society, and they urge professionals to bring about a more just and vital society through the types of interventions and services being provided to the identified individuals and their families.

A recent review of the child maltreatment prevention literature yielded 298 documents. The studies or program reports included all types of child maltreatment (i.e., general, sexual, physical, or emotional abuse, and neglect) and all levels of preventive activities, targeting the general population as well as groups at risk of maltreatment

(Beatty and Booth, 1991). Interestingly, seven states yielded the highest number of child maltreatment prevention documents: California, Colorado, Illinois, Michigan, New York, Pennsylvania, and Washington (Beatty and Booth, 1991). Several recommendations for specific prevention activities to enhance the effectiveness of prevention programs were formulated by Beatty and Booth (1991). These recommendations are as follows:

1. Programs should focus on physical abuse, emotional maltreatment, and neglect.
2. Programs should aim at secondary and tertiary prevention.
3. Methods should aim to increase awareness.
4. Evaluations should measure the effectiveness of prevention programs.

For example, one sexual abuse prevention program conducted by professionals in Nebraska attempted to evaluate its effectiveness in its aim to increase the perceptions of risk of sexual abuse of seventy-four second- and sixth-grade students (Hashima, Jacobs, and Kenning, 1991). The evaluation, using a pretest/posttest design and two risk-perception tasks, yielded several important conclusions (Hashima et al., 1991). First, the children's estimates of their risk of sexual abuse before enrolling in the prevention program were consistent with a prevalence rate of 38% reported in the literature, but these children's estimates are likely to increase after their participation in the sexual abuse prevention program. Second, the younger (second-grade) children reported greater increases after their participation. Third, the goal to increase children's awareness of the general risks should be reformulated to increase children's awareness of specific risks associated with situational factors such as private situations rather than public spaces and adolescents and familiar adults rather than older adults or strangers.

LEGAL ISSUES AND FUTURE TRENDS

Most states passed legislation pertaining to criminal sexual assault, frequently using such terms as "accused," "bodily harm," "family member," "force or threat of force," "sexual conduct," "sexual penetration," and "victim." Certain legal issues have since been challenging various professionals. R. Alexander (1995) observed: "The result of increased attention and legal changes is that more individuals have been convicted and imprisoned for lengthy prison sentences" (p. 229). Some cases, however, have been dismissed or reversed because of improper investigative procedures or inappropriate expert testimony. Therefore, professionals need to be sensitive to several key legal issues: hearsay, protection, testimony, and investigation.

The first three of these issues pertain to the adjudication stage, where the judiciary occupies the primary role (Kirkwood and Mihaila, 1995). First, hearsay is characterized by the testimony of a third person, based on a sexually abused child's report, regarding the conduct and verbalizations of an alleged offender. R. Alexander (1995) reported that some long-standing exceptions to the hearsay rule render some hearsay admissible in court. This is significant because a very young child may report the abuse to a third person. As long as the utterances of a child to this adult or doctor are "excited," then the hearsay testimony of this adult is admissible because the nature of excited utterances from a child can generally be regarded as truthful.

The second key issue involves the protection of the well-being of the child accuser or plaintiff and the preservation of the right of a defendant to confront his or her accusers. A child may be frightened by the court proceedings or the prospect of confronting his or her abuser (Kirkwood and Mihaila, 1995). In CSA cases, extraordinary protective measures in courtroom procedures had been enacted for the child plaintiff only when "a mental health professional examined the child and concluded that the child would be severely traumatized by testifying in open court" (R. Alexander, 1995, p. 232). These legislative initiatives or protective measures included allowing children to be assessed for competency in the judge's chambers without the defendant present, to testify behind a screen in open court, or to testify in a separate room and viewed by video in the courtroom (R. Alexander, 1995).

The third issue involves the expert testimony of child protection workers. R. Alexander (1995) found that the courts almost universally denounced some forms of expert testimony that exceed the prescribed bounds. A reliance on the diagnosis of child sexual abuse accommodation syndrome can encroach on the province of a jury charged with the responsibility of ascertaining facts. The courts reasoned that the original use of this syndrome was for treatment purposes and not for the certification of the truthfulness of the diagnosis and, by extension, the defendant's guilt. In sum, the courts' decisions clearly stated an opinion that a child sexual abuse accommodation syndrome, even if it had developed in a child, could not be considered as adequate and sufficient evidence to prove that sexual abuse had indeed occurred. For expert testimony to be proper, "the scope of the social worker's testimony must be based on the literature . . . and general professional experience with victims as a class" (R. Alexander, 1995, p. 235).

The fourth issue pertains to the criminal investigation process (Kirkwood and Mihaila, 1995). Even though changes in court proceedings had taken place to allow convictions of CSA offenders to be made, the validity of the evidence gathered during the investigation can have an impact on the subsequent prosecution of the offender. As Goldstein (1987) emphasized, "The major reason for seeking evidence in these cases is to prove that a crime occurred, corroborate the child's testimony, prevent as many avenues of defense as possible, and identify the responsible offender(s)" (pp. 304–305). Furthermore, it is the responsibility of the investigators to move quickly to protect and preserve any other direct or physical evidence in addition to recording the victim and witness statements. R. Alexander (1995) also cautioned against carelessness on the part of child protection workers: "While improper expert testimony may be correctable upon any retrial, a child witness contaminated by improper investigatory procedures may likely result in irreparable harm to the case or to an innocent person" (p. 239).

A community model of dividing responsibilities among professionals emerged in the substantiation of alleged CSA (Bagley and King, 1990). These responsibilities include (1) police officers who evaluate criminal evidence and protective custody needs, (2) social service workers who address the issue of protection, (3) nurses or doctors who evaluate the degree of the abuse and determine the treatment and clinicians who carry out psychotherapeutic services, and (4) lawyers who attend to the trial issues (Goldstein, 1987). As Goldstein (1987) stressed: "The investigator must determine if the child has been molested or exploited, then determine if the child is at risk and/or needs protection. This determination, and *protecting the best interests of the child* during the investigative and prosecutorial process, have the highest priority" (pp. 291–292).

Most complaints originate from the general public and are reported to a law enforcement or child protection agency. In most states, the receiving agency must also report the case to at least one other agency to ensure that the case is properly handled and that the various agencies are well coordinated. Once assigned to investigate a case, the team must be sensitive to the needs of the family members, in particular those of the child victim, who may be susceptible to further traumatization. Other professionals, such as rape crisis counselors or psychologists or other therapists, may be introduced to the family as additional sources of support for the family and child at this time. Unfortunately, protective measures can be a source of further trauma because the practice of removing the victim from her home and then placing her in a foster home is akin to locking up the victim (Kirkwood and Mihaila, 1995).

Goldstein (1987) discussed other concerns that the investigators need to consider to ensure a successful criminal investigation. During the initial contacts, the investigators need to determine an appropriate way to interview the child victim and to determine whether or not the child needs to be taken to the hospital for medical examination and treatment. Within seventy-two hours of the disclosure, biological evidence should be collected by a physician. The selected medical procedures typically include a colposcopic examination, a semen identification method, or a physical examination. To avoid any contamination of accounts, witnesses need to be identified and interviewed separately. The staff and students of the victim's school should be interviewed in the case of extrafamilial CSA. In the case of intrafamilial CSA, the siblings and any other individuals who live in the home as well as the parents should be interviewed. In all cases, all the children with whom the offender associated should be identified to determine whether or not they had been victimized. Interviewing the offender requires preparation. It is advisable to check records for warrants with other state and federal government agencies where the offender might be known.

Significant inroads have been made along the lines of professional beliefs and attitudes, research focus and methods, intervention and treatment methods, and prevention strategies. Most professionals are now aware of the criminal nature of CSA. Blume (1990) asserted:

> Let us avoid the tendency to attempt to decide whether incest is "bad" by its consequences. Are enough survivors depressed in their later life? Are they depressed enough? . . . Incest, like rape, is bad in and of itself. . . . We do not need to measure the degree of

trauma caused by a burglary, for instance, to bring it to legal judgment; the act is evaluated on its own terms. So, too, should we view sexual robbery. (p. 17)

Most professionals also maintain an open-mindedness and guard against a need for denial in their work. Herman (1990) said that witnesses, as much as victims, are subject to the dialectic of trauma, to deny unspeakable violations of the human social compact and to proclaim them aloud: "The knowledge of horrible events periodically intrudes into public consciousness, but is rarely retained for long. To speak publicly about one's knowledge of atrocities is to invite the stigma that attaches to victims" (p. 290).

As the pervasive negative effects of CSA are documented to induce necessary social action, more recent evidence has been accumulating to show that a substantial portion of individuals who have a history of CSA appear to be well adjusted, living well and loving well, and often excelling in one or more areas. Given the numerous studies on the association between CSA and later psychopathology, a partial shift in focus to "resiliency in the face of adversity"—what abilities or characteristics are involved in resilient behaviors that result in adaptation—represents a positive development. Researchers in this nascent, but rapidly expanding, area of resiliency propose that certain variables such as self-esteem and social support act as mediating influences that help to ameliorate the effects of the CSA trauma (Lam and Grossman, 1997; Long and Jackson, 1993) or stressful life events (Rutter, 1985; Werner and Smith, 1982).

Sanford (1990) wrote about "ordinary adults with extraordinary childhoods" (p. 5) who have managed not only to survive their childhood trauma, but also to break the cycle of intergenerational abuse. This author pointed to the methodological limitation of highly biased sampling as being a primary culprit of the view that the long-term effects of CSA are pervasively negative and damaging. If the bulk of these investigations were composed of survivors largely from criminal justice, mental health, social service, or chemical dependency centers, however, then it is possible that the strengths or resilience of a substantial number of those survivors who were not involved with these centers had gone unnoticed and therefore undocumented. Sanford (1990) proposed a salutogenic approach to the study of the long-term effects of CSA as an important approach to adopt, given that the weight of the accumulated evidence to date is on the "disease" end rather than the "healthy" end of the continuum. This approach has challenged the notion that survivors are doomed to a wide array of dysfunctional outcomes. It has also raised the issue of identifying origins of health that have allowed some survivors to transform themselves into healthy adults. As Felsman and Vaillant (1987) observed, "What goes right is more important than what goes wrong" (p. 50).

Due to numerous methodological limitations inherent in most published investigations, Browne and Finkelhor (1986) concluded that causal inferences between a history of CSA and later adult psychopathology cannot be drawn with any confidence. Mrazek and Mrazek (1987) were among the first to propose detailed descriptions of personal and social characteristics that help to nurture resiliency in the lives of children who experienced child maltreatment. These children had certain characteristics: they respond quickly to danger, seek out relevant information, form and use relationships, maintain positive projective anticipation, take decisive risks, have a conviction of being loved, restructure painful experiences cognitively, and nurture optimism and hope. These personal characteristics were often augmented and strengthened by life circumstances or social factors. The children were located in middle- to upper-class family environments that were generally supportive, excluding the obvious trauma of CSA. As such, these families had access to good health, education, and social welfare services, an important mediating variable in the event that CSA was disclosed to the appropriate authorities. In addition, these families typically had additional support such as additional caregivers or available relatives (especially grandparents) and neighbors for instrumental and emotional support.

Given the prevalence of CSA and the magnitude of its impact on individuals, the search for mediators such as resiliency in the context of CSA takes on a heightened urgency. Grossman, Culhane, Moore, Lam, and Paniesen (1994) studied the resiliency specifically in the context of CSA survivors' lives. On the basis of an extensive literature review and an ongoing analysis of responses from the research participants of the Boston University Resiliency Project, Grossman et al. conceptualized resilience in the context of CSA as capacities to (1) continue to function in the world, (2) demonstrate adaptive characteristics, (3) convert childhood defensive strategies into unusual adulthood strengths, (4) transform relational style to rewarding and reciprocal from abusive and destructive, and (5) make meaning of the CSA to benefit oneself and others (Grossman and Moore, 1994; Grossman et al., 1994).

CONCLUSION

CSA is a prevalent phenomenon with long-term consequences for individuals, families, and society. Numerous negative aftereffects as well as resilient manifestations are likely to be detected in the adult lives of individuals with histories of CSA. CSA is far reaching and touches us all in some way. Now that the dimensions and correlates of CSA are known, one must act on behalf of children who are not yet developmentally able to articulate their own needs. Indeed, professionals from many disciplines work to identify, intervene, treat, empower, and heal victims, survivors, offenders, and families of CSA. Furthermore, conducting rigorous research directed toward increasing the understanding of CSA and its aftereffects and implementing social programs directed toward prevention and social change to limit further occurrences of CSA and its consequences are goals that numerous professionals are working to achieve.

EDITORIAL SUMMARY

Child sexual abuse is a well-documented phenomenon, yet individuals, professionals, and society still have the tendency to deny its prevalence. It is emotionally easier and safer to believe that the sexual abuse of children is rare or that it happens to those who are different from us.

Although the Child Abuse Prevention and Treatment Act of 1974, Public Law (P.L.) 93-247, provides a legal definition of sexual abuse, there is a lack of agreement among researchers and clinicians concerning an operational definition of child sexual abuse. The two types of sexual abuse are incest or intrafamilial abuse and extrafamilial abuse. Incest or intrafamilial sexual abuse involves a perpetrator who is a family or extended family member. In cases of extrafamilial abuse, the perpetrator is someone who is outside of the child's family.

Research has suggested that negative, long-term aftereffects of child sexual abuse include depression, self-destructive behavior, anxiety, isolating and stigmatized feelings, low self-esteem and self-concept, repeated victimization, and substance abuse. Correlates of child sexual abuse include cultural, environmental, family, and individual factors.

Approximately 90% of offenders are males. Child molesters are divided into two broad categories: situational and preferential. The majority of victims of child sexual abuse are girls (about 85%), and approximately one-third of offenders are relatives of the victim. It is believed that children become and remain victims of child sexual abuse as a result of various characteristics inherent to their developmental stages.

Prevention strategies that focus on social programs and societal changes are needed to decrease instances of child sexual abuse. Research on resilient behaviors may identify variables that serve as mediating factors that help to ameliorate the potential negative affects of child sexual abuse.

REFERENCES

Alexander, P. D. (1985). A systems theory conceptualization of incest. *Family Process, 24,* 79–88.

Alexander, R. Jr. (1995). Recent legal trends in child sexual abuse cases: Direction for child protection workers. *Child and Adolescent Social Work Journal, 12*(3), 229–240.

American Psychiatric Association. (1994). *Diagnostic and Statistical Manual of Mental Disorders* (4th ed.). Washington, DC: American Psychiatric Association.

Armstrong, L. (1978). *Kiss Daddy Goodnight: A Speak-Out on Incest.* New York: Pocket Books.

Bagley, C., and King, K. (1990). *Child Sexual Abuse: The Search for Healing.* New York: Routledge.

Bagley, C., and Thurston, W. (1988). *Child Sexual Abuse: Critical Reviews of the Research Literature.* Ottawa: Federal Health and Welfare.

Bass, E., and Thornton, R. (1983). *I Never Told Anyone: Writings by Women Survivors of Child Sexual Abuse.* New York: Harper and Row.

Beatty, L., and Booth, J. (1991, August). *An Analysis of the Child Maltreatment Prevention Literature.* Poster session presented at the annual meeting of the American Psychological Association, San Francisco.

Beitchman, J. H., Zucker, K. J., Hood, J. E., DaCosta, G. A., Akman, D., and Cassavia, E. (1992). A review of the long-term effects of child sexual abuse. *Child Abuse and Neglect, 16,* 101–118.

Bender, L., and Blau, A. (1937). The reaction of children to sexual relations with adults. *American Journal of Orthopsychiatry, 7,* 500–518.

Blume, S. E. (1990). *Secret Survivors: Uncovering Incest and Its Aftereffects in Women.* New York: Wiley.

Briere, J., and Runtz, M. (1990). Differential adult symptomatology associated with three types of child abuse histories. *Child Abuse and Neglect, 14,* 357–364.

Briere, J., and Runtz, M. (1993). Childhood sexual abuse: Long-term sequelae and implications for psychological assessment. *Journal of Interpersonal Violence, 8*(3), 312–330.

Browne, A., and Finkelhor, D. (1986). Impact of child sexual abuse: A review of the research. *Psychological Bulletin, 99*(1), 66–77.

Butler, S. (1985). *Conspiracy of Silence: The Trauma of Incest* (2nd ed.). San Francisco: Volcano Press.

Caplan, G. (1964). *Principles of Preventive Psychiatry.* New York: Basic Books.

Department of Health and Human Services, Office of Human Development Services, Administration for Children, Youth and Families, and National Center on Child Abuse and Neglect. (1986). *A Report to the Congress: Joining Together to Fight Child Abuse.* Washington, DC: Superintendent of Documents.

Edwards, J. J., and Alexander, P. C. (1992). The contribution of family background to the long-term adjustment of women sexually abused as children. *Journal of Interpersonal Violence, 7*(3), 306–320.

Faller, K. C. (1988). *Child Sexual Abuse: An Interdisciplinary Manual for Diagnosis, Case Management, and Treatment.* New York: Columbia University Press.

Feldman, W., Feldman, E., Goodman, J., McGrath, P., Pless, R., Corsini, L., and Bennett, S. (1991). Is childhood sexual abuse really increasing in prevalence? An analysis of the evidence. *Pediatrics, 88*(1), 29–33.

Felsman, J. K., and Vaillant, G. E. (1987). Resilient children as adults: A 40-year study. *Advances, Institute for the Advancement of Health, 4* (4), 45–61.

Ferenczi, S. (1949). Confusion of tongues between the adult and the child (the language of tenderness and passion). *International Journal of Psychoanalysts, 49,* 692–697. (Original work published in 1933.)

Finkelhor, D. (1979). *Sexually Victimized Children.* New York: Free Press.

Finkelhor, D., and Browne, A. (1985). The traumatic impact of child sexual abuse. A conceptualization. *American Journal of Orthopsychiatry, 55,* 530–541.

Fromuth, M. E. (1986). The relationship of childhood sexual abuse with later psychological and sexual adjustment in a sample of college women. *Child Abuse and Neglect, 10*, 5–15.

Gagnon, J. (1965). Female victims of sex offenses. *Social Problems, 13*, 176–192.

Ganzarain, R. C., and Buchele, B. J. (1988). *Fugitive of Incest: A Perspective from Psychoanalysis and Group.* Madison, CT: International Universities Press.

Garbarino, J. (1980). What kind of society permits child abuse? *Infant Mental Health Journal, 1*, 270–280.

Gebhard, P., Gagnon, J., Pomeroy, W., and Christenson, C. (1965). *Sex Offender: An Analysis of Types.* New York: Harper and Row.

Gelinas, D. (1983). The persisting negative effects of incest. *Psychiatry, 46,* 313–332.

Goldstein, S. L. (1987). *The Sexual Exploitation of Children: A Practical Guide to Assessment, Investigation, and Intervention.* New York: Elsevier.

Grossman, F. K., Culhane, K., Moore, R. P., Lam, J. N., Paniesen, R. (1994). *Resiliency in Survivors of Childhood Sexual Abuse: A Review of the Literature.* Unpublished manuscript, Boston University.

Grossman, F. K., and Moore, R. P. (1994). Against the odds: Resiliency in an adult survivor of childhood sexual abuse. In C. E. Franz and A. J. Stewart (Eds.), *Women Creating Lives: Identities, Resilience, and Resistance* (pp. 71–82). New York: Guilford Press.

Groth, A. N. (1978). Patterns of sexual assault against children and adolescents. In A. W. Burgess, A. N. Groth, L. L. Holmstrom, and S. M. Sgroi (Eds.), *Sexual Assault of Children and Adolescents* (pp. 3–24). Lexington, MA: Lexington Books.

Hashima, P. Y., Jacobs, J. E., and Kenning, M. (1991, August). *Sexual Abuse Prevention Programs and Children's Perceptions of Risk.* Poster session presented at the annual meeting of the American Psychological Association, San Francisco.

Herman, J. (1981). *Father-Daughter Incest.* Cambridge, MA: Harvard University Press.

Herman, J. (1990). Discussion. In R. P. Kluft (Ed.), *Incest-Related Syndromes of Adult Psychopathology* (pp. 289–293). Washington, DC: American Psychiatric Press.

Higgins, G. O. (1994). *Resilient Adults: Overcoming a Cruel Past.* San Francisco: Jossey-Bass.

Kempe, C. H., Silverman, F. N., Steele, B. F., Droegemueller, W., and Silver, H. K. (1962). The battered-child syndrome. *Journal of the American Medical Association, 181,* 17–24.

Kendall-Tackett, K. A., Williams, L. M., and Finkelhor, D. (1993). Impact of sexual abuse on children: A review and synthesis of recent empirical studies. *Psychological Bulletin, 113*(1), 164–180.

Kinsey, A. C., Pomeroy, W. B., Martin, C. E., and Gebhard, P. (1948). *Sexual Behavior in the Human Female*. Philadelphia: W. B. Saunders.

Kirkwood, L. J., and Mihaila, M. E. (1995). Incest and the legal system: Inadequacies and alternatives. In B. Finkelman (Ed.), *Child Abuse, Vol. 2: A Multidisciplinary Survey* (pp. 79–105). New York: Garland.

Kluft, R. P. (1990). *Incest-Related Syndromes of Adult Psychopathology*. Washington, DC: American Psychiatric Press.

Lam, J. N. (1989). *Review of the Clinical and Empirical Literature on the Effects of Child Sexual Abuse from a Systems Perspective*. Unpublished manuscript, Roosevelt University at Chicago.

Lam, J. N., and Grossman, F. K. (1997). Resiliency and adult adaptation in women with and without self-reported histories of childhood sexual abuse. *Journal of Traumatic Stress, 10*(2), 175–196.

Long, P. J., and Jackson, J. L. (1993). Childhood coping strategies and the adult adjustment of female sexual abuse victims. *Journal of Child Sexual Abuse, 2,* 23–39.

Lustig, N., Dresser, J., Spellman, S., and Murray, T. (1966). Incest: A family group survival pattern. *Archives of General Psychiatry, 14,* 31–40.

Mey, B., and Neff, R. (1982). Adult-child incest: A review of research and treatment. *Adolescence, 107*(68), 717–735.

Mrazek, P. J., and Haggerty, R. J. (Eds.). (1994). *Reducing Risks for Mental Disorders: Frontiers for Preventive Intervention Research*. Washington, DC: National Academy Press.

Mrazek, P. J., and Mrazek, D. A. (1987). Resilience in child maltreatment victims: A conceptual exploration. *Child Abuse and Neglect, 11,* 357–366.

Russell, D. E. H. (1983). The incidence and prevalence of intrafamilial and extrafamilial sexual abuse of female children. *Child Abuse and Neglect, 7,* 133–146.

Rutter, M. (1985). Resilience in the face of adversity: Protective factors and resistance to psychiatric disorder. *British Journal of Psychiatry, 147,* 598–611.

Sanford, L. T. (1990). *Strong at the Broken Places*. New York: Random House.

Summit, R. C. (1983). The child sexual abuse accommodation syndrome. *Child Abuse and Neglect, 7,* 177–193.

Summit, R. C., and Kryso, J. (1978). Sexual abuse of children: A clinical spectrum. *American Journal of Orthopsychiatry, 48,* 237–251.

Wattenberg, E. (1985). In a different light: A feminist perspective on the role of mothers in father-daughter incest. *Child Welfare, 64*(3), 203–951.

Weinberg, S. (1955). *Incest Behavior*. Secaucus, NJ: Citadel Press.

Werner, E. E., and Smith, R. S. (1982). *Vulnerable, but Invincible: A Longitudinal Study of Resilient Children and Youth*. New York: McGraw-Hill.

Westerlund, E. (1986). Freud on sexual trauma: An historical review of seduction and betrayal. *Psychology of Women Quarterly, 10,* 297–310.

Wind, T. W., and Silvern, L. (1992). Type and extent of child abuse as predictors of adult functioning. *Journal of Family Violence, 7* (4), 261–281.

Wolfe, D. A. (1985). Child-abusive parents: An empirical review and analysis. *Psychological Bulletin, 97*(3), 462–482.

Wyatt, G. E., and Peters, S. D. (1986). Issues in the definition of child sexual abuse in prevalence research. *Child Abuse and Neglect, 10,* 231–240.

3

Child Neglect

Shaffdeen A. Amuwo, Ph.D.
Community Health Sciences
School of Public Health
University of Illinois at Chicago

Jacqueline B. Hill, MSW, MPH, ACSW
Department of Behavioral Sciences
Purdue University Calumet

Child neglect is a form of child maltreatment that, unlike child abuse which relates to *commission* by the parents or caretaker, is an *omission* in meeting the basic needs of children, resulting in their being harmed or being put in harm's way. It is a serious, chronic, endemic problem in the United States and the rest of the world. This is the most prevalent of all types of child maltreatment and endangers children over three times more often than physical abuse (National Center on Child Abuse and Neglect, 1988). In some instances, it leads to more developmental and educational problems (Erickson, Egeland, and Pianta, 1989; Eckenrode, Laird, and Doris, 1993; Leiter and Johnsen, 1994) and produces an equal or a greater number of fatalities (Jackson, 1984) than other maltreatment groups.

HISTORICAL RECOGNITION OF NEGLECT

Although interest in child neglect has existed since the 1970s because of its association with child abuse, it is really not a new phenomenon. Nor have its constructs remained constant over time. As far as is known, child neglect is one of the best-kept secret "diseases," yet it pervades every society known to humans. This is not to say that child neglect was not an area of concern in the United States before 1900 (Folks, 1902; Wolock and Horowitz, 1984). What is more appalling, however, is the relative disregard for the problem by professionals in comparison with child physical and sexual abuse (Dubowitz and Black, 1994; Wolock and Horowitz, 1984). The lack of attention paid to child neglect is due to many factors, including (1) a lack of empirical knowledge of its consequences, (2) the direct implications of parental deficits, (3) a reluctance to intrude into the everyday caretaker role of the parents, (4) a lack of a universal definition, and (5) a possible linkage to the economic status of the parents.

This attitude occurs among some professionals even though the history of child neglect parallels and sometimes coexists with the history of child physical and sexual abuse, both of which receive more coverage from academics and the media. At a minimum, and depending on the kind of neglect, the history of child maltreatment, including neglect, can be traced to biblical times. In fact, the Roman Law of the Twelve Fables forbade rearing of children with disabilities (Radbill, 1974). The neglect of children—including its ultimate form, abandonment—was not an uncommon phenomenon during the precolonial and colonial days (Hunt, 1970), during slavery (Anderson, 1994; Wyatt, 1985), and during the Industrial Revolution (deMause, 1974; Radbill, 1974).

In ancient times, the birth of babies was intricately linked to omens of good and evil; abandonment, infanticide, and fillicide were therefore of little concern (Broch, 1988). In nineteenth-century Asia, Europe, and America, it was not uncommon, particularly in impoverished communities, to abandon or kill unwanted children (Radbill, 1974). During the Industrial Revolution, exposure to harm was common, both as part of working conditions based on maximizing profits and in competing for food and shelter.

Historically, most societies regarded children as properties of their parents who therefore could be treated in any way. Quite often, the needs and the resources of the parents and their psychological and belief state determined the conditions of child rearing. The treatment could be a lack of attention to the needs of the child in many areas, such as education, nurturing, supervision, nutrition, medical concerns, housing, and protection from harm.

ORGANIZED EFFORTS AGAINST THE NEGLECT OF CHILDREN

The maltreatment of children is a form of human degradation. Therefore, organized efforts to reduce or ameliorate its impact in cases of abuse, neglect, abandonment, infanticide, or any other forms of child maltreatment parallels history.

Although child neglect is not a new phenomenon, it has not received as much attention from scholars as physical and sexual forms of maltreatment. Political consideration plays a great role in suppressing the exposure of child neglect as a disease entity that is worthy of studying with the same fervor as other forms of maltreatment.

Despite the paucity of data to ensure the continuation and refinement of studies, the phenomenon has been elevated to the level of social policy interest, perhaps because its understanding involves research from many disciplines. Neglected children are deprived of the protection, nurturing, education, and skills necessary to survive.

Given its relative lack of recognition in many parts of the world, worldwide statistics on child neglect prove extremely challenging. Estimates, however, put the number of neglected children in the hundreds of millions. Because the "neglect" of children has become so common in every society and because of growing awareness of the need to ensure the safety of children, in November 1954 the United Nations adopted and proclaimed a Declaration of the Rights of the Child (Barnen, 1990; Defrick, 1992). This declaration provides a worldwide framework for the treatment of children and emphasizes the rights of the child to develop in a healthy and caring environment and to be provided with all the privileges of a human being, including nutrition, security, health care, and freedom from exploitation. Furthermore, in 1989 the United Nations General Assembly adopted an International Convention on the Rights of the Child. These U.N. declarations and the subsequent affirmations by other world political bodies affect all types of child maltreatment in all nations under the U.N. charter.

In the United States, the primary focus of earlier organized efforts was toward criminal prosecution followed by punishment of the offender if found guilty and the removal of children from harm's way (Bremner, 1970). The literature, however, suggests that actions by authority were a rarity except in severe cases that resulted in homicide or in which "punishment was grossly unreasonable in relation to the offense when parents inflicted cruel and merciless punishment, or when the punishment permanently injured the child" (Thomas, 1972, p. 304). Because the earlier cases focused on the severity of the consequences, whatever the type of maltreatment, it is important to consider the history of child abuse and neglect along parallel lines. This chapter focuses on child neglect with the understanding that both phenomena often occur to the same individual. In addition, the lateness in recognizing child neglect within the context of child maltreatment does not preclude the acknowledgment of its presence in earlier cases.

The earliest record of what is now known as organized efforts against child maltreatment in the United States, according to Watkins (1996), dated back as early as 1665 when, in the state of Massachusetts, "a master was found guilty of maltreatment that resulted in the death of his 12-year-old apprentice" (p. 500). It is not clear whether the case was considered within the context of child labor law, as the twelve-year-old apprentice was not his son, or if it was just a case of criminality against a person regardless of their relationship. What is certain is that this finding of Bremner (1970), as presented by Watkins (1996), attempts to put to rest many years of claims that the first known prosecutorial case involving child abuse was that of maltreatment of Mary Ellen Wilson. Furthermore, Watkins asserted that Bremner cited two additional cases in the same state in the 1670s concerning two children removed from unsuitable homes. Watkins also cited a case in the state of Tennessee where a parent was sanctioned by the court for inflicting excessive punishment on a child.

Additionally, Lavaritz and Shelman (1996) noted that prior to Mary Ellen Wilson's case was the case of Emily Thompson. Although Emily Thompson was maltreated by her custodian, she denied that she was ever beaten and neglected, a characteristic quite common among child victims of maltreatment because of fear of further reprisal. Therefore, despite corroborative evidence provided by neighbors and the support of the American Society for the Prevention of Cruelty to Animals (ASPCA), she was returned to her abuser by the judge. Not until further publicity, ironically berating the ASPCA for equating humans with animals, and sudden the appearance of her grandmother was she removed from her abuser.

According to the literature (although disputed by some [Watkins, 1996]), the extraordinary importance of the ASPCA is that, at least until the end of the first quarter of the nineteenth century, there were no organized efforts to protect children, even though efforts were well under way to protect animals. Established in 1874, the ASPCA embraced the inclusion of children by invoking the habeas corpus law to protect Mary Ellen Wilson from the wrought of an abusive caretaker. By arguing successfully that Mary Ellen Wilson was indeed an "animal," the girl, who had experienced gross maltreatment evidenced by severe bruises on her neck and face, was taken away and the abuser jailed.

The successful prosecution of Mary Ellen Wilson, prompted by community and intellectual concerns and the recognition of the abuse, gave birth to the New York Society for the Prevention of Cruelty to Children (SPCC) in 1875. This marked the beginning of the child protection movement, at least outside of the labor industry. In the ensuing years, similar organizations were formed in San Francisco, Boston, Rochester, Baltimore, Buffalo, and Philadelphia. By 1900, the SPCC had 161 organizations and affiliates in the United States (Folks, 1902). By 1876, New York State's child protection law was enacted. Laws to stop the abuse of children in their own homes were enacted in Britain in 1884, upon the organization of Britain's National Society for the Prevention of Cruelty to Children.

Clearly, organized efforts were well under way, although the consistency of the efforts and scholarly articulation of the problems could not be determined. There was little involvement of the medical and public health community; therefore, the legal community and social service agencies led the way in recognizing the maltreatment of children. The number of such organizations declined to fewer than 50 by the mid 1930s, however, followed by a decline in public interest (Nelson, 1984).

MEDICAL COMMUNITY'S RECOGNITION OF CHILD ABUSE AND NEGLECT

The early 1960s saw the resurgence of interest in child abuse and neglect due to the work of medical professionals. Dr. Henry Kempe's seminal paper on "the battered-child syndrome" (Kempe, Silverman, Steele, Droegemeller, and Silver, 1962) by far provided the first extensive clinical conditions in young children who had been physically abused. Kempe's writing, and studies by others within the medical profession, provided the lightning rod of respectability necessary for the identification and diagnosis of child abuse. Although there was an acknowledgment of emotional neglect secondary to physical and sexual abuse, high-profile interest, respectability, devotion, and intensity were not available specifically for child neglect. Nevertheless, this paper aroused public and congressional interest and spurred the establishment of child abuse and neglect reporting laws in all states by 1967. In fact, the Children's Bureau of the U.S. Department of Health, Education, and Welfare sponsored a child abuse issue conference the same year that Kempe published his findings. A major and predicted outcome of that conference was the recommendation for the adoption of laws that would require professionals to report suspected child abuse and neglect cases to appropriate authorities. Shortly after, in 1971, the U.S. Senate Subcommittee on Children and Youth was established. Despite this attention, child neglect still lagged behind other areas of child maltreatment in terms of recognition and research. Thus, many of the writings focused primarily on physical and sexual abuse. This happened even though, for the most part, child neglect coexisted with other forms of maltreatment and constituted 52% of total maltreatment statistics (U.S. Department of Health and Human Services, Administration for Children and Families, 1996).

LEGAL DEFINITIONS OF CHILD NEGLECT

Since its "discovery," the definition of child neglect has been changing amid the prevailing political, social, economic, and cultural contexts of child rearing. Because the definition varies across cultures, professions, economic considerations, and prevailing political mores, it is necessary to consider the legal definition of child neglect within many settings.

Global Definition

The General Assembly of the United Nations, although it has no binding laws, approved a resolution recognizing the Rights of the Child in 1954 and expected all member-nations to honor the ordinance regarding the treatment of children. Furthermore, in 1989, the General Assembly unanimously adopted the creation of an International Year of the Child. By the end of 1992, 120 countries, including the United States, had ratified the convention (Defrick, 1992). The resolution covers many areas, such as the duty of the state and the community to preserve the integrity and dignity of children and the establishment of an international minimum standard for the survival of children and their protection against all forms of exploitation and abuse (United Nations International Children's Emergency Fund, 1989). Also covered in the resolution are avenues to prevent (1) the inducement or coercion of a child to engage in any unlawful sexual activity, (2) the exploitative use of children in prostitution or other unlawful sexual practices, and (3) the exploitative use of children in pornographic performance and materials (Munir, 1993).

A challenging attribute of child neglect globally is the position of the child in a society as well as the prevailing culture and social economic status of the family. For instance, practices common to Western culture—weaning the child, the use of infant formula, child and parents sleeping in separate rooms or not sharing the same bed— might be construed as child neglect in some nonwesternized cultures, especially those of Africa. Therefore, the universal definition of child neglect will be dependent on the extent to which cultural and historical traditions similar to those of the Western nations are considered (deMause, 1974; Solomon, 1973; Steele, 1970). According to Poffenberger (1981), "what might be considered child neglect or deprivation includ-ing abuse by some Western standards may also fulfill a normative function in child rearing practices in some culture" (p. 72). What the U.N. declaration did, however, was to provide "legal" context to a global issue, given the variations that occur from place to place, and engineer a contextual framework for interacting with the child.

Definition of Child Neglect in United States

Although legal definitions vary from state to state, in the United States universal governing principles for the protection of children have evolved over time. Serving as a template for the current definition of child neglect was the adoption of laws that required professionals to report cases of child abuse and neglect. This recommenda-tion was made by conferees convened by the Children's Bureau of U.S. Department of Health, Education, and Welfare after the presentation of Kempe's seminal paper of 1962. Professionals working with children mandated to report any suspected abuse or neglect include educators, physicians, nurses, mental health professionals, social workers, and day-care providers (Myers, 1992). Between 1963 and 1967, all fifty states had some form of reporting laws.

CHILD ABUSE PREVENTION AND TREATMENT ACT

In January 1974, the Congress of the United States enacted Public Law 93-237, the Child Abuse Prevention and Treatment Act (CAPTA). At its inception, this law allo-cated $60 million in federal funds to help states and local communities develop pro-grams and services for abused and neglected children. One of the primary conditions of funding was to require states to establish systems for identifying and reporting suspected cases of abuse and neglect and for responding to the needs of children and families. Although it has been modified several times, CAPTA provides legislation for compliance by the states for funding eligibility. The state laws were therefore established to meet congressional guidance, at a minimum. Many states' definitions far exceed the guidelines provided by CAPTA, however.

CAPTA was established within the Department of Health and Human Services, the National Center on Child Abuse and Neglect (NCCAN):

> NCCAN conducts activities designed to assist and enhance national, state and commu-nity efforts to prevent, identify, and treat child abuse and neglect. These activities include: conducting research and demonstrations; supporting service improvement projects; gathering, analyzing, and disseminating information through a national clear-inghouse; and awarding grants to eligible states to develop, strengthen, and carry out

child abuse and neglect prevention and treatment programs and programs relating to the investigation and prosecution of child abuse cases. (U.S. Department of Health and Human Services, Administration for Children and Families, 1996, pp. 30748–30749)

Within the context of CAPTA, child neglect can be defined as a type of maltreatment that refers to the failure to provide needed, age-appropriate care.

Some researchers have divided acts of neglect by the parents into eight subgroups: physical health care, mental health, supervision, substitute child care, housing hazards, household sanitation, personal hygiene, and nutrition (Pecora, Whitaker, Mallucio, Barth, and Plotnick, 1992). Most professionals, however, have defined four types of neglect: physical, emotional, educational, and medical (National Child Abuse and Neglect Data Systems, 1994). Physical neglect accounts for most of the cases of maltreatment. Reports from National Child Abuse and Neglect Data Systems show an estimate of 8 of every 1,000 children in this category. Physical neglect is an act of omission and may include medical care, child abandonment, inadequate supervision, rejection of a child leading to expulsion from the home, and failure to provide adequately for the child's safety, emotional needs, and physical needs. Some of the consequences of physical neglect include severe disruption to child development causing failure to thrive, malnutrition, serious illnesses, physical harm in the form of cuts, falls that may result in head injury or broken bones, bruises, burns due to lack of supervision, and a lifetime of low self-esteem and retardation. Failure to thrive (FTT) may be caused by extreme physical neglect or other medical problems (Schmitt and Mauro, 1989). That this was recognized early in the 1900s shows that neglect existed then, as manifested clinically by FTT. Children with FTT exhibit marked stunted growth coupled with reactive attachment disorder of infancy (American Psychiatric Association, 1994). Educational neglect occurs when a child is not monitored to ensure that he or she attends school regularly (resulting in chronic truancy), is of mandatory school age but not enrolled in school or not receiving school training adequate for his or her development, or is not receiving any needed special educational training. Educational neglect can lead to hopelessness, underachievement in acquiring necessary basic skills, dropping out of school, antisocial behaviors, and low self-esteem. It is estimated that 4.5 of every 1,000 children are victims of educational neglect (National Child Abuse and Neglect Data Systems, 1994).

Emotional neglect involves activities that may affect a child's psychological being. The activities may include disruptive behavior of the parents such as severe fights or spousal abuse, allowing a child to use drugs or alcohol, calling a child names and focusing on his or her failures or shortcomings, refusing or failing to provide needed psychological care, constant belittling, and withholding affection. Severe neglect of infants can result in nonbonding with the parents or any adult, which may lead to a lack of respect or empathy for life. Failure to monitor infants may result in the infant failing to thrive and may even lead to infant death.

Medical neglect involves failing to provide for appropriate health care and disease prevention needs of the child or withholding health care, although financially able to obtain treatment. In 1993, 23,009 cases of medical neglect were reported to authorities (National Child Abuse and Neglect Data Systems, 1994). Medical neglect may result in a child not being immunized properly against childhood diseases such as measles, mumps, diphtheria, and rubella, resulting in chronic health problems, including death. Although withholding health care needs because of religious beliefs may not constitute neglect in some states, authorities have gone to court to force medical treatment if the life of the child is threatened.

OVERVIEW OF OTHER RESEARCH IN THE FIELD

Since Polansky, Hally, and Polansky (1975) published their profile of neglect, and since neglect as a form of maltreatment has become more pronounced, only a very small number of articles per year specifically devoted to the area of neglect have been produced. In addition, monographs from symposia or other scientific gatherings have been scarce. As a result, a literature review of the discipline of neglect can be quite adventurous compared with other maltreatment areas. Child neglect is an indictment of the social fabric and the economic structure of even the most advanced country in the world. Given the continued growth in the world economy and advancement in technical knowledge, one might expect a growth in human potential. This, however, has not been the case. There has been greater disparity between the average income and the income of the poor (United Nations Development Program, 1996). This phenomenon will obviously spur continued examination of poverty as a risk factor for child neglect.

Therefore, it is suspected that child neglect will continue to increase beyond proportions. Of course, the increase in incidence will be dependent on the prevailing definitions. To this extent, scholars might want to pay particular attention to the evolving definition of neglect, both conceptually and operationally, to ensure that definitions do not continue to change to the degree that the attention to the plight of possibly millions of children who will be victimized will be reduced or limited. As scholarly work proceeds in the area of definition, specific avenues of neglect pertaining to incidence and prevalence should be addressed.

An outline of the interest of scholars in the area of child neglect was provided in response to NCCAN's announcement for comments on priority areas for research and documentation (U.S. Department of Health and Human Services, Administration for Children and Families, 1996). The responses included research interest and program development in the areas of (1) families with substance abuse and addiction problems, (2) families experiencing domestic violence, (3) parents with mental retardation, (4) families that have children with social needs, (5) impact of community-based family support, and (6) families with adopted children. Although major interest will focus on population groups and families, several exploratory, well-designed experimental studies using large populations sponsored by NCCAN could help not only quantify but also articulate the extent of neglect. Furthermore, addressing neglect within the context of human needs and potential loss to the future of the country will help spur further research and subsequent publications in many areas, including (1) social and environmental effects on social functioning mediating neglect, (2) community organizational context contributing or resilient to neglect, (3) governmental and institutional policy analyses or adoption impacting on neglect, and (4) exploration of domains of influence on children that might mediate neglect.

Several studies are under way that might contribute immensely to the field. Examples include studies going on at the Erickson Institute for Advanced Study in Child Development, Chicago. Some of the studies at the Erickson Institute focus on social impoverishment, community dimensions of child maltreatment, and examination of low- and high-risk families within the context of child maltreatment (Garbarino and Crouter, 1978; Garbarino and Kostelny, 1992). Other examples of studies under way with potential to addressing neglect include studies at the Kempers Institute in Colorado, the eight-year study on human development currently being conducted by the Harvard School of Public Health in Chicago communities, and the Minnesota Mother-Child Interaction Project designed to develop an integrative model for examining the antecedents of child maltreatment. Although some of these studies do not directly focus on neglect, they nevertheless are organized and implemented to unveil human potential in deprived communities and address the context of ameliorating and preventing violence against and among youth. Obviously, the neglect of children is a major aspect of violence against youth. In addition, given the proliferation of managed care and that more than 20 million U.S. children suffering from a variety of chronic conditions may be at risk in transition to managed care, policy implications on child neglect need to be thoroughly studied.

CORRELATES OF CHILD NEGLECT

The complexity surrounding the definition of abuse also makes its correlates quite challenging. A single factor is not likely to stand out as a correlate. Several models, however, have been postulated to provide a general framework of the phenomenon of child neglect. Such models are necessary to assist clinicians and policy makers in addressing prevention and intervention issues. Prominent among these models is the ecological model (Giovannoni and Billingsley, 1970; Pelton, 1989; Young, 1964). Many circumstances including social, psychological, education, age, stress, family settings, size of family, and parental dysfunction have led to neglect of children (Belsky, 1993; Gelles and Straus, 1988). The ecological model provides a comprehensive picture of correlates of neglect and, within such contextual framework, other multiple factors that contribute to the occurrence of neglect (Belsky, 1980; Crouch and Milner, 1993; Newberger and Newberger, 1981). Proponents of the ecological perspectives generally focus on the contextual issues relating to parental understanding of the needs of children, the role of poverty, social adjustment, social difficulties (Dubowitz, Black, Starr, and Zuravin, 1993), and status of the children.

Parental Understanding

Determining the basic needs of children is very complex, varying across several dimensions and requiring a good understanding by the parent. Yet using the Childhood

Level of Living scale, Polansky and Chalmers's (1987) studies have shown strong agreement about the basic elements of child care (Polansky, Ammons, and Weathersby, 1983; Polanksy and Williams, 1978). Parental understanding of the needs of children is very crucial to applying the necessary nurturing and responses. Many parents, however, lack these attributes because of their own young age as parents, immaturity, social isolation, unfulfilled dependency needs, or poor knowledge of child development (Connelly and Strauss, 1992; Meier, 1964; Wiehe, 1996).

Poverty

Studies have shown that neglect occurs more frequently among parents from impoverished communities (Gabarino and Kostelny, 1992). Within these communities and among other communities, the poorest are generally the ones with the highest risk of neglect (Giovannoni and Billingsley, 1970; Wise and Meyers, 1988). The issue of poverty is at the forefront of correlates of neglect because it compounds additional stress that might impact on parenting responsibilities of nurturing, caring, and meeting basic needs of the child. Associated with poverty are major areas of neglect, such as (1) poor housing conditions due to the presence of lead and inadequate bathroom and cooking facilities, (2) limited or lack of access to health care due to ineligibility or during waiting period for benefits and no insurance coverage, (3) inadequate nutrition due to no cooking facilities, and (4) inability to respond adequately to educational deficits of the child due to isolation and a lack of resources. Although poverty is not the only correlate of neglect, and neglect can be found among "well-to-do" families, studies show that it is by far the most important contributing factor in the ecological pathway of neglect (Giovanoni and Billinglsey, 1970; Kotch et al., 1995; Wolock and Horowitz, 1984).

Social Difficulties

Social difficulties of the caretaker and the child have been associated with neglect. The social difficulties of the caretaker include poor parenting style, disturbed parent-child attachment, and anxiety among parents and neglected children (Egeland and Stroufe, 1981; Egeland, Stoufe, and Erickson, 1983). Parents of neglected children also exhibit deficits in communication, decreased social behavior, and low prosocial behaviors (Crittenden, 1992). In addition, parents who were neglected when they were children seem to have the tendency to neglect their children because of their own reduced attachment and other psychological stress (Polansky, Chalmers, Buttenweiser, and Williams, 1980; Starr, MacLean, and Keating, 1991).

Substance Abuse

Alcohol and drug abuse have been directly tied to an increased risk of child abuse and neglect (Wright, Garrison, Wright, and Stimmel, 1991). Studies have shown high correlation between parental substance abuse and child neglect (Famularo, Kinscherff, and Fenton, 1992; Kropenske et al., 1994). Although alcohol is implicated in a wide range of birth defects and developmental disabilities, the National Institute on Drug Abuse estimated that 60% of women of child-bearing age consume alcohol during pregnancy. U.S. juvenile courts experienced approximately a 3,000% increase in drug-related abuse and neglect petitions between 1984 and 1989 (Brady, Posner, Lang, and Rosati, 1994).

INTEGRATED MODEL OF CHILD NEGLECT

The determination of correlates must be based on a combination of reports from many sources and from validated experimental research. From the review of literature and sources identified earlier, it can be said that neglect occurs within a set of four domains, with each of the four domains of influence interacting with each other at one time or the other. Therefore, the likelihood of one domain acting independently is extremely small. Moreover, correlating factors within each domain become even more complex when one considers that different forms of neglect may overlap and that the consequence may be more intensive in one domain than the other (Ammerman, Cassissi, Hersen, and VanHasselt, 1986; Clausen and Crittenden 1991; Briere and Runtz, 1989). The four domains of influence on child abuse and neglect are individual, parents and caretakers, community, and society.

Individual

The term "individual" is being used here to refer to a child of up to eighteen years old, which fits into the operational definition of a dependent child. Because of the complex psychological and biological process of development that takes place during the span of these eighteen years, it is important that the problems of the neglected child be addressed within the context of several stages of development. Thus, correlates of neglect with regard to an infant might be markedly different from those of late adolescence. Therefore, the development of the child can be divided into four stages: infancy, preschool years, school-age or preadolescent years, and adolescent years.

Infancy and Preschool Years   For the most part, the arrival of a baby carries with it much joy and happiness, and extraordinary feelings of accomplishment for having provided for the continuation of the human race by producing a progeny. In fact, in most cultures, the arrival of a baby is regarded as the most important phase of life (Korbin, 1981). This arrival also causes stressful conditions, however. Humans are in the class mammalia, of which there are more than 400 species. Within this class, there is no other mammal whose young is more dependent than human beings. A newborn is defenseless and imposes some structural psychological stress, as everything has to be done for that child. He or she has neither been trained to be cooperative nor to have meaningful social interactions. That the child is a psychological and biological being imposing on his or her caretakers sets off several complex circumstances. These circumstances increase the vulnerability of the child to neglect between infancy and preschool years. The correlates of maltreatment at this time period include weak neck muscles, weak bone structure, helplessness, smallness, ultimate dependency, structural stress on the family, economic burden, and vulnerability to shaking or whiplashing (Hendee, 1991).

According to Erickson's (1968) theory of psychosocial development, infancy represents the "age of basic trust versus mistrust" (p. 97). The child learns that others, especially the parents and caretakers, can be trusted to provide an intimate nurturing environment that includes feeding and satisfaction of all bodily and emotional needs. Deviation from this process or any mistrust that develops may leave the child unbonded and lacking in affection. Although the intrinsic behavior of the parent toward the child is most important, the child is also able to recognize and approve others who provide the child's basic needs. With the repetitive actions of adults, the child becomes psychologically attached. During infancy, however, according to Freudian development theory, the primary source of tension and pleasure for the infant is the mouth (Hendee, 1991). Thus, the child uses cries, especially during infanthood, to elicit response. A baby's cry, on the other hand, has been suggested to contribute to the vulnerability of the child to maltreatment by the caretaker (Frodi and Lamb, 1985). The child maltreatment data (approximately 53% of which is neglect) for 1994 shows that the five-year average rate of victimization among children less than one year of age had the highest rate, with 16 victims per 1,000 children of the same age. At one year of age, the rates dropped to 14 victims per 1,000. Among children eight to nine years, the rates are 12 per 1,000, whereas they are nine per 1,000 among sixteen-year-olds (U.S. Department of Health and Human Services, Administration for Children and Families, 1996). Thus, there is an inverse relationship between the age of the child and abuse and neglect.

Preadolescent Years   Erickson (1968) described this period as "industry versus inferiority" (p. 123). Children at this phase of life derive pleasure through completing tasks and learning new skills. Their moral judgment is generally tied to good versus bad: good if they conform to fixed rules of others and bad if they are not able to. Conformity is therefore very important to them.

This age represents the age of first experiences in school and in interacting socially and educationally with peers and adults outside the family. Such children seek approval and admiration of peers and others through negative or positive attention seeking. Unacceptable social behaviors may begin to manifest at this time if unchecked with concrete guidance. The maltreatment rate of 14 to 15 victims per 1,000 is generally stable during this period (U.S. Department of Health and Human Services, Administration for Children and Families, 1996).

Adolescent Years   The adolescent period represents a developmental phase between childhood and adulthood characterized by physical, sexual, and psychological developments. This period could be called the "freedom" years in the sense that it represents a phase in which a child grows intellectually and emotionally and seeks opportunity and friendship while spared of the adult responsibilities that come with such opportunities. To many adolescents, these are the most troubling years, because they also represent turbulence, peer dominance, and a search for autonomy. This period is transitional, contextual, and highly influenced by many factors that include relationship with peers, family, community, culture, ethnic background, geographic location, religious practice, beliefs, political climate, moral values, and economic status (Hendee, 1991).

Accompanying the adolescent period is the period of puberty, a dynamic biological process primarily related to the acquisition of reproductive functioning that results in manhood or womanhood and the development of relationship skills. Although the variability that takes place here between females and males and between individuals is enormous, this period is essentially accompanied by qualitative and quantitative changes in the hormonal system, pituitary glands, and adrenal glands that result in the development of primary sex characteristics. For obvious reasons, no two adolescents are alike, and the rapid changes that take place by themselves also put an adolescent at risk of being neglected and maltreated, especially sexually. Provocative attempts by adolescents at this time to become "normal" or like everybody else may make them more vulnerable to emotional, physical, and sexual abuse. The physical changes are said to have some effects on attitude, emotional behavior, and interaction of the adolescent with the family and the community, resulting in mood swings that often are incongruent with the apparent provocation. In essence, this increases their exposure to harm's way and to vulnerability.

Parents and Caretakers

In nearly all instances, parents and caretakers are the guilty parties in substantiated cases of neglect. In fact, some scholars' definition of neglect directly implicates the parents and caregivers despite their own vulnerability, needs, and mental and physical state (Gaudin, 1993). Several others, however, consider the status of the parents and caretakers as a domain of influence on child neglect. An extensive review of the literature conducted by Connelly and Straus (1992) identified a number of characteristics of young mothers associated with increased risk of abusive behavior. These correlates of social dysfunction could also be attributed to neglect. They are multifactorial and include single parenthood, inadequate support systems, insufficient knowledge of and experience in child rearing, inadequate education, early repeated pregnancy, poverty, minority group membership, perinatal difficulties, failure to secure prenatal care during the first trimester, immaturity, unfulfilled dependency needs, poor knowledge of child development, marital violence and discord, and the use of physical punishment. Other correlates of neglect that might be attributed to the vulnerability of the parents and caretakers include having unrealistic expectations of children's behavior and emotional development (Polansky, Gaudin, Ammons, and Davis, 1985), alcohol and substance abuse (Brady et al., 1994), and family and religious beliefs (Dubowitz et al., 1993). The greater the number of the conditions stated, the greater the likelihood that the child will be neglected.

The child's characteristics, such as being born after a difficult pregnancy, illness during infancy, difficult personality, or mannerisms that provoke anger in the parent or caretaker can also place the child at risk for neglect and abuse. Children who do not meet developmental expectations of parents and caretakers—like timely toilet training, acquisition of speech and language skills, and other comparative behaviors—are likely targets for differential treatment.

Community

The ecological model of child neglect has as its core the social dimensions of the community. Garbarino and Kostelny (1992) described child maltreatment as a community problem and attempted to further articulate the role of the social environment on family functioning. Their study, which was part of an extensive research design to study human ecology, involved the seventy-seven community areas of Chicago. Using the correlation between low income and child maltreatment (U.S. Department of Health and Human Services, Administration for Children and Families, 1996), they showed in a series of case studies that (1) poverty, violence, and poor housing appear to be congruent with negative community climate and lack of community identity (Garbarino and Kostelny, 1992); (2) there are higher levels of child maltreatment in high-risk areas than in low-risk areas; (3) there is a very high sense of disassociation in high-risk communities; and (4) services and resources are more available in low-risk areas where child maltreatment is lower.

The community as a domain of influence is further supported by the work of Earls, McGuire, and Shay (1994) in their effort to evaluate a community intervention to reduce the risk of child abuse. Their study was designed to build a caring Boston community with families empowered to break patterns of abusive and neglectful behavior. Using population markers and several questionnaires, they were able to determine that (1) in a community where extensive cultural diversity predominates, there is also a language barrier, social isolation, street violence, and negative health indicators that impact on the vulnerability of families with young children; and (2) there is a strong association between the cultural background of parents and their child disciplinary practices.

The above studies illustrate the tremendous role that communities and neighborhoods play as correlates of child maltreatment. Communities that are poor, disorganized, and at a high risk for antisocial behaviors also experience high levels of child neglect. The extent of the problems, however, is generally only known by the residents themselves, whereas authorities are, for the most part, oblivious until celebrated or highly publicized cases occur.

On February 8, 1994, while investigating an alleged drug deal, police in Chicago swept into an apartment at 219 North Keystone Avenue, on the west side of Chicago. There they found nineteen children living in squalor. According to television news and newspaper accounts, the children were living on top of each other on a pair of dirty mattresses or were sprawled on the apartment's cold floor amid food scraps, cigarette butts, and human excrement. Most of the children were in dirty diapers or underwear. According to police accounts, one boy was later found to have cerebral palsy and had bruises, belt marks, and cigarette burns on his body, while two of the children who were awake were sharing a neck bone with a dog.

One might think that the above case is very rare and extreme. Yet drug-abusing women participating in an intervention project near the 219 North Keystone address said shortly after the discovery that the case was not as isolated as it seemed, especially in an area very much entrenched in drug abuse (personal communication). Parental substance abuse can lead to any type of maltreatment, including neglect. The type of neglect could be multifactorial, encompassing all forms of neglect, and in combination with other forms of maltreatment, including physical and sexual abuse.

Society

Upon examining what goes on in a community, the role that society plays in child neglect becomes clear. A society implies a political, social, and economic context. The political context dictates the definition of neglect and provides an avenue to safeguard children and protect families. That child neglect is a political concept underscores many cases, because the legal definition is modified to suit society's outcry. The case of Baby Jane Doe is a good example.

Baby Jane Doe was an infant with extensive congenital problems that required long-term hospitalization and expensive treatments. Given her poor prognosis, her parents requested that physicians not proceed with any treatment. The parents' request caused a great deal of furor in the court of public opinion. The state of Indiana (where the case occurred), sued the parents as well as the medical provider in order to force provision of service and to invoke the Child Abuse Amendment Act of 1984. However, the state child neglect statues provided for governmental intervention only in medical treatment decision-making for nondisabled children. The U.S. Congress later modified the definition of maltreatment to include the withholding of food or medical treatment for handicapped children. The controversial modification, commonly called the "Baby Doe Compromise," transfers the decision to provide or not to provide medical service to the professional and ethical judgment of the physician. Thus, the political issue practically changed the definition of neglect. Furthermore, Nelson (1984) illustrated the role that political consideration played in the congressional approval of CAPTA.

The social context of neglect is that it is more prevalent and reported in communities with "low social value." This is not to say, however, that it is only limited to poor communities. As for the economic context, the high-risk communities studied by Garbarino and Kostelny (1992) are generally poor communities with low investments and therefore low economic returns.

CHARACTERISTICS OF OFFENDERS AND VICTIMS

Based on a review of the literature and on the work of the authors, the offender in child neglect is not always the parent or the caretaker (Paget, Philip, and Abramczyk, 1993; Ryan, 1977). As indicated under the correlates of neglect and in looking at the ecological context of neglect, the culprits also include the society, neighborhood characteristics, culture, and the prevailing political context (Garbarino and Kostelny, 1992; Nelson, 1984).

Socioeconomic Status of the Caretaker or Parent

Socioeconomic status has been identified as a very strong predictor of child neglect. The majority (approximately 51%) of children confirmed as neglected come from homes headed by single females. In addition, most of them are either unemployed

(42%), have very low income, or are dependent on public assistance (American Association for Protecting Children, 1988; U.S. Department of Health and Human Services, National Center on Child Maltreatment, 1996). The review by Claussen and Crittenden (1991) suggested that lower-income-level parents are associated with the most severe forms of neglect and that higher-income-level parents are associated with less severe forms of neglect. There appears to be no other maltreatment that correlates more with poverty than neglect. That poor women, regardless of color, have the greater likelihood of being perpetrators of neglect calls into question society's expectations of single, vulnerable, powerless, and poor women to support families.

Access of Parents and Caregivers to Support Systems

Quite a number of families do not have access to the supportive resources of extended families. Therefore, at times they have to leave their children under the care of siblings for periods ranging from short to long term. The question of concern is, When does such action become neglect?

Race of Victims

According to data from the American Association for Protecting Children (1988) data, an overwhelming number of neglected children, approximately 63%, are Caucasians. Yet African Americans and Hispanics, representing, respectively, 20% and 12% of neglect cases, have higher risk. The statistics are also closely related to total maltreatment figures for 1990–1994 from forty states (U.S. Department of Health and Human Services, Administration for Children and Families, 1996). This report shows maltreatment victims to be 56% white, 27% African American, and 10% Hispanic.

Age of Victims

Available data appear to show that the younger a child is, the more likely he or she will be neglected. Data from the NCCAN show that 54% of neglected children are less than five years of age, and 34% of cases reported are for infants. The average age of neglected children, however, is six years (American Association for Protecting Children, 1988). The age of the victim also depends on the type of neglect. As might be expected, older children are more likely to suffer from educational neglect than younger ones. Medical neglect, however, may be more common among preschool-age children but may not be discovered until noticed by school authorities.

Gender of Victims

There have not been substantial studies conducted that associate gender with neglect. The U.S. Department of Health and Human Services (1996) report showed that 52% of reported cases were males and 48% were females. These figures are also congruent with the U.S. Department of Health and Human Services' five-year (1990–1994) report on data collected from forty-five states regarding victims of maltreatment.

PREVENTION AND TREATMENT

The prevention and intervention of child neglect needs to be addressed within the context of public health. Such contexts focus on primary, secondary, and tertiary prevention. The public health context is even more crucial now than ever before, given the urgency of addressing the myriad long-term social problems created by the impact of dehumanizing children through neglect. Paradoxically, despite the paucity of data on child neglect, some essential stages of public health endeavors are already in progress. These endeavors include (1) developing surveillance systems for morbidity and mortality associated with child neglect, (2) identifying risk groups using knowledge from the correlates of child neglect, (3) applying case control methods to be able to identify risk factors that could be modified, and (4) designing rigorously evaluated studies. The results of these endeavors would substantially help in identifying all the domains of influence on children and would provide avenues for focusing on prevention and intervention strategies.

The focus of primary prevention is to address the antecedents of child neglect ecologically. This will involve the society, the community, the individuals, and the parents. The major focuses here are to address human needs and to create resources. Enacting laws to protect children, providing adequate housing and nutrition, and educating parents and caretakers to ensure an understanding of their role in appropriately nurturing their children are important interventions. Immunization services for children, providing access to medical care, teaching prosocial behaviors to children, and reducing negative influences on their environments are some examples of preventive measures. Primary prevention efforts also include the implementation of specialized programs to address the needs of the family, given the chaotic state of some communities.

Several home visitation programs being developed and implemented throughout the country for new parents are examples of primary prevention. An excellent example of the home visitation strategy is Hawaii Healthy Start (Hawaii Department of Health, 1991), which has prevented neglect among participants and showed great potential for application in other areas of the country. Some features of Hawaii Healthy Start include:

1. Systematic hospital-based screening

2. Community-based home visiting family support services

3. Individualized intensive service based on the family's need and level of risk

4. Linkage to health-care services

5. Coordinated health and social services for at-risk families

6. Continuous follow-up with the family until the child reaches age five

7. A structured training program in the dynamics of abuse and neglect, early identification of families at risk, and home visiting

8. Collaboration with other programs to serve children through age three who are at risk of developmental delay

9. Staff selection and retention

Using Hawaii Healthy Start as a model, the Chicago Model for Child Abuse Prevention was developed and implemented in 1994 for use in Chicago neighborhoods (Amuwo and Rashid, 1994). This model, along with several other Illinois initiatives, has become a cornerstone of Healthy Families of Illinois (HFI) (Illinois Department of Public Health, 1995) Project. The goals of HFI are to strengthen family functioning, enhance child development, promote positive parenting, enhance parent-child interaction, and link families with community health and other resources.

Secondary prevention involves the application of strategies to families identified as "at risk" for neglect before the occurrence of neglect. Programs like Healthy Families of Illinois are also targeted at such families because they are at high risk for neglect. Because of the success of home visitations, the Ronald McDonald Children's Charities in partnership with the National Committee to Prevent Child Abuse have now developed Healthy Families of America in more than twenty-two states.

Tertiary prevention aims at providing protective services for children who have experienced neglect and providing necessary services such as nutrition, education, prenatal care, and psychological treatment to the affected families. In addition, provision of basic human needs—for example, adequate employment, housing, and nutrition—for affected families will reduce recidivism and preserve families.

LEGAL ISSUES AND FUTURE TRENDS

As indicated earlier, the definitions of child neglect will continue to form an important legal issue. Future trends will be driven by the political context of the day. For instance, in some states identified "cocaine babies" delivered by substance-abusing women or cases of fetal alcohol syndrome warrant criminal prosecution of the mother as an abuser. Such accusations immediately establish that the authorities are labeling the abusive parent. The fetus is recognized as an unborn child and creates tension between right-to-life groups and abortion rights and protective services workers. On the other hand, a prosecutor might charge a mother with child neglect if, for example, the mother continued to use drugs during pregnancy and therefore allowed the fetus to be affected by a drug or alcohol. This could be considered a punishable offense. Thus, future trends will involve many political and socially conscious groups becoming interested in providing services to the mother and her unborn child in a positive, nonpunitive manner.

Another trend is the continued recognition of the child as the ultimate responsibility of the parent. By such recognition, the degree to which society is involved in the care of children will be curtailed. In addition, any action by child protection services to remove children from a dysfunctional home could be seen as violating the privacy of the family. The rise in teenage pregnancy sends an alarm to professionals concerned about the developmental needs of teenagers when their own maturity is questionable. Although vigilance is warranted in cases of suspected or documented neglect, the resources of child protection services are often diverted to cases of severe abuse. This bifurcation of resources will continue until the impact of neglect is absorbed and understood by families and communities.

In its report Neighbors Helping Neighbors, the U.S. Advisory Board on Child Abuse and Neglect (1993) made a number of recommendations that favor strengthening neighborhoods and improving the quality and quantity of services available for families. Furthermore, the importance of neighborhoods in combating neglect was emphasized in the 1994 Kids Count Data Book, issued by the Annie Casey Foundation. To this extent, future trends on the study of child neglect will focus on the recommendations of the U.S. Advisory Board on Child Abuse and Neglect (1993). The recommendations include (1) participation of neighborhood residents in planning and managing services that address issues of neglect, (2) empowering community residents to own their own homes, (3) implementing prevention zones through public and private partnerships, and (4) funding more family resource centers. The new directions of the U.S. Advisory Board on Child Abuse and Neglect will spur research and program implementation in areas of neglect relevant to neighborhood issues. Furthermore, there will be greater proliferation of home visitation services and evaluations of their impact.

CONCLUSION

Understanding the context in which neglect occurs is essential to developing an appropriate assessment for intervention. When neglect is primarily a result of individual dysfunctional behavior instead of community or environmental factors, carefully constructed risk assessment measures are necessary. Interventions to remedy neglect should focus on the provision of supportive resources that include nurturing neglectful parents, professional services, treatment/service plans, emergency financial assistance, and family preservation services.

EDITORIAL SUMMARY

Child neglect involves an act of omission in which the basic needs of a child have not been met. Although neglect is the most prevalent of all types of child maltreatment and its consequences are as serious as child physical and sexual abuse, it receives far less attention than abuse.

Definitions of neglect tend to change amid the prevailing political, social, economic, and cultural contexts of child rearing. Researchers have identified four general types of neglect: physical, emotional, educational, and medical. Acts of neglect have been further divided into eight subgroups: physical health care, mental health care, inadequate supervision, substitute child care, housing hazards, household sanitation, personal hygiene, and nutrition.

No other type of child maltreatment correlates more closely with poverty than neglect. Poverty, however, is not the only factor associated with neglect, and the ecological model provides a comprehensive explanation of the multiple factors that contribute to its occurrence. The developmental stage of the child, the parents and caregivers, the community, and society are four domains that may also influence neglect.

Offenders tend to be parents or caregivers, but society, neighborhood characteristics, culture, and the prevailing political context may also contribute to the neglect of children. Younger children face a greater risk of being neglected than older children. The development of prevention strategies that focus on children and their parents, the community, and society will ultimately help to address human needs and create the resources necessary to obliterate child neglect.

REFERENCES

American Association for Protecting Children. (1988). *Highlights of Official Child Neglect and Abuse Reporting, 1986.* Denver: American Humane Association.

American Psychiatric Association. (1994). *Diagnostic and Statistical Manual of Mental Disorders* (4th ed.). Washington, DC: American Psychiatric Association.

Ammerman, R. T., Cassissi, J. E., Hersen, M., and VanHasselt, V. B. (1986). Consequences of physical abuse and neglect in children. *Clinical Psychology Review, 6,* 291–310.

Amuwo, S. A., and Rashid, J. R. (1994). *Chicago Model for Child Abuse Prevention Study in Healthy Families of Illinois* (1995). Report of the Healthy Families, Illinois Steering Committee to Governor Jim Edgar and the general assembly. Springfield: Illinois Department of Public Health.

Anderson, C. (1994). *Black Labor, White Wealth.* Edgewood, MD: Duncan and Duncan.

Barnen, R. (1990). *The International Convention: What It Says and How It Can Change the Status of Children Worldwide.* New York: United Nations.

Belsky, J. (1980). Child maltreatment: An ecological integration. *American Psychologis, 35,* 320–335.

Belsky, J. (1993). Etiology of child maltreatment: A developmental-ecological analysis. *Psychological Bulletin, 114,* 413–434.

Brady, J. P., Posner, M., Lang, C., and Rosati, M. J. (1994). *Risk and Reality: The Implications of Prenatal Exposure to Alcohol and Other Drugs* (U.S. Department of Health and Human Services). Washington, DC: U.S. Government Printing Office.

Bremner, R. H. (Ed.). (1970). *Children and Youth in America: A Documentary History, 1600–1865* (Vol. 1). Cambridge, MA: Harvard University Press.

Briere, J., and Runtz, M. (1989). Multivariate correlates of childhood psychological and physical maltreatment among university women. *Child Abuse and Neglect, 12,* 331–341.

Broch, H. (1988). Abandonment, infanticide, and fillicide. *Pediatric Perspectives, 142,* 1058–1060.

Bureau of Justice Statistics, Department of Justice (1988). *National Incidence Based Reporting System Handbook.* Washington, DC: U.S. Government Printing Office. (Produced annually.)

Claussen, A. H., and Crittenden, P. M. (1991). Physical and psychological maltreatment: Relations among types of maltreatment. *Child Abuse and Neglect, 15,* 5–18.

Connelly, C. D., and Strauss, M. A. (1992). Mother's age and risk for physical abuse. *Child Abuse and Neglect, 12,* 295–304.

Crittenden, P. M. (1992). Children's strategies for coping with adverse home environments: An interpretation using attachment theory. *Child Abuse and Neglect, 16,* 329–343.

Crouch, J. L., and Milner, J. S. (1993). Effects of child neglect on children. *Criminal Justice and Behavior, 20,* 49–65.

Defrick, S. (Ed.). (1992). *The United Nations Convention on the Rights of the Child: A Guide to Travant Preparatoires.* London: HMSO.

deMause, L. (Ed). (1974). *The History of Childhood.* New York: Harper and Row.

Dubowitz, H., and Black, M. (1994). Child neglect. In R. M. Reece (Ed.), *Child Abuse: Medical Diagnosis and Management.* (pp. 279–297). Philadelphia: Lea and Febiger.

Dubowitz, H., Black, M., Starr, R. H., Jr., and Zuravin, S. (1993). A conceptual definition of child neglect. *Criminal Justice and Behavior, 20,* 1–5.

Earls, F., McGuire, J., and Shay, S. (1994). Evaluating a community intervention to reduce the risk of child abuse: Methodological strategies in conducting surveys. *Child Abuse and Neglect, 5,* 473–485.

Eckenrod, J., Laird, M., and Doris, J. (1993). School performance and disciplinary problems among abused and neglected children. *Developmental Psychology, 29,* 53–62.

Egeland, B., and Stroufe, A. (1981). Developmental sequale of maltreatment in infancy. *New Directions for Child Development, 11,* 77–92.

Egeland, B., Stroufe, L. A., and Erickson, M. F. (1983). The developmental consequences of different patterns of maltreatment. *Child Abuse and Neglect, 7,* 459–469.

Erickson, E. H. (1968). *Identity: Youth and Crisis.* New York: Norton.

Erickson, M. F., Egeland, B., and Pianta, R. (1989). The effects of maltreatment on the development of young children. In D. Cichetti and V. Carlson (Eds.), *Child Maltreatment* (pp. 647–684). Cambridge, MA: Harvard University Press.

Famularo, R., Kinscherff, R., and Fenton, T. (1992). Parental substance abuse and the nature of child maltreatment. *Child Abuse and Neglect, 16,* 475–483.

Folks, H. (1902). *Care of Destitute, Neglected, and Delinquent Children.* New York: Macmillan.

Frodi, A., and Lamb, M. (1985). Child abusers' responses to infant smiles and cries. *Child Development, 51,* 238–241.

Garbarino, J., and Crouter, A. (1978). Defining the community context for parent-child relations: The correlates of child maltreatment. *Child Development, 49,* 604–616.

Garbarino, J.,and Kostelny, K. (1992). Child maltreatment as a community problem. *Child Abuse and Neglect, 16,* 455–464.

Gaudin, J. M. (1993). Effective intervention with neglectful families. *Criminal Justice and Behavior, 20,* 66–89.

Gelles, R. J., and Strauss, M. A. (1988). *Intimate Violence.* New York: Simon and Schuster.

Giovannoni, J., and Billingsley, A. (1970). Child neglect among the poor: A study of parental inadequacy in families in three ethnic groups. *Child Welfare, 19,* 196–204.

Hawaii Department of Health (1991). *Hawaii Healthy Start.* Honolulu: Hawaii Family Stress Center.

Hendee, W. R. (Ed.). (1991). *The Health of Adolescents.* Chicago: American Medical Association.

Hunt, D. (1970). *Parents and Children in History.* New York: Basic Books.

Illinois Department of Public Health (1995). *Healthy Family Illinois Initiative.* Report of the Healthy Families, Illinois Steering Committee to Governor Jim Edgar and the general assembly. Springfield: Illinois Department of Public Health.

Jackson, A. (1984). *Child neglect: An Overview.* In *Perspectives on Child Maltreatment in the Mid-'80s* (pp. 15–17). Washington, DC: Children's Bureau, National Center on Child Abuse and Neglect, U.S. Department of Health and Human Services.

Kempe, C. H., Silverman, F. N., Steele, B. F., Droegemueller, W., and Silver, H. K. (1962). The battered-child syndrome. *Journal of the American Medical Association, 181,* 17–24.

Korbin, J. E. (1981). Conclusions. In J. E. Korbin (Ed.), *Child Abuse and Neglect: Cross-Cultural Perspectives* (pp. 205–210). Berkeley: University of California Press.

Kotch, J., Browne, D., Ringwalt, C., Stewart, P., Ruina, E., Holt, K., Lowman, B., Jung, J., and Libow, J. (1995). Risk of child abuse or neglect in a cohort of low-income children. *Child Abuse and Neglect, 19,* 1115–1130.

Kropenske, V., Howard, J., Breitenbach, C., Dembo, R., Edelstein, S. B., McTaggart, K., Moore, A., Sorensen, M. B., and Weiss, V. (1994). *Protecting Children in Substance-Abusing Families.* Washington, DC: U.S. Department of Health and Human Services.

Lavaritz, L., and Shelman, E. (1996). Before Mary Ellen. *Child Abuse and Neglect, 20,* 235–237.

Leiter, J., and Johnsen, M. C. (1994). Child maltreatment and school performance. *American Journal of Education, 102,* 154–189.

Meier, E. (1964). Child neglect. In N. Cohen (Ed.), *Social Work and Social Problems* (pp. 153–200). New York: National Association of Social Workers.

Munir, A. B. (1993). Child protection principles and applications. *Child Abuse Review, 2,* 119–126.

Myers, J. E. B. (1992). *Legal Issues in Child Abuse and Neglect.* Newbury Park, CA: Sage.

National Center on Child Abuse and Neglect, Administration on Children and Families, U.S. Department of Health and Human Services. (1988). *Findings: Study of National Incidence and Prevalence of Child Abuse and Neglect, 1988.* Washington, DC: U.S. Government Printing Office.

National Child Abuse and Neglect Data Systems, National Center on Child Abuse and Neglect, Administration on Children and Families, U.S. Department of Health and Human Services (1994). *Data Trends.* Washington, DC: U.S. Government Printing Office.

Nelson, B. (1984). *Making an Issue of Child Abuse: Political Setting for Social Problems.* Chicago: University of Chicago Press.

Newberger, C. M., and Newberger, E. H. (1981). The etiology of child abuse. In N. S. Ellerstein (Ed.), *Child Abuse and Neglect: A Medical Reference.* New York: Wiley.

Paget, K. D., Philip, J. D., and Abramczyk, J. W. (1993). Recent developments in child neglect. In T. H. Ollendick and R. J. Prinz (Eds.), *Advances in Clinical Child Psychology* (Vol. 15, pp. 121–174). New York: Plenum Press.

Pecora, P. J., Whitaker, J. K., Maluccio, A. N., Barth, R. P., and Plotnick, R. D. (1992). *The Child Welfare Challenge.* New York: Aldine Gruyter.

Pelton, L. H. (1989). *For Reasons of Poverty.* New York: Praeger.

Poffenberger, I. (1981). *Child rearing and social structure in rural India: Toward cross-cultural definition of child abuse and neglect.* In J. Korbin (Ed.), *Child Abuse and Neglect: Cross-Cultural Perspectives* (p. 72). Berkeley: University of California Press.

Polansky, N. A., Ammons, P. W., and Weathersby, B. L. (1983, September–October). Is there an American standard of child care? *Social Work, 28,* 341–346.

Polansky, N. A. and Chalmers, M. A. (1978) Assessing adequacy of child caring: An urban scale. *Child Welfare, 57* (7); 439–449.

Polanksy, N., Chalmers, M. A., Buttenweiser, E., and Williams, D. P. (1980, revised 1991). *Damaged Parents: Anatomy of Child Neglect.* Chicago: University of Chicago Press.

Polansky, N. A., Gaudin, J. M., Ammons, P. W., and Davis, K. B. (1985). The psychological ecology of the neglectful mother. *Child Abuse and Neglect, 9,* 265–275.

Polansky, N. F., Hally, C., and Polansky, N. A. (1975). *Profile of neglect: A Survey of the State of Knowledge of Child Neglect.* Washington, DC: Community Services Administration, Department of Health, Education, and Welfare.

Polansky, N. A., and Williams, D. P. (1978). Class orientation to child neglect. *Social Work, 23,* 397–405.

Prino, C. T., and Peyrot, M. (1994). The effect of child physical abuse and neglect on aggressive, withdrawn, and prosocial behavior. *Child Abuse and Neglect, 18,* 871–884.

Radbill, S. (1974). A history of child abuse and infanticide. In R. E. Helfer and C. H. Kempe (Eds.), *The Battered Child* (2nd ed.), (pp. 3–17). Chicago: University of Chicago Press.

Ryan, W. (1977). *Blaming the Victim.* New York: Vintage Books.

Schmitt, B. D., and Mauro, R. D. (1989). Nonorganic failure to thrive: An outpatient approach. *Child Abuse and Neglect, 13,* 235–248.

Solomon, T. (1973). History and demography of child abuse. *Pediatrics, 51*(4), 773–776.

Starr, R. H., Jr., MacLean, D. J., and Keating, D. P. (1991). Life-span developmental outcomes of child maltreatment. In R. H. Starr, Jr. and D. A. Wolfe (Eds.), *The Effects of Child Abuse and Neglect: Issues and Research.* New York: Guilford Press.

Steele, B. F. (1970). Violence in our society. *Pharos of Alpha Omega, 33*(2), 42–48.

Thomas, M. P. (1972). Child abuse and neglect. Part 1: Historical overview, legal matrix, and social perspectives. *North Carolina Law Review, 50,* 293–349.

United Nations Development Program. (1996). *Human Development Report.* New York: Oxford University Press.

United Nations International Children's Emergency Fund (1989). *Report on the State of the World's Children.* New York: United Nations.

U.S. Advisory Board on Child Abuse and Neglect, Administration for Children and Families, U.S. Department of Health and Human Services (1993). *The Continuing Child Protection Emergency: A Challenge to the Nation (Third Report).* Washington, DC: U.S. Government Printing Office.

U.S. Department of Health and Human Services, Administration for Children and Families. National Center on Child Abuse and Neglect. *Federal Register (1996).* Washington, DC: U.S. Government Printing Office.

U.S. Department of Health and Human Services, National Center on Child Maltreatment. *1994: Reports from the States to the National Center on Child Abuse and Neglect.* (1996). Washington, DC: U.S. Government Printing Office.

Watkins, S. A. (1996). The Mary Ellen myth: Correcting child welfare history. *Social Work, 35*(6), 500–503.

Westat Associates. (1988). *Study of the National Incidence and Prevalence of Child Abuse and Neglect.* Washington, DC: U.S. Government Printing Office.

Wiehe, V. R. (1996). *Working with Child Abuse and Neglect.* Thousand Oaks, CA: Sage.

Wise, P. H., and Meyers, A. (1988). Poverty and child health. *Pediatric Clinics of North America, 35,* 1169–1186.

Wolock, T., and Horowitz, B. (1984). Child maltreatment as a social problem: The neglect of neglect. *American Journal of Orthopsychiatry, 54,* 530–542.

Wright, L. S., Garrison, J., Wright, N. B., and Stimmel, D. (1991). Childhood unhappiness and family stressors recalled by adult children of substance abusers. *Alcoholism Treatment Quarterly, 8*(4), 67–80.

Wyatt, G. E. (1985). The sexual abuse of Afro-American and white American women in childhood. *Child Abuse and Neglect, 9,* 507–519.

Young, L. (1964). *Wednesday's Children: A Study of Child Neglect and Abuse.* New York: McGraw-Hill.

4

Dating Violence as a Social Phenomenon

Carroy U. Ferguson, Ph.D.
College of Public and Community Service
University of Massachusetts at Boston

Historically, dating is a distinctly modern phenomenon. What are recognized as dating patterns of the 1990s did not really appear on the social scene until the beginning of the twentieth century. Not until the 1920s were young people afforded a leisurely adolescence whereby courtship and dating habits could evolve (Garrett, 1982). In the next several decades, despite the Great Depression and World War II, the number of young people entering colleges steadily increased. With this change came greater freedom of action, especially in courting habits (Parsons, 1965). The casual date emerged as an everyday event. Gradually, dating patterns worked out by college students and other young adults filtered down to change the behavior of students in high school and junior high (Handlin and Handlin, 1971). The dating process in America has therefore been an evolving social phenomenon.

It is in this evolving historical context that recognition of dating violence as a social phenomenon has emerged. Also in this evolving historical context have emerged research on dating violence as a social phenomenon, efforts to define dating violence and to determine its correlates, efforts to develop prevention and treatment strategies, and forums and articles debating legal and related issues likewise. Although dating violence and what has come to be known as date rape have often been addressed as separate problems in the emerging literature on dating violence, this chapter focuses on dating violence as a social phenomenon that includes sexual dating violence as part of a continuum of minor to severe forms of violence in dating relationships. Yet because the identification of date rape as a social phenomenon with subsequent social research has served to highlight dating violence as a social phenomenon, an overview of date rape's emergence in the literature and in society as a special case of dating violence is presented.

HISTORICAL RECOGNITION OF DATING VIOLENCE

One of the earliest historical references to dating violence as a social phenomenon in America appears in court records from the colonial period. The Court records indicate a significant number of illegitimate births and trials for sexual offenses involving single persons (Demos, 1971). Dating in colonial times often involved a custom known as "bundling," which was very popular in New England. Bundling originated in northern Europe (Tomassen, 1970; Stone, 1979), where long winter nights, great distances between the homes of courting persons, and inadequate heating systems made courting difficult. Bundling involved a young man and woman sharing the same bed for the evening, allowing them to talk privately, to keep warm, and to avoid night travel by the young man; in the eighteenth century, the girl's parents often placed a board between the boy and the girl, hoping to minimize the forbidden physical contact (Garrett, 1982). Court records indicate that male violators of the norm were sometimes prosecuted for sexual offenses.

In a traditional society, dating or courtship was rare or was conducted in groups under strict community controls (Shorter, 1977). Courtship was viewed as an opportunity for marriage that could result in the preservation or increase of family assets. The rich were especially careful in controlling patterns of courtship because they had fortunes to preserve (Stone, 1979). If dating violence occurred in this context, it is likely that it was minimized or overlooked if it threatened matters such as lineage, inheritance, and power relations (Goode, 1973). According to Garrett (1982), European youth then broke away from family and community controls by moving to the cities in great numbers. New patterns of courtship arose almost immediately. In America, attitudes toward courtship behaviors were more flexible. Consequently, couples in the New World enjoyed at least some independence in selecting a courting and marriage partner (Kett, 1977). The new patterns, however, would not be devoid of a continuation of cultural norms based on patriarchy, the institutionalization of male dominance over women in both the public and private spheres (Gamache, 1991; Dobash and Dobash, 1979). Some researchers have theorized (i.e., the patriarchy theory) that this kind of cultural context explains how some men come to believe that violence against their female partners will be supported or at least tolerated (Pence, 1987; Gelles and Straus, 1988).

Because of cultural norms and attitudes surrounding dating practices, historically dating violence has been largely an unrecognized or "hidden" social phenomenon. Not until the late 1970s and early 1980s would dating violence be somewhat recognized as a social phenomenon and as a significant area or problem for social research. During the nineteenth century in America, dating evolved through the following patterns: (1) bundling died out as the population moved westward, and courtship turned toward more conventional practices (e.g., meeting at dances, barn or house raisings, churches, picnics, outings); (2) lower-class engagements were short, and couples knew relatively little about each other before they married; and (3) courtship for the wealthy lasted longer and included many more pleasant diversions than for the lower classes (Greven, 1977). During this period, adolescence and young adulthood as distinct periods of human development and dating as a distinct social phenomenon for purposes other than marriage were not recognized. These developments gained greater legitimacy during the 1920s. From the 1940s on, the automobile dramatically affected the dating habits and sexual conduct of American youth (Cummins, 1978; Bettelheim, 1965). Many dates began with a movie, a school dance, or a private party and ended by parking on lover's lane (Hollingshead, 1975). During the 1950s and early 1960s, an elaborate system of formal rules guided dating practices (e.g., exchanging rings to "go steady"). From the mid 1960s to the early 1980s, courtship patterns were far less oriented toward marriage than ever before; even the terminology changed (e.g., "going steady" changed to "going with someone" or "going out"). Fewer couples made formal dates or expected the boy to call for the girl at a particular time or place or to accompany him to a specific event (Garrett, 1982). This pattern may have reversed somewhat today (terminology of the 1990s includes "seeing" and "going together"), but not to the level of the 1950s. Throughout this evolving history of dating practices, dating violence as a social phenomenon was not a subject for much discussion. If mentioned or acknowledged at all, it was largely anecdotal.

A number of landmark studies and social events have focused attention on dating violence as a social phenomenon, even though it continues to remain a relatively "hidden" phenomenon. The first landmark study in the scholarly literature on dating violence was by Kanin (1957), who looked at male aggression in dating-courting relationships. Interestingly, the study took place against the backdrop of the more elaborate dating patterns of the 1950s. He found that 30% of the women surveyed reported experiencing attempted or completed forced sexual intercourse while on a high school date. In two subsequent studies, Kanin found in 1967 that more than 25% of the male college students surveyed indicated that they had attempted to force sexual intercourse on a woman to the point that she cried or fought back. Kanin and Parcell in 1977 found that 26% of the men surveyed indicated that they had tried to force intercourse on a woman. The importance of these studies is that they indicate a relatively consistent pattern for male sexual aggression in dating relationships, despite the changing dating patterns over the years.

For more than two decades after Kanin's study (1957), however, one of the most severe forms of dating violence was marginally studied as a significant social problem, with the implication that other forms of violence such as emotional (verbal) or physical violence or threats were also prevalent in dating relationships. Research on emotional and physical forms of dating violence would emerge in the early 1980s. Regardless of whether or not a full range of minor to severe violence has been included as a focus of study, the prevalence of dating violence in the general population and attitudes about it have not been firmly conclusive and continue to be subjects of intense discussion in the literature at present.

Makepeace's 1981 study on courtship violence among college students often has been credited with stimulating other social researchers to define and conceptualize dating violence as a social phenomenon. He estimated that 21% of his college-age respondents reported that they had either engaged in or sustained violence within their dating relationships during their lifetime. Other studies have reported lifetime estimates from 9% (Roscoe and Callahan, 1985) to 60% (Laner, 1983; McKinney, 1986). Most studies have found higher minor assault rates than severe assault rates (Arias, Samios, and O'Leary, 1987; Lane and Gwartney-Gibbs, 1985; Makepeace, 1982). Interestingly, most studies have reported that women in contrast to men have higher levels of both inflicting and sustaining dating violence. Five studies (Makepeace, 1981, 1982; McKinney, 1986; Sigelman, Barry, and Wiles, 1984; Yllo and Straus, 1981) found higher rates of males inflicting violence (being the aggressor), but a majority of studies have reported either mutuality or higher rates for women inflicting violence (being the aggressor) (Arias et al., 1987; Plass and Gessner, 1983; Bernard and Bernard, 1983; Billingham and Sack, 1987; DeMaris, 1987; Lane and Gwartney-Gibbs, 1985; Marshall, 1987; Marshall and Rose, 1987; O'Keefe, Brockopp, and Chew, 1986; Cate, Henton, Koval, Christopher, and Lloyd, 1983; Henton, Cate, Koval, Lloyd, and Christopher, 1993). Studies are more consistent in reporting that women have a higher prevalence rate of sustaining violence in a dating relationship than men (Bernard and Bernard, 1983; Billingham and Sack, 1987; Lane and Gwartney-Gibbs, 1985; Makepeace, 1982; Marshall, 1987; Marshall and Rose, 1987; O'Keefe et al., 1986). One study found most dating violence to be mutual but with males more inclined to perceive it as mutual (Laner and Thompson, 1982). Lane and Gwartney-Gibbs (1985) found males to use more violence than females. Males were also more likely to perpetuate sexual assault than their female counterparts.

From a historical perspective, these studies provide an overview of a social research process in the 1980s to recognize dating violence as a social phenomenon and to determine its prevalence in American society. Several methodological factors have influenced the inconsistency and generalizability of these studies with respect to prevalence rates. Makepeace (1986) pointed out several of these factors:

1. Most reports have been based on small samples.

2. Highly varied indicators of victimization have been used, including acts committed, perceived role ("victim" versus "offender"), mutuality versus unilaterally, and initiation (who struck first).

3. Some studies have not differentiated reports of males and females, even though studies have found that the sexes differ in perceptions of courtship (Bernard, 1973; Feldman, 1967; Turk and Bell, 1970) and in their subjective perceptions of battering situations (Edleson, Eisikovits, and Guttmann, 1985).

Two other factors have also been noted by Sugarman and Hotaling (1991): the widespread use of nonrandom college samples precluding generalization to society-at-large and decisions about the type of violent act to be included (verbal, physical, sexual), the referent period of the survey (lifetime versus one-year estimates), and the role that the respondent had within the violent interaction (perpetrator versus victim). Finally, there may be some question about the use of the Conflict Tactics Scales (CTS) (Straus, 1979), a self-report instrument designed to measure intrafamily conflict and violence, to study violence in dating relationships. Many studies using the CTS have found symmetrical results for men and women as aggressors (e.g., Arias and Johnson, 1989; Arias et al., 1987; Cate et al., 1982; DeMaris, 1987; Lane and Gwartney-Gibbs, 1985; Laner and Thompson, 1982; Makepeace, 1986; Marshall and Rose, 1988; Sigelman et al., 1984). Other studies rely more on data from court records, police, and women's shelters (Martin, 1976; Dobash and Dobash, 1978, 1979). Despite the methodological concerns, the most frequently cited estimate for the prevalence of dating violence is that 28% of dating individuals were involved in intimate violence during their dating careers (Sugarman and Hotaling, 1991; Family Research Laboratory at the University of New Hampshire, 1996).

After Makepeace's 1981 study, Pirog-Good and Stet's (1989) *Violence in Dating Relationships: Emerging Social Issues* and Levy's (1991) *Dating Violence: Young Women in Danger*, two often-cited seminal books, served to crystallize the idea of dating violence as a recognized and legitimate social phenomenon and as a legitimate topic for social research. To a large extent, the former book summarized the status of social research on dating violence, categorizing it and the nature of the relevant research into physical abuse and sexual abuse. The latter book updated the status of social research on dating violence, broadened the definition, and extended the discussion to include intervention strategies and remedies to address the now recognized social problem. In short, researchers, professionals, activists, and young people themselves now provided a comprehensive cross-cultural view of dating violence as a social phenomenon.

THE EMERGENCE OF DATE RAPE AS A SPECIAL CASE OF DATING VIOLENCE

Susan Brownmiller's 1976 historical treatise on rape, *Against Our Will: Men, Women, and Rape*, was a landmark book that coined the term "date rape". In 1979, a landmark two-part study by Giarrusso, Johnson, Goodchilds, and Zellman found that a significant percentage of teenagers believed forced sex on dates was sometimes acceptable. In that same year, a popular soap opera, *General Hospital*, portrayed a story line on date rape, where Luke raped Laura and she then left her husband to marry him. What has come to be known as acquaintance rape or date rape thus emerged in the 1980s for study as a special aspect of dating violence (e.g., Koss and Oros, 1982, 1985; Estrich, 1987; Warshaw, 1988). A landmark study on dating violence by Malamuth (1981) found that 35% of college men indicated some likelihood that they would rape if they could be assured of getting away with it. Kanin (1984) found that 25% of the women reported that they had suffered attempted or completed rape. These early studies focused on sexual dating violence, which other studies on dating violence sometimes excluded (e.g., Bernard and Bernard, 1983; Billingham and Sack, 1987; Lane and Gwartney-Gibbs, 1985; Makepeace, 1981).

In the 1980s and into the 1990s, other significant works, in addition to the studies cited above, that highlighted dating violence as a social phenomenon were also produced. Many of these other works again focused on sexual dating violence. A *Ms.* magazine article (Koss and Oros, 1982) based on Dr. Mary Koss' research is credited as being the first widely read national magazine to use the term "date rape" in defining it as a social problem. Koss's nationwide survey with more than 6,100 students on thirty college campuses, published later in 1985, reported that one in four college women had experienced rape or attempted rape. Harvard Law School Professor Susan Estrich's *Real Rape: How the Legal System Victimizes Women Who Say No* (1987) was heralded as a landmark book about how acquaintance rape is treated by the legal system. Robin Warshaw's 1988 book, *I Never Called It Rape* (based on Koss's nationwide survey), was the first book on acquaintance rape written for the general public. It was followed by two other important books, Parrot and Bechhofer's *Acquaintance Rape: The Hidden Crime* in 1991 and Parrot's *Coping with Date Rape and Acquaintance Rape* in 1993. In 1993, Carol Bohmer and Andrea Parrot's *Sexual Assault on Campus: The Problem and the Solution* was cited as another landmark book that helped to focus attention on dating violence on college campuses.

Lundberg-Love and Geffer (1989) summarized the scholarly research on the prevalence of date rape and other forms of sexual aggression, ranging from 2% (Dhaenens and Farrington, 1987) to 77% of women and 57% of men who had been involved (Muehlenhard and Linton, 1987). Lundberg-Love and Geffer (1989) proposed a four preconditions theoretical model of date rape. The model included (1) factors that enhance motivation to sexually abuse (power and control, miscommunication about sex; sexual arousal, emotional incongruence, and imbalance in power differential); (2) factors that reduce internal inhibitions (attitudes related to traditional sex roles such as acceptance of violence, endorsement of rape myths, and adversarial relationships, and prior abusive acts); (3) factors that reduce external inhibitions (date location, mode of transportation, date activity, and alcohol or substance use); and (4) factors that reduce victim resistance (passivity, poor self-defense techniques and strategies, traditional attitudes, and poor sexual knowledge). A block at any point may deter date rape. The prevalence of date rape and acquaintance rape, however, has not gone unchallenged in the literature.

According to Maglin and Perry (1996), charges of "date-rape hype" on college campuses first appeared in a *Playboy* article by Stephanie Guttman (1990). Gilbert (1991b) and Paglia (1991) took up her critique, which was reiterated by Roiphe (1993a, 1993b) and Will (1993). Katie Roiphe's book, *The Morning After: Sex, Fear, and Feminism on Campus* (1993c), however, has been credited with stirring up much of the debate, particularly within the feminist community. Roiphe questioned Koss's methodology and findings and argued that such feminist discussion confuses young women into mislabeling a wide array of normal, often unpleasant, sexual experiences as rape. "Her thesis is that the battle against date rape is a symptom of young women's general anxiety about sex ... which they displace onto a fear of rape"

(Maglin and Perry, 1996, p. 141). Maglin and Perry (1996) called critiques such as Roiphe's "antifeminist backlash" and suggested that Roiphe uses a narrow definition of what constitutes a "real" rape (versus just "bad sex"). Warshaw (1988, p. 4) noted that acquaintance rape remains largely hidden because few people identify it for what it is and because the assault occurs between individuals who know each other, within the context of the often confused personal and sexual relationships between men and women.

In addition, a number of landmark social events have surfaced on the national scene to bring attention to the issue of dating violence and acquaintance rape or date rape. The reemergence of the women's movement in the 1970s was an important social development, because domestic and sexual violence was made a significant agenda for the movement. According to Bohmer and Parrot (1993), rape laws began to change to allow easier prosecution in 1975. In 1978, the *Rideout* case in Oregon was the first case where a husband still effectively living with his wife was tried for marital rape. In 1984, *The Phil Donahue Show* was the first syndicated television talk show to do a program on the subject of date rape. In 1985, Cathleen Crowell Webb admitted to falsely accusing Gary Dotson of rape after he spent eight years in prison for the alleged crime, reinforcing the perception that women may charge rape falsely. In 1986, Syracuse University found a football player innocent of any wrongdoing after he pleaded guilty to sexual misconduct when he was charged with rape and sexual assault. Jodie Foster won an Academy Award in 1988 for the role she played in the film *The Accused*, a film about acquaintance gang rape. A made-for-television documentary, *Against Her Will*, was aired in 1989, focusing on date rape on college campuses. In 1989, a jury in *State of Florida v. Lloyd* acquitted a defendant on rape charges because the victim was wearing lace "short shorts" and no underwear. In 1989, a made-for-television, prime-time movie, *When He's Not a Stranger*, about date rape on a college campus was aired. In 1990, football players at Glen Ridge High School were charged with gang rape, as were lacrosse players at St. John's University in 1991. William Kennedy Smith was tried and acquitted for date rape in Florida in 1991. In 1992, Mike Tyson was convicted for date rape of a Miss Black America beauty pageant contestant, the Tailhook Naval harassment scandal occurred (seven naval officers were fired as a result), and members of the Cincinnati Bengals football team were named in a civil suit for either participating in or watching a gang rape. In 1996, yet another sex scandal involving the U.S. armed forces occurred, as Army drill sergeants were accused of sexual assaults during boot camp. These landmark social events have helped to sharpen national focus on the issues of dating violence and acquaintance rape or date rape.

Complicating the issue of date rape has been the emergence of what has been called "the date rape drug." The newest and most popular drug used now is Rohypnol (brand name for flunitrazepam, a benzodiazepine). Street names for this drug include "roofies," "ruffies," "roche," "R-2," "rib," and "rope." It is an extremely strong tranquilizer, often mixed with some other drink or drug. The effects begin within thirty minutes, peak within two hours, and may last for up to eight hours, depending on the size of the dosage. When the drug is taken, the person may wake up not remembering anything that happened and may feel sluggish, possibly thinking that he or she drank too much. Adverse effects include decreased blood pressure, memory impairment, drowsiness, visual disturbances, dizziness, and confusion. "Roofies" are usually mixed with alcohol, marijuana, or cocaine to produce a very dramatic "high," making them very popular on college campuses and in high schools. Some women have reported waking up in fraternity houses with no clothes on, finding themselves in unfamiliar surroundings with unfamiliar people, or having been sexually assaulted while under the influence of the drug. Because of the drug, they were unable to stop or resist the attack and often pass out, waking up only to vaguely remember what happened (Butler and Nakahara, 1996).

Despite the recognition of dating violence as a social phenomenon, including the more severe forms of physical and sexual assault, young people in the 1990s do not seem to talk about it as a problem or seek help. Lynn Harris in the "The Hidden World of Dating Violence" (*Parade Magazine,* 1996) clearly illustrated how dating violence as a social phenomenon is "the problem teenage girls are afraid to talk about." Her research found that many young women hide the problem from friends, parents, and other adults. Some of the reasons identified for why they keep quiet about their experiences include:

1. They do not want to be pressured into breaking up so that they can appear to be popular.
2. They fear losing the freedom they have already been able to get and do not want their parents to think that they have poor judgment.
3. They are trying to separate from their parents, making them unlikely to open up to their parents when they are in trouble.
4. They have difficulty accepting that there is in fact a problem and confuse jealousy and possessiveness to mean "he loves me."
5. They may believe that they deserve to be abused and take it for granted, perhaps having encountered it as a norm in their homes.

It remains to be seen whether or not dating violence will become less "hidden" now that it is recognized as a social phenomenon. Currently, it is often unreported and underreported, remaining largely hidden in the context of illusory dating norms and expectations.

WHAT IS DATING VIOLENCE? DOES IT HAVE LEGAL STATUS AS A SOCIAL PHENOMENON?

The above historical context has established that dating violence is a recognized social phenomenon, even though there are debates and varied estimates about its prevalence in American society. So, what is dating violence? And, what is its status as a legal phenomenon? Currently, "dating violence" is not recognized as a legal category, nor are the terms "acquaintance rape" or "date rape." But many of the violent acts (e.g., physical assaults, rape) that constitute dating violence and that take place in the context of the dating relationship are subject to legal remedies. When young people are involved, emancipated minors or minors with a guardian ad litem do have access to these legal remedies. The legal status of dating violence, to some extent, is a conceptual and definitional issue. Social researchers have offered a number of conceptualizations of dating violence, but social research definitions and legal definitions have not yet fully met.

One of the first issues that surrounds a definition of dating violence is that in the social research literature, the terms "dating" and "courtship" are used interchangeably and often refer to a variety of dyadic interactions (Sugarman and Hotaling, 1991). Thompson (1986), for example, includes a focus on the process of mate selection as characteristic of "dating," its initial purpose during pre- and postcolonial days up to the 1920s. Carlson (1987), on the other hand, suggests that these terms may refer to any romantically involved, unmarried couple. Sugarman and Hotaling (1991) argue that both of these definitions are insufficient because "dating can involve married individuals (that is, extramarital affairs) and the functions of dating often involve more than mate selection, . . . a couple can date as 'friends,' or they may view the relationship as having the potential of leading to marriage, . . . and 'dating' applies to homosexual as well as heterosexual relationships" (pp. 102–103).

Notwithstanding the efforts by social researchers to conceptualize dating, the ultimate legal issue is that most domestic violence laws do not currently include dating relationships in the definition of domestic violence. "Only Colorado, California and Pennsylvania allow people who have experienced dating violence to apply for domestic violence restraining orders, and they do not limit the orders to adults. In all other states, a dating relationship is not considered 'domestic'" (Kuehl, 1991, p. 217).

A second issue in defining dating violence surrounds the term "violence" and what types of abuse to include in the definition. Thompson (1986) defined courtship violence as "any acts and/or threats that physically and/or verbally abuse another" (p. 166) in the context of "any interaction related to the dating and/or mate selection process" (p. 165). Carlson's (1987) definition included "violence in unmarried couples who are romantically involved" (p. 17). Puig (1984) used the term "courtship partner" in a definition of dating violence, defining courtship partner abuse as "acts of physical aggression directed at one dating partner by another dating partner" (p. 268). Makepeace (1981; 1986) includes sexual assault, physical injury, and emotional trauma in his definition of courtship violence. Harris (1996) noted that dating violence "can involve anything from verbal attacks to punching, physical threats or worse" (p. 4). She acknowledged that "though date rape is addressed as a separate problem, [dating violence] is often accompanied by unwanted sexual pressure or abuse" (p. 4). Harris also noted that girl-on-boy abuse—usually verbal—does occur, but the perpetrators of physical violence are overwhelmingly male. Currently, physical assaults and injury are more related to legal definitions of violence than verbal assaults in most states.

Levy (1993) offered the following descriptive definition of dating violence in abusive teen relationships:

> In a violent dating relationship, a person repeatedly threatens to, or actually acts in a way that physically, sexually or verbally injures their boyfriend or girlfriend. It does not just happen once, but happens again and again. It is not the same as getting angry or having fights. In a violent dating relationship, one person is afraid of and intimidated by the other. Being abused by someone you love means being mistreated by them. This may be emotional or physical or sexual, or all three. (p. 31)

There are numerous examples of what constitutes *emotional abuse* (e.g., jealousy, possessiveness, and suspiciousness that leads to verbal harassment, isolation, or throwing your things at you or destroying them), *physical abuse* (e.g., pushing, hitting, slapping, kicking, beatings with a fist, choking, attacks with an object or a weapon), and *sexual abuse* (e.g., mistreatment by sexual acts, demands, or insults; violently forced to have sex; coerced or manipulated to have sex; forced to have sex with others or to watch your boyfriend or girlfriend have sex with someone else; forced to have sex without protection).

Rowe (1993) defined dating violence in the context of dating as a sociocultural phenomenon:

> Going on a date can mean different things to different people. Dates are often group activities, while other dates involve only a couple. A dating partner can vary from being a casual acquaintance to a steady relationship, sometimes referred to as "going together" to engagement. Some married couples go on "dates" as a way to add vitality to their relationship. A dating relationship may be as short as one meeting, or may result in a lifetime commitment.

Rowe thus defines dating violence in the context of an array of forms of abuse and violations against a dating partner. He includes (1993, pp. 2–3):

1. *Physical abuse:* kicking, biting, choking, hitting, battering (beating up), or threatening to use a gun, knife, or other weapon. For instance, Nebraska law defines physical abuse as "any attempt to intentionally, knowingly or recklessly cause bodily injury with or without a deadly weapon, or placing by physical menace another in fear of imminent serious bodily injury."

2. *Emotional abuse:* any verbal or nonverbal communication intended to cause psychological pain to another person; common forms include insulting remarks and cursing the partner, public humiliation and intimidation, treating the partner as inferior, trying to control what the partner does, yelling and screaming, excessive teasing about a partner's faults, and manipulations with false accusations and threats. (Most states do not have laws punishing this form of abuse.)

3. *Economic exploitation:* stealing, damaging, or destroying a partner's money or property. Examples are threatening to take money, forcing a date to pay solely for items that are to be shared, or stealing money or property (belonging to a partner or members of a partner's family).

4. *Alcohol and drug abuse:* abuse associated with increased levels of violence among dating couples. An example is being forced to ride with a driver under the influence of drugs or alcohol while on a date.

5. *Unwanted sexual contact:* often forced on dating partners. Some may fail to resist sexual advances for fear of being physically or emotionally battered, whereas others may go along for the sake of popularity.

Although some research studies have equated violence with injuries such as being beaten, knifed, or shot (e.g., Makepeace, 1988), others limit acts to physical violence (Puig, 1984) or include acts or threats of both physical and verbal violence (Thompson, 1986). The definition of dating violence in the literature therefore has reflected both a narrow perspective and a broader perspective. Sugarman and Hotaling (1991) note that "broader definitions may include acts and threats of physical, verbal, sexual and psychological violence, regardless of their perceived severity" (p. 101), but that they prefer "a more moderate definition of violence—the use or threat of physical force or restraint that has the purpose of causing injury or pain to another individual" (p. 101).

The most common usages of the term in the field appear to find the broader perspective more meaningful for defining dating violence. Programs such as New Hope for Women use the following definition of dating violence: "It is what happens in a teen dating relationship when one person uses abuse to gain power and keep control over their partner. This abuse can be physical, emotional, or sexual." The National Clearinghouse on Family Violence (1990) explains dating violence as follows: "Dating violence is the sexual, physical, or emotional abuse of one partner by the other in a dating relationship where the couple is not living together. While incidents of violence against men do occur, violence against women is more pervasive, more systematic, and usually more severe" (p. 1). To understand and appreciate the phenomenon of dating violence as a social phenomenon and its connection to a legal status more fully, this discussion has therefore preferred the broader perspective.

There are a number of implications for using narrower definitions of dating violence versus broader definitions with respect to its connection to a legal status. First, if acts of psychological abuse (e.g., verbally demeaning or humiliating you by following you around or phoning you continually to harass, alarm, or annoy you) are excluded from a definition of dating violence, then recipients of such abuse may be limited in taking advantage of existing criminal law and using the grounds of criminal harassment. If sexual abuse is excluded from a definition of dating violence, then recipients of such abuse in a dating relationship may be reluctant, even more so than they currently are, to take advantage of existing criminal law and to use the grounds of sexual assault.

Assault, beating, sexual coercion, and rape are all illegal. They are crimes. By using a broad definition of dating violence, then, violent boyfriends or girlfriends can be charged with (Kuehl, 1991, p. 214; Levy, 1993, p. 85):

- *Criminal harassment:* subjecting you (others) to physical contact, following you around or phoning you continually if it is done to harass, alarm, or annoy you, if it has that effect, or if the behavior occurs with no legitimate purpose

- *Reckless endangerment:* placing you in serious fear or apprehension of bodily injury or death
- *Assault:* intentionally or negligently causing or attempting to cause bodily injury
- *Aggravated assault:* intentionally or negligently causing or attempting to cause grave injury, as with a weapon
- *Rape or attempted rape:* sexual intercourse (penetration of the vagina) forced by violence or threat of violence
- *Sexual assault:* touching, rubbing, stroking, or using objects in a sex act forced by violence or the threat of violence; also, touching, rubbing, or stroking by an adult of someone who is under eighteen
- *Sodomy:* forced penetration of the anus
- *Forced oral sex*

Further, using the broader definitions of abuse, recipients of dating violence may also take advantage of civil law by seeking a restraining order and in a few states may take advantage of domestic violence laws. Although dating violence does not currently have legal status as a category in law, social research definitions and legal definitions regarding dating violence as a social phenomenon currently meet through existing criminal law, civil law, and domestic violence law if the recipient of abuse accesses these laws, and with adult advocates when the recipient of dating violence is considered a minor.

OVERVIEW OF OTHER RESEARCH IN THE FIELD

One area of research often cited with research on dating violence is family (domestic) violence and spousal (marital) violence. Some research indicates that dating violence and spousal violence are about as commonplace as one another (Carlson, 1987; Cate et al., 1982; Lane and Gwartney-Gibbs, 1985; Laner and Thompson, 1982; Makepeace, 1981; Yllo and Straus, 1981). These early studies noted that unmarried couples experienced a rate of physical violence equivalent to married couples. Bergman (1992), in a study of dating violence among high school students, found that the pattern of dating violence seemed to "mirror" the typical pattern of domestic violence. That is, the violence tended to occur within the context of a relatively long-term relationship, did not cause an end to the relationship, and tended to recur in the relationship. This finding departed from Roscoe and Callahan's (1985) portrayal of the short-lived violent incidents among their subjects. Bergman (1992) suggested that the finding depicts violent high school dating relationships in a fashion similar to what has been depicted in courtship and marital violence, in which partners adapt to the violence as part of their relationship.

Descriptions of spousal abuse extend as far back as recorded history, including the Roman Empire, the Middle Ages, and modern times (Davis, 1971). Family researchers point out that in Blackstone's codification of the English common law

(1768), a husband had the right to physically "chastise" an errant wife provided the stick was no bigger than his thumb and that this rule was upheld by an appellate court in North Carolina in 1867. Some historians argue that the subjugation of women by men in the ancient world served as a model for the development of later forms of oppression and that public policies enlarging women's rights have not changed the nature of male-female relations within the family (Lerner, 1986) and by extension outside the family into dating relationships. Spousal abuse was ignored until the 1970s, when the women's movement made battering a central issue and gave it wide publicity (Straus and Gelles, 1988). Subsequently, research on what were called the "battered wife syndrome" (Langley and Levy, 1977; Dobash and Dobash, 1979), and the "battered husband syndrome" (Steinmetz, 1977, 1978) to accompany earlier research on the "battered child syndrome" (Kempe, 1962) emerged in the literature. This kind of research set the stage for exploring violence in relationships beyond the family context, leading to expanded research interest for studying violence in dating relationships. Currently, however, there is not a large body of research.

A more specific area of research in the literature on dating violence has focused on acquaintance rape and date rape. One study found that date rape accounts for 67% of sexual assaults reported by adolescents and college women (Ageton, 1983). Warshaw (1988) noted that young women between the ages of fourteen and seventeen represent an estimated 38% of those victimized by date rape. In reviewing the context of date rape and relevant literature, Bateman (1991) points out that "one of the major differences between studies on courtship violence and those on date rape is that the former frequently find similar rates of victimization for males and for females. Sexual aggression, however, remains an almost exclusively male province" (p. 95). Early studies (Kanin, 1957; Kanin and Parcell, 1977) appear to report similar results as later studies in this regard (Koss, 1987; Levy, 1984). Even using the CTS, Sigleman, Berry, and Wiles (1984) found only rare reports of female-committed sexual violence. A ratio of eight to one was reported by Makepeace (1986) regarding females to males feeling that they were victims of forced sex.

A cultural explanation is theorized by Courtois (1988) to understand the gender disparity in sexual dating violence studies. That is, from a cultural point of view, the theory is that men and women are conditioned into roles of power and dominance (men) and passivity and dependence (women), which create a context for condoning sexual violence toward women. In this context, reporting rates by adolescents (and other women) for sexual assaults or date rapes are rare (Koss, Gidycz, and Wisniewski, 1987; Miller, 1988). A lack of recognition that a sexual assault or rape has occurred or even an attitude of some tolerance is also highly likely.

Many young women may experience unwanted sex as part of what happens on dates. In a study by Miller and Marshall (1987), 27% of the young women interviewed indicated that they had engaged in unwanted sex because of their boyfriends' psychological pressure and did not consider it to be rape. One of every six interviewees believed that it is impossible for her to stop a sexually aroused man or for him to stop himself. Miller (1988) found that 56% of adolescent girls interviewed agreed that under certain circumstances, it is okay for the man to use force to obtain sex. Fisher (1986) showed that women with more traditional values are more accepting of forcible sex as well as less sure of what rape is, believing that they are responsible for satisfying a man's sexual urges. Several studies found that some men share similar beliefs (Koss and Leonard, 1984; Mahoney, Shively and Traw, 1985) and would sexually force a woman to have sex under certain circumstances (Malamuth, 1981; Briere and Malamuth, 1983).

It has been theorized that sexual dating violence may stem from "overconformity" to masculinity in the socialization process as young men are encouraged to focus on *quantity* of sexual experiences rather than *quality* (Kanin, 1985; Mahoney et al., 1985). DeKeseredy's (1988) argument for the relevance of social support theory to explain female abuse in dating relationships, whereby male social networks may perpetuate and legitimate various means of female abuse, also may be significant here. Further, there may be huge male-female perceptual gaps in assumptions about the willingness to have sex and the cues that are used to determine willingness. Muehlenhard (1988), for example, found that among college student respondents, the following cues were used to determine that the woman was willing to have sex: her initiating the date, allowing the man to pay for the date, or going to the man's apartment. When asked if he would be justified in forcing sexual intercourse if it turned out that she definitely did not want sexual intercourse, 27.5% of the men and 17.5% of the women said that forced sex would be justified. Batemen (1991) thus theorized that there is an "acceptability of rape" in the culture and that confusion occurs in the context of paradoxical and adversarial expectations related to women playing the "gatekeeper" role and men the "initiator" role surrounding sex. Arguably, perhaps nowhere do these expectations get played out more consistently than on college campuses.

Date rape (the most common type of rape on college campuses) and acquaintance rape are estimated to happen to one-fifth of college women, whereas one-quarter of college women will experience either attempted or completed forced sex (often during the woman's first college year) (Koss et al., 1987; Bohmer and Parrot, 1993). At colleges where first-year students live on campus and then move off campus during their sophomore year, the incidence of sexual assaults reportedly increases (Parrot, 1985). Further, gang rape, although not unique to college campuses, is yet another form of sexual assault that the literature in the field is beginning to note and to connect to dating violence. One study found that of the documented cases of alleged gang rape by college students from 1980 to 1990, 55% were committed by fraternity members, 40% were committed by members of sports teams (football, basketball, and lacrosse), and only 5% were committed by men who were not affiliated with formal organizations (O'Sullivan, 1991). Another study showed that a majority of gang rapes committed on college campuses occur in fraternity houses (Tierney, 1984). Groth and Birnbaum (1979) found that many of the people involved in gang rape are "followers" rather than "initiators." Sanday (1990) reported that gang rape may occur when women who are believed to be "easy" are imported from off campus for this purpose. Suffice it to say that gang rape has been especially difficult to prove because of the unwillingness of collaborators to provide evidence. As a potential outcome of dating violence, however, it is an important area for further research.

Another body of research that may have relevance to the field and the study of dating violence has been labeled "close relationships" research (Hendrick, 1989). Research on long-term, close personal relationships (excluding marriage) is relatively new. Between 1969 and 1978, there were very few references in the literature with the title "personal relationships" or "close relationships." Between 1979 and 1988 there were about thirty (Duck and Pond, 1989), and the number increased in the 1990s. The relevance of this body of literature is that some of the underlying dynamics for understanding how violence may emerge in close dyadic relationships may be more closely examined. For example, researchers now look at personal needs and personal relationships (McAdams, 1988); functions of nonverbal behavior in close relationships (Patterson, 1988); ontogeny, phylogeny, and relationships (Nash, 1988); persuasion in personal relationships (Miller and Boster, 1988); quality of communication (Montgomery, 1988); loneliness (Rook, 1988); and violence between intimate partners (Cardarelli, 1997). One study, using the framework of close relationships, developed a theoretical model of the causes of date rape in developing close relationships (Shotland, 1989). In this context, Makepeace (1997) likewise has proposed a developmental theory of courtship violence, viewing courtship violence as a process in the context of an innate need for intimacy and an innate disposition to aggress in response to frustration in fulfilling normative cultural prescriptions for intimacy during courtship and dating.

Shotland's (1989) theoretical model includes what he calls "early date rape," "beginning date rape," and "relational date rape." According to the model, early date rape occurs after the couple has had several dates but before the couple has established a relationship. In beginning date rape, a man may date a woman with the intent to rape her, realizing that such an action is less likely to be labeled as rape than would the action of raping a stranger on the street. It has been found that most college students do not expect to have sexual intercourse during their first few dates and that the average male does not expect sexual intercourse until roughly the fifth date (Knox and Wilson, 1981). Couples who have established a relationship usually understand their partner's position regarding sex (Peplau, Rubin, and Hill, 1977), and so miscommunication is not likely to be a cause of a rape. Relational date rape then occurs within the context of a variety of exchange and social comparison processes. An analysis of relational date rape combines the elements of differential lifestyle, misperceptions of sexual intent between males and females, personality characteristics, and social attitudes. Shotland's theoretical model holds a great deal of promise for better understanding the nature of date rape and for developing better preventive strategies for this kind of assaultive behavior. It illustrates the utility of the emerging body of research on close relationships and the implications of this research for better understanding the nature of dating violence and the dating relationship.

In terms of close relationships and dating violence in general, Makepeace's (1997) developmental theory of courtship violence adds the perspective that it is the frustration of the desire to fulfill developmental normative prescriptions (internalized cultural norms that prescribe expected attitudes, behaviors, and forms of courtship according to age, development, and standing with respect to the collateral institutions of family, education, and economy) that is the principal cause of courtship violence, "when the preconscious and innate disposition to aggress in response to frustration has not been sufficiently extinguished via socialization" (p. 46). He acknowledges that this is a first step in developing a more comprehensive theory.

Studies exploring the connection between sexual and physical violence in dating relationships, as well as between sexual preferences and physical violence, are also emerging in the literature. With regard to the former connection, Stets and Pirog-Good (1989) found a nonsignificant relationship for men, but a significant relationship for women. Sigelman et al. (1984) earlier found that men inflict more physical and sexual violence than women. In regard to the latter connection, studies have explored the extent of violence in adult lesbian relationships (Minnesota Coalition for Battered Women, 1990; Morrow and Hawxhurst, 1989) and have found that, compounded by societal pressures, lesbians batter their partners to gain power and control over intimates (Hart, 1986) and in response to society's pressures (Heron, 1983; Hunter and Schaechter, 1987; Slater, 1988; Whitlock, 1989). Finally, there is emerging literature on what are called false rape allegations and the connection between sexual and physical violence in courtship (Kanin, 1994). Studying these kinds of connections helps to clarify the parameters of dating violence further.

One other interesting body of information related to research on dating violence has been found on the Internet. In a preliminary study of five databases on the Internet, Ferguson (1996) found 344,728 references to dating violence on one database, 129,797 references on a second database, 20,299 references on a third database, 12,121 references on a fourth database, and 5 references on a fifth database. Research data included reports by the American Medical Association (1995), articles for electronic journals, information on facts and prevention strategies from researchers and various programs, and information about correlates of abuse for dating violence.

CORRELATES OF ABUSE FOR DATING VIOLENCE

Unique aspects of adolescent abusive relationships and characteristics of dating violence have been identified (e.g., Bergman, 1992; Sugarman and Hotaling, 1991; Levy, 1991, 1993; McFarland, 1989). In the 1990s, unique aspects of adolescent abusive relationships include the following:

1. Gender role definitions, derived from peer group norms (e.g., DeKeseredy, 1988; Kanin, 1985), that often fit extreme and stereotyped patterns of dominance and passivity (e.g., Dobash and Dobash, 1989; Levy, 1991, 1993), such as the women's caretaking role, the women's responsibility for the success of the relationship, her social dependence on the man, and the man's insistence on having the woman's attention on demand, including sexual attention.

2. Sexism inherited in norms such that a "girlfriend" may be expected to give up activities, talents, and other relationships and give priority to her boyfriend, and a "boyfriend" may be expected to be sexually aggressive, make all the decisions

in the relationship, and be domineering and controlling of her activities and behavior (e.g., Gomache, 1991; Schechter, 1982).

3. Romanticizing about love and relationships such that jealousy, possessiveness, and abuse are often interpreted as signs of love (e.g., Roscoe and Callahan, 1985; Makepeace, 1986, 1987).

4. When frightening occurrences happen; not expecting, asking for, or getting support from their families with whom they may have conflict or from whom they may be isolated (e.g., Henton et al., 1983; Roscoe and Benaske, 1985; Stets and Pirog-Good, 1987); in turn, adults do not always take adolescents seriously and may assume that they are overreacting, acting out, or going through a phase.

5. The risk of violence to both adult and adolescent women is higher when they are pregnant (McFarlane, 1989), pregnant or parenting adolescents also have fewer resources than adults, their reactions to peers may make them reluctant to use sources of help or they may engage in self-blame and feelings of helplessness when abused, or an abusive boyfriend may use a young woman's pregnant or parenting status as a reason for abuse.

6. Young lesbians are vulnerable to relationship violence because confusion about norms and roles may be acted out in a relationship (Lobel, 1986; Waterman, Dawson, and Bologna, 1989).

7. Special circumstances for adolescents such as the disruption and trauma of immigration, immigration status, or coming from cultures in which dating and sexuality are restricted and possible sources of shame may create vulnerability for violence in relationships (Levy, 1991).

8. If a young woman feels that her options for succeeding in her education or career are limited by racism and discrimination, she may count on the relationship to define her future and become vulnerable to abuse in the relationship (White, 1991).

Based on a variety of studies already cited (e.g., Sugarman and Hotaling, 1989; Ageton, 1983; Warshaw, 1988) and others, the characteristics of dating violence can be summarized as follows:

1. Dating violence is not unique to one class, community, or ethnic group, nor to heterosexual women (diversity) (e.g., Makepeace, 1987; O'Keefe et al., 1986; Plass and Gesser, 1983; Hart, 1986).

2. There is no consensus among researchers (e.g., Arias et al., 1987; Matthews, 1984; Roscoe and Callahan, 1985; Makepeace, 1986) and practitioners regarding the relationship between gender and dating violence; researchers indicate that both men and women can be the recipient of dating violence, but practitioners report that they are seeing only women and that young men are only hit when the women fight back.

3. There is consistency among researchers and practitioners regarding the "hidden" nature of dating violence (Harris, 1996; Levy, 1993).

4. There is consistency among researchers (e.g., Warshaw, 1988; Parrot and Bechhofer, 1991) and practitoners (e.g., NiCarthy, 1991; Harris, 1996) that young people do not define dating violence as a problem.

5. The patterns of abuse in dating relationships are similar to adult battering, whereby control and jealousy are enforced by verbal and physical abuse (DeMaris, 1987; Thompson, 1986; Sigelman et al., 1984).

6. Although documentation of date rape has brought attention to the issue of sexual assault and sexual coercion that take place in intimate relationships (particularly on college campuses), it has yet to dispel the disbelief about the prevalence of such repeated acts (White and Humphrey, 1991).

7. Although there is not a causal connection between substance abuse and dating violence, the two often coexist (Kantor and Straus, 1987; Makepeace, 1986).

There is an implied correlation between the unique aspects of dating and the characteristics of dating violence cited above. Bergman (1992), in his study of dating violence among high school students and using severe violence as a dependent variable, found other correlates. The sample was limited to females only. He found that the number of dating partners was the most significant positive correlate of dating violence, that self-reported grade point average was the second best predictor (a negative correlate) of violence, and that dating frequency was the third best predictor (a positive correlate). The conclusion was that the incidence of severe violence is related to the number of dating partners, poor academic performance, and frequency of dating. The person's age and the age at which dating began were not found to be significantly related. Bergman (1992) also looked at differences among students from three different communities. He found that the highest incidence of dating violence was consistently found in the suburban school, the second highest in the inner-city school, and the third highest in the rural school. This trend was consistent for physical violence, sexual violence, severe violence, and any violence. How much these correlates are the result of or are antecedent to dating violence requires further study. The findings do suggest, however, that teens who are preoccupied with and highly invested in dating relationships and are less focused on other major aspects of their lives such as school attendance, homework, and achievement may become vulnerable for dating violence.

Sugarman and Hotaling (1991) have identified what they call contextual factors and risk markers as correlates of dating violence. Contextual factors refer to variables that are associated with the assaultive act and can be assessed only if the respondent has been a participant (perpetrator, victim, or both) in an act of dating violence (e.g., time and location of assault, reported conflict preceding the assault, victim's and perpetrator's interpretation of the violence, actions taken by both parties after the violence occurred) (pp. 104–105). Risk markers are correlates of being in a violent dating relationship, require comparison groups on a specific variable (e.g., self-esteem), and can be related either to origins or consequences of the dating violence.

Contextually, both men and women report that their partner was the initiator or that they are jointly responsible for the violence. Men, however, are more likely to report being the aggressor in the violent interaction, whereas women label themselves as being victims. In accord with attribution theory (Tedeschi, Smith, and Brown, 1974), interpretations of this phenomenon may relate to perception of role with respect to the conflict that led up to the violence, perception of role of "aggressor" and "victim" with respect to initiator of the violence, and perception of role with respect to the outcome of the violent interaction (e.g., beaten up, gives in to the other). Jealousy and uncontrollable anger are cited consistently in various studies as the most frequent or the primary causes of dating violence for both men and women (e.g., Makepeace, 1986; Roscoe and Callahan, 1985; Makepeace, 1981). The causes for males' violent interaction are perceived by them to be more instrumental, particularly regarding sexual denial (e.g., to intimidate, frighten, or force the other to give something), whereas for women they perceive their violence resulting from uncontrollable anger, jealousy, self-defense, and retaliation. Anger, confusion, and violence representing love describe the prominent emotional states of the aggressor in dating violence (e.g., Cate et al., 1982; Henton et al., 1983). In terms of responses to dating violence, contextually, there is an underuse of professional helpers (e.g., a teacher, counselor, clergy, or law officer), and physical violence may not result in the end of the relationship, despite the emotional trauma (Olday and Wesley, 1983; Henton et al., 1983).

The risk markers identified by Sugarman and Hotaling (1989, 1991) include:

1. Intrapsychic factors (i.e., attitudes toward intimate violence, sex-role attitudes, personality variables, particularly self-concept). Research currently provides a mixed picture.

2. Self-concept and other personality constructs. Currently the only consistent association that has been found is between lowered self-concept and being a victim of dating violence.

3. Alcohol usage. Although implicated as a contextual factor of dating violence in several studies, its status as a correlate of intimate violence is unclear.

4. Experiencing and witnessing violence in the family of origin. Although violence in the family of origin has found consistent association with husband-to-wife violence, the dating violence literature presents a less consistent picture with some studies reporting a significant positive association (e.g., Bernard and Bernard, 1983; DeMaris, 1987; Laner and Thompson, 1982) and others reporting no significant association (e.g., O'Keefe et al., 1986; Stets and Pirog-Good, 1987).

5. Interpersonal factors (i.e., level of commitment that includes relational phase, measures of love and liking, length of time in the relationship, number of dates with the partner, and living arrangements). There are contradictory results regarding relational phase. Level of love was found to be uncorrelated with violence involvement (Arias et al., 1987), but violence-involved women reported higher levels of dislike.

6. Stress (e.g., academic problems, job loss, role loss, financial problems). Currently, there are inconsistent findings in the literature (see Makepeace, 1982, 1987, and Marshall, 1987).

7. Sociodemographic factors (i.e., race, family income, religion, age, place of origin). The literature in this area is scarce and no discernible patterns emerge (see Makepeace, 1989; O'Keefe et al., 1986; Plass and Gessner, 1983; Sigelman et al., 1984; Lane and Gwartney-Gibbs, 1985).

Despite the inconsistency of findings in some of the literature on dating violence, various theoretical models based on correlates that can be empirically tested are slowly emerging in the literature. Riggs and O'Leary (1989), for example, have introduced a comprehensive theoretical model of courtship aggression based on social learning theory (Bandura, 1973). The model includes two components: (1) a contextual component with seven constructs (models of aggression in intimate relationships; parental aggression toward the child; acceptance of aggression as an appropriate response to conflict, frustration, or threat; psychopathology and neuropathology; arousability and emotionality; personality; and prior use of aggression) and (2) a situational component with five major predictors of courtship aggression (the expectation of a positive outcome to the aggression, stress, the use of alcohol, the partner's use of aggression, and relationship conflict). Five constructs are related to relationship conflict (relationship problems, problem-solving ability, couple communication, relationship satisfaction, relationship level and intensity) rather than to the aggression itself. The importance of this kind of model is that it recognizes the multivariate nature of dating violence as a social problem and presents testable variables.

Drawing on the above social learning model, Tontodonato and Crew (1992) empirically tested via a multivariate analysis the predictive value of some of the constructs. They found that parent-child violence, drug use, and knowledge of the use of dating violence by others predicted the use of courtship violence by females. Belief that violence between intimates is justifiable, drug use, and parental divorce were found to be related to perpetuation of dating aggression by males. Although the methodology employed the somewhat controversial Conflict Tactics Scale (Straus, 1979), the study does represent a major step forward with regard to theory development and an empirical approach for better understanding the predictive value of various correlates of dating violence. In addition to lending support to the relevance of social learning theory, these findings may also give support to DeKeseredy's (1988) male social support model of dating violence and Makepeace's (1997) developmental theory of intimate violence.

Much more research, however, is required to identify consistent patterns of correlates of dating violence and to elucidate various theoretical models further. Although there are some consistent correlational factors that have been identified, currently there are mixed results in the literature.

CHARACTERISTICS OF OFFENDERS AND VICTIMS

One observation that has been reported consistently by researchers on dating violence and practitioners in the field is that many recipients of dating violence do not recognize that they are being abused. A variety of authors have presented profiles of the offender and recipient of dating violence. Following is a synthesis of some of these presentations.

Victims or recipients of dating violence tend to exhibit some or all of the following characteristics:

- They are frightened of their boyfriend's or girlfriend's temper.
- They are afraid to disagree with him or her.
- They find themselves apologizing to themselves or others for their boyfriend's or girlfriend's behavior when they are treated badly.
- They are frightened by his or her violence toward others.
- They have been hit, kicked, or shoved or have had things thrown at them.
- They do not see friends or family as much because of their boyfriend's or girlfriend's jealousy.
- They have been forced to have sex.
- They have been afraid to say no to sex.
- They are forced to justify everything they do, every place they go, and every person they see to avoid their boyfriend's or girlfriend's temper.
- They are unable to go out, get a job, or go to school without their boyfriend's or girlfriend's permission.
- They have become secretive, ashamed, or hostile to their parents because of this relationship.

If a person is emotionally or verbally abusive, it is common that the person may believe that he or she is also a victim or recipient of violence. The person often believes that others cause the problems and cause the violence. The person often lacks awareness about his or her role in the relationship as an abuser. Abusers tend to exhibit some or all of the following characteristics:

- They are extremely jealous and possessive.
- They have an explosive temper or have a history of fighting or bragging about mistreating others or show unpredictable behavior.
- They consistently ridicule, criticize, or insult their girlfriend or boyfriend or try to control a dating partner by being bossy, giving orders, making all the decisions, or not taking the other person's opinion seriously. They may blame a dating partner when they mistreat the partner, indicating that they were provoked or that the partner made them do it, pressed their buttons, or led them on.
- They become violent when they drink or use drugs. They may pressure a dating partner to take drugs or alcohol.
- They break their partner's things or throw things at him or her.
- They hit, push, kick, or otherwise injure their partner when they are angry.
- They threaten to hurt or kill their partner or someone close to them, or they use or own weapons.
- They force their partner to have sex or intimidate him or her so that he or she is afraid to say no. They may think women are sex objects, attempt to manipulate for sex, or get too serious about the relationship too quickly.
- They threaten to kill themselves if their partner leaves or will not accept breaking up.

- They make their partner account to them for every moment the partner is away from them.
- They spy on their partner or call him or her constantly to check up on that person.
- They accuse their partner of seeing others.
- They blame others for their faults or blame circumstances for their problems.
- They may have a history of "bad" relationships and blame the other person for all the problems.
- They may have been raised in a home where there was violence.
- They must win arguments, no matter what the cost.
- They believe that they cannot control their temper or anger.
- They ask for a second chance, again and again, often stating that they will change, and will not do it again, but they do not act on their promise.
- Their way is the only way, and their way is law.

Other correlates of abuse have been pointed out for sexual assaults in America, both generally and as they pertain to dating violence and date rape. The American Medical Association (1995), for example, outlined the following sociocultural factors:

- Sociocultural influences that contribute to the incidence and prevalence of sexual assault include increased acceptance of interpersonal violence, adversarial stereotypes of male-female relationships, prevalent myths about rape, and sex-role stereotyping (Schwartz, 1991). Some victims of attacks meeting the legal definition of rape do not label their experience as sexual assault (Illinois Coalition Against Sexual Assault, 1991).
- Common myths surrounding rape include that only women can be sexually assaulted, that victims who truly resist cannot be raped, that no really doesn't mean no, that nice girls don't get raped, and that "she asked for it." Male rape victims may feel that others will question their sexuality if they report the incident or that they in fact subconsciously desired and complied with their assault. Each of these beliefs can lead to confused attitudes, emotions, and behavior, both among victims and others. Blame can be shifted from perpetrator to victim, leading to a process of "secondary victimization," which in turn leads to lack of support for and even condemnation of the victim (Schwartz, 1991).
- Surveys have suggested that adolescents in particular have complicated views about forced sexual behavior. For example, surveys of American youth have found that boys and girls justify forced sex under a variety of circumstances, including the boy spending money on the girl, the girl being "sexually experienced," a history of dating for six months or more, "when a girl gets a guy sexually excited," or when a girl agrees to sex and then changes her mind (Schwartz, 1991; White and Humphrey, 1991).
- Use of alcohol and drugs also contributes to the risk of sexual assault. A study of sexual assault among college students found that 73% of the assailants and 55% of the victims had used drugs, alcohol, or both immediately before the assault.

Individuals who exhibit some or all of the above characteristics may be caught up in what has been called a cycle of violence (Steinmetz, 1977; Levy, 1993). It involves three cyclical stages: the tension-building stage, the explosion stage, and the honeymoon stage. During the tension-building stage, the abuser becomes more and more temperamental, edgy, critical, and explosive. He or she becomes jealous, possessive, and accusatory, trying to control the other person. The potential recipient of the abuse tries to keep the peace during this stage, becoming more tense and nervous and sometimes withdrawn, depressed, and distracted. The tension-building stage ends with a violent explosion, with the abuser verbally or physically (or both) attacking the dating partner. The abuser calls the dating partner names, hits, and will not let the person get away. After the sudden release of tension, the abuser always feels sorry and is afraid that the dating partner will leave. The recipient of the abuse may or may not leave at this point. Following the explosion, a honeymoon stage sets in, whereby the abuser is apologetic, romantic, or passionate. The recipient of the abuse is often seduced by the appearance of romance, because the person remembers the things that he or she loves about the abuser when he or she is not abusive. The rationalization is that the recipient of the abuse loves the abuser and that the abuser needs him or her. The dating pair may even develop rationalizations to justify the violence, believing that the violence was a "misunderstanding" and will not happen again. The rationalizations maintain the relationship until the tension builds up again. The honeymoon stage keeps the couple a couple.

In "Recognizing abuse tough task for teens" (*Times*, 1995), Amy French noted that it is not uncommon for men to suffer abuse, but women more commonly are the recipients of abuse, partly because abusers see violence as a means of control and men are expected to control family and social situations. She presented a theoretical model of a cycle of abuse that centers around power and control exerted primarily by men. The elements of the cycle of abuse include (1) using male privilege, (2) using economic abuse, (3) using coercion and threats, (4) using intimidation, (5) using emotional abuse, (6) using isolation, (7) minimizing, denying, and blaming, and (8) using children.

The profiles above identify characteristics that represent danger signals for dating violence. Individuals who identify with or have experienced some or all of these issues may be vulnerable to dating violence and the cycles of violence or abuse. The significance of developing profiles is that they help in developing prevention and treatment strategies for both the recipients of violence in the dating relationships as well as for the perpetrators of violence.

PREVENTION AND TREATMENT

A variety of prevention and treatment strategies have emerged to address the problem of dating violence. Most prevention strategies focus on educating young people about what dating violence is and how to recognize it. Because dating violence tends to be "hidden" or unrecognized, most practitioners in the field suggest that it is important to reach out to adolescents and young people as well as to others who may experience dating violence.

The majority of the prevention program models throughout the United States and Canada are carried out in high schools by school staff or by community-based domestic violence programs. The models include:

> (1) classroom education, with curricula that usually cover facts about and definitions of dating violence, relationship skills (e.g., conflict management, communication, handling jealousy and anger), and resources for help; (2) speak-outs for youth; (3) saturation of the school environment with policy-setting so that violence is not tolerated, an intervention plan for students and school personnel, and coordination among parents, police and health and mental health agencies; (4) support groups or workshops for high-risk young men and women that focus on nonviolent relationship skills; (5) theater troupe or other dramatic presentations to students by students; and (6) peer leadership/counseling and presentations. (Levy, 1991, p. 16)

A number of model dating violence prevention programs exists. An example of a theater model was created by Brown University students; they conduct a theatrical piece, *Love's Not Suppose to Hurt,* followed by an interactive experience with the audience. The actors remain in character for a question-and-answer period in which many of the complex and controversial issues surrounding dating violence are addressed. The students are then split up into single-sex discussion groups followed by a mixed-sex discussion group. An example of a model prevention education program is the Dating Violence Intervention Program run by Carole Sousa in Cambridge, Massachusetts. This comprehensive program includes classroom education, a peer leadership program, a theater troupe, support groups, and education and planning with school personnel. The model of using support groups to empower young abused women in dating relationships is increasingly popular in schools and in domestic violence shelters. An example of this model is the school-based support groups conducted by the Center for Battered Women Teen Dating Violence Project in Austin, Texas. NiCarthy's (1991) "Addictive Love" workshops are a special version of the support group model. An example of a teacher-training model is the strategy developed by the Minnesota Coalition for Battered Women. Teachers are viewed as resources who can be most effective in reaching out to young people in high school. These are but a few examples of the prevention models that have been developed to address dating violence.

Intervention strategies for those involved in dating violence include the use of friends, relatives, community resources, domestic violence programs, and clinical intervention. Intervention requires patience, nonjudgmental support, and sensitivity to cultural and cross-cultural norms and sexual preferences. Other intervention strategies involve legal remedies, as previously noted (Kuehl, 1991).

The following strategies are offered for what you can do to be safe if you are being abused (Levy, 1993; NiCarthy, 1991):

1. Take it seriously. Let your abuser know that emotional, sexual, and physical abuse are all serious and dangerous and that it will not be tolerated.

2. Plan for your safety. If you are not ready to break up, think of a safety plan for when the abuser is violent; if you are ready to break up, think of a safety plan for his or her explosive reaction or harassment to try to get you back.

3. Use self-defense. Let your abuser know loudly and clearly that you will not be hit, or that you will not have sex unless it's agreeable to you.

4. Use the legal system. Refer to the charges listed elsewhere in this discussion.

5. If a minor, tell an adult about the violence. Telling your parents or sometimes a coworker, a neighbor, or a friend's parent can be helpful.

6. Call a hotline for information. Most cities have teen hotlines, domestic violence and rape hotlines, or crisis hotlines; the National Domestic Violence Hotline number is 1-800-333-7233.

7. Find a counselor or support group to help you sort out your confused feelings and become stronger in coping with the violence.

Graham and Rawlings (1991) discuss what they call the Stockholm syndrome (a pattern of bonding in violent dating relationships) that may require clinical intervention.

Trauma often accompanies date rape, and a person may need clinical treatment for posttraumatic stress disorder. A therapeutic technique called "flooding" has sometimes proved helpful (Gallers and Lawrence, 1991). Again, however, legal remedies can and should also be accessed in these circumstances.

LEGAL ISSUES AND FUTURE TRENDS

Dating violence as a social phenomenon has been framed largely as a problem for teenagers and young adults who date, even though dating is not an age-specific phenomenon. In the context of teenagers who date, a number of legal issues that currently exist impact on the availability and use of legal remedies to address dating violence.

Kuehl (1991) outlined a variety of obstacles for minors who are victims of dating violence. First, in most states, minors (persons under the age of eighteen) do not have a legal presence and need to have a guardian ad litem (parent, counselor, or advocate) to access existing laws. (Emancipated minors who have properly filed papers with the court and live independently can also access existing laws.) A minor can file a police complaint and can testify in a criminal case but needs an adult present to file a case on her or his behalf. As previously noted, domestic violence laws do not recognize dating relationships (except in Colorado, Pennsylvania, and California) and are set up for adult intimate relationships. Second, teens face the obstacle of not being taken seriously by a judge in juvenile court proceedings, which tend to be informal. The court may try to use alternative sentencing instead of sending a perpetrator to detention (minors are not sent to jail), and a judge may minimize problems as youthful indiscretion or "teenage love." Third, because they tend to distrust adults and authorities or may feel ashamed, minors may be torn between a desire for safety and a desire to protect a boyfriend or girlfriend from the legal system. Fourth, the lack of response from authorities when reports are made at colleges and high schools tend to make teens and young adults reluctant to view and pursue legal remedies as viable options. One trend is an increasing number of advocates and availability of resources for teens who are involved in abusive relationships; these advocates can be helpful to youths in accessing legal remedies.

Any action that is a crime if committed by an adult (robbery, rape, murder, battery) is also a crime if committed by a minor. The juvenile courts handle cases involving minors and even though minors are not sent to jail, they may be put in juvenile detention, released to their parents, or put on probation. They may also receive "alternative dispositions" (e.g., being ordered to go to another school or to leave the victim alone). If battering is reported to the police, even if the relationship is not covered by laws criminalizing domestic violence, the abuser may be charged with the crimes previously outlined as various state criminal laws are accessed. One trend that appears to be emerging is increased activism with and by legislators to file preventive legislation as precursors to having to access criminal laws. The goal is to provide teens with more advocates. For example, Harris (1996) noted that the lawmakers in Massachusetts have filed a bill requiring training in intervention for teachers, police, and social workers with respect to dating violence.

Legal issues regarding acquaintance rape may command more serious attention in the legal system. The U.S. Department of Justice and the National Institute of Justice now recognize acquaintance rape as an emerging issue in law. In a 1994 report by the National Institute of Justice, it was noted that "acquaintance rape . . . surfaced during the 1980s as [one of the] issues that [is] likely to have a profound influence on the investigation and prosecution of future rape cases" (p. 65). The report also notes that

> during the past two decades most States have reformed their rape laws and broadened the definition of rape to include any type of sexual penetration. These rape laws remove corroboration and resistance requirements and make the victim's sexual history inadmissible as evidence. They also emphasize the offender's acts rather than the victim's history, and they draw attention to rape's violent aspects, as opposed to its sexual ones. In some States, the term "rape" is being replaced by "sexual assault," "sexual battery," and other terms that emphasize its violent nature. . . . New statutes now define some rapes as gender-biased hate crimes, allowing for increased criminal penalties or civil actions. Federal legislation defining some rapes as hate crimes against women has also been introduced, and Federal legislation to reduce the incidence of rape on college campuses has been enacted. (p. 7)

Examples of recent federal legislation include the Campus Sexual Assault Victim's Bill of Rights (passed in July 1992), the Student Right-to-Know and Campus Security Act of 1990, the Hate Crimes Statistics Act of 1990, and the Victims of Crime Act of 1984.

Sensitivity to the issue of sexual assault is such that most colleges now have sexual harassment policies. Antioch College in Yellow Springs, Ohio, has expanded its approach to include what is called a sexual consent policy. It was sought by a feminist group on campus, Womyn of Antioch, after two rapes were reported on campus that year, neither of which were prosecuted, and was issued in 1992. The policy has generated much debate in academia, and the nature of this debate is presented in the 1995 book *Rape on Campus*. Whether or not the experiment at Antioch College becomes a trend or is ultimately viewed as an overreaction remains to be seen.

CONCLUSION

In the context of an evolving history of dating practices, dating violence has emerged as a social phenomenon. Although there is inconsistent data in the field regarding prevalence, it is widely recognized today as a "hidden" problem. It is framed largely as a teen problem, although it can be found in all dating relationships. Many authors have found correlates and characteristics of dating violence and have explored causation and effect; theoretical models, which can be empirically tested, are just beginning to emerge. Dating violence continues to be an emerging phenomenon, however, because it does not have legal status. Much more work is required to educate youth in recognizing it as a problem, to educate legislators and the legal system about the nature and seriousness of the problem, and to engage the public in creating a climate for healing these abusive relationships.

EDITORIAL SUMMARY

From pre- and post-colonial days up to the late 1950s, dating violence surfaced only anecdotally, if mentioned or acknowledged at all. In the late 1950s and later in the 1970s and 1980s, landmark social research and social events involving violence in dating relationships emerged in the literature and in the culture to focus attention, legitimize, and crystallize dating violence as a social phenomenon. To some extent, the emergence of date rape as a special case of dating violence sharpened the focus. Today, dating violence is framed largely as a teen problem, although it can be found in all dating relationships. Many authors have found correlates and characteristics of dating violence and have explored causation and effect; theoretical models, which can be empirically tested, are just beginning to emerge. Treatment and prevention programs have also been developed. Dating violence continues to be an emerging phenomenon, however, because it does not have legal status. Much more work is required to educate youth in recognizing dating violence as a problem, to educate legislators and the legal system about the nature and seriousness of the problem, and to engage the public in creating a climate for healing these abusive relationships.

REFERENCES

Ageton, S. S. (1983). *Sexual Assault Among Adolescents.* Lexington, MA: Heath.

American Medical Association. (1995, November 6). *Sexual Assault in America.* [On-line]. http://www.ama-assn.org/public/releases/assault/action.htm.

Arias, I., and Johnson, P. (1989). Evaluations of physical aggression among intimate dyads. *Journal of Interpersonal Violence, 4*(3), 298–307.

Arisas, I., Samios, M., and O'Leary, K. D. (1987). Prevalence and correlates of physical aggression during courtship. *Journal of Interpersonal Violence, 2*(1), 82–90.

Bandura, A. (1973). *Aggression: A Social Learning Analysis.* Englewood Cliffs, NJ: Prentice-Hall.

Bateman, P. (1991). The context of date rape. In B. Levy (Ed.), *Dating Violence: Young Women in Danger* (pp. 94–99). Seattle: Seal Press.

Bergman, L. (1992). Dating violence among high school students. *Social Work: Journal of the National Association of Social Workers, 37*(1), 21–27.

Bernard, J. (1973). *The Future of Marriage.* New York: Bantam.

Bernard, M. L., and Bernard, J. L. (1983). Violent intimacy: The family as a model for love relationships. *Family Relations, 32,* 283–286.

Bettelheim, B. (1965). The problem of generations. In E. K. Erikson (Ed.), *The Challenge of Youth* (pp. 76–109). Garden City, NY: Doubleday.

Billingham, R. E., and Sack, A. R. (1987). Conflict resolution tactics and the level of emotional commitment among unmarrieds. *Human Relations, 40,* 59–74.

Bohmer, C., and Parrot, A. (1993). *Sexual Assault on Campus: The Problem and the Solution.* New York: Lexington.

Briere, J., and Malamuth, N. A. (1983). Predicting self-reported likelihood of sexually abusive behavior: Attitudinal versus sexual explanations. *Journal of Research in Personality, 17,* 315–323.

Brownmiller, S. (1975). *Against Our Will: Men, Women, and Rape.* New York: Simon and Schuster.

Burkhart, B. R., and Stanton, A. L. (1985). Sexual aggression in acquaintance relationships. In G. Russell (Ed.), *Violence in Intimate Relationships.* New York: Spectrum Press.

Butler, K., and Nakahara, S. (1996). "Date rape drug" becoming a major concern on college campuses. *UMF Mainstream.* [On-line]. Available from UMF Mainstream Online.

Cardarelli, A. P. (Ed.) (1997). *Violence between Intimate Partners: Patterns, Causes, and Effects.* Boston: Allyn and Bacon.

Carlson, B. (1987). Dating violence: A research review and comparison with spouse abuse. *Social Casework: The Journal of Contemporary Social Work, 68*(1), 16–23.

Cate, R. M., Henton, J. M., Koval, J., Christopher, F. S., and Lloyd, S. (1982). Premarital abuse: A social psychological perspective. *Journal of Family Issues, 3,* 79–91.

Courtois, C. (1988). *Healing the Incest Wound.* New York: W. W. Norton.

Cummins, M. (1978). Police and petting: Informal enforcement of sexual standards. In J. M. Henslin and E. Segarin (Eds.), *The Sociology of Sex* (pp. 123–139). New York: Schocken Books.

Davis, E. G. (1971). *The First Sex.* New York: Putnam.

DeKeseredy, W. S. (1988). Woman abuse in dating relationships: The relevance of social support theory. *Journal of Family Violence, 3*(1), 1–13.

DeMaris, A. (1987). The efficacy of a spouse abuse model in accounting for courtship violence. *Journal of Family Issues, 8*(3), 291–305.

Demos, J. (1971). *A Little Commonwealth: Family Life in Plymouth Colony.* New York: Oxford University Press.

Dhaenes, R. A., and Farrington, K. (197). *A Study of Stereotyped Attitudes Toward Rape.* Paper presented at the Third National Family Violence Research Conference, Durham, NH.

Dobash, R. E., and Dobash, R. (1978). Wives: The "appropriate" victims of marital violence. *Victimology, 2*(3–4), 426–442.

Dobash, R. E., and Dobash, R. (1979). *Violence Against Wives.* New York: Free Press.

Duck, S., and Pond, K. (1989). Friends, Romans, countrymen, lend me your retrospections. In C. Hendrick (Ed.), *Close Relationships.* Newbury Park, CA: Sage.

Edelson, J. L., Eisikovits, Z., and Guttman, E. (1985). Men who batter women. *Journal of Family Issues, 6,* 229–247.

Epstein, J., and Langenbahn, S. (Eds.). (1994, May). The criminal justice and community response to rape. *Issues and Practices in Criminal Justice.* Washington, DC: National Institute of Justice, U. S. Department of Justice.

Estrich, S. (1987). *Real Rape: How the Legal System Victimizes Women Who Say No.* Cambridge, MA: Harvard University Press.

Feldman, H. (1967). *Development of the Husband-Wife Relationship.* Ithaca, NY: Cornell University Press.

Ferguson, C. (1996). *Review of Information about Dating Violence on the Internet.* Unpublished manuscript, University of Massachusetts at Boston.

French, A. (1995). Recognizing abuse tough task for teens. *Times.* [On-line] http://www.htimes.com/htimes/today/dvpart2.html.

Fisher, G. J. (1986). College student attitudes toward forcible date rape: I. Cognitive predictors. *Archives of Sexual Behavior, 15*(6), 457–467.

Gallers, J., and Lawrence, K. J. (1991). Overcoming post-traumatic stress disorder in adolescent date rape survivors. In B. Levy (Ed.), *Dating Violence: Young Women in Danger* (pp. 172–183). Seattle: Seal Press.

Gamache, D. (1991). Domination and control: The social context of dating violence. In B. Levy (Ed.), *Dating Violence: Young Women in Danger* (pp. 69–83). Seattle: Seal Press.

Garrett, W. (1982). *Seasons of Marriage and Family Life.* New York: Holt, Rinehart and Winston.

Gelles, R. J., and Straus, M. A. (1988). *Intimate Violence.* New York: Simon and Schuster.

Giarrusso, R., Johnson, P. B., Goodchilds, J. D., and Zellman, G. (1979, April). *Adolescent Cues and Signals: Sex and Assault.* Paper presented at the meeting of the Western Psychological Association, San Diego.

Gilbert, N. (1993, June 29). The wrong response to rape. *Wall Street Journal,* p. 19.

Gilbert, N. (1991a, June 27). The campus rape scare. *Wall Street Journal,* p. 10.

Gilbert, N. (1991b). The phantom epidemic. *Public Interest, 103,* 54.

Goode, W. (1973). *Explorations in Social Theory.* New York: Oxford University Press.

Graham, D. L., and Rawlings, E. I. (1991). Bonding with abusive dating partners: Dynamics of Stockholm Syndrome. In B. Levy (Ed.), *Dating Violence: Young Women in Danger,* (pp. 119–135). Seattle: Seal Press.

Greven, P. (1977). *The Protestant Temperament: Patterns of Child-Rearing, Religious Experience, and the Self in Early America.* New York: Knopf.

Groth, N., and Birnbaum, H. J. (1979). *Men Who Rape.* New York: Plenum Press.

Guttman, S. (1990, October). Date rape: Does anyone really know what it is? *Playboy,* pp. 48–56.

Handlin, O., and Handlin, M. (1971). *Facing Life: Youth and the Family in American History.* Boston: Little, Brown.

Harris, L. (1996, September). The hidden world of dating violence. *Parade Magazine,* pp. 4–6.

Hart, B. (1986) Lesbian battering: An examination. in K. Lobel (ed.), *Naming the Violence* (pp. 173–189). Seattle: Seal.

Hendrick, C. (1989). *Close Relationships.* Newbury Park, CA: Sage.

Henton J. M., Cate, R., Koval, J., Lloyd, S., and Christopher, S. (1983). Romance and violence in dating relationships. *Journal of Family Issues, 4,* 467–482.

Heron, A. (1983). *One Teenager in Ten: Testimony by Gay and Lesbian Youth.* New York: Warner.

Hollingshead, A. B. (1975). *Elmtown's Youth and Elmtown Revisited.* New York: Wiley.

Hunter, J., and Schaecher, R. (1987) Stresses on lesbian and gay adolescents in schools. *Social Work in Education, Spring,* 180–190.

Illinois Coalition Against Sexual Assault. (1991). Acquaintance rape. *Sexual Violence: Facts and Statistics.* Springfield: Illinois Coalition Against Sexual Assault.

Kanin, E. J. (1957). Male aggression in dating-courtship relationships. *Journal of Sociology, 63,* 197–204.

Kanin, E. J. (1984). Date rape: Unofficial criminals and victims. *Victimology: An International Journal, 9,* 93–108.

Kanin, E. J. (1985). Date rapists: Differential sexual socialization and relative deprivation. *Archives of Sexual Behavior, 14*(3), 219–231.

Kanin, E. J. (1994). False rape allegations. *Archives of Sexual Behavior, 23*(1), 81–90.

Kanin, E. J., and Parcell, S. R. (1977). Sexual aggression: A second look at the offended female. *Archives of Sexual Behavior, 6,* 67–76.

Kantor, G. K., and Straus, M. A. (1987). The drunken bum theory of wife abuse. *Social Problems, 34,* 213–230.

Kempe, R. S. (1962). *The Battered Child.* Chicago: University of Chicago Press.

Kett, J. (1977). *Rites of Passage: Adolescence in America 1790 to the Present.* New York: Basic Books.

Knox, D., and Wilson, K. (1981). Dating behaviors of university students. *Family Relations, 30,* 255–258.

Koss, M. P. (1985) The hidden rape victim: Personality, attitudinal, and situational characteristics. *Psychology of Women Quarterly, 9,* 193–212.

Koss, M. P. (1987) *Outrageous Acts and Everyday Seductions: Sexual Aggression and Victimization Among College Students.* Paper presented at Romance, Rape and Relationships: A Conference on Teen Sexual Exploitation, Seattle.

Koss, M. P., Gidycz, C. A., and Wisniewski, N. (1987). The scope of rape: Incidence and prevalence of sexual aggression and victimization in a national sample of higher education students. *Journal of Consulting and Clinical Psychology, 55,* 162–170.

Koss, M. P., and Leonard, K. E. (1984). Sexually aggressive men. In N. A. Malamuth and E. Donnerstein (Eds.), *Pornography and Sexual Aggression.* Orlando, FL: Academic Press.

Koss, M. P., and Oros, C. J. (1982). Sexual experiences survey: A research instrument investigating sexual aggression and victimization. *Journal of Counseling Psychology, 50*(2), 455–457.

Kuehl, S. J. (1991). Legal remedies for teen dating violence. In B. Levy (Ed.), *Dating Violence: Young Women in Danger* (pp. 209–220). Seattle: Seal Press.

Lane, K. E., and Gwartney-Gibbs, P. A. (1985). Violence in the context of dating and sex. *Journal of Family Violence, 6*(1), 45–59.

Laner, M. R. (1983). Courtship abuse and aggression: Contextual aspects. *Sociological Spectrum, 3,* 69–83.

Laner, M. R., and Thompson, J. (1982). Abuse and aggression in courting couples. *Deviant Behavior, 3,* 229–244.

Langley, R., and Levy, R. C. (1977). *Wife Beating: The Silent Crisis.* New York: Pocket Books.

Leone, B., and de Koster, K. (Eds.), (1995). *Rape on Campus.* San Diego: Greenhaven Press.

Lerner, G. (1986). *The Creation of Patriarchy.* New York: Oxford University Press.

Levy, B. (Ed.). (1991). *Dating Violence: Young Women in Danger.* Seattle: Seal Press.

Levy, B. (1993). *In Love and in Danger: A Teen's Guide to Breaking Free of Abusive Relationships.* Seattle: Seal Press.

Levy, P. (1984). Courtship often a violent time. *Minneapolis Tribune.*

Lobel, K. (1986). *Naming the Violence: Speaking Out about Lesbian Battering.* Seattle: Seal Press.

Lundberg-Love, P. and Geffer, R. (1989). Date rape: Prevalence, risk factors, and a proposed model. In M. A. Pirog-Good and J. E. Stets (Eds.), *Violence in Dating Relationships: Emerging Social Issues,* (pp. 166–184). New York: Praeger.

Maglin, N., and Perry, D. (1996). *"Bad Girls," "Good Girls": Women, Sex, and Power in the Nineties.* New Brunswick, NJ: Rutgers University Press.

Mahoney, E. R., Shively, M., and Traw, M. (1985). Sexual coercion and assault: Male macho and female chance. *Sexual Coercion and Assault, 1*(1), 2–7.

Makepeace, J. (1981). Courtship violence among college students. *Family Relations, 30,* 97–102.

Makepeace, J. (1982). Life events, stress and courtship violence. *Family Relations, 32,* 101–109.

Makepeace, J. (1986). Gender differences in courtship violence victimization. *Family Relations, 35,* 383–388.

Makepeace, J. M. (1987). Social factors and victim offender differences. *Family Relations, 36* (1), 87-91.

Makepeace, J. (1988). The severity of courtship violence injuries and individual precautionary measures. In G. T. Hotaling, D. Finkelhor, J. T. Kirkpatrick, and M. A. Straus (Eds.), *Family Abuse and Its Consequences: New Directions in Research* (pp. 297–311). Newbury Park, CA: Sage.

Makepeace, J. (1989). Dating, living together, and courtship violence. In M. A. Pirog-Good and J. E. Stets (Eds.), *Violence in Dating Relationships: Emerging Social Issues* (pp. 95–107). New York: Praeger.

Makepeace, J. (1997). Courtship violence as process: A developmental theory. In A. P. Cardarell (Ed.), *Violence between Intimate Partners: Patterns, Causes, and Effects.* Boston: Allyn and Bacon.

Malamuth, N. M. (1981). Rape proclivity among males. *Journal of Social Issues, 37*(4), 138–157.

Malamuth, N. M. (1984). Aggression against women. In N. A. Malamuth and E. Donnerstein (eds.), *Pornography and Sexual Aggression.* Orlando, FL: Academic Press.

Marshall, L. L. (1987, July). *Gender Differences in the Prediction of Courtship Abuse from Family of Origin Violence, Anxiety Proneness and Recent Positive and Negative Stress.* Paper presented at the Third National Conference on Family Violence Research, University of New Hampshire, Durham, NH.

Marshall, L. L., and Rose, R. (1987). Gender, stress and violence in adult relationships of a sample of college students. *Journal of Social and Personal Relations, 4,* 299–316.

Marshall, L. L., and Rose, R. (1988). Family of origin and courtship violence. *Journal of Counseling and Development, 66*(9), 414–418.

Martin, D. (1976). *Battered Wives.* San Francisco: Glice.

Matthews, W. L. (1984). Violence in college couples. *College Student Journal, 18,* 150–158.

McAdams, D. P. (1988). Personal needs and personal relationships. In S. W. Duck (Ed.), *Handbook of Personal Relations* (pp. 7–22). Chichester: John Wiley.

McFarlane, J. (1989). Battering in pregnancy: The tip of the iceberg. *Women and Health, 15*(3), 69–84.

McKinney, K. (1986). Measures of verbal, physical, and sexual dating violence by gender. *Free Inquiry into Creative Sociology, 14*(1), 55–60.

Miller, B. (1988). Date rape: Time for a new look at prevention. *Journal of College Student Development, 29,* 553–555.

Miller, B., and Marshall, J. (1987). Coercive sex on the university campus. *Journal of College Student Personnel, 28*(1), 38–47.

Miller, G. R., and Boster, F. (1988). Persuasion in personal relationships. In S. W. Duck (Ed.), *Handbook of Personal Relationships* (pp. 275–288). Chichester: John Wiley.

Minnesota Coalition for Battered Women. (1990). *Confronting Lesbian Battering: A Manual for the Battered Women's Movement.* M.C.B.W., 570 Asbury Street, #201, St. Paul, MN 55104.

Montgomery, B. M. (1988). Quality communication in personal relationships. In S. W. Duck (Ed.), *Handbook of Personal Relationships* (pp. 343–359). Chichester: John Wiley.

Morrow, S. L., and Hawxhurst, D. M. (1989). Lesbian partner abuse: Implications for therapists. *Journal of Counseling and Development, 68,* 58–62.

Muehlenhard, C. L. (1988). Misinterpreted dating behaviors and the risk of date rape. *Journal of Social and Clinical Psychology, 6*(1), 20–37.

Nash, A. (1988). Ontogeny, phylogeny and relationships. In S. W. Duck (Ed.), *Handbook of Personal Relationships* (pp. 121–141). Chichester: John Wiley.

National Clearinghouse of Family Violence. (1990). *Dating Violence and Acquaintance Rape.* [On-line]. Lycos, National Clearinghouse on Family Violence, Health and Welfare.

NiCarthy, G. (1991). Addictive love and abuse: A course for teenage women. In B. Levy (Ed.), *Dating Violence: Young Women in Danger* (pp. 240–257). Seattle: Seal Press.

O'Keefe, N., Brockopp, K., and Chew, E. (1986). Teen dating violence. *Social Work, 31,* 465–468.

Olday, D., and Wesley, B. (1983). *Premarital Courtship Violence: A Summary Report.* Unpublished paper, Moorhead State University, Moorhead, MN.

O'Sullivan, C. (1991). Acquaintance gang rape on campus. In A. Parrot and L. Bechhofer (Eds.), *Acquaintance Rape: The Hidden Crime* (pp. 140–156). New York: Wiley.

Paglia, C. (1991, February 15). Feminists lead women astray on the threat of rape. *Philadelphia Inquirer*, p. 23.

Parsons, T. (1965). Youth in the context of American society. In E. Erickson (Ed)., *The Challenge of Youth*, pp. 110–142. Garden City, NY: Doubleday.

Parrot, A., and Bechhofer, L. (1991). *Acquaintance Rape: The Hidden Crime.* New York: Wiley.

Parrot, A. (1985). *Comparison of Acquaintance Rape Patterns Among College Students in a Large Co-ed University and a Small Women's College.* Presented at the annual meeting of the Society for the Scientific Study of Sex, San Diego, CA.

Patterson, M. L. (1988). Functions of nonverbal behavior in close relationships. In S. W. Duck (Ed.), *Handbook of Personal Relationships* (pp. 41–56). Chichester: John Wiley.

Pence, E. (1987). *In Our Best Interest.* Duluth: Minnesota Program Development, Inc.

Peplau, L. A., Rubin, Z., and Hill, C. T. (1977). Sexual intimacy in dating relationships. *Journal of Social Issues, 33*(2), 86–109.

Pirog-Good, M. A. , and Stets, J. E. (1989a). The help-seeking behavior of physically and sexually abused college students. In M. A. Pirog-Good and J. E. Stets (Eds.), *Violence in Dating Relationships: Emerging Social Issues* (pp. 108–125). New York: Praeger.

Pirog-Good, M. A., and Stets, J. E. (Eds.) (1989b). *Violence in Dating Relationships: Emerging Social Issues.* New York: Praeger.

Plass, M. S., and Gessner, J. C. (1983). Violence in courtship relations: A Southern example. *Free Inquiry in Creative Sociology, 11,* 198–202.

Puig, A. (1984). Predomestic strife: A growing college counseling concern. *Journal of College Student Personnel, 25,* 268–269.

Riggs, D. S., and O'Leary, K. D. (1989). A theoretical model of courtship aggression. In M. A. Pirog-Good and J. E. Stets (Eds.), *Violence in Dating Relationships: Emerging Social Issues* (pp. 53–71). New York: Praeger.

Roiphe, K. (1993a). Gender differences in courtship violence victimization. *Family Relations, 35,* 383–388.

Roiphe, K. (1993b). Life events, stress, and courtship violence. *Family Relations, 32,* 101–109.

Roiphe, K. (1993c). *The Morning After: Sex, Fear, and Feminism on Campus.* Boston: Little, Brown, and Company.

Rook, K. S. (1988). Toward a more differentiated view of loneliness. In S. W. Duck (Ed.), *Handbook of Personal Relationships* (pp. 571–589). Chichester: John Wiley.

Roscoe, B., and Benaske, N. (1985). Courtship violence experienced by abused wives: Similarities in patterns of abuse. *Family Relations, 34,* 419–424.

Roscoe, B., and Callahan, J. E. (1985). Adolescents' self-report of violence in families and dating relationships. *Adolescence, 20,* 545–553.

Rowe, G. P. (1993). *Dating: The benefits and risks.* [On-line]. Internet: NF 93–123, http://famwww.unl.edu/fam/pub/nebfacts/nf93-123.html.

Sanday, P. (1990). *Fraternity Gang Rape.* New York: New York University Press.

Schechter, S. (1982). *Woman and Male Violence: The Visions and Struggles of the Battered Women's Movement.* Boston: South End Press.

Schwartz, I. L. (1991). Sexual violence against women: Prevalence, consequences, societal factors, and prevention. *American Journal of Preventative Medicine, 7*(6), 363–373.

Shorter, E. (1977). *The Making of the Modern Family.* New York: Basic Books.

Shotland, R. S. (1989). A model of the causes of date rape in developing and close relationships. In C. Hendrick (Ed.), *Close Relationships* (pp. 247–270). Newbury Park, CA: Sage.

Sigelman, C. K., Berry, C. J., and Wiles, K. A. (1984). Violence in college students' dating relationships. *Journal of Applied Social Psychology, 14*(6), 530–548.

Slater, B. (1988). Essential issues in working with lesbian and gay male youths. *Professional Psychology: Research and Practice, 19*(2), 226–235.

Steinmetz, S. K. (1977). *The Cycle of Violence: Assertive, Aggressive, and Abusive Family Interaction.* New York: Praeger.

Steinmetz, S. K. (1978). The battered husband syndrome. *Victimology, 2,* 499–509.

Stets, J. E., and Pirog-Good, M. A. (1987). Violence in dating relationships. *Social Psychology Quarterly, 50*(3), 237–246.

Stets, J. E., and Pirog-Good, M. A. (1989). Patterns of physical and sexual abuse for men and women in dating relationships: A descriptive analysis. *Journal of Family Violence, 4*(2), 161–180.

Stone, L. (1979). *The Family, Sex, and Marriage in England 1500–1800.* (Abridged ed.) New York: Harper and Row.

Straus, M. A. (1979). Measuring intrafamily conflict and violence: The conflict tactics scale. *Journal of Marriage and the Family, 41,* 75–88.

Straus, M. A., and Gelles, R. J. (1988). Violence in American families: How much is there and why does it occur. In E. W. Nunnally, C. S. Chilman, and F. M. Cox (Eds.), *Troubled Relationships* (pp. 141–162). Newbury Park, CA: Sage.

Sugarman, D. B., and Hotaling, G. T. (1989). Dating violence: Prevalence, context, and risk markers. In M. A. Pirog-Good and J. E. Stets (Eds.), *Violence in Dating Relationships: Emerging Social Issues.* (pp. 3–32). New York: Praeger.

Sugarman, D. B., and Hotaling, G. T. (1991). Dating violence: a review of contextual and risk factors. In B. Levy (Ed.), *Dating Violence: Young Women in Danger* (pp. 100–118). Seattle: Seal Press.

Tedeschi, J. T., Smith, R., and Brown, R. (1974). A reinterpretation of research on aggression. *Psychological Bulletin, 81,* 540–562.

Thompson, W. E. (1986). Courtship violence: Toward a conceptual understanding. *Youth and Society, 18*(2), 162–176.

Tierney, B. (1984). Gang rape on college campuses. *Response to Violence in the Family and Sexual Assault, 7*(2), 1–2.

Tomassen, R. (1970). *Sweden: Prototype of Modern Society.* New York: Random House.

Tontodonato, P., and Crew, B. K. (1992) Dating violence, social learning theory, and gender: A multivariate analysis. *Violence and Victims, 7*(1), 3–14.

Turk, J. L., and Bell, N. (1970). *The Measurement of Family Behavior: What They Perceive, What They Report, and What We Observe.* Paper presented at the annual meeting of the American Sociological Association.

Warshaw, R. (1988). *I Never Called It Rape: The Ms. Report on Recognizing, Fighting, and Surviving Date and Acquaintance Rape.* New York: Harper and Row.

Waterman, C. K., Dawson, L. J., and Bologna, M. J. (1989). Sexual coercion in gay male and lesbian relationships: Predictors and implications for support services. *Journal of Sex Research, 26*(1), 118–124.

White, E. (1991). The abused black woman: Challenging a legacy of pain. In B. Levy (Ed.), *Dating Violence: Young Women in Danger* (pp. 84–93). Seattle: Seal Press.

White, J. W., and Humphrey, J. A. (1991). Young people's attitudes toward acquaintance rape. In Parrot and Bechhofer (Eds.), *Acquaintance Rape: The Hidden Crime.* New York: Wiley.

Whitlock, K. (1989). *Bridges of Respect: Creating Support for Lesbian and Gay Youth.* Philadelphia: American Friends Service Committee.

Will, G. (1993, October 4). Sex amidst semi-colons. *Newsweek,* p. 92.

Yllo, K., and Straus, M. A. (1981). Interpersonal violence among married and cohabiting couples. *Family Relations, 30,* 339–347.

5

Wife Abuse

Michael P. Brown, Ph.D.,
and James E. Hendricks, Ph.D.
Department of Criminal Justice and Criminology
Ball State University

Although evidence of wife abuse can be found throughout the annals of recorded history, not until the 1970s was it considered a social problem worthy of rigorous scholarly attention. Hence, wife abuse is a relatively new area of social scientific inquiry. Fraught with methodological limitations, however, research on wife abuse is hindered by the very nature of the act itself, frequently hidden behind the doors of private residences (Saunders, 1993).

Unable to gather information that may be generalizable to all victims of wife abuse, an understanding of this crime tends to be based on official criminal justice documents such as arrest reports, court documents, or victim assistance and advocate program records as well as autobiographies, diaries, and personal interviews with victims who are willing to "speak out." These sources of information fail to reflect the "true" nature of the untold number of abusive marital relationships that never come to the attention of criminal justice officials or are never told in other written forms. Nevertheless, the information that has been gathered has engendered numerous social programs that provide services to meet the social, psychological, and physical needs of victims of wife abuse; inspired innovative treatment modalities to address the psychological needs of offenders; and encouraged the passage of laws to protect the abused and to express indignation toward the act of wife abuse and its perpetrators.

This chapter attempts to provide the most comprehensive and up-to-date information on wife abuse available. The terms "domestic violence" and "wife abuse" are used interchangeably. They are intended to denote violence toward women by their husbands. This chapter provides a general overview of diverse issues related to wife abuse, from the history of wife abuse to its legal definition and from the nature and extent of wife abuse to its correlates. Profiles of offenders and victims are also provided. Prevention and treatment methods are delineated, and future trends are described.

HISTORY OF WIFE ABUSE

Centuries ago, laws existed that regulated the use of physical violence by husbands toward their wives. These laws should in no way suggest, however, that women were protected from physical abuse from their husbands. On the contrary, physical violence was a socially accepted method of expressing a husband's disapproval with his wife, and existing laws did nothing more than regulate the extent to which a husband could use physical force. Moreover, these early laws went as far as to provide justification for husbands to assault their wives.

For example, English common law, the historical basis for many of the laws in the United States, gave husbands the unabashed right to use physical violence—albeit with "restraint"—to control their wives and "maintain" the family unit (Dobash and Dobash, 1979; Walker, 1990a). The well-known "rule of thumb" was a guiding principle for many early laws that made it permissible to strike one's wife as long as the rod or stick was no thicker than the husband's thumb. Husbands who failed to practice restraint rarely faced formal legal sanctions. Instead, informal sanctions, such as spiritual direction by the clergy or retaliatory violence from family members of the battered wife, were the norm (Pleck, 1979).

In 1641, the Puritans enacted the first laws that explicitly forbade wife abuse (Pleck, 1987). Several years later, in 1672, the Pilgrims of Plymouth Colony passed a similar law (Pleck, 1987). Yet these laws, like those that preceded them, were largely symbolic. Puritans and Pilgrims allowed for the use of "moderate" physical violence against one's wife for the greater good of society or to provide direction to a wayward wife who had temporarily lost her way from the path of salvation (Pleck 1979). Hence, although wife abuse was forbidden by statute, social norms left anti-wife abuse legislation virtually unenforced.

From the late eighteenth century to the mid-nineteenth century, the criminal justice system continued to be apathetic toward controlling wife abuse. In those rare cases when a husband was charged with wife abuse, judges commonly dismissed the charge on the grounds that a husband had the right to chastise his wife (Lerman, 1981). The long-standing common law right of a husband to strike his wife remained an influential factor in criminal court decision making.

Rapid social change in the late nineteenth century brought about by the Civil War and a growing immigrant population (considered by many to be the dangerous underclass) (Boyer, 1978) provided the catalyst to call into question the long-held belief that what a husband did to correct his wife in private was beyond the jurisdiction of government authorities (Pleck, 1989). In place of this common law protection arose the demand for increased government (i.e., criminal justice) intervention into the private lives of U.S. citizens to establish social order and create a sense of safety and security. In 1871, an Alabama court, responding to what was then considered the esprit de corps, rendered the following decision:

> The privilege, ancient though it may be, to beat [one's wife] with a stick, to pull her hair, choke her, spit in her face or kick her about the floor, or to inflict upon her like indignities, is not now acknowledged by our law. . . . In person, the wife is entitled to the same protection of the law that the husband can invoke for himself. (cited in Hart, 1992, p. 22)

Hopes were dashed, however, that the nation had indeed arrived at a unified position regarding the proper role of the government in the private lives of U.S. citizens when a mere three years later, in 1874, another court rendered the following decision in a domestic violence case:

> If no permanent injury has been inflicted, nor malice, cruelty nor dangerous violence shown by the husband, it is better to draw the civilian, shut out the public gaze, and leave the parties to forget and forgive. (cited in Hart, 1992, p. 22)

As the nation entered the twentieth century, concerns waned over the common law right of husbands to beat their wives (Pleck, 1989; Rothman, 1980). Activists instead set their sights on "larger" social issues, such as suffrage and the temperance movement (Buzawa and Buzawa, 1996). Moreover, the criminal justice system's role in domestic violence situations was legally obstructed with nearly every state codifying the common law requirement that specifies that arrests for misdemeanor offenses were to be henceforth restricted to those committed in the presence of law enforcement officials.

Simultaneously, a movement was under way to decriminalize wife abuse. The establishment of family courts was considered a means to achieve that end, that is, to remove wife abuse cases from criminal court calendars and place them within the jurisdiction of family courts. These courts were purposely designed to address family-related issues. Imposing criminal sentences on abusers was not the intent of family courts, but rather the pursuit of reconciliation and rehabilitation (Pleck, 1987).

The cultural norms that, in the past, perpetuated wife abuse and shielded it from criminal justice intervention are still influential today. A criminal justice response to wife abuse continues to be an unpopular medium for dealing with violence between intimates (Zimring, 1989; Martin, 1976). Research conducted by Hirschel, Hutchinson, and Dean in 1992 estimated that only about half of all women who are victims of domestic violence report the incident to the police. Of those women who seek a formal criminal justice response, only about 1% of the cases ever end with the arrest of the abuser (Dutton, 1987). In many people's eyes, wife abuse remains a matter that should be dealt with in private by the involved parties.

This position, although predominant, appears to be less influential In the United States today. States have enacted legislation that affords police officers more power to arrest alleged abusers in misdemeanor battery cases when the offense did not occur in an officer's presence (Hendricks, 1992). Moreover, a network of legal and social service agencies with the express purpose of dealing with wife abuse has developed. For example, wife abuse, in addition to being considered a criminal justice issue, is now viewed as a civil rights problem of significant proportions (U.S. Commission on Civil Rights, 1982). In addition, legal services agencies, many of which are funded by public monies, have been instituted to assist victims of wife abuse find satisfaction within the criminal justice system (see, for example, Buzawa and Buzawa, 1996). Also, the passage of the Violence Against Women Act of 1993, which has committed millions of dollars in support of promoting policies and establishing programs to combat domestic violence and protect victims, may signal the federal government's commitment to making wife abuse a national priority (for a thorough discussion, see Buzawa and Buzawa, 1996).

LEGAL DEFINITION OF WIFE ABUSE

Providing a legal definition of wife abuse may appear to be a relatively simple endeavor. Wife abuse might be defined as an assault within a marital relationship, where the wife is the victim. As simple as this may seem, a recent national survey of domestic violence legislation reveals that providing a general definition of wife abuse is far more difficult than it appears.

That national survey, conducted by Hendricks (1992) in the late 1980s, demonstrated that there is no uniform definition of what constitutes abuse. For example, five states fail to provide any legal definition of abuse. The forty-five state statutes that define abuse tend to differ considerably by the degree to which harm is inflicted on the victim. In a few state statutes, physical harm is not even necessary for abuse to have occurred. Connecticut, for example, defines family violence as verbal abuse that may lead to the expression of physical violence (Hendricks, 1992).

In addition, Hendricks (1992) found that the definition of the abused partner, the marital status of the victim, and the relationship of the victim to the abuser tend to be broadly defined by state statutes. For instance, only six state statutes require that the victim of domestic violence be a marital partner. In thirty-eight states, however, marriage is not required for an assault to be covered by their domestic violence legislation. Victims may be relatives (e.g., spouses, children, parents, or grandchildren) or ex-spouses. The remaining six states offer no indication whatsoever as to who is covered by their domestic violence legislation.

The manner in which the federal government is approaching violence against women offers a glimmer of hope in establishing a general definition of domestic violence and wife abuse in particular. In so doing, the quest for an effective, unified approach to combat wife abuse may be institutionalized, thereby affording legal redress for a crime that has been all too often ignored in the legal arena and legitimized by societal norms. Based on Title VII of the Civil Rights Act of 1964 and later expounded upon in Title III of the Violence Against Women Act of 1993, victims of gender-based violent crimes are empowered to seek a civil remedy in federal court against offenders who have committed gender-motivated crimes. In the Violence Against Women Act of

1993, it is reasoned that traditional state laws have proven to be difficult avenues for women to seek proper recourse for the criminal harms they have encountered over the course of history and that wife abuse is not only a criminal act but an act of discrimination. As Neuborne (1991) stated in a hearing before 101st Congress: "Placing this violence in the context of the civil rights laws recognizes it for what it is—a hate crime."

Although the Violence Against Women Act of 1993 may be viewed by some as a monumental step in the direction of protecting women from abuse, it has notable limitations that bear mentioning. First, this act "does not expand Federal jurisdiction to all attacks against women, nor does it supplant all State tort law" (Violence Against Women Act of 1993, p. 51). Second, "a plaintiff must prove that the crime of violence—whether an assault, a kidnapping, or a rape—was gender-motivated" (Violence Against Women Act of 1993, p. 51). "Whether a particular crime is, in fact, gender-motivated will be a question of fact for the court or jury to decide" (Violence Against Women Act of 1993, p. 50).

Notwithstanding these comments, the seriousness of wife abuse is not depreciated by the apparent limitations of this act. In fact, this act provides an opportunity to seek recompense on a level not previously afforded to victims of violent crimes, that is, "a civil rights claim redresses an assault on a commonly shared ideal of *equality*" (Violence Against Women Act of 1993, p. 51, emphasis added). On this basis alone (i.e., the ideal of equality), a civil rights remedy for wife abuse seems to be a logical, legal avenue for making inroads to fighting wife abuse.

THE NATURE AND EXTENT OF WIFE ABUSE

Underreported and hidden from the public eye, the nature and extent of wife abuse is an unknown and incomprehensible social calamity. Estimates put the number of violent domestic encounters by women in their own homes at as many as 4 million annually (Bureau of Justice Assistance, 1993). The National Crime Victim Survey (NCVS) reports that women are disproportionately the victims of domestic violence, constituting 95% of the reported violent confrontations (Bachman, 1994). One study found that domestic violence toward women is so pervasive that an adult female is more likely to be a victim of a violent crime by her male partner at home than anywhere else or by anyone else (Gelles and Straus, 1988).

Furthermore, according to NCVS data, more than 50% of all couples experience at least one assaultive incident during the course of their relationship, with women experiencing more than ten times the number of violent incidents than men (Feld and Straus, 1989). Many of these violent incidents are serious. The National Family Violence Resurvey found, for example, that 39% of all violent encounters involved the wife being punched with a fist, kicked, bitten, or attacked with a knife or gun (Gelles and Straus, 1988). Approximately 1.5 million of these women required medical attention for the injuries they incurred from these violent encounters, with about half of them needing either to visit or to stay overnight at a hospital (Straus and Gelles, 1986).

Many domestic violence encounters end with women losing their lives. In 1991 alone, approximately 4,400 persons were killed by family members (Federal Bureau of Investigation, 1992). In that same year, 28% of all homicide victims died at the hands of their male partner (Federal Bureau of Investigation, 1992). Moreover, the Federal Bureau of Investigation (1992) reported that between 1980 and 1991, over 50% of all women murdered (eighteen years of age and older) were victims of their husbands, ex-husbands, or boyfriends.

CORRELATES OF WIFE ABUSE

Three perspectives exist on the causes of domestic violence (or wife abuse): individual, societal, and feminist. These perspectives attribute wife abuse to distinctly different phenomena. Each perspective is presented on its own merits, and no attempt is made to show that one perspective is necessarily superior to the others.

The Individual Perspective

The individual perspective is ostensibly concerned with the characteristics of the abuser. How the victim may precipitate the abuse is also a part of this perspective, but to a much lesser extent than the focus on the offender (see, for example, O'Leary, 1993). The central tenet of this perspective is that domestic violence arises from personal characteristics, prior life experiences, and biological propensities. Regardless of the specific source(s) of violence, however, it is believed that abusers have the capacity to control the impulse to act violently. Thus, it is proposed that men who have low self-control are more likely to abuse their wives than are those who exhibit high self-control.

Research conducted from this perspective approaches domestic violence as a complex phenomenon, consisting of a variety of factors that interact to bring about an increased likelihood of abusive behavior. For example, some research suggests that one of the best predictors of family violence is the interaction between a history of violent relationships and personal characteristics. Riggs and O'Leary (1992), for instance, found that abuse is more likely when there is an interaction between the belief that aggressive behavior is normative and the individual characteristics of impulsivity and defensiveness, and the tendency to take offense with or be overly sensitive to the words or actions of others. Also, Straus (1980) suggested that abusers may have learned to associate "love" with the expression of violence during their formative years when caregivers used physical chastisement to correct their conduct.

An examination of the changing status of women in American society may likewise provide insight into wife abuse. As women have slowly gained social standing in the workplace and consequently have become increasingly economically independent, the relationship between men and women (or, for that matter, between husbands and wives) has changed. Husbands who have felt a sense of power over their wives— as a consequence of economic dependence—may begin to feel as if they are losing control of their relationship as wives have gained economic independence (see, for example, Green, 1984). Physical violence may be employed as a last-ditch effort to regain a sense of control (Coleman and Straus, 1986; Kahn, 1984). This is especially the case when offenders are (1) unable to articulate deep emotional feelings,

(2) psychologically immature, (3) suffering from depression, (4) schizophrenic, (5) afflicted by other severe character disorders (Steinmetz, 1980), or (6) diagnosed as having antisocial personality disorders (Jacobsen, 1994).

Furthermore, violent tendencies may be enhanced chemically. Inhibitor-reducing substances, such as alcohol and illegal drugs, have been found to be related to domestic violence (Kantor and Straus, 1987). Moreover, higher than average levels of testosterone appear to be predictive of violent behavior (Dabbs, Jurkovic, and Frady, 1991).

The Societal Perspective

Grounded in family-oriented and sociologically based theories, the societal perspective places the psychological factors addressed by the individual perspective into a broader framework that includes social institutions and social structures (Gelles, 1993). The central tenet of this perspective is that, ideally, society in general and the family in particular help suppress violent tendencies through a network of support systems such as friends and extended family members. With today's nuclear family and the relative ease with which families are able to move from one geographic region to another, however, such support systems—that is, inhibitors of violence— tend to be lacking (Steinmetz, 1980). Therefore, the extent to which such inhibitors are absent from today's families appears be proportionate with the level of violence found within a family unit (Steinmetz, 1980).

Moreover, the socialization function of families cannot be underestimated. Research has consistently found evidence supporting the notion of intergenerational transmission. For example, male children who witness their fathers beat their mothers tend to emulate that behavior when they marry (Finkelhor, Hotaling, and Yllo, 1988; Hotaling and Sugarman, 1990). The same has been found to be true of female children who witness violence between their parents (Buzawa and Buzawa, 1996).

Social and occupational stress have been likewise found to be correlated with domestic violence. Social stressors, such as poverty and failed marriages, contribute to family violence (Steinmetz, 1980). Occupational stressors, primarily a function of job tasks—such as those associated with police work—are also predictive of family violence (Steinmetz, 1980).

The Feminist Perspective

The feminist perspective examines violence against women from a social structural level of analysis. Therefore, domestic violence is considered endemic to cultures influenced by patriarchal religions such as Christianity and Judaism (Hart, 1992). In such cultures, physical violence is but one form of abuse. Women, as members of the underclass, are also abused through economic deprivation, sexual exploitation, and various forms of intimidation such as that achieved through stalking or isolation (Yllo, 1993).

At the center of this perspective is the axiom that domestic violence is used to maintain coercive control over women (Jones and Schechter, 1992). Patriarchal families are simply a reflection of male-dominated societies where physical abuse and oppression are justified on religious grounds as the duties of husbands (Hart, 1992).

Such gender inequality leaves women essentially powerless in the family unit and society at large (Schechter, 1982). As Eitzen (1988) stated:

> This [sex role] differentiation ranks the sexes in such a way that women are unequal in power, resources, prestige, or presumed worth. At the same time, both women and men are denied the full range of human and social possibilities. The social inequalities created by sex differentiation have far-reaching consequences for the society at large. (p. 352)

In societies where gender equality exists, there is less abuse toward women than in other societies. Levinson (1989), after an exhaustive examination of cultures around the world, found that domestic violence is rare when husbands and wives jointly make decisions on household and financial matters, peaceful conflict resolution and marital stability are cultural priorities, and premarital sexual freedoms are equal for both males and females. The feminist perspective argues, then, for cultural change through the removal of obstacles to a gender-neutral social structure.

CHARACTERISTICS OF OFFENDERS AND VICTIMS

Research indicates that abusers and victims share a number of common characteristics (Mickish, 1996). That is not to say that persons who possess these characteristics will necessarily abuse their wives. At best, the following characteristics predict the likelihood of domestic violence.

Low Self-Esteem

Both offenders and victims in abusive relationships tend to have low self-esteem. For the abuser, feelings of insecurity and a low self-esteem culminate in a sense of fear that his marital partner will leave or abandon him (Mickish, 1996). The abuser, threatened by his wife's attention being diverted anywhere but toward him—such as during pregnancy (Hendricks and McKean, 1995)—creates crises that force the focus of attention on him. Attempts to isolate the victim from friends and family members also serve to ensure that the husband has his wife's full attention (Mickish, 1991). Operating on the extremes, abusers commonly lavish their victims with affection and expensive gifts in the attempt to compensate for the harm that has been done (Mickish, 1991).

A victim of abuse—confronted by a violent partner and socialized within a culture that teaches women to be passive, dependent, and supportive of their marital partner—feels a sense of limited self-worth (Mickish, 1996). She not only feels trapped in a violent marriage but considers herself a failure as a wife, comforter, and peacemaker. Consequently, victims may contemplate suicide as the only way out of the abusive relationship and as a way to end feelings of low self-worth (Hendricks and McKean, 1995).

Violent Family Background

Both abusers and victims are likely to have been raised in abusive families, thus having a high tolerance for violence (Hendricks and McKean, 1995). Within this environment, children learn to confront normal, everyday nuisances and conflicts from an aggressive stance. Abused, oppressed, and deprived as children, abusers have poorly developed self-concepts, and the expression of violence may be a means by which they derive feelings of power, importance, security, and control over their lives. Likewise, victims have low self-concepts that may be rooted in their childhood. Mickish (1991) wrote:

> The more she was hit by her parents and/or siblings, the more likely that she will stay [in an abusive relationship]. In other words, she learned at an early age that it is okay to hit someone you love when they have done something "wrong." (p. 66)

Traditional and Stereotypical Beliefs

It is common that both the abuser and victim share traditional beliefs about the role of husband and wife and their responsibilities in the home. The abuser may consider the use of violence as justified on the grounds that it maintains family unity by reinforcing traditional role responsibilities (Hendricks and McKean, 1995). The victim may hold similar beliefs and consequently view violence as a way to resolve conflict. The victim may be further compelled to continue her participation in an abusive relationship when divorce or separation are not considered acceptable avenues of escape. She may therefore want to believe the hollow promises of the abuser that he will turn from his abusive ways (Hendricks and McKean, 1995).

Denial

The psychological defense mechanism used most by the abuser and victim is denial. For the abuser, denial serves many psychological purposes. For example, denying personal responsibility for the violent encounter serves to reduce, if not replace, feelings of guilt. The victim also uses denial to her personal benefit, but it is the flip side of the same coin. As Hendricks and McKean (1995) pointed out: "The victim is likely to feel guilty about the battering thinking that in some fashion she could avoid it or that there is a magical solution to the problem" (p. 142).

Self-Defeating and Unhealthy Sexual Conduct

Whereas the abuser may find sex to be a cathartic release of hostility, the victim may use sex to obtain the intimacy she is lacking. At the same time, using sexual intimacy in this manner, the abuser may find that he feels powerful or self-aggrandized (Hendricks and McKean, 1995).

Isolation

Abusers commonly isolate their victims from interpersonal contact with others (Ewing, Lindsey, and Pomerantz, 1984). Abusers may likewise isolate themselves from others. As a consequence of their isolation, neither the abuser nor the victim may view their violent relationship as a problem (Mickish, 1991). The abuser frequently gains a sense of power and control from the isolation of the victim. Moreover, it provides a sense of security that the abuser is searching for, since it satisfies the commonly held concern that his partner will leave or abandon him (Hendricks and McKean, 1995).

Stress and Stress-Related Problems

High levels of stress and psychophysiological reactions are common among abusers and victims. Abusers tend to find external releases such as the use of alcohol to deal with their feelings of anger, guilt, and inadequacy. In turn, the abuser may point to the consumption of alcohol as the source of violence instead of accepting personal responsibility for his actions. Victims of abuse, on the other hand, may attempt to internalize their anger and feelings of guilt, which may manifest themselves in the form of health-related problems, from headaches to gastrointestinal ailments (Hendricks and McKean, 1995). Moreover, in the event that the victim is unavailable as a target of his aggression, abusers may turn their anger on others, inanimate objects, or even themselves (Hendricks and McKean, 1995).

PREVENTION AND TREATMENT

Several different models of intervention have developed over the years to deal with domestic violence. First, there are informal efforts. The battered women's shelter movement of the 1970s, for example, developed out of the efforts of community leaders, battered women themselves, and women's rights advocates (Schechter, 1982). This movement culminated in the establishment of twenty-four-hour hotlines that provide emotional support and information regarding services available to abused women. Emergency shelters and an extensive network of volunteer host homes also developed to serve as safe havens for abused women and their children, and a place for women to receive social, psychological and legal support services (Roberts, 1981). Today, liter-•lly thousands of intervention programs exist to help abused women (Roberts, 1995).

Police officers may, in the performance of their official duties, attempt to resolve domestic disputes informally. Although an argument could be made that such efforts are appropriate in given situations, they are subject to intense scrutiny. Most police officers are not adequately trained to determine the level or type of intervention necessary to diffuse violence in domestic contexts. Moreover, such intervention efforts may leave victims in potentially volatile situations.

A second form of intervention is formal mediation with professional intermediaries. The primary purpose of mediation is to show those in violent domestic relationships how to resolve differences without resorting to inappropriate or violent conduct (Buzawa and Buzawa, 1996). For this type of intervention to be successful, there must be cooperation between abusers and victims: they must desire to reach an agreement. An impartial mediator helps to facilitate the resolution. Moreover, when used in conjunction with criminal justice processing, mediation can help both the offender and the victim understand the criminality of the abuser's conduct, an important issue frequently denied by both parties.

The question of whether mediation programs are effective in reducing abuse requires further investigation. One study found that mediation reduces recidivism, but to no greater an extent than traditional court processing (Bethel and Singer, 1981–1982). Research, however, indicates rather consistently that both abusers and victims tend to rate mediation more favorably and as being more fair to both parties than traditional court processing (Smith, 1983). The criminal justice system also benefits from intervention in the form of mediation. Mediation tends to be less costly and time consuming than traditional justice system processing (Buzawa and Buzawa, 1996).

Notwithstanding these facts, however, mediation may increase the risk of further abuse to victims. If mediation is ineffective at stopping violence, or at the very least reducing the offender's potential of violence, the victim may find herself in a far worse situation than that which existed prior to the mediation experience (Pirro, 1982). Research conducted by Smith (1983) indicated that about one-third of victims reported increased violence or fear of revenge subsequent to a mediation experience.

The third form of intervention takes the form of counseling. Counseling may be initiated by the abuser and the victim, without justice system processing, mandated as a condition of pretrial diversion, or made a part of criminal sentencing. Counseling, however, is rarely sought by violent partners voluntarily. Moreover, when abusers and victims voluntarily participate in counseling, they are more likely to "drop out" than court-mandated participants (Green, 1984).

Counseling attempts to bring about rehabilitation, a long-term change in the behavior of the abuser. Rehabilitation assumes that changes in the attitudes, perceptions, and interpersonal skills of abusers precede behavioral change (Hamberger and Hastings, 1993). This is not a simple endeavor. The specific needs of abusers and victims must be taken into consideration before a specific type of counseling is employed. Moreover, counseling should not be used as the sole source of intervention. Consideration should also be paid to making counseling just one component of an overall intervention strategy that might also include shelter services, legal consultation, and housing and financial services (Hendricks and McKean, 1995).

Jurisdictions vary considerably in how counseling is used in conjunction with a criminal justice response to domestic violence. For example, some jurisdictions suspend prosecution if abusers participate in counseling. After successfully completing the counseling regimen, a prosecutor may drop all charges if no further abusive instances come to the attention of the justice system during a specified period of time (Rebovich, 1996). On the other hand, some prosecutors refuse to suspend formal justice system processing. Instead, they may make counseling a condition of a plea bargain or a part of a criminal sentence (Rebovich, 1996).

Mixed results have been reported by investigators regarding the success of court-mandated counseling. Pirog-Good and Stets (1986) estimated that nationally about 60% of offenders mandated to obtain counseling actually complete their programs. Gondolf (1984) reported a slightly lower completion rate (52%).

Regarding the recidivist activities of abusers who successfully complete a counseling program, Hamberger and Hastings (1993) found recidivist abuse to be as low as 4%; Dutton (1986) found a much higher rate of recidivism, 47%. Such disparities in findings are probably attributed to the demographic characteristics of the abusers participating in the counseling programs under review (Saunders and Parker, 1989).

LEGAL ISSUES AND FUTURE TRENDS

Domestic violence is one of only a few social problems in which policy initiatives can be traced to social scientific research findings. The Minneapolis Domestic Violence Experiment (Sherman and Berk, 1984) is perhaps the most notable example of how research has brought about substantial change in the criminal justice response to domestic violence. That study revealed that when police officers arrested a suspected wife abuser, the abuser was less likely to repeat his actions than when no arrest was initiated. Based upon the results of the "Minneapolis Experiment," jurisdictions throughout the United States established "preferred" or "mandated" arrests as the norm in response to domestic violence calls (Sherman and Cohn, 1989).

One would be remiss not to mention the pronounced and influential presence of the feminist movement in bringing about the changing criminal justice response to wife abuse. As Mederer and Gelles (1989) pointed out, the feminist movement in conjunction with an increasingly conservative American society and a genuine concern with police liability in domestic violence situations are but a few of many factors that have led to substantial changes in the criminal justice response to domestic violence. Overall, the criminal justice system takes a more punitive position toward domestic violence than in the past, and changing social attitudes toward family violence suggest that such a response is likely to carry over well into the future.

The information presented in this chapter suggests other specific changes in the manner in which the criminal justice system responds to domestic violence. For example, there is a continuing trend toward further widening the avenues for victims to pursue abuse charges through both criminal and civil remedies. The widespread passage of victims' bills of rights will assist in bringing about these changes.

The police response to domestic calls will continue to change. In addition to becoming more firmly committed to preferred or mandatory arrest procedures, with the trend toward community-based policing will come an increased emphasis on interpersonal communication skills that will bring about a more proactive response when police are called to intercede in domestic violence situations. With the increasing emphasis placed on domestic violence, it would come as no surprise if specialized training were to become a priority in many police training academies.

Furthermore, an increasingly sensitive police response to domestic violence, in combination with the contemporary conservative movement, will likely result in a substantial increase in the number of domestic violence cases coming to the attention of the courts. The consequence of this will likely be a noticeable backlog of cases. Specialized courts, akin to drug courts, may be established to deal with the unique nature of the crime of wife abuse. If this occurs, there will be a need for counselors, mediators, and other professionals with specialized training in the area of domestic violence. Relationships among the police, courts, social service agencies, and other support service agencies will need to be forged to meet the distinctive needs of both abusers and victims.

Central to meeting those needs are an appreciation for and an understanding of the battered woman syndrome. Battered woman syndrome poses a special challenge to the justice system because women, attempting to adapt to repeated abuse, seek merely to survive the battering relationship (Walker, 1990b). The focus on survival is characterized by learned helplessness; escape is not seen as a viable option because with the passage of time, the abuser gains power over his wife. Consequently, a criminal justice response is not considered to be an avenue of escape (Browne, 1987; Walker, 1979). On the contrary, the abused may view a formal justice system response as putting her at risk of further victimization. Feeling helpless and merely wanting to survive the violent relationship, the abused may find herself trying to protect the one person who poses the greatest threat to her safety and security: the abusive husband.

A more efficient and effective police and court response to domestic violence will in turn increase the number of domestic abuse offenders under correctional control. Incarceration sentences will likely be reserved for the most serious cases or for the abuser who demonstrates a long history of abuse. Probation, uniquely fashioned to meet the needs of offenders, will probably be the most common sanction. Intensive probation supervision will be used for those offenders who pose too great a risk for traditional probation sentences yet are not serious enough to require incarceration sentences.

CONCLUSION

The history of the criminal justice response to domestic violence is filled with the neglect of victims of abuse. There is, however, reason to believe that a foundation has been laid for a more equitable and reasoned response to domestic violence. Although cultural beliefs about the status of women in society, the relative social value of women in relationship to that of men, and the belief that the government should not have the authority to intervene in the private lives of citizens have served to perpetuate domestic violence, they appear to be less influential today than in the past.

There are now both criminal justice and civil rights remedies in place for women who seek relief from domestic violence. In addition, there are diverse social programs that provide support for women who feel powerless and often do not know where to turn for help. The future response to domestic violence, assuming that the culture does not drastically change or fiscal constraints do not derail the justice system from its current course, will be more humane toward the female victim than in the past.

EDITORIAL SUMMARY

Wife abuse has existed throughout history. Yet only during the 1970s was it recognized as a legitimate social problem. Although it has been given a great deal of attention, its definition remains ambiguous. Currently, there is no universal definition of wife abuse. State definitions vary from verbal abuse to physical violence.

Different theoretical approaches on wife abuse include the individual perspective, the societal perspective, and the feminist perspective. The individual perspective concentrates on personal characteristics, life experiences, and biological tendencies of abusers. The societal perspective draws on sociological theories examining social institutions, particularly the family, in explaining wife abuse. The feminist approach posits that wife abuse is rooted in a patriarchal culture. Women are viewed as the underclass living in a male-dominated society.

The vast amount of research on wife abuse has shown that abusers and victims share common characteristics. Each tends to have low self-esteem, to have grown up in violent families, to possess traditional stereotypical beliefs in gender roles, and to express high levels of stress.

Various efforts have been made to assist victims of wife abuse. Shelters have been developed to provide safety to women in need. Formal mediation programs have also been created in attempt to resolve conflict between abuser and victim. In addition, formal and informal counseling are available to the husband and wife. It is through research that these programs exist. Thus, scholars must continue their research to provide additional innovative techniques.

REFERENCES

Bachman, R. (1994). *Violence Against Women.* Washington, DC: U.S. Department of Justice, Bureau of Justice Statistics.

Bethel, C. A., and Singer, L. R. (1981–1982). A new remedy for causes of domestic violence. *Vermont Law Review, 6,* 2.

Bethel, C. A., and Singer, L. R. (1981–1982). A new remedy for causes of domestic violence. *Vermont Law Review, 7,* 1.

Boyer, P. (1978). *Urban Masses and Moral Order in America, 1820–1920.* Cambridge, MA: Harvard University Press.

Browne, A. (1987). *When Battered Women Kill.* New York: Free Press.

Bureau of Justice Assistance. (1993). *Family Violence: Interventions for the Justice System.* Washington, DC: U.S. Department of Justice, U.S. Government Printing Office.

Buzawa, E. S., and Buzawa, C. G. (1996). *Domestic Violence: The Criminal Justice Response* (2nd ed.). Thousand Oaks, CA: Sage.

Civil Rights Act of 1964. 42 U.S.C., 2000e.

Coleman, D. H., and Straus, M. A. (1986). Marital power, conflict, and violence in a nationally representative sample of American couples. *Violence and Victims, 1,* 141–157.

Dabbs, J. M., Jurkovic, G. J., and Frady, R. L. (1991). Salivary testosterone and cortisol among late adolescent male offenders. *Journal of Abnormal Child Psychology, 19*, 469–478.

Dobash, R., and Dobash, R. (1979). *Violence Against Wives*. New York: Free Press.

Dutton, D. (1986). Wife assaulters' explanations for assault: The neutralization of self-punishment. *Canadian Journal of Behavioral Science, 18*, 381–390.

Dutton, D. (1987). *The Predictors of Recidivism in a Population of Wife Assaulters*. Paper presented at the Third National Family Violence Conference, Durham, NH.

Eitzen, D. S. (1988). *In Conflict and Order: Understanding Society*. Boston: Allyn and Bacon.

Ewing, W., Lindsey, M., and Pomerantz, J. (1984). *Battering: An AMEND Manual for Helpers*. Denver: Abusive Men Exploring New Directions.

Federal Bureau of Investigation. (1992). *Crime in the U.S.: 1991*. Washington, DC: U.S. Government Printing Office.

Feld, L. S., and Straus, M. (1989). Escalation and desistance of wife assault in marriage. *Criminology, 27*, 141–161.

Finkelhor, D., Hotaling, G. T., and Yllo, K. (1988). *Stopping Family Violence: Research Priorities for the Coming Decade*. Newbury Park, CA: Sage.

Gelles, R. J. (1993). Through a sociological lens: Social structure and family violence. In R. J. Gelles and D. R. Loseke (Eds.), *Current Controversies on Family Violence* (pp. 31–46). Newbury Park, CA: Sage.

Gelles, R., and Straus, M. (1988). *Intimate Violence*. New York: Simon and Schuster.

Gondolf, E. W. (1984). *Men Who Batter: An Integrated Approach to Stopping Wife Abuse*. Homes Beach, FL: Learning Publications.

Green, H. W. (1984). *Turning Fear to Hope*. Nashville, TN: Thomas Nelson.

Hamberger, L., and Hastings, J. (1993). Court mandated treatment of men who assault their partner. In N. Z. Hilton (Ed.), *Legal Responses to Wife Assault: Current Trends and Evaluation* (pp. 182–129). Newbury Park, CA: Sage.

Hart, B. (1992). *State Codes on Domestic Violence: Analysis, Commentary, and Recommendations*. Reno, NV: National Council of Juvenile and Family Court Judges.

Hendricks, J. E. (1992). Domestic violence legislation in the United States: A survey of the states. In E. C. Viano (Ed.), *Intimate Violence: Interdisciplinary Perspectives* (pp. 213–226). Washington, DC: Hemisphere.

Hendricks, J. E., and McKean, J. B. (1995). *Crisis Intervention: Contemporary Issues for On-Site Interveners* (2nd ed.). Springfield, IL: Charles C Thomas.

Hirschel, J. D., Hutchinson, I. W., and Dean, C. W. (1992). The failure of arrest to deter spouse abuse. *Journal of Research in Crime and Delinquency, 20*, 7–33.

Hotaling, G. T., and Sugarman, D. B. (1990). The primary prevention of wife assault. In R. T. Ammerman and M. Herson (Eds.), *Treatment of Family Violence: A Source Book* (pp. 23–47). New York: Wiley.

Jacobsen, N. J. (1994). Rejoinder to Lipchik and Geffner. *Family Therapy News, 25*, 2.

Jones, A., and Schechter, S. (1992). *When Love Goes Wrong*. New York: HarperCollins.

Kahn, A. S. (1984). The power war: Male response to power loss underequality. *Psychology of Women Quarterly, 6*, 234–247.

Kantor, G., and Straus, M. (1987). The "drunken bum" theory of wife beating. *Social Problems, 34*, 213–230.

Lerman, L. (1981). *Prosecution of Spouse Abuse Innovations in Criminal Justice Response*. Washington, DC: Center for Women Policy Studies.

Levinson, D. (1989). *Family Violence in Cross-Cultural Perspective*. Newbury Park, CA: Sage.

Martin, D. (1976). *Battered Wives*. San Francisco: Glide.

Mederer, H. J., and Gelles, R. J. (1989). Compassion or control: Intervention in cases of wife abuse. *Journal of Interpersonal Violence, 4*, 23–43.

Mickish, J. E. (1991). Domestic Violence: Spouse Abuse. In J. E. Hendricks (Ed.), *Crisis Intervention in Criminal Justice/Social Service* (pp. 41–84). Springfield, IL: Charles C Thomas.

Mickish, J. E. (1996). Spousal abuse. In. J. E. Hendricks (Ed.), *Crisis Intervention in Criminal Justice/Social Service* (pp. 52–91). Springfield, IL: Charles C Thomas.

Neuborne, B. (1991). *Violence Against Women: Victims of the System*. Hearings before the Committee on the Judiciary, U.S. Senate, 101st Congress, 2d session, April 9.

O'Leary, K. D. (1993). Through a psychological lens: Personality traits, personality disorders and levels of violence. In R. Gelles and D. Loseke (Eds.), *Current Controversies on Family Violence* (pp. 7–31). Newbury Park, CA: Sage.

Pirog-Good, M. A., and Stets, J. (1986). Program for abusers: Who drops out and what can be done. *Response, 9*(2), 17–19.

Pirro, J. (1982). Domestic violence: The criminal court response. *New York State Bar Journal, 54*, 352–357.

Pleck, E. (1979). Wife beating in nineteenth-century America. *Victimology, 4*, 60–74.

Pleck, E. (1987). *Domestic Tyranny*. Oxford, UK: Oxford University Press.

Pleck, E. (1989). Criminal approaches to family violence, 1640–1980. In L. Ohlin and M. Tonry (Eds.), *Family Violence* (pp. 19–58). Chicago: University of Chicago Press.

Rebovich, D. J. (1996). Prosecution response to domestic violence: Results of a survey of large jurisdictions. In E. S. Buzawa and C. G. Buzawa (Eds.), *Do Arrest and Restraining Orders Work?* (pp. 176–191). Thousand Oaks, CA: Sage.

Riggs, D. S., and O'Leary, K. D. (1992). *Violence between Dating Partners: Background and Situational Correlates of Courtship Aggression.* Unpublished manuscript.

Roberts, A. R. (1981). *Sheltering Battered Women.* New York: Springer.

Roberts, A. R. (1995). *Crisis Intervention and Time-Limited Cognitive Treatment.* Thousand Oaks, CA: Sage.

Rothman, D. J. (1980). *Conscience and Convenience: The Asylum and Its Alternatives in Progressive America.* Boston: Little, Brown.

Saunders, D. (1993). Husbands who assault: Multiple profiles requiring multiple responses. In N. Z. Hilton (Ed.), *Legal Responses to Wife Assault* (pp. 9–36). Newbury Park, CA: Sage.

Saunders, D. G., and Parker, J. C. (1989). Legal sanctions and treatment follow through among men who batter: A multivariate analysis. *Societal Work Research and Abstracts, 23*, 21–29.

Schechter, S. (1982). *Women and Male Violence: The Visions and Struggles of the Battered Women's Movement.* Boston: South End.

Sherman, L. W., and Berk, R. A. (1984). The specific deterrent effects of arrest for domestic assault. *American Sociological Review, 49*, 261–272.

Sherman, L. W., and Cohn, E. (1989). The impact of research on legal policy: The Minneapolis Domestic Violence Experiment. *Law and Society Review, 23*, 117–144.

Smith, B. E. (1983). *Non-stranger violence. The criminal court's response.* Washington, DC: Department of Justice, National Institute of Justice.

Steinmetz, S. K. (1980). Violence prone families. *Annals of New York Academy of Sciences, 347*, 351–365.

Straus, M. A. (1980). Wife beating: How common and why. In M. A. Straus and G. T. Hotaling (Eds.), *Social Causes of Husband Wife Violence.* Minneapolis: University of Minnesota Press.

Straus, M., and Gelles, R. (1986). Social change and change in family violence from 1971 to 1985 as revealed by two national surveys. *Journal of Marriage and the Family, 48*, 465–479.

U.S. Commission on Civil Rights. (1982). *Under the Rule of Thumb: Battered Women and the Administration of Justice.* Washington, DC: National Institute of Justice.

Violence Against Women Act of 1993. 103rd U.S.C., 1st session.

Walker, L. (1979). *The Battered Woman.* New York: Harper and Row.

Walker, L. (1990a). Psychological assessment of sexually abused children for legal evaluation and expert witness testimony. *Professional Psychology: Research and Practice, 21*, 344–353.

Walker, L. (1990b). *Terrifying Love*. New York: Harper and Row.

Yllo, K. A. (1993). Through a feminist lens: Gender, power, and violence. In R. J. Gelles and D. R. Loseke (Eds.), *Current Controversies on Family Violence* (pp. 47–62). Newbury Park, CA: Sage.

Zimring, F. E. (1989). Toward a jurisprudence of family violence. In L. E. Ohlin and M. Tonry (Eds.) *Family Violence* (pp. 547–570). Chicago: University of Chicago Press.

6

Husband Battering: A Review of the Debate over a Controversial Social Phenomenon

Sylvia I. Mignon, Ph.D.
Criminal Justice Department
University of Massachusetts at Boston

Although all types of family violence elicit negative reactions, husband battering is perhaps the most emotionally charged. A primary concern is that a focus on husband battering may eclipse the problem of wife battering and divert attention and resources from what many consider to be the more significant problem. The study of husband battering, however, has not developed beyond the debate about how much of it actually exists. This chapter reviews the nature of debate in the 1970s, 1980s, and 1990s and identifies some of the relevant issues. There are primarily two views on this controversial social phenomenon: those who view husband battering as a significant social problem and those who see husband battering as a substantially smaller and less serious problem. In the debate, husband battering is juxtaposed against wife battering in terms of value, importance, and prevalence. This chapter examines the controversial issues more closely, including correlates of husband abuse, profiles of offenders and victims, and treatment and prevention issues.

HISTORICAL RECOGNITION OF HUSBAND BATTERING

In the mid 1970s, the women's movement exerted pressure to acknowledge wife beating as a serious social problem (Pleck, 1987). Newspapers began reporting wife abuse in 1974. During 1977, the *New York Times* published forty-four articles on wife beating. In 1976, the first state laws on this subject were introduced; these laws included funding for shelters, improved reporting, and more effective court response (Pleck, 1987). Against this historical backdrop, husband battering emerged as a controversial issue in the late 1970s.

Although there has been much disagreement about the prevalence of husband battering, many agree that the best-known researcher on the topic of husband battering is Suzanne K. Steinmetz. Steinmetz's article "The Battered Husband Syndrome" published in *Victimology* (1977–1978) is considered the classic work that started the debate over the existence and prevalence of this problem. Steinmetz offered a review of empirical data from her own work as well as her work with Straus and Gelles in the 1975 National Family Violence Survey. Steinmetz also offered a historical review of cartoons that she cited as evidence of the existence of the problem of husband battering. She emphasized findings that reflected "that not only the percentage of wives having used physical violence often exceeds that of husbands, but that wives also exceed husbands in the frequency with which these acts occur" (p. 503). Steinmetz claimed that battered husbands have been ignored because it is more stigmatizing to be a battered husband than a battered wife. She offered several reasons for why wife battering has been given much attention and husband battering so little: lack of empirical data, "selective inattention" on the part of researchers and the media, more serious and more visible physical injury to women, and the reluctance of males to admit their victimization by women (1977–1978, p. 504). Steinmetz concluded that her work was not meant to "de-emphasize the importance of providing services to beaten wives, but to increase our awareness of the pervasiveness of all forms of family violence" (p. 507).

In a response to Steinmetz, also published in *Victimology* (1978), Fields and Kirchner stated that Steinmetz's work was full of "baseless conjecture" (p. 216). They criticized Steinmetz for not accurately interpreting her own data and for concluding that wives exceed husbands in "almost all" categories of violence. Steinmetz (1977–1978) presented seven categories of violence:

1. throwing things
2. pushing and shoving
3. hitting and slapping
4. kicking
5. hitting with something,
6. threatening with a knife or gun
7. using a knife or gun

She used these seven categories in her early work with Straus and Gelles and, in addition, had previously included a "beat up" category. According to Fields and Kirchner (1978), Steinmetz omitted the "beat up" category in her article "The battered husband syndrome" (1977–1978). The effect of Steinmetz's modification was that it reduced the perception of the prevalence of wife battering and increased the perception of the prevalence of husband battering. Fields and Kirchner (1978) stated that categories such as the "beat up spouse" and "used knife or gun" are the types of serious violence used primarily by men against their partners. Fields and Kirchner also reviewed data showing that wives are overwhelmingly the victims in domestic disputes; they collected data from the New York City Crisis Centers and Brooklyn Legal Services. They found that wives victimized by husbands sought medical and legal assistance about 225 times more frequently than men. Fields and Kirchner concluded, as do others (Pagelow, 1984; Pleck, Pleck, Grossman, and Bart, 1977), that a "battered husband syndrome" does not exist. The findings do not deny that husbands can be victimized; they suggest that husband battering occurs on a far smaller scale than wife battering.

Pagelow (1984) offered a comprehensive review of the controversy created by Steinmetz's work. She criticized Steinmetz's (1977–1978) calculations that estimated that there are 250,000 battered husbands in the United States. She pointed out that Steinmetz identified no battered husbands in her sample of fifty-seven couples and identified only two male victims in a sample of twenty-six police-involved spousal assault cases. Pagelow (1984) documented how husband battering as a social phenomenon began to receive greater publicity than wife battering. One result was an exaggerated newspaper account in Norway reporting that the United States had 12 million battered husbands. Pagelow (1984) concluded: "Almost all writers who discuss the question of wife abuse versus husband abuse come to the conclusion that the proportions of male victims are minuscule compared to female victims" (p. 272). The concern is that exaggerating the prevalence and severity of husband battering prevents the public from taking seriously the legitimate problem of wife beating (Cose, 1996).

The deep disapproval for Steinmetz's work is clearly seen through the considerable personal and professional harassment she endured during this period, reportedly from radical women's groups (Dunn, 1996; Sherven and Sniechowski, 1996). Steinmetz and her family received threatening telephone calls, efforts were made to deny her tenure and promotion, and bomb threats were made to a branch of the American Civil Liberties Union where she had been invited to speak (Dunn, 1996; Sherven and Sniechowski, 1996; Straus, 1990).

To place the controversy over the prevalence of husband battering in context, it is important to examine the results of the national surveys of family violence by Straus and Gelles. The National Family Violence Survey of 1975 was the first effort to document family violence on a national scale. It comprised a nationally representative sample of 2,143 married and living together couples (Straus, 1977–1978). One finding indicated gender differences regarding the forms of domestic violence by husbands and wives. Wives, for example, were more likely to "kick, bite, hit with fist," and "hit or try to hit with something" than men. These acts were described as less dependent on physical size and strength than other acts (Straus, 1977–1978; Straus, Gelles, and Steinmetz, 1980). Of the many important findings of this research, it documented that "women are about as violent in the family as men" (Straus and Gelles, 1986, p. 470). The 1985 National Survey of 3,520 couples confirmed the same finding. In 1975, 12.1% of men and 11.6% of women reported violent acts toward their partners. In 1985, the overall violence was reported as 11.3% of men and 12.1% of women who were violent toward their partners. The differences between the findings in 1975 and the findings in 1985 were not statistically significant (although some writers such as McNeely and Robinson-Simpson [1988] do not acknowledge the lack of statistical significance), nor were the differences between rates of husbands' violence toward women and wives' violence toward men (Straus and Gelles, 1986).

The 1985 National Study did ask respondents who hit first (Straus and Gelles, 1990). Husbands responded that they hit first in 44% of cases, their wives hit first in 45% of cases, and in 11% of the cases husbands could not remember or were unclear who struck the first blow. Wives perceived that their husbands hit first in 53% of cases, wives perceived that they hit first in 42% of cases, and in 5% of cases the perception of who hit first was unclear. Clearly, spouses have different perceptions of abusive events. Dobash, Dobash, Wilson, and Daly (1992) and others criticized this work for not taking into consideration the context in which the violence occurred and the meaning attached to the episode by the participants.

Research in the 1980s continued, with some supporting the existence and prevalence of a "battered husband syndrome" and others denying its existence. The next significant event that occurred was the publication in 1987 of McNeely and Robinson-Simpson's article, "The truth about domestic violence: A falsely framed issue," in *Social Work.* The title alone appeared to invite a hostile response, and indeed that is what occurred. McNeely and Robinson-Simpson (1987) reviewed the literature on husband battering. They focused on the national studies of Straus and Gelles in 1975 and 1985 and on works that pointed to women being just as violent toward their partners as men were to their partners (Straus and Gelles, 1986; Nisonoff and Bitman, 1979). McNeely and Robinson-Simpson (1987) concluded that husband battering is a significant social problem and that "domestic violence is a two-way street" (p. 488). In their conclusion, however, they made a particularly troublesome and controversial statement that "men increasingly are defenseless when allegations of domestic violence are made" (p. 488). The authors were convinced that the public and policy makers are operating from the false assumption that only women are victims of spousal abuse and therefore will not acknowledge and respond to men's needs. According to McNeely and Robinson-Simpson (1987), the unresponsiveness to victimized men can result in their "social and legal defenselessness" (p. 485).

Saunders (1988) responded to McNeely and Robinson-Simpson (1987) and understandably criticized them for claiming to have uncovered the "truth." (In their rebuttal to Saunders' [1988] criticisms, McNeely and Robinson-Simpson [1988] pointed out that their original manuscript had placed the word "truth" in the title in quotes, which were removed by the *Social Work* editorial staff.) Saunders's (1988) criticisms focused on their overlooking methodological problems with Steinmetz's

(1977, 1977–1978) work, ignoring conflicting research findings, and "relying heavily on conjecture, opinion, and anecdotal evidence" (p. 179). Saunders (1988) concluded that "false portrayals of women as vindictive initiators of violence will only add to their oppression" (p. 181). There were also very strong letters to the editor of *Social Work* ("Continued Debate," 1988) that heavily criticized the McNeely and Robinson-Simpson (1987) article. The editors included their own note in the journal, stating that there was considerable controversy generated by the NcNeely and Robinson-Simpson (1987) article. The editors reported that the majority of letters challenged the position of the authors (p. 191).

The debate over the prevalence of husband battering as a social problem continued into the 1990s. Straus (1996) exemplified the current view of those who see husband battering as very important and termed it a "serious social problem" (p. 50). He stated that although women are more likely to receive injuries, men are more likely to be victimized by their wives. Although previously indicating that wives become violent in response to their own victimization (Straus and Gelles, 1986), Straus apparently no longer believed this to be the case. He suggested that women also initiate violence. He explained that minor physical abuse by wives can result in placing women in danger. That is, any level of violence, no matter how minimal, sets up a situation for the husband to assault his wife. The husband can justify his retaliation because his wife has set a precedent in using physical abuse. It can mean immediate and serious retaliation or can allow the husband to rationalize his abusive behavior whenever he sees his wife as difficult or obstinate. According to Straus and Gelles (1990), it is therefore important for women to end their own abuse of their partners so as to end physical abuse against women.

Dobash et al. (1992) best exemplified the argument that husband battering is not a significant social problem. They presented a well-documented article entitled "The myth of sexual symmetry in marital violence." Dobash et al. (1992) argued that reports of symmetrical violence are exaggerated and are based on self-reports of respondents surveyed as perpetrators and victims of abuse. They claim that the Conflict Tactics Scale (CTS) (Straus, 1979), devised to measure the number and types of violent acts between partners, is not reliable and valid. They note that the CTS contributes to erroneous assumptions of symmetry in spousal violence.

The new men's movement of the 1980s and 1990s has not dealt with husband battering as an issue. The men's movement has focused on the difficulties of conforming to the expectations of the traditional male role as well as advocacy in child custody cases. But it has given almost no attention to husbands' victimization by their wives, another telling sign that husband battering may not be a significant problem (Lucal, 1995).

DEFINITIONS OF HUSBAND BATTERING

For all the attention now devoted to family violence, there is no one clear definition of the term. Gelles and Straus (1979) reviewed existing definitions of family violence and offered the following: "an act carried out with the intention or preconceived intention of causing physical pain or injury to another person" (Feld and Straus, 1990, p. 490). Miller and Wellford (1996) defined intimate violence as "violence committed by those individuals one is more likely to trust and have continuing social relations with" (p. 17). Rasche (1988) pointed out that definitions of abuse vary for different racial and ethnic groups. Dobash et al. (1992) pointed to the subjectivity in determining a definition of violence. They stated that it is the desire to reduce subjectivity that led to the development of the CTS (Straus, 1979) to objectify and count the number of violent acts.

A literature review revealed no specific effort to define husband battering. There are suggestions, however, that there are differences between the violence men use against their wives and the violence wives use against their husbands. Within a general societal context, men have been found to be far more aggressive and violent than women. Men are substantially more likely to be victimized by another man than by their wives (Browne, 1996). Men also commit murder of strangers far more often than women (Straus, 1996).

The CTS (Straus, 1979) is frequently used in research to measure types and amounts of family violence and to examine disparities between male violence and female violence in the home. Although the CTS has been used to show symmetry in wife battering and husband battering, this is problematic (Szinovacz, 1983). Straus et al. (1980) acknowledged that the CTS does not measure the intent or purpose of the violence. It, therefore, provides no information whether a woman is acting in self-defense against her abuser or whether she is the initiator of violence. The CTS also does not measure injuries resulting from physical abuse, nor does it address psychological abuse (Dobash et al., 1992; Miller and Wellford, 1996; Straus et al., 1980). As pointed out by Berk, Berk, Loseke, and Rauma (1983): "When injuries are the concern, spousal violence is about the harm men inflict on women" (p. 210). Although acknowledging the considerably higher rate of injury among women, Straus (1996) said it is problematic to examine rates of injury. Newer laws and police policies do not rely on injury to determine official involvement, but rely on reported behavior or "probable cause" to believe violence took place (Straus, 1996). Straus was also concerned that a focus on injury excludes 97% of husband assaults in which no physical injury occurs. Straus maintained that this is still a serious problem.

The consensus is that women are far more likely to engage in "minor" rather than "severe" violence and that violence by women is not intended to injure the husband. Of course, it can be hard to define what constitutes "severe" or "major" violence as opposed to "minor" violence (Feld and Straus, 1990). Women are more likely to engage in pushing, shoving, slapping, or throwing things, whereas men may more often use punching, kicking, or attacks with objects or weapons. Stets and Straus (1990) found that men and women engage in equal amounts of "minor" violence. Interviews with the female respondents in the study, however, revealed substantially higher rates of "severe" violence on the part of men than the men admitted. A study of the issue of a woman's defense or retaliation currently does not exist, nor are there studies that conclusively link husband battering with psychological abuse. Such studies are needed to clarify the nature of the debate.

It has been assumed that a wife's physical response to her husband's assault will deter him from future assaults (Feld and Straus, 1990; Pagelow, 1984). The Bowker (1983) reported that some wives felt that aggressive defense of themselves thwarted future abuse from their husbands, whereas other wives reported being further victimized. Currently, no research has determined whether the wife's chosen defense strategy deters or escalates violence by her husband. The wife's actions, however, may well be viewed by some as husband battering, rightly or wrongly. Feld and Straus (1990) found that minor assaults by wives were associated with subsequent severe victimization by husbands. This speaks to the importance of paying attention to minor violence as an indicator of increased risk. It also speaks to the problem of defining husband battering. Does the minor violence constitute husband battering, or is the effect more important than what initiated the violence?

Another critical distinction between the abuse perpetrated by men and women is in the area of sexual assault. Research shows that sexual abuse can be part of the pattern of abuse against wives, and in the most violent attacks by husbands upon their wives, wives are physically and sexually assaulted (Browne, 1996). Cases of women sexually assaulting their partners are very rare.

Dobash et al. (1992) raised the issue of whether women and men have the same motives for engaging in physical abuse. They stated that those who adhere to the view of symmetry in violence between men and women assume that the genders think and act alike, which certainly contrasts with the different socialization processes for men and women. Actually, power differentials and socialization processes have been implicated as contributing to the problem of family violence. It is more realistic to expect that the motives for abuse do differ for men and women because the greater size and strength of men can certainly affect the outcome of the violent episode (Dobash et al., 1992). Some clarity about motives, then, may contribute to a definition of husband battering.

OVERVIEW OF OTHER RESEARCH IN THE FIELD

It is evident from the above historical perspective that not much progress has been made in the years of discussion about husband battering. The disconcerting aspect of this history is that the discussion has not changed much and continues to focus only on the existence or prevalence of husband battering as a social phenomenon. One result is that very little attention has been given to identifying the characteristics of victimized men, the correlates of abuse, and treatment and prevention efforts.

Some comparisons can be made between the opposing viewpoints of battering as a significant problem and those who perceive it as a less significant problem than wife battering. One body of research reflects the view that marital violence is equally committed by husbands and wives against one another (McLeod, 1984; McNeely and Mann, 1990; Meredith, Abbott, and Adams, 1986; Nisonoff and Bitman, 1979; Rouse, Breen, and Howell, 1988; Steinmetz, 1977, 1977–1978; and Straus and Gelles, 1986). This has been called the "family violence" perspective (Kurz, 1993; Stalans and Lurgio,

1995). Research that concludes that there is symmetry in spouse battering often focuses on the accurate measurement of type and amount of violence and relies on use of the CTS (Brush, 1990; Dobash et al., 1992).

A larger body of research has found that wives are far more often the victims of spousal violence than are men (Berk et al., 1983; Brush, 1990; Cleek and Pearson, 1985; Dobash and Dobash, 1979; Dobash et al., 1992; Gaquin, 1977–1978; Gondolf, 1988; Harlow, 1991; Lucal, 1995; Pagelow, 1984; Pleck et al., 1977; Saunders, 1988; Schwartz, 1987). This has become known as the feminist perspective. It emphasizes a long history of women's subordination to men. This perspective is critical of the CTS for not taking into consideration the context of the violence or the resulting injuries that women are far more likely to suffer than men (Dobash and Dobash, 1979; Brush, 1990; Saunders, 1988).

There are also those working in the field of family violence who frame the problem in terms of "mutual violence" (Stacey, Hazlewood, and Shupe, 1994; Straus, 1996). Berk et al. (1983), however, criticized a mutual violence perspective. They stated that terms such as "mutual combat" are inappropriate and that it is "downright pernicious" (p. 210) to think that a few battered husbands stack up against the enormous number of battered women.

Many of the research findings reflect that wife battering is a far more significant problem than husband battering. Dobash and Dobash (1979) found the ratio of husband to wife abuse to be sixty-six to one. Brush (1990) found that women reported that they were hurt 2.75 times more often than men. In an analysis of National Crime Survey data, Gaquin (1977–1978) found that only 3% of the cases involved a woman's assault on her male partner. McLeod (1984) found that men accounted for 6% of all self-reported victims of spousal assault. Holmes, Mignon, and Headley (1993) found that women were perpetrators of any type of domestic abuse in only 12% of cases reported to law enforcement. Berk et al. (1983), in an analysis of domestic disturbance police calls, found that in 3% of the cases, men were the only victims. Schwartz (1987) found that 93% of those receiving treatment from a private physician for injuries incurred in a domestic dispute were women. In a study of divorce, Cleek and Pearson (1985) found that women listed abuse as a cause of divorce much more frequently than men. Although not an exhaustive list, these studies provide considerable evidence for the disparity between amounts of wife battering and husband battering.

So what are the issues that have been involved in the debate over the prevalence of husband battering? How can researchers come up with radically different conclusions about husband battering? Several factors have influenced the nature of the debate: underreporting of abuse by men, the greater physical strength of men, and the societal dynamic that men have more options available to them than women. Methodological concerns and problems, including questions about the use of the CTS in various studies, have also contributed to different conclusions about the significance of husband battering. The context in which violence occurs and the question of who hits first are other factors that some researchers ignore and others find critical in determining the extent of husband battering.

A number of researchers have noted the problem of men underreporting abuse (Edleson and Brygger, 1986; Jouriles and O'Leary, 1985; Stets and Straus, 1990; Straus, 1977–1978; Szinovacz, 1983). The problem of men underreporting abuse is likely to contribute to the appearance of symmetrical marital abuse (Edleson and Brygger, 1986; Jouriles and O'Leary, 1985; Szinovacz, 1983). According to Szinovacz (1983), wives were more likely to acknowledge victimization as well as their own violence toward their husbands. The study also found that husbands may not report their wives' abusive behavior because they did not take it seriously enough to remember it. Jouriles and O'Leary (1985) found that of couples receiving marital therapy, husbands reported lower levels of violence than did their wives. Edleson and Brygger (1986) found differences in reporting threats of violence rather than actual violence. High levels of agreement were achieved when no violence occurred. Men underreport due to a fear of court action, a fear of delay in reuniting with family, and a denial or minimization of their assaultive behavior so that they do not have to face the seriousness of their behavior (Edleson and Brygger, 1986).

One reason frequently given for why husband battering is not a significant problem is that men have more alternatives available to them than do battered women. No one can deny that men, in general, tend to have more marketable occupational skills, make more money even for comparable work, and are less likely to have care of the children than women (Durkin, 1996; Pagelow, 1984).

Another reason frequently cited for viewing husband battering as far less significant a problem than wife beating is that differences in physical size tip the scales in favor of men (Berk et al., 1983; Browne, 1996; Pagelow, 1984). Men are bigger and stronger than women, and as Straus (1977–1978) points out, a single beating can ensure the dominance of the male in the relationship.

Methodological issues and problems are apparent in the study of domestic violence in general and husband battering in particular (Hornung, McCollough, and Sugimoto, 1981). Problems with the CTS related to the finding of husband and wife symmetry in spousal violence were discussed in the previous section. Another problem is that most studies that use the CTS rely on respondents who are unrelated (Szinovacz, 1983). Szinovacz advocates for the use of couple data, that is, using husbands and wives from the same marriage. This is especially important because it is known that relatively objective questions can bring very different responses from spouses (Szinovacz, 1983). Although some research points to methodological problems such as ambiguous questions, social desirability bias, and respondents' inability to recall events accurately, Szinovacz identified several substantive reasons for different husband and wife responses. They include different interests and perceptions of marriage, lack of empathy, and marital conflict. Edleson and Brygger (1986) supported the view that researchers need to obtain data on family violence from both the perpetrator and the victim.

A number of researchers point to the importance of qualitative research methods for a more accurate understanding of the meaning attached to a violent episode and the context in which it occurred (Brush, 1990; Dobash and Dobash, 1983; Dobash et al., 1992; Margolin, 1987). Although not rejecting quantitative data, Dobash and Dobash (1983) emphasized the use of historical analysis, examination of police and court records, and in-depth interviews (of two to twelve hours' duration) with battered women. A respectful and trusting relationship between the interviewer and the respondent is also important (Brush, 1990). Qualitative data can add a richness to family violence research that quantitative data alone cannot provide.

An examination of patterns of spousal homicide has also been used to bolster the viewpoint that marital violence is symmetrical (Dobash et al., 1992). Steinmetz and Lucca (1988) cited Wolfgang's 1958 study showing almost equal rates of marital homicide by men and women. In his study in Philadelphia, Wolfgang (1958) found that between 1948 and 1952, fifty-three men killed their wives and forty-seven women killed their husbands. FBI Uniform Crime Reports statistics also have pointed toward an almost equal rate of spousal killing. Simply looking at rates, however, does not tell the complete story. According to Dobash et al. (1992), men kill their wives after long periods of physically abusing them. Men kill their wives and children together; women do not. Men track down and kill women who have left them; women do not. Men kill their wives as a part of a murder-suicide; women do not. Dobash et al. (1992) considered the evidence "overwhelming" (p. 81) that a significant proportion of wives killing their husbands is in self-defense, hardly ever the reason men kill their wives. In contrast to men, women kill after their own prolonged abuse with a pattern of increased severe injury, when they perceive lack of options, and when their own lives have been threatened (Browne, 1987, 1996).

Recent evidence shows greater disparity between the prevalence of husband and wife homicide. Between 1988 and 1991, 64% of marital homicides were women who were killed by male partners and 36% were men killed by female partners (Browne, 1996). Women rarely kill; they account for 11.5% of adult homicides, with men committing 88.5% of homicides. It is true, however, that if women kill, they are most likely to kill their partners (Browne, 1996).

Importantly, Browne (1996) points out that the FBI Uniform Crime Reports contain only a brief description of the homicide, the method used to kill the victim, and the relationship between the victim and the perpetrator, if it is known to the police. The Uniform Crime Reports do not contain information about the history of the couple; therefore it is not possible to determine a national estimate of homicides that have a history of physical violence. Browne (1996) has found that more detailed studies on the local level do point to the wife who kills her husband as having a history as a battered woman. Such studies may suggest that husband battering may be a reactive pattern to other violent dynamics in the history of the couple.

The number of women who killed their male partners showed a 25% decrease from 1976 through 1984 (Browne, 1996). This has been attributed to an increase in legislation and expansion of services for battered women. Unfortunately, from 1976 to 1987, there was an increase in men killing their female partners. But even though the national rate of husbands killing their wives has declined since the mid 1980s, it is not the significant decline seen in the rates of wives killing their husbands (Browne, 1996). In general, it may be inappropriate to link spousal homicide with husband battering, because spousal homicide rates cannot give an accurate picture of the prevalence and nature of husband battering.

CORRELATES OF ABUSE

Very little work has been done on a theoretical formulation for husband battering, or for family violence in general, although a number of researchers have noted this as a problem (Dobash et al., 1992; Lucal, 1995; Miller and Wellford, 1996). Dobash et al. (1992) argued that the reason researchers incorrectly say there is symmetry in marital violence is because they "too often operate without sound (or indeed any) theoretical visions of marital relationships, of interpersonal conflicts, or of violence" (p. 83). Although many studies deal primarily with correlates of abuse, there has been insufficient attention to formulating integrated theoretical models that incorporate and explain the different types of family violence (Cardarelli, 1996).

In the current state of knowledge, explanations for family violence can be grouped into three major approaches: the individual psychopathology model, the family dysfunction model, and the feminist model (Miller and Wellford, 1996). The individual psychopathology model focuses on the individual personality characteristics of the abuser and, at times, the victim of abuse. These explanations tend to focus on the major mental disorders and the importance of individual diagnosis and treatment of the perpetrator. A plethora of research, however, shows that persons with severe mental illness are not more likely to commit serious crimes or be more violent than the general population (Bartol, 1991). Alcohol and drugs are also implicated here, yet, as will be discussed, the relationship is not a causal one. Gelles and Straus (1988) pointed out that perceiving mental disorders and substance abuse as causes of family violence is a "myth." Locating the cause of the problem within the individual means a lack of attention to socialization effects and broader societal issues and pressures.

Most research on family violence has been within the individual psychopathology model, which can be attributed to being easiest to measure these variables than other variables (Margolin, Sibner, and Gleberman, 1988). Although no specific effort has been made to examine theoretical formulations of husband battering, the individual psychopathology approach tends to be used in explanations of husband battering. Because no research exists, one can only speculate on the individual characteristics of abusive wives. It is possible that some wives who batter may suffer from a major mental disorder and that some may have substance abuse problems that can be confounding factors. It is also likely that women who batter have considerable anger and have not learned to channel or appropriately deal with anger.

The family dysfunction model focuses on violence as learned behavior and examines the history of the perpetrator's family of origin (Miller and Wellford, 1996). This model highlights that many abusers either witnessed abuse as a child or were abused themselves. This has been described as the "cycle of violence" or the intergenerational transmission of violence. Miller and Wellford (1996) point out that research on this model has been mixed. A history of violence in a battering man's family of origin, however, is often noted as an important factor. Although no special research effort has been made to examine husband battering within the family dysfunction model, women who are physically abusive toward partners are likely to come from a violent family background (Steinmetz and Lucca, 1988). For women, however, a history of violence in the family of origin is probably more likely to be related to becoming a victim of family violence rather than a perpetrator.

The feminist or structural conditions approach is also known as the patriarchal model. The key to this approach is understanding the historical subordination of women to men. Women are viewed as the property of men. From this perspective, the societal structure is designed to condone, perhaps encourage, and perpetuate the superordination of men over women. This perspective has been successful to such a degree that male domination can readily be seen in all major social institutions. Dobash and Dobash (1979) have long been known for their view that a patriarchal society encourages violence toward women; violence against women is an extension of male domination. Although there are no data linking husband battering directly to the patriarchal model, one could make the argument that women batter their husbands as a response to societal male domination. That is, the avenues for women to display anger toward the larger male-dominated society may not be available; therefore, women may direct their anger and aggression toward their husbands because husbands are more readily available as a specific target. Again, there are no data pointing in this direction, nor is this perspective likely to emerge as a believable explanation for violence within a particular family.

Socioeconomic status may have an impact on husband battering. Historically, socioeconomic status was considered to be significantly related to family violence. Efforts were then made to underscore that family violence is a problem within all socioeconomic classes (Gelles and Straus, 1988). It does appear, however, that there is more family violence in lower socioeconomic groups (Moore, 1996). The theory that there is universal risk for family violence is not adequate. Because there is no specific research in this area, one can speculate that, in the same way that wife battering is found more often among those in lower socioeconomic groups than in other groups, the same case may hold for husband battering as well.

Alcohol and drug use have also been correlated with domestic violence, but the relationship is a murky one. Until recently, assumptions were made that substance abuse causes domestic violence. This assumption is no longer held to be true. Family violence and substance abuse are now seen as coexisting problems, each one of which needs treatment. The connection between substance abuse and family violence, however, is one of the most difficult issues to understand in the family violence literature (Leonard and Jacob, 1988). The majority of studies looking at the relationship between family violence and substance abuse have focused on findings obtained from female victims. Carlson (1977), in interviews with 101 women, found that 60% of male perpetrators abused alcohol, with 21% abusing other drugs. In a study of working-class women admitted to a shelter, Labell (1979) found that 72% reported that their husbands had drinking problems, and 28% reported drug problems on the part of their husbands. In interviews with 270 battered women, one-half reported that their husbands had a drinking problem (Fagan, Stewart, and Hansen, 1983). Browne's (1987) study of battered women who killed their abusers found that 78% of the deceased men were intoxicated every day or almost every day.

A particularly difficult area to study is the relationship between family violence and substance abuse on the part of the victim. Several studies report high rates of substance abuse on the part of victims of family violence. In their study of battering parolees, Miller et al. (1990) found that 56% of female victims had alcohol problems and 40% used some type of illegal drug on a regular basis. Although there is no specific research on the role of alcohol and drugs and their relationship to husband battering, substance abuse is so often a part of family violence incidents that it may be fair to say that substance abuse is likely to be involved in situations where men may be battered.

A fair amount of professional attention has been given to why women stay in battering relationships. Recently, some have suggested that the question should be changed from the victim-blaming "Why do battered women stay?" to "Why do men batter?" (Ferraro, 1996). The focus has indeed been on why victims stay in the relationships. Some reasons offered include fear, lack of options, financial problems, lack of marketable skills, and concern for the children. Steinmetz and Lucca (1988) pointed out that some of the same mechanisms may operate to keep men in an abusive relationship.

According to Steinmetz and Lucca (1988), "minor" violence on the part of wives may not be a significant concern to husbands. A husband may be more likely to stay in the relationship if the violence affects him alone. Husbands may be more likely to consider leaving an abusive wife if she is abusive toward the children. Some men, however, feel that they are protecting the children by staying in the relationship. Some may feel that it is best for the children for the couple to remain together, no matter how serious the abuse. Steinmetz and Lucca also pointed out that although men have more financial security, leaving the home and obtaining a separate living arrangement can result in a lower standard of living for men.

Steinmetz and Lucca (1988) also addressed the issue of why men do not protect themselves from the physical attacks of their wives. One reason they give is that men have been taught that hitting a woman is wrong. Another reason is that men recognize that a physical response on their part could result in serious injury to the woman. Steinmetz and Lucca said that a "self-serving" (p. 243) reason is that the wife feels guilty about her abuse, which a man can see as a form of punishment for the wife.

Although it is known that women sustain greater injuries than men, Stets and Straus (1990) suggested several reasons this may be the case. In addition to greater physical size and strength, and hence the ability to inflict greater harm, men are more likely than women to have professional obligations that preclude them from taking the time to recover from their injuries. Women may have more flexibility than men in work situations, but women are also more likely to have greater household responsibilities than men. Although Stets and Straus suggested that women's more flexible schedules make it more likely they will care for themselves when they are sick, this is questionable. Stets and Straus also suggested that the socialization of women may make them more sensitive to physical discomfort and more likely to seek help than men. Male socialization, on the other hand, encourages them to tolerate pain and not to seek help from others.

In general, there has been little effort to arrive at theoretical formulations of husband battering and little effort made to examine correlates of abuse as they specifically pertain to husband battering. Speculation on the topics, such as those offered above, should encourage the development of a framework for future research in these areas.

CHARACTERISTICS OF OFFENDERS AND VICTIMS

As indicated, very little data are available on characteristics of battered men and their wives. The reality is that there is not much research on a sample of battered men (Pagelow, 1984; Lucal, 1995). There does seem to be the assumption that the same mechanisms of intimidation, power, and control issues that battered wives suffer are also endured by battered men (Durkin, 1996). Much of what is known, however, is anecdotal. It also appears that there is more attention given to physical assaults than to psychological abuse.

It is known that a constellation of attitudes and behaviors develop into a pattern of wife battering. Browne (1996) reviewed the warning signs and behaviors associated with men battering their partners: intrusion, isolation, possession, jealousy, prone to anger, and a history of violence. Browne noted that milder forms of some of these characteristics are actually part of a romantic tradition in our culture. A man who batters is intrusive and wants his partner to account to him for where she is at all times. Isolation is acknowledged to be a critical issue: isolating a wife from family and friends can ensure that she is less likely to be able to extricate herself from the battering relationship. The husband comes to believe that his wife is his possession, that she is an extension of himself, and that she exists to satisfy his own needs. Jealousy is taken to extreme levels and tends to underlie the most violent assaults of men against their partners (Browne, 1996). The profile also includes men who are prone to display anger that is disproportionate to the situation. These men also have a history of aggression and violent behavior. Are the same or different dynamics at work for husband battering?

Because no research evidence exists regarding profiles of wives who batter their husbands, how these women compare with men who batter is only speculative. Intrusion, possession, and jealousy may be issues for women who batter, but these qualities are far less likely to be factors for women than for men who batter. These characteristics in this society are more likely to be associated with male rather than female socialization. The isolation husbands who batter impose on their wives is a critical characteristic in a developing battering pattern. Even in nonbattering relationships, husbands have historically been able to make sure that their wives do not work, if that is the husband's desire. It is almost unheard of that a wife would demand that her husband not have a job. Even if an abusive wife is able to restrict her husband's contacts with family and friends, she is not likely to be able to envelope her husband in total isolation, because his link to the outside world is preserved through his work. As indicated previously, abusive wives are likely to have problems dealing with anger and channeling their anger appropriately.

Although there is little information available on the characteristics of battered men, anecdotal evidence does suggest that low self-esteem is very likely an issue, just as it is for battered women. Some claim that battered husbands suffer more shame and embarrassment than battered wives. The greater embarrassment men feel is used as an explanation for why male victims comprise very small numbers in official statistics such as police reports and court data (Guerin, 1983; Straus; 1996). A chief probation officer in a suburban Boston district court, where only 5% of battering cases involve wives assaulting husbands, has not found that men experience more shame or embarrassment than battered women (personal communication, December 23, 1996). The qualities of shame and embarrassment are certainly subjective, making them difficult to quantify. It is unclear how fruitful it is to debate whether female or male victims suffer more shame and embarrassment as a result of their victimization. Stets and Straus (1990) did find that wives who were victims of assault by husbands suffered more stress and depression than abused husbands, although the data did not prove that the assaults caused psychological injury.

Interestingly, clinicians almost always seem to remember cases in which a husband is battered because these situations are so unusual. Anecdotal reports obtained from conversations with clinicians reveal several cases where the woman was physically much bigger and stronger than the man. A clinician reported that her only case of husband battering involved undiagnosed mental illness. In an example of the individual psychopathology model, the clinician reported that in treating a man who was physically abused by his wife, the wife, who came for one assessment interview, appeared to suffer from bipolar mental disorder (personal communication, December 21, 1996).

One self-reported case of husband battering is available on the Internet ("Battered husband," 1990). The man claimed that he was an abused husband, yet during divorce proceedings the judge did not believe or did not act on this information. This man's ex-wife obtained custody of the children and would not allow him to see his children. Although the reasons remain unclear, the man committed suicide. In one of his postings on the World Wide Web, the man described the two factors he felt allowed him to be abused by his wife. The first was low self-esteem, which he said kept him from dating others. He said he ended up settling for someone inappropriate instead of remaining alone. The second factor identified by this man was the role of caretaker or codependent, in which he said he took more responsibility than he felt he should; he kept hoping that his love and compassion could make a difference, apparently, in his wife's abusive behavior.

Some self-reports of battered men raise the issue of whether men are innocent victims of abuse. One story obtained through the Internet (Christopher, "Domestic violence," 1995) gave details as to how a girlfriend kicked and slapped her boyfriend. Early in his account, however, Christopher described the emotional abuse the partners heaped on one another for a period of time. Although casting himself in the role of the victim, Christopher described punching his partner. He seemed genuinely surprised that he should end up with an official charge of assault.

In the California case of *People v. Walker* (1983), a partial transcript of the appeal showed that Mr. Walker tried to use the defense that he was an emotionally battered husband. Mr. Walker described that his wife controlled everything and that he was forced to give up hobbies such as dancing. His wife significantly curtailed his activities, leaving him with the feeling that he had no choice but to kill her, which he did in 1981 by beating her with a heavy lead fishing weight. He failed in a battered husband defense; it was shown that he clearly had planned the murder and enlisted the assistance of someone else in carrying out the killing and trying to make it appear to be a burglary. Mr. Walker's first-degree murder conviction was upheld on appeal. Rather than viewing the case as a failure of a battered husband defense, it shows that some cases are not appropriate for a battered spouse defense (Guerin, 1983).

This section has speculated on some characteristics likely to be found in victims and perpetrators of husband battering. This material serves as a reminder that little is known about husband battering and that more research would be useful in making explicit the dynamics of husband battering.

PREVENTION AND TREATMENT

The twenty-year debate over the seriousness of husband battering has precluded efforts to learn more about who these men are and what needs they have for services. Lucal (1995) correctly pointed out that the debate has been essentially confined to the academic world. Clinicians are remarkably absent from the debate, focusing instead on the treatment of any clients who come to them for assistance, female and male.

Improvements in documenting, assessing, and treating wife abuse continue, although most family abuse still does not come to the attention of law enforcement (Flowers, 1996). The effectiveness of family violence interventions may be questioned, however; law enforcement and the court system are now at their most responsive with greater access to restraining orders, court-mandated treatment, and a national movement toward mandatory arrest laws (Davis and Smith, 1995; Mignon and Holmes, 1995; Sullivan, 1996). Some feel that emphasis on services for women has precluded concern for male battering victims, whereas others fear that attention to male victims will dilute efforts to help battered women.

For any victim of abuse, physical safety comes first. It is known that male perpetrators follow their victims, whereas women are much less likely to do so (Browne, 1996). Male victims are more likely than female victims to be able to leave an abusive situation without needing the assistance of shelter services due to the likelihood of greater financial independence. It is mostly through the efforts in treating the problems of battered men that the small numbers are seen. In fact, the few shelters established for male victims of battering have not fared well. The only battered men's shelter in Great Britain opened in November 1992 and closed very shortly after that (Durkin, 1996). One shelter that was available to both battered women and men had five men stay within a three-year period. "Fear of ridicule" was suggested as the reason so few men availed themselves of services (Cose, 1996). In December 1993, a shelter for battered men opened in St. Paul, Minnesota. A *Newsweek* story in August 1994 reported that the director stated that services were provided to fifty-four men. This work was clouded by controversy involving the director's personal history and his own statement that he had thirteen restraining orders against him (Cose, 1996).

For those who do clinical work with victims and perpetrators of family violence, the issue is not how prevalent the problem is. Rather, the treatment needs of these clients and how those needs can best be met must be determined. Nadean Verdicchio, program director of the Unity House Families in Crisis Program in Troy, New York, estimates that 5% of the clients receiving services from this comprehensive agency are male (personal communication, November 4, 1996). Services include shelter, housing assistance, and individual and group counseling. Verdicchio focuses on the importance of providing assistance to all victims of family violence: elderly, young, women, and men. Male clients not only receive the same services as women, but they participate in the programs alongside female clients, including group therapy. According to Verdicchio, this model works very well, with no problems resulting.

CONCLUSION

The debate about the prevalence of husband battering is not heading in a direction that is likely to be fruitful. An academic debate over numbers may be interesting but cannot lead to treatment and prevention efforts. The primary concern about considering husband abuse a legitimate social problem is that it will reduce or deny services to the far greater number, and more seriously injured group, of battered women. Indeed, several writers acknowledged that emphasizing husband battering at the expense of wife battering has led to the denial of funding for services for female victims (Fields and Kirchner, 1978; Pagelow, 1984). Straus and Gelles (1986, 1990) stated, without giving any details, that the data showing symmetry in abuse by men and women in the 1975 National Family Violence Survey have been used in court against battered women and have been used to minimize the need for services for battered women. At this point, the trend of the ongoing debate about husband battering, therefore, continues to be one that focuses on whether husband battering should be considered a significant social problem.

Straus (1977–1978), for example, earlier offered a number of reasons why it is important to give more policy attention to wives as victims of domestic violence. As already indicated, men underreport their own violence. Husbands have higher rates of inflicting injury ("beating up" and "using a knife or gun") and repeat violent acts more often than women. (Note that later Straus [1996] said that women are more violent than men.) The greater physical strength makes women much more likely to be injured than men. Straus (1977–1978) also reaffirms the critical point that data do not reveal how many violent acts on the part of women are in retaliation for abuse they have suffered. Straus (1977–1978) emphasized that a large number of attacks occur while the wife is pregnant and represent danger to both the woman and the unborn child (see also Browne, 1996). Historically, economic and social constraints limit the options women have available to them to free themselves from an abusive relationship. These are and should continue to be critical issues, reaffirming the need for social policy emphasis to be placed on the protection of women. On the other hand, the debate over the existence and prevalence of husband battering should not be used to detract from these issues. Rather, the debate must begin to focus on ways to heal all forms of domestic violence, regardless of their prevalence.

Some have suggested that the major issue for the stagnation of the debate is the inability to define husband battering as a significant social problem. Straus and Gelles (1986) stated that the victimization of men has not received public attention and funds because "it has not been defined as a problem" (p. 472). Straus's (1996) current work appears designed to contribute to the effort to have husband battering be redefined as a social problem.

Lucal (1995) pointed out that the attention to wife battering has been consistent through the years, whereas attention to husband battering has been inconsistent and frequently negative. Lucal (1995) noted that husband battering has not been defined as a social problem for several reasons: (1) there has been no organized effort on behalf of male victims, (2) there has been a lack of media attention to the subject, and (3) there are stereotypical gender images of women as weak and men as strong. The perception that "men do not make good victims of domestic violence" (Lucal, 1995, p. 107) contributes to the inability to define husband battering as a social problem.

A critical missing piece is that treatment and prevention efforts can be far more successful if a clinical picture emerges of the experiences of victimized men, their financial issues, emotional issues, their role in caring for children, and the effects on children. Thus far, research efforts have overlooked the individual victims in pursuit of the numbers game. Acknowledging that the problem of husbands as victims is much smaller than that of battered women does not mean that no attention should be paid to male victims. It may certainly be a truism that husband battering may not be a significant problem, but for an individual male victim, it most certainly is significant. Qualitative research, including interviews with husbands who have been victimized and with clinicians who treat them, could make a concrete and major contribution to treatment and prevention efforts as well as to the nature of the debate.

EDITORIAL SUMMARY

The study of husband battering emerged in the 1970s and continues today. It has not, however, developed beyond a debate about the prevalence of the problem. Attention has only focused on whether husband battering should be considered a significant social problem. No research attention has been given to the dynamics of husband battering, the characteristics of victimized men, correlates of abuse, and treatment and prevention efforts. The lack of a theoretical formulation further hampers attempts to understand husband battering. Ignoring these issues precludes the development of effective treatment and prevention strategies for those cases of husband battering that do exist.

REFERENCES

Berk, R. A., Berk, S. F., Loseke, D. R., and Rauma, D. (1983). Mutual combat and other family violence myths. In D. Finkelhor, R. J. Gelles, G. T. Hotaling, and M. A. Straus (Eds.), *The Dark Side of Families* (pp. 197–212). Beverly Hills, CA: Sage.

Bartol, C. R. (1991). *Criminal Behavior: A Psychosocial Approach*. Englewood Cliffs, NJ: Prentice Hall.

Battered Husband—Divorce—Suicide. (1990). [On-line]. Internet: www.isc.org/men/wells/index.html and www.isc.org/men/wells/26175.

Bowker, L. E. (1983). *Beating Wife-Beating*. Lexington, MA: Lexington Books.

Browne, A. (1987). *When Battered Women Kill*. New York: Free Press.

Browne, A. (1996). Violence in marriage: Until death do us part? In A. P. Cardarelli (Ed.), *Violence between Intimate Partners: Patterns, Causes, and Effects* (pp. 48–69). Needham Heights, MA: Allyn and Bacon.

Brush, L. D. (1990). Violent acts and injurious outcomes in married couples: Methodological issues in the national survey of families and households. *Gender and Society, 4*, 56–67.

Cardarelli, A. P. (1996). Confronting intimate violence: Looking toward the twenty-first century. In A. P. Cardarelli (Ed.), *Violence between Intimate Partners: Patterns, Causes, and Effects* (pp. 178–185). Needham Heights, MA: Allyn and Bacon.

Carlson, B. E. (1977). Battered women and their assailants. *Social Work, 22*, 455–460.

Christopher. (1995, January). *Domestic Violence—A Story*. [On-line]. Internet: www.isc.org/men/battery/testimony/robinhood.html.

Cleek, M. G., and Pearson, T. A. (1985). Perceived causes of divorce: An analysis of interrelationships. *Journal of Marriage and Family, 47*, 179–183.

Continued debate: The truth about domestic violence. (1988). [Letters to the editor]. *Social Work, 33*(2), 189–191.

Cose, E. (1996). The problem of domestic violence for men is exaggerated. In K. L. Swisher (Ed.), *At Issue: Domestic Violence* (pp. 86–88). San Diego: Greenhaven Press. (Reprinted from Truths about spouse abuse in *Newsweek*, August 8, 1994.)

Davis, R. C., and Smith, B. (1995). Domestic violence reforms: Empty promises or fulfilled expectations? *Crime and Delinquency, 41*(4), 541–552.

Dobash, R. E., and Dobash, R. P. (1979). *Violence Against Wives: A Case Against the Patriarchy*. New York: Free Press.

Dobash, R. P., and Dobash, R. E. (1983). The context-specific approach. In D. Finkelhor, R. J. Gelles, G. T. Hotaling, and M. A. Straus (Eds.), *The Dark Side of Families* (pp. 261–276). Beverly Hills, CA: Sage.

Dobash, R. P., Dobash, R. E., Wilson, M., and Daly, M. (1992). The myth of sexual symmetry in marital violence. *Social Problems, 39*(1), 71–91.

Dunn, K. (1996). Women are responsible for domestic violence. In K. L. Swisher (Ed.), *At Issue: Domestic Violence* (pp. 76–79). San Diego: Greenhaven Press. (Reprinted from Truth abuse in *The New Republic*, August 1, 1994.)

Durkin, T. (1996). Domestic violence harms both men and women. In K. L. Swisher (Ed.), *At Issue: Domestic Violence* (pp. 65–70). San Diego: Greenhaven Press. (Reprinted from The myth of the violent femme in *Mademoiselle*, April 1994.)

Edleson, J. L., and Brygger, M. P. (1986). Gender differences in reporting of battering incidences. *Family Relations*, *35*, 377–382.

Fagan, J. A., Stewart, D. K., and Hansen, K. V. (1983). Violent men or violent husbands: Background factors and situational correlates. In D. Finkelhor, R. J. Gelles, G. T. Hotaling, and M. A. Straus (Eds.), *The Dark Side of Families* (pp. 49–67). Beverly Hills, CA: Sage.

Feld, S. L., and Straus, M. A. (1990). Escalation and desistance from wife assault in marriage. In M. A. Straus and R. J. Gelles (Eds.), *Physical Violence in American Families: Risk Factors and Adaptations to Violence in 8,145 Families* (pp. 489–505). New Brunswick, NJ: Transaction. (Reprinted from *Criminology, 27*, 1989, 141–161.)

Ferraro, K. J. (1996). Battered women's strategies for survival. In A. P. Cardarelli (Ed.), *Violence between Intimate Partners: Patterns, Causes, and Effects* (pp.124–140). Needham Heights, MA: Allyn and Bacon.

Fields, M. D., and Kirchner, R. M. (1978). Battered women are still in need: A reply to Steinmetz. *Victimology: An International Journal*, *3*(1–2), 216–226.

Flowers, R. B. (1996). The problem of domestic violence is widespread. In K. L. Swisher (Ed.), *At Issue: Domestic Violence* (pp.10–21). San Diego: Greenhaven Press. (Reprinted from *The Victimization and Exploitation of Women and Children: A Study of Physical, Mental and Sexual Maltreatment in the United States.* Jefferson, NC: McFarland and Company, 1994.)

Gaquin, D. A. (1977–1978). Spouse abuse: Data from the national crime survey. *Victimology: An International Journal*, *2*, 632–643.

Gelles, R. J., and Straus, M. A. (1979). Determinants of violence in the family: Towards a theoretical integration. In W. R. Burr, R. Hill, F. I. Nye, and I. L. Reiss (Eds.), *Contemporary Theories about the Family.* Chapter 21. Vol. 1. New York: Free Press.

Gelles, R. J., and Straus, M. A. (1988). *Intimate Violence: The Causes and Consequences of Abuse in the American Family.* New York: Simon and Schuster.

Gondolf, E. W. (1988). [Letter to the editor]. *Social Work*, *33*(2), 190.

Guerin, N. L. (1983). People v. Walker—The battered husband defense. *Criminal Justice Journal*, *7*(1), 153–170.

Harlow, C. (1991). *Female Victims of Violent Crime.* Washington, DC: Office of Justice Programs.

Holmes, W. M., Mignon, S. I., and Headley, T. (1993). *Mandatory Arrest and Domestic Violence in Massachusetts.* Boston: Massachusetts Committee on Criminal Justice.

Hornung, C. A., McCullough, B. C., and Sugimoto, T. (1981). Status relationships in marriage: Risk factors in spouse abuse. *Journal of Marriage and the Family, 43*, 675–692.

Jouriles, E. N., and O'Leary, K. D. (1985). Interspousal reliability of reports of marital violence. *Journal of Consulting and Clinical Psychology, 53*, 419–421.

Kurz, D. (1993). Social science perspectives on wife abuse: Current debates and future directions. In P. B. Bart and E. G. Moran (Eds.), *Violence against Women: The Bloody Footprints* (pp. 252–269). Newbury Park, CA: Sage.

Labell, L. S. (1979). Wife abuse: A sociological study of battered women and their mates. *Victimology: An International Journal, 4*, 258–267.

Leonard, K. E., and Jacob, T. (1988). Alcohol, alcoholism, and family violence. In V. B. Van Hasselt, R. L. Morrison, A. S. Bellack, and M. Hersen (Eds.), *Handbook of Family Violence* (pp. 383–406). New York: Plenum Press.

Lucal, B. (1995). The problem with "battered husbands." *Deviant Behavior: An Interdisciplinary Journal, 16*, 95–112.

Margolin, G. (1987). The multiple forms of aggressiveness between marital partners: How do we identify them? *Journal of Marital and Family Therapy, 13*, 77–84.

Margolin, G., Sibner, L. G., and Gleberman, L. (1988). Wife battering. In V. B. Van Hasselt, R. L. Morrison, A. S. Bellack, and M. Hersen (Eds.), *Handbook of Family Violence* (pp. 89–117). New York: Plenum Press.

McLeod, M. (1984). Women against men: An examination of domestic violence based on an analysis of official data and national victimization data. *Justice Quarterly, 1*, 171–193.

McNeely, R. L., and Mann, C. R. (1990). Domestic violence is a human issue. *Journal of Interpersonal Violence, 5*, 129–132.

McNeely, R. L., and Robinson-Simpson, G. (1987). The truth about domestic violence: A falsely framed issue. *Social Work, 32*(6), 485–490.

McNeely, R. L., and Robinson-Simpson, G. (1988). The truth about domestic violence revisited: A reply to Saunders. *Social Work, 33*(2), 184–188.

Meredith, W. H., Abbott, D. A., and Adams, S. L. (1986). Family violence: Its relations to marital and parental satisfaction and family strengths. *Journal of Family Violence, 1*, 299–305.

Miller, B. A., Nochajski, T. H., Leonard, K. E., Blane, H. T., Gondoli, D. M., and Bowers, P. M. (1990). Spousal violence and alcohol-drug problems among parolees and their spouses. *Women and Criminal Justice, 1*(2), 55–71.

Miller, S. L., and Wellford, C. F. (1996). Patterns and correlates of interpersonal violence. In A. P. Cardarelli (Ed.), *Violence between Intimate Partners: Patterns, Causes, and Effects* (pp. 16–28). Needham Heights, MA: Allyn and Bacon.

Mignon, S. I., and Holmes, W. M. (1995). Police response to mandatory arrest laws. *Crime and Delinquency, 41*(4), 430–442.

Moore, A. (1996). Intimate violence: Does socioeconomic status matter? In A. P. Cardarelli (Ed.), *Violence between Intimate Partners: Patterns, Causes, and Effects* (pp. 90–100). Needham Heights, MA: Allyn and Bacon.

Nisonoff, L., and Bitman, I. (1979). Spouse abuse: Incidence and relationship to selected demographic variables. *Victimology: An International Journal, 4,* 131–140.

Pagelow, M. D. (1984). *Family Violence.* New York: Praeger.

People v. Walker. 145 Cal. App. 3d 886; 193 Ca. Rptr. 812 (1983).

Pleck, E. (1987). *Domestic Tyranny: The Making of Social Policy Against Family Violence from Colonial Times to the Present.* New York: Oxford University Press.

Pleck, E., Pleck, J. H., Grossman, M., and Bart, P. B. (1977). The battered data syndrome: A comment on Steinmetz' article. *Victimology: An International Journal, 2,* 3–4, 680–683.

Rasche, C. E. (1988). Minority women and domestic violence: The unique dilemmas of battered women of color. *Journal of Contemporary Criminal Justice, 4,* 150–171.

Rouse, L., Breen, R., and Howell, M. (1988). Abuse in intimate relationships. A comparison of married and dating college students. *Journal of Interpersonal Violence, 3,* 414–429.

Saunders, D. G. (1988). Other "truths" about domestic violence: A reply to McNeely and Robinson-Simpson. *Social Work, 33*(2), 179–183.

Schwartz, M. D. (1987). Gender and injury in spousal assaults. *Sociological Focus, 20,* 61–75.

Sherven, J., and Sniechowski, J. (1996). Men and women both cause domestic violence. In K. L. Swisher (Ed.), *At Issue: Domestic Violence* (pp. 83–85). San Diego: Greenhaven Press. (Reprinted from Women are responsible, too, *Los Angeles Times,* June 21, 1994.)

Stacey, W. A., Hazlewood, L. R., and Shupe, A. (1994). *The Violent Couple.* Westport, CT: Praeger.

Stalans, L. J., and Lurgio, A. J. (1995). Responding to domestic violence against women. *Crime and Delinquency, 41*(4), 387–398.

Steinmetz, S. K. (1977). *The Cycle of Violence: Assertive, Aggressive, and Abusive Family Interaction.* New York: Praeger.

Steinmetz, S. K. (1977–1978). The battered husband syndrome. *Victimology: An International Journal, 2*(3–4), 499–509.

Steinmetz, S. K., and Lucca, J. S. (1988). Husband battering. In V. B. Van Hasselt, R. L. Morrison, A. S. Bellack, and M. Hersen (Eds.), *Handbook of Family Violence* (pp. 233–246). New York: Plenum Press.

Stets, J. E., and Straus, M. A. (1990). Gender differences in reporting marital violence and its medical and psychological consequences. In M. A. Straus and R. J. Gelles

(Eds.), *Physical Violence in American Families: Risk Factors and Adaptations to Violence in 8,245 Families* (pp. 151–166). New Brunswick, NJ: Transaction.

Straus, M. A. (1977–1978). Wife beating: How common and why? *Victimology: An International Journal, 2*(3–4), 443–448.

Straus, M. A. (1979). Measuring intrafamily conflict and violence: The conflict tactics scales. *Journal of Marriage and the Family, 51,* 75–88.

Straus, M. A. (1990). The national family violence surveys. In M. A. Straus and R. J. Gelles (Eds.), *Physical Violence in American Families: Risk Factors and Adaptations to Violence in 8,145 Families* (pp. 3–16). New Brunswick, NJ: Transaction.

Straus, M. A. (1996). Domestic violence is a problem for men. In K. L. Swisher (Ed.), *At Issue: Domestic Violence* (pp. 67–80). San Diego: Greenhaven Press. (Reprinted from Physical assaults by wives: A major social problem. Chapter 4 in R. J. Gelles and D. R. Loseke (Eds.), *Current Controversies on Family Violence*, Newbury Park, CA: Sage, 1993.)

Straus, M. A., and Gelles, R. J. (1986). Societal change and change in family violence from 1975 to 1985 as revealed by two national surveys. *Journal of Marriage and the Family, 48,* 465–479.

Straus, M. A., and Gelles R. J. (1990). How violent are American families? Estimates from the national family violence resurvey and other studies. In M. A. Straus and R. J. Gelles (Eds.), *Physical Violence in American Families: Risk Factors and Adaptations to Violence in 8,145 Families* (pp. 95–112). New Brunswick, NJ: Transaction.

Straus, M. A., Gelles, R. J. and Steinmetz, S. K. (1980). *Behind Closed Doors: Violence in the American Family.* Garden City, NY: Anchor/Doubleday.

Sullivan, C. R. (1996). Societal collusion and culpability in intimate male violence. In A. P. Cardarelli (Ed.), *Violence between Intimate Partners: Patterns, Causes, and Effects* (pp. 154–164). Needham, Heights, MA: Allyn and Bacon.

Szinovacz, M. E. (1983). Using couple data as a methodological tool: The case of marital violence. *Journal of Marriage and the Family, 45,* 633–644.

Wolfgang, M. E. (1958). *Patterns in Criminal Homicide.* Philadelphia: University of Philadelphia Press.

7

Male-to-Male Gay Domestic Violence: The Dark Closet

Tod W. Burke, Ph.D.
Department of Criminal Justice
Radford University

I thought I was going to die. He had his hands around my throat and was squeezing tighter and tighter. I could feel myself blacking out and I tried to fight him off but it was no use. He started to bang my head against the hall mirror. The last thing I remember is feeling something warm pouring down the back of my neck. Then I must have passed out. (Kirby, 1994, p. 46)

Male-to-male gay domestic violence is not isolated to the above incident. In fact, "experts estimate that between 25 [and] 30% of all gay men and lesbians in intimate relationships are victims of domestic abuse" (Letellier, 1994b, p. 16). A survey administered by the Gay and Lesbian Community Action Council revealed that 17% of the 1,000 gay men surveyed reported having been involved in a physically violent gay relationship (Elliott, 1996). Island and Letellier (1991a) noted that out of the approximately 12 million adult gay males, as many as 500,000 are victims of domestic violence. Greg Merrill, coordinator of the Community United Against Violence in San Francisco, stated "that domestic violence occurs in a quarter to a third of gay . . . relationships—approximately the same proportion as among heterosexuals" (Tuller, 1994, p. A8).

Gay domestic violence is a serious concern. Domestic violence now ranks only behind substance abuse and acquired immunodeficiency syndrome (AIDS) as the major health crisis among gay men (Island and Letellier, 1991b). Some specialists believe that the causes of domestic violence are similar among heterosexuals and homosexuals (Senk, 1995), yet there are some distinct characteristics. This chapter examines some of these characteristics, with particular attention devoted to historical recognition, legal definitions and concerns, and profiling offenders and victims. Prevention and treatment strategies and future trends and recommendations are also highlighted.

BRIEF HISTORY OF SAME-SEX DOMESTIC VIOLENCE

Same-sex domestic violence has existed as long as same-sex relationships; little attention, however, has been devoted to this topic. Prior to the women's movement during the late 1960s and early 1970s, research often focused on "victim blaming," which minimized domestic violence. Today, resources and program strategies for women are well established (Merrill, 1996). As Elliott (1996) wrote:

> For well over 25 years, heterosexual women have received advocacy, support and intervention for the battered women's movement when they have sought help. While the hundreds of battered women's programs around the country have championed the cause of healthy relationships for heterosexual women . . . most of the nation's programs still refuse to deal with gay male couple violence. (p. 6)

According to Elliott (1996), the women's movement proved successful in attempting to combat sexism, but as a consequence, it has excluded homosexuals, particularly gay males. The myths that males cannot be victims of domestic violence and that the only violence that occurs to gay males is in the form of "gay bashing" exist (Letellier, 1995). Island and Letellier (1991a, pp. 16–24) have identified fifteen common myths about violence against gays:

1. Gay men are never the victims of domestic violence.
2. Domestic violence is more common in heterosexual relationships.
3. Gay men's domestic violence is a "fair fight" between two men.
4. When two men fight it is just "boys being boys."
5. Gay men's domestic violence is just a "lovers'" quarrel.
6. The batterer will always be bigger and stronger than the victim.
7. Men who are abusive while under the influence of alcohol and/or drugs are not responsible for their actions.
8. AIDS is a cause of domestic violence.
9. Gay men's domestic violence is sexual behavior enjoyed by the victim.
10. The law does not protect gay men from domestic violence.

11. Victims often provoke the violence—they get what they deserve.

12. Victims are simply exaggerating the violence. If it were really bad, they would leave.

13. It is easy for gay male victims of domestic violence to leave their partners.

14. Gay men's domestic violence occurs only to those who hang out at gay bars, are of lower income, or [are] people of color.

15. Victims of domestic violence are co-dependents.

Contrary to popular belief, gay men are more likely to be killed by their partner than by a gay basher (Letellier, 1995). For example, in San Francisco between 1991 and 1992, one-third of the gay men murdered were killed by their partners and one-third were killed by what was recorded as their "roommate" (Letellier, 1995). Until recently, "the domestic violence movement historically has focused almost exclusively on the battering of heterosexual women" (Letellier, 1994a, p. 95).

The lack of attention to same-sex domestic violence is not limited to the women's movement. The gay community may also be responsible for keeping same-sex domestic violence closeted. The reasons for silence may include shame, fear of future victimization due to homophobia, and denial. Some gays maintain the illusion that homosexuals would not resort to the same uncivilized behavior as heterosexuals (Elliott, 1996).

Perhaps another reason for silence within the gay community is that many gay males are simply unaware that domestic violence occurs in same-sex relationships. This lack of knowledge may be due in part to how society defines and perceives domestic violence.

DEFINITION OF DOMESTIC VIOLENCE

Definitions of domestic violence vary and play a significant role in the development of legal standards. Farley (1985) states that domestic violence is "an act of aggression, either psychological or physical, that is an attempt by the perpetrator to intimidate or harm another in an intimate relationship, out of real or perceived frustration with a given situation" (p. 231). Although this definition appears to be accurate, it may be too restrictive. Farley (1985) assumes that domestic violence occurs as a result of frustration (real or imagined) "with a given situation." Domestic violence may not be situation specific. Rarely does domestic violence "just happen." Instead, it is the result of one person attempting to control another for gain over a period of time. It is the perpetrator who must be held accountable, not the situation.

Island and Letellier (1991a) indicate that a key element to domestic violence is "power." It is the use of power that allows the offender to control the victim physically, psychologically, or materially (material abuse includes possession of goods and destruction of personal property).

Walber (1988) notes that domestic violence "is any pattern to coerce, dominate or isolate within a relationship" (p. 250). Because domestic violence assumes that the individuals involved are in some sort or relationship (lovers or dating, whether living together or not) (Island and Letellier, 1991a), it is often assumed that battering or other abuse is isolated to those individuals. That assumption may be misleading. Gay men may "be battered or abused by a lover, ex-lover, roommate or family member" (Walber, 1988, p. 250). In addition to physical, psychological, and material abuse, gay domestic violence may include the restriction of one's freedom, heterosexist control (threats to reveal gay identity to others, or "outing"), economic control, or sexual control (Walber, 1988).

In this chapter, gay domestic violence will be defined as a means to control others through power, including physical and psychological threats (verbal and nonverbal) or injury (to the victim or to others), isolation, economic deprivation, heterosexist control, sexual assaults, vandalism (destruction of property), or any combination of methods.

Many states have worded their domestic violence laws to be gender specific. For instance, Witzer (1993, in Lundy)

> notes that nine states—Alabama, Arizona, Delaware, Georgia, Michigan, New Jersey, North Carolina, Oregon, and South Carolina—have domestic violence laws that apply only to heterosexual couples, and that Oregon's domestic violence law provides for warrantless searches in cases of heterosexual domestic violence only. The states of Washington and Indiana both provide for the creation of shelters for battered women but limit the use of such shelters to either heterosexual couples (Washington) or spouses and former spouses (Indiana). (p. 292)

California and Massachusetts provide gender-neutral definitions of domestic violence that allow individuals involved in same-sex relationships access to the same legal rights as heterosexuals, such as access to family courts, the ability to obtain restraining orders, and the opportunity to press charges and prosecute the batterer (Kingston, 1996). As a result of legal restraints placed on gays in many jurisdictions, the recent passage of the bill prohibiting the recognition of gay marriages (in those states that fail to recognize gay marriages) appears significant.

In understanding gay domestic violence, it is important to examine legal definitions and specific categories of abuse and violence. It is not uncommon for people to use the terms "assault and battery," "abuse," and "neglect" interchangeably within domestic violence encounters. Most states, however, make individual distinctions.

An assault is the unlawful attempt or threat to inflict harm upon another, whereas a battery is the actual unlawful or harmful touching of another (Reid, 1995). For example, if someone threatens to hurt another, it is an assault; if someone physically injures that person in any unlawful manner, it is a battery.

Neglect and abuse, although often associated with children, apply to gay domestic situations as well. Negligence is the failure to do what is reasonable. Those who are negligent are thoughtless, irresponsible, or inconsiderate (by legal standards) (Statsky, 1985). One may be legally negligent if he or she fails to provide the needed personal or medical care to another (Karmen, 1990). For instance, if a partner failed to provide his lover suffering from AIDS the necessary medication to sustain life, he may be charged with criminal negligence (and possibly more, depending on the jurisdiction).

Abuse includes physical assaults, sexual assaults, and psychological mistreatment with the purpose to injure, degrade, harm, assault, batter, slander, disgrace, or exploit. Physical abuse includes hitting, choking, slapping, grabbing, kicking, scratching, burning, shoving, and hitting with objects or weapons (Island and Letellier, 1991a; Sonkin and Durphy, 1989; Walber, 1988). Sexual abuse includes forced sexual activity (rape, sodomy), assaulting sexual body parts with objects, forced nonmonogamy, and forced sexual contact with animals (Reed, 1989; Sonkin and Durphy, 1989; Walber, 1988). Psychological mistreatment includes criticizing, intimidating, isolating, humiliating, ridiculing, ignoring, harassing, lying, degrading, insulting, name calling, manipulating, blaming, and threatening ultimatums (to leave, to hurt themselves or others) (Island and Letellier, 1991a; Sonkin and Durphy, 1989; Walber, 1988).

As noted within the definition, gay domestic violence can include isolation, economic deprivation, heterosexist control, and vandalism. According to Walber (1988), isolation is a means of restricting one's movement by controlling personal and social contacts as well as by prohibiting the victim from participating in activities that include others. For example, the abuser may forbid his lover to see friends or family members.

Economic deprivation may vary, but the result remains the same: power and control. The abuser may attempt to control the finances by placing all monies into an account that either he (the abuser) controls directly or one that requires dual signatures for withdrawals. Another means of economic control is stealing money from the victim or accruing substantial debt in the name of the victim (e.g., credit cards) (Walber, 1988).

Heterosexist control is the threat to "out" the victim to family members, friends, coworkers, employers, and so forth. (Walber, 1988). Although this may appear trivial to some, many gays wish to keep their sexual orientation private for fear of retaliation, which may include loss of job, loss of friends, and isolation from family.

Vandalism is not uncommon in gay domestic violence. Some common methods of control through property destruction include destroying mementos; breaking furniture; throwing or smashing objects; burning, discarding, or destroying clothing; vandalizing a vehicle; selling or hiding of personal belongings, and injuring or threatening to injure pets of the victim (Island and Letellier, 1991a; Walber, 1988).

SPECIAL CONCERNS

In addition to legal concerns, some issues pose particular interest within the gay community. Domestic violence among gays is often complicated by homophobia and the specific problems associated with human immunodeficiency virus (HIV) and AIDS. Furthermore, gay domestically abused people of color suffer additional strain.

Homophobia is a fear of homosexuals. Despite the progress made in the latter part of the twentieth century, homophobia remains a valid concern (Blumenfeld, 1992; Byrne, 1996). According to Lundy (1993),

the same-sex batterer frequently uses homophobia as a means to maintain control and power imbalance in the relationship. . . . Gay batterers . . . may use homophobia to control their mates by threatening to "out" the victim (i.e., disclose the victim's homosexuality) to friends, family, employers, or others unless the victim complies with the batterer's demands. (p. 282)

Using homophobia as a tool for control often produces feelings of self-hate and fear in the victim (Byrne, 1996). This emotional blackmail makes leaving the abusive relationship problematic.

Another reason some victims fail to leave an abusive relationship concerns HIV/AIDS. According to the Centers for Disease Control (1993), approximately 62% of the estimated 1 million Americans infected with HIV are gay (and bisexual) men. Many of these men are involved in relationships (Barrett, 1993).

The rationale for staying in an abusive relationship when one or both partners are HIV positive (or have AIDS) varies. According to Merrill (Smith, 1994), victims remain in an abusive relationship because (1) they may be physically or financially dependent on their partner, (2) they fear dying alone, or (3) they believe that they could not find another lover due to their illness. Letellier (1996) added that, due to homophobia, family members provide little or no assistance and society members do not recognize gay domestic violence as valid. The victim often feels isolated. Because many lives have been lost to AIDS, close friends are no longer available for support.

Letellier (1996) stated that abuse may include rape and sexual assaults. Research indicates that some HIV positive abusers have deliberately infected their partner to prevent him from leaving. Others use the "guilt card" to maintain control. For instance, the HIV positive abusive partner may feign illness to prevent the other partner from leaving or to entice him back (if he left). Some remain in the relationship because they do not wish to abandon their partner in time of need.

Some abusers have withheld medication or prevented their HIV positive partner from seeking the necessary medical attention. Others have threatened to communicate the status of their ill partner to supervisors, parents, or health-care providers (for possible loss of insurance coverage) (Letellier, 1996).

According to Lundy, "People of color are not only vulnerable to racism in the larger society, but also frequently are targets of homophobia in their minority community" (pp. 288–289), which becomes particularly apparent for those individuals who are victims of both male battering and AIDS. The lack of resources for gay people of color is well noted (Mendez, 1996).

Many gay men are isolated from the community by their abusive partners, thereby making communication about possible resources unattainable. The lack of resources is magnified when the abused gay male is a person of color, lower income, or a gay youth (most literature concerning gay resources is targeted toward white, middle-class gay males) (Letellier, 1996; Lundy, 1993; Peterson and Marin, 1988).

Gay domestic violence is not caused by homophobia, HIV, or race. It is the result of an abusive person controlling another. In addition to control, what common characteristics do most abusers possess? Why do they abuse their partners? Do victims possess common characteristics? Although there are no simple answers, profiling the batterer and victim may assist in understanding both the abuser and the victim of gay domestic violence.

CHARACTERISTICS OF OFFENDERS AND VICTIMS

Before providing a general profile of the batterer and victim, it is important to understand the purpose and limitations of profiles. Profiling is a process whereby people are placed into special categories based on certain characteristics shared by others. According to Geberth (1981), profiling is an educated attempt to provide a personality composite of unknown subjects. Although profiling may prove useful for classification and possible identification, it should not be used as a crystal ball. Caution should be used in attempting to draw any conclusions merely because certain personality traits have been identified.

The Batterer

Gay male batters can come from all socioeconomic, racial or ethnic, educational, occupational, and religious backgrounds, and the age of the gay batterer cannot be determined with any degree of certainty (Farley, 1996; Sonkin and Durphy, 1989). Furthermore, being abusive is not determined by a gay man's size or strength (Walber, 1988). Batterers do, however, possess certain shared characteristics. For instance, many gay batterers minimize or deny their use of violence (Bernard and Bernard, 1984; Island and Letellier, 1991a; Sonkin and Durphy, 1989); they blame the victim for their behavior (known as victim blaming) (Island and Letellier, 1991a; Reed, 1989; Sonkin and Durphy, 1989; Walber, 1988); they are often loners (do not have close friends) (Sonkin and Durphy, 1989); they possess explosive personalities or tempers (Sonkin and Durphy, 1989); they have low self-esteem (Hotaling and Sugarman, 1986; Rouse, 1984; Sonkin and Durphy, 1989); they lack proper communication skills (Sonkin and Durphy, 1989); and they feel a lack of control over their lives, thus feeling a need to control others (Island and Letellier, 1991a; Sonkin and Durphy, 1989).

Alcohol and drugs are significant factors in profiling gay domestic batterers. Studies have indicated that, when compared to the general population, gays have a higher incidence of substance abuse (Farley, 1996). Gottfredson and Gottfredson (1988) stated that alcohol and drug use may influence the likelihood of harm in violent situations. Island and Letellier (1991a, p.248) added that "since alcohol is expected to and actually does relax inhibitions, the perpetrator may also attack more strongly and viciously than when sober, causing more serious injury to victims." Sonkin and Durphy (1989) estimated that 70% to 80% of all battering occurs while the perpetrator is under the influence of drugs, alcohol, or both. Roberts (1988) similarly found that 70% of abusers were under the influence of drugs, alcohol, or both during domestic violent episodes.

The effects that drugs and alcohol may have in contributing to violence is debatable. Roberts (1988) and Sonkin and Durphy (1989) noted that battering appeared more severe when drugs and alcohol were used in combination. The most common drugs of choice among male batterers include marijuana and cocaine (Amaro, Fried, Cabral, and Zuckerman, 1990). Some studies indicate that severe intoxication actually decreases the risk of violence (Coleman and Straus, 1983). Buikhuisen, Van Der

Plas-Korenhoff, and Bontekoe (1988) found that in small amounts, alcohol reduces aggression, thereby decreasing the amount of violent activity. Furthermore, "with respect to alcohol, the drink often does what the drinker expects it to do" (Renzetti, 1992, p. 61). In other words, if someone expects that an alcoholic drink will make him or her more cheerful, that person's behavior will often reflect that mood. Alcohol serves as an aid to a self-fulfilling prophecy. Regardless of the effects alcohol and drugs play in gay domestic violence, voluntary intoxication is merely an excuse to violence, not the cause.

Another characteristic often found among batterers is jealousy. Because it may lead to future violence, the power of jealousy should not be underestimated. According to Sonkin and Durphy (1989), jealousy is described as a fear of losing a partner's time, attention, closeness, and sexual encounters to someone else:

> A man whose self-worth is shaky, or who fears abandonment, is especially vulnerable to jealousy in battering relationships. . . . A man will try to protect against the deep pain of loss by controlling his partner through threats, intimidation, or even violence. (p. 84)

Island and Letellier (1991a, pp. 76–81) profile a gay batterer as follows:

1. There is a preexisting tendency in the abuser to manipulate, control, and dominate others.

2. Violence among abusers is progressive, therefore becoming more intense and frequent.

3. The abuser is unable to manage his own anger and frustration.

4. The abuser will often attempt to restrict the freedom of the victim.

5. The batterer will use cruel, demeaning, and aggressive behavior to achieve his ends, including physical, psychological, sexual and material intimidation, and terror.

6. The batterer has the specific intent to commit violence.

7. The abuser will attempt to stifle the victim (via threats and battery) to prevent others from learning of the violence.

8. The batterer will use victim blaming as a means to justify the violence.

9. The batterer will possess certain behavioral characteristics including (but not limited to) low self-esteem; self-hatred; depression; justification; denial; possessing unrealistic expectations for self and partner; jealousy; being critical of others; being insecure; lacking trust; deceit; showing a fascination with violence, including weapons, injury, or torture; and strong feelings of failure.

10. The abuser will exhibit a pattern of emotional dependency (towards the victim).

11. The perpetrator will obsess about the victim.

12. The batterer most likely (1) has a history of battering and violence; (2) has been abused as a child; (3) witnessed routine physical and psychological abuse;

(4) had an abusive parent; (5) had a history of cruel, demeaning, or violent behavior toward others; (6) was neglected as a child; or (7) has a history of substance abuse.

13. The abuser may have a pattern of failed relationships, academic or occupational difficulties, or financial problems.

14. The abuser will most likely possess poor communication skills

15. The batterer may perceive himself as "macho."

16. The batterer will suffer from some form of psychological disorder.

17. The batterer will only target those he perceives as "weaker." Rarely will a batterer display violence toward people in positions of authority or higher status.

18. The batterer will be reluctant to seek outside assistance for his problem(s).

The above profiles originate from a number of theories. These theories are presented for critical analysis only and do not relieve the abuser of his responsibility.

The most frequently cited theory of gay male domestic violence focuses on socialization. According to the social learning theory, batterers learn their violent behavior from others. Studies indicate that "men who both witnessed violence and suffered directly from it are even more likely to be domestically violent" (Campbell, 1995, pp. 70–71). The family violence perspective (which originated from the social learning theory) reveals that men learn from childhood experiences, the media, and social norms that violence is an acceptable means to resolve disputes (Stalans and Lurigio, 1995).

The developmental theory supports the view that developmental impairment contributes to gay domestic violence. Island and Letellier (1991a) state that when batterers were children, they failed to develop proper cognitive skills necessary for effective decision making, including the skills necessary to control anger and frustration.

The communication theory posits that men who abuse their lovers failed to acquire adequate communication skills (Island and Letellier, 1991a). This view is reflective of those who indicate that most abusers suffer poor communication skills.

The sociopolitical theory advocates that gay male domestic violence may result from a male-dominated society (Island and Letellier, 1991a). The assumption here is that domestic violence is a power and gender issue. The male uses this power to dominate, intimidate, and control to meet his needs. The difficulty concerning this theory in gay domestic violence is that the gender is the same, thus creating the possibility of a greater power struggle.

The Victim

Many believe that victims of gay domestic violence are weak and lack control over their lives. On the contrary, "victims of domestic violence . . . are often strong and powerful people who are in control of every aspect of their lives, except that they are in a relationship with an abusive partner" (Island and Letellier, 1991a, p. 88). Profile characteristics common in many gay male victims (Sonkin and Durphy, 1989) include (1) anger toward partner, (2) withdrawal, (3) lack of trust, (4) fear, (5) self-blaming, (6) frustration, (7) depression, or (8) low self-esteem. Sonkin and Durphy (1989) added that codependency is a trait found among abused subjects.

A codependent "is someone who has let another person's behavior affect him . . . and who is obsessed with controlling that person's behavior" (Beattie, 1987, p. 31). Codependents possess feelings of low self-worth and have a need to be needed (Sonkin and Durphy, 1989). Island and Letellier (1991a) do not support the codependency theory of victimization. In fact, they stated that "codependency is totally inappropriate, ineffective, and even dangerous when used in an attempt to understand or label domestic violence" (p. 225). Domestic violence is a criminal act, not a relationship problem. It occurs because one person is abusive and violent toward another, which has nothing to do with codependency (Frank, 1989; Island and Letellier, 1991a).

Island and Letellier (1991a) outlined the profile characteristics of gay domestic abuse victims (both current and potential). Victims may:

1. Have not been exposed to prior abuse (in a relationship or otherwise)

2. Overestimate their ability to handle domestic violence

3. Tend to blame themselves for the interpersonal problems

4. Show an uneasiness with disagreement

5. Tend to take responsibility for other people's actions

6. Possess low self-esteem and self-worth

7. Trivialize or deny abuse

8. Not perceive that they are being controlled, manipulated, and dominated by the abuser

9. Make attempts to leave the relationship, only to return later

10. Find leaving extremely difficult

11. Believe that they are trapped in the relationship

12. Believe that they must simply endure the violence

13. Develop coping strategies to avoid or control the violence, including appeasing the abuser, avoiding the abuser, or justifying the abuse

14. Attempt to seek some assistance for himself or the abuser, although the abuser may ridicule and reject these attempts

15. Stay in the relationship hoping the violence will cease

CYCLE OF VIOLENCE

A victim profile would be incomplete without a basic understanding of the cycle of violence. Walker (1979) outlined the three stage cycle of violence: the tension-building stage, the acute battering stage, and the calm stage.

The tension-building stage can last anywhere from days to years. In this stage, tension results in constant arguing or in the silent treatment. Simple assaults (violence causing minor injuries) may also be noted.

The acute battering stage may last anywhere from a few minutes to days. Here, violence has escalated to severe battering of the victim (aggravated assault or maiming)—including punching, kicking, slapping, and choking—resulting in bruises, broken bones, or both. It is not uncommon for weapons to be used during the assaults.

During the calm, loving, respite stage, the abuser is apologetic for his actions and will shower the victim with gifts and promises in an attempt to seek forgiveness. During this stage, the victim often feels sorry for the abuser and believes that his "acts of kindness" are reflective of his love. This stage, however, eventually fades and the cycle continues.

As the frequency of the cycle increases, the severity of violence will likely increase. In other words: (1) the more times the cycle is completed, the less time it takes to complete; (2) the longer the cycle continues, the greater the violence; and (3) the longer the cycle goes uninterrupted, the shorter the duration of the final stage (Sonkin and Durphy, 1989).

Repeated victimizations may lead to shock, numbness, fear, anger, and helplessness. The cumulating effect may result in depression, substance abuse, posttraumatic stress disorder, suicide, or murder (Dutton, 1988; Sonkin and Durphy, 1989).

Profiling is merely a tool to assist in the possible identification of a victim or a batterer. Although some argue that domestic violence profiling is difficult and inaccurate (Limandri and Sheridan, 1995; Saunders, 1995; Walber, 1988), it may prove useful for prevention and treatment strategies.

PREVENTION AND TREATMENT

Prevention and treatment of gay male domestic violence can take many forms. Island and Letellier (1991a) identified two models that they believe are necessary for effective prevention strategies: the legislative response and public and private action.

The legislative response focuses on government intervention, including governmental hearings, for the enactment of laws and law enforcement. In other words, this response says that gay domestic violence needs to be addressed by governmental officials when defining and enforcing domestic violence flaws. This strategy would include expanding the language of domestic violence statutes to ensure that all victims are equally protected (the Fourteenth Amendment) regardless of gender or sexual orientation. Funding must be allocated to provide for shelters, outreach programs for the gay and lesbian communities, training and education (seminars), and medical and legal services.

Private and public action includes education and training of social service personnel, health-care professionals, criminal justice personnel, and the gay community. Social service personnel (therapists, social workers, psychologists, psychiatrists, etc.) and health-care professionals (doctors, emergency room personnel, nurses, etc.) need a better understanding of gay domestic violence. Following therapy and treatment, victims of gay domestic violence are often released back into the setting where the violence occurred, thus allowing the cycle to continue. Proper and required training and education may reduce this violent trend.

Criminal justice personnel also need adequate training and education concerning gay domestic violence. Police officers need to be more sensitive to the needs of the gay community, particularly when enforcing domestic violence laws. Police officers are often unsure how to handle gay domestic violence. Witzer (1993) discovered that several officers were unaware that domestic violence occurred in same-sex relationships. If they are aware, "they tend to make double arrests, or arrest the wrong person, or won't arrest anyone" (Smith, 1994, p. 13).

The problem is magnified in those areas where the police are distrusted by the gay community (Kirby, 1994). Letellier (1994b. p. 18) stated that "calling the police . . . remains unthinkable for most gay men given the widespread homophobia of many police departments." Reed (1989) found that some male victims of gay domestic violence are revictimized by the police, sometimes verbally or physically. Letellier (1994b) reported that approximately 20% of gays have been victimized by police.

Some police agencies have incorporated specialized training into academies and in-service programs to educate officers in proper methods of handling gay domestic situations (Senk, 1995). Witzer (1993), however, found that some officers during training failed to take the issue seriously. Crowe (1995) recommends that the police assist in transporting victims (to a medical facility or shelter) (due to department policy, many police agencies forbid the transportation of victims and injured subjects via police cruiser), providing information concerning available services, assisting victims develop a safety plan, and helping victims obtain restraining orders against the abuser.

When an arrest is made, prosecutors may be reluctant to press charges due to a lack of sufficient evidence, the victim may be unwilling to testify against the abuser for fear of later retribution, or the prosecutor may believe that it is in the best interest of justice not to prosecute. In other words, gay domestic violence may be perceived as merely a "lovers' quarrel" that will rectify itself without court intervention.

Judges also possess discretionary powers. They may dismiss a case based on the same criteria afforded the prosecutor. Some judges fail to understand the critical nature of same-sex domestic violence. For instance, judges may provide restraining orders for both parties without ascertaining the facts (Lundy, 1993). One judge modified an abused gay man's restraining order from one year to three months when the judge discovered that the victim possessed a black belt in Karate. The judge assumed that the victim could "take care of himself" (Lundy, 1993).

There is some debate as to the effectiveness of restraining orders. Island and Letellier (1991a) strongly supported the use of restraining orders to prevent the abuser from making contact with the victim. Grau, Fagan, and Wexler (1984), however, reported that restraining orders failed to cease assaults but did reduce harassment (in less serious cases).

Some recommend mandatory arrests for domestic assaults, but the effectiveness of those arrests is debatable. The Minneapolis Experiment (Sherman and Berk, 1984) found that arrests were more effective in deterring future violence than mediation (or no arrest). In attempting to verify these findings, the National Institute of Justice funded six replication studies. "In contrast to the Minneapolis Experiment . . . none of the six replications found arrest to be a more effective deterrent than other methods of police response" (Muraskin and Roberts, 1996, p. 81). These studies indicate that mandatory arrests may not necessarily be in the best interest of the victim. Although arrest offers a temporary reprieve from the violence, other alternatives may prove useful.

The gay community also needs to understand the importance of domestic violence. Many gays believe that domestic violence only occurs in the "heterosexual world" and therefore that gays are immune. Gay male domestic violence is quite prevalent and needs to be openly addressed. Island and Letellier (1991a) proposed that gay newspapers and gay leaders and politicians "speak out" and condemn gay domestic violence.

Prevention and treatment strategies should include a variety of services to gay male victims. Such strategies include information concerning domestic violence; referrals (therapists, health care providers, legal services, etc.); twenty-four-hour hotlines; long-term support services, and individual and group counseling (Island and Letellier, 1991a).

The availability of therapy is critical in the treatment of the victim. A distinction must be made, however, between effective and ineffective therapy. Effective therapy includes individual or group counseling or a combination of the two. Couple's counseling is considered by most experts to be ineffective for domestic violence treatment (Farley, 1985; Island and Letellier, 1991a; Reed, 1989; Sonkin and Durphy, 1989; Walber, 1988). Unfortunately, judges frequently order couple's counseling as a means to reduce violence and seek treatment for the parties. Due to stereotyping, the courts often assume that because two men are involved in the dispute, there is equal power in the relationship. The presumption is not only unproductive but dangerous. Victims often fear reprisal from the batterer and thus may be reluctant to participate openly during the counseling session. In other words, as a result of any comments made during those sessions, the victim may be placed in direct physical and emotional jeopardy. Furthermore, violence may actually intensify. For proper counseling to occur, the therapist (or other social service professional) must have the requisite formal training, should be sensitive to gay issues and concerns (not necessarily be gay himself or herself), should possess extensive knowledge pertaining to domestic violence, should not be treating the batterer, must be supportive of victims of domestic violence, and must not have a sexual interest in the parties involved (Island and Letellier, 1991a).

Group counseling serves the needs of both the victim and the abuser. For the abused, group counseling provides a place for victims to meet other victims to allow a free exchange of ideas. Group counseling also provides victims emotional support that may reduce the victim's feelings of isolation (Island and Letellier, 1991a).

The batterer will also benefit from group counseling. Group counseling is designed to assist the batterer in understanding that he is accountable for his actions and that his behavior has a direct (and indirect) impact on others. For example,

group therapy is effective because it forces perpetrators to break through their denial and own responsibility for their behavior. . . . With gay men and lesbians, the group format aids in confronting any denial regarding same-sex battering. It also provides a safe environment to explore the other issues . . . that may exacerbate their behavior. (Purdy and Nickle, in Farley, 1981, pp. 235–236).

Whether one uses individual or group therapy, the central theme—healing—remains the same. For the victim, the healing process begins with the recognition of gay domestic violence. Once this is accomplished, the victim must terminate the relationship immediately. Although difficult, it is essential. Island and Letellier (1991a) outlined the steps necessary for leaving an abusive partner: "(1) Admit that you are being abused; (2) start telling people about the violence; (3) find a safe-space; (4) develop a 'mental map'; (5) pack a bag; (6) get a post office box; (7) open your own bank account and (8) leave, leave, leave" (pp. 128–129).

The batterer must come to terms with his behavior and accept full responsibility for his actions. He must understand that his behavior is not only socially repulsive but illegal. The batterer must recognize that blaming others will no longer be tolerated, and he needs to develop new behavior patterns if the treatment and healing processes are to be effective.

FUTURE TRENDS AND RECOMMENDATIONS

According to Island and Letellier (1991a), "The gay male community, comprised of at least 12 million American males, a population roughly equal to the entire continent of Australia, must now contend with its own domestic violence" (p. 276). It is estimated that a "gay man is abused by his lover every 90 seconds" (Island and Letellier, 1991a, p. 266). In the East Bay area of San Francisco, the Gay Men's Domestic Violence Project receives about 400 calls annually concerning domestic related issues (Senk, 1995). Although these statistics appear alarming, same-sex domestic violence will likely increase unless needed attention is devoted to this topic.

It is strongly recommended that:

1. Legislation should expand the language of domestic violence laws to ensure equal representation of victims, including gender- and sexual-orientation-neutral terminology.

2. Resources—including information concerning gay domestic violence, referrals, hotlines, long- and short-term support, safe houses (places where a victim can stay at a location unknown to the abuser), shelters, and individual and group counseling—should be made available to the entire gay community (including lower-income gays, gay people of color, and gay youth).

3. Training and education concerning gay domestic violence issues should be required for all medical and health-care personnel as well as legal and social services personnel.

4. Police agencies should incorporate education and training via academy, in-service programs, and standard operating procedure manuals explaining proper methods of handling gay domestic disputes. Prosecutors should prosecute domestic violence cases and judges should issue restraining orders and avoid sentence disparity based on gender and sexual orientation. Perhaps a team of specially trained judges could be assembled to handle domestic violence cases, similar to that recently incorporated in Washington, DC (Miller, 1996).

5. The gay community must be prepared to discuss same-sex domestic violence openly. Communication can be made through supportive politicians, gay newspapers, and gay clubs. The signs for AIDS awareness reading "Silence = Death" may also be applicable to domestic violence.

6. Services should be made available to the abuser, including support groups and counseling.

CONCLUSION

Little attention has been devoted to male-to-male domestic violence. Domestic violence is not isolated to the heterosexual community. Gay men are being victimized in record numbers. Victimization includes physical, sexual, and psychological threats and assaults, isolation, economic sanctions, heterosexist control, and vandalism. Within the gay community, victimization is complicated by homophobia, HIV and AIDS, and racism.

Research has revealed that gay male batterers come from all socioeconomic, racial and ethnic, educational. occupational, and religious backgrounds. Age, size, and strength are not valid battery-prediction indicators. Some shared characteristics among batterers include denial of violence and responsibility, victim blaming, failure to develop close friendships, violent temper, low self-esteem, poor communication skills, insecurity, jealousy, deceitfulness, and emotional dependency toward the victim. While batterers may be under the influence of drugs or alcohol, the contributory effects remain debatable. A number of theories shed light on the behavior of batterers, including the social learning theory, the developmental theory, the communication theory, and the sociopolitical theory.

Common characteristics of the victim include anger toward the partner, withdrawal, lack of trust, fear, self-blame, frustration, depression, low self-esteem and self-worth, and feeling "trapped" in the relationship. Codependency is an inappropriate label when profiling domestic violence. To better understand domestic violence, Walker's Cycle of Violence was addressed.

Strategies to prevent and treat gay male domestic violence include either legislative or public and private action; components of such action include governmental intervention, education and training, better arrest procedures, judicial discretion, restraining orders, media attention referrals, support, and counseling. Future research needs to be conducted and should include quantitative studies that may shed light into the dark closet that remains.

EDITORIAL SUMMARY

Male-to-male gay domestic violence is a new area of study. Historically, scholars explored traditional heterosexual relationships within intimate violence research. Studies that did examine gay violence concentrated exclusively on "gay bashing." Because little is known about gay domestic violence, its definition remains vague. This chapter defines violence between intimate male partners as any acts of control, including physical and psychological threats or injury, isolation, economic deprivation, sexual abuse, and destruction of property. Most states define domestic violence in gender-specific terms, focusing on heterosexual couples. Thus, male gay domestic violence does not legally exist.

Although there are no specific traits that clearly identify batterers, common characteristics are shared among these perpetrators. Batterers may have low self-esteem and communication problems and may feel a sense of loss of control over their lives. Alcohol, drug abuse, and jealousy are also often found among many gay batterers.

The cycle of violence theory developed to explain wife abuse could be applied to gay domestic violence as well. Victims experience three stages of violence: the tension-building stage, the acute battering state, and the calm stage. The cycle helps explain why victims remain in violent relationships.

Private and public action is necessary to minimize and treat this neglected problem. One approach to reduce gay domestic violence is through education. Awareness is vital in recognizing the problem as well as its treatment.

REFERENCES

Amaro, H., Fried, L., Cabral, H., and Zuckerman, B. (1990). Violence during pregnancy and substance use. *American Journal of Public Health, 80*(5), 575–579.

Barrett, D. C. (1993). *The Influence of Multiple Identities on the Health Behavior of Gay Men.* Unpublished doctoral dissertation, Indiana University.

Beattie, M. (1987). *Codependent No More.* New York: Harper and Row.

Bernard, J., and Bernard, M. (1984). The abusive male seeking treatment: Jekyll and Hyde. *Family Relations, 33,* 543–547.

Blumenfeld, W. J. (1992). *Homophobia: How We All Pay the Price.* Boston: Beacon Press.

Buikhuisen, W., Van Der Plas-Korenhoff, C., and Bontekoe, E. H. M. (1988). In T. E. Moffit and S. A. Mednick (Eds.), *Biological Contributions to Crime Causation* (pp. 261–276). Dordrecht, Netherlands: Martinus Nijhoff.

Byrne, D. (1996). Clinical models for the treatment of gay male perpetrators of domestic violence. *Journal of Gay and Lesbian Social Services, 4*(1), 102–116.

Campbell, J. (1995). *Assessing Dangerousness: Violence by Sexual Offenders, Batterers, and Child Abusers*. Newbury Park, CA: Sage.

Centers for Disease Control. (1993, February). *HIV/AIDS Surveillance Report*. Atlanta: U.S. Department of Health and Human Services.

Coleman, D., and Straus, M. (1983). Alcohol abuse and family violence. In E. Gottheil, K. A. Druley, T. E. Skoloda, and H. M. Waxman (Eds.), *Alcohol, Drug Abuse and Aggression* (pp. 104–124). Springfield, IL: Charles C Thomas.

Crowe, A. H. (1995, August). Stopping terrorism at home. *State Government News*, 18–22.

Dutton, D. (1988). Profiling of wife assaulters: Preliminary evidence for a trimodal analysis. *Violence and Victims, 3*(1) 5–29.

Elliott, P. (1996). Shattering illusions: Same-sex domestic violence. In C. Renzetti and C. Miley (Eds.), *Violence in Gay and Lesbian Domestic Partnerships* (pp. 1–8). New York: Haworth Press.

Farley, N. (1985). *Not a Myth, a Fact: An Overview of Same-Sex Domestic Violence*. Unpublished master's thesis. Norwich University, Northfield, VT.

Farley, N. (1996). A survey of factors contributing to gay and lesbian domestic violence. In C. Renzetti and C. Miley (Eds.), *Violence in Gay and Lesbian Domestic Partnerships* (pp. 35–42). New York: Haworth Press.

Frank, P. (1989). *Domestic Abuse Couple Counseling Policy Statement*. New York: Volunteer Counseling Service of Rockland County, Inc.

Geberth, V. (1981, September). Psychological profiling. *Law and Order*, pp. 46–52.

Gottfredson, D., and Gottfredson, S. (1988). Strikes and risks in the prediction of violent criminal behavior. *Violence and Victims, 3*(4), 247–262.

Grau, J., Fagan, J., and Wexler, S. (1984). Restraining orders for battered women: Issues of access and efficacy. *Women and Politics, 4,* 13–28.

Gutierrez, F., and Dworkin, S. (1992). *Counseling Gay Men and Lesbians*. American Association for Counseling and Development.

Hotaling, G., and Sugarman, D. (1986). An analysis of risk markers in husband to wife violence: The current state of knowledge. *Violence and Victims, 1,* 101–124.

Island, D., and Letellier, P. (1991a). *Men Who Beat the Men Who Love Them*. New York: Harrington Park Press.

Island, D. and Letellier, P. (1991b, Spring/Summer). The scourge of domestic violence. *Rainbow Ventures*, pp. 11–14.

Karmen, A. (1990). *Crime Victims: An Introduction to Victimology*. Wadsworth.

Kingston, T. (1996, May 9). Queer domestic violence: The unspoken epidemic. *S.F. Frontiers, 15*(1), 12–14.

Kirby, N. (1994). Love hurts. *British News Magazine Attitude, 1*(3), 46–50.

Letellier, P. (1994a). Gay and bisexual male domestic violence victimization: Challenges to feminist theory and responses to violence. *Violence and Victims, 9*(2), 95–106.

Letellier, P. (1994b, April). Identifying and treating battered gay men. *San Francisco Medicine,* pp. 16–19.

Letellier, P. (1995, March/April/May). Same-sex male battering. *Visions,* p. 8.

Letellier, P. (1996). Twin epidemics: Domestic violence and HIV infection among gay and bisexual men. In C. Renzetti and C. Miley (Eds.) *Violence in Gay and Lesbian Domestic Partnerships* (pp. 69–81). New York: Haworth Press.

Limandri, B., and Sheridan, D. (1995). Prediction of intentional interpersonal violence: An introduction. In J. Campbell (Ed.) *Assessing Dangerousness: Violence by Sexual Offenders, Batterers and Child Abusers* (pp. 1–19). Newbury Park, CA: Sage.

Lundy, S. (Ed.). (1993, Winter). Abuse that dare not speak its name: Assisting victims of lesbian and domestic violence in Massachusetts. *New England Law Review, 20,* 273–311.

Mendez, J. M. (1996). Serving gays and lesbians of color who are survivors of domestic violence. In C. Renzetti and C. Miley (Eds.) *Violence in Gay and Lesbian Domestic Partnerships* (pp. 53–59). New York: Haworth Press.

Merrill, G. S. (1996). Ruling the exceptions: Same-sex battering and domestic violence theory. In C. Renzetti and C. Miley (Eds.), *Violence in Gay and Lesbian Domestic Partnerships* (pp. 9–21). New York: Haworth Press.

Miller, B. (1996, November 5). Domestic violence gets new priority in district. *Washington Post,* p. B3.

Muraskin, R., and Roberts, A. (1996). *Visions for Change: Crime and Justice in the Twenty-First Century.* Upper Saddle River, NJ: Prentice Hall.

Peterson, J. L., and Marin, G. (1988). Issues in the prevention of AIDS among black and Hispanic men. *American Psychologist, 43,* 871–877.

Purdy, F. and Nickle, N. (1981). Practice principles for helping men who batter. In N. Farley (Ed.) *Not a Myth: An Overview of Same-Sex Domestic Violence.* Unpublished master's thesis, Norwich University, Northfield, VT.

Reed, J. (1989, April 16–22). Naming and confronting gay male battering. *Gay Community News,* pp. 8–10.

Reid, S. (1995). *Criminal Law.* Upper Saddle River, NJ: Prentice Hall.

Renzetti, C. (1992). *Violent Betrayal: Partner Abuse in Lesbian Relationships.* Newbury Park, CA: Sage.

Roberts, A. (1988). Substance abuse among men who batter their mates: The dangerous mix. *Journal of Substance Abuse Treatment, 5,* 83–87.

Rouse, L. (1984). Models, self-esteem, and locus of control as factors contributing to spouse abuse. *Victimology, 9*(1), 130–141.

Saunders, D. (1995). Prediction of wife assault. In J. Campbell (Ed.), *Assessing Dangerousness: Violence by Sexual Offenders, Batterers and Child Abusers* (pp. 68–95). Newbury Park, CA: Sage.

Senk, A. S. (1995, January 9). New law recognizes lesbian, gay abuse. *Contra Costa Times,* p. 3A.

Sherman, L., and Berk, R. (1984). The specific deterrent effects of arrest for domestic assault. *American Psychological Review, 49,* 261–272.

Smith, B. (1994, September 29). When the hand that holds you in public hurts you in private. *S.F. Frontiers,* pp. 12–14.

Sonkin, D., and Durphy, M. (1989). *Learning to Live without Violence.* San Francisco, CA: Gay Community News Volcano Press.

Stalans, L., and Lurigio, A. (1995). Responding to domestic violence against women. *Crime and Delinquency,* pp. 387–398.

Statsky, W. (1985). *Legal Thesaurus/Dictionary.* New York: West.

Tuller, D. (1994, January 3). When gays batter their partners. *San Francisco Chronicle,* pp. A1, A8.

Walber, E. (1988). *Behind Closed Doors: Battering and Abuse in the Lesbian and Gay Community.* Washington, DC: National Lesbian and Gay Health Foundation.

Walker, L. (1979). *The Battered Woman.* New York: Harper and Row.

Witzer, E. (1993). Seeing the invisible victims: Domestic violence in lesbian relationships: A guide for judges and others in the legal community. In S. E. Lundy (Ed.), Abuse that dare not speak its name: Assisting victims of lesbian and gay domestic violence in Massachusetts. *New England Law Review, 20,* 273–311.

8

Lesbian Battering: The Other Closet

Nicky Ali Jackson, Ph.D.
Purdue University Calumet

Although the issue of lesbian battering is a relatively new field of study, it is not a new phenomenon. Historically, domestic violence research focused on traditional heterosexual marital relationships. Subsequently, scholars expanded research on spousal abuse to violence among nonmarried populations: dating and cohabiting couples. Interest in intimate violence is clear given the vast amount of scholarly literature and media coverage dedicated to the topic. Little attention, however, has been given to homosexual battering, in part due to a homophobic society. If studied, gays are recognized as a legitimate population that threatens a proheterosexual nation.

Another explanation for the scant research on same-sex battering lies within the gay community. Homosexuals maintain a private, secluded lifestyle. This is evident in major cities where there is a large concentration of homosexuals residing in a specific area, creating a unique subculture. Whether their isolation is by choice or is unintentional, the impact remains the same. Their separation from mainstream society results in misconceptions and low tolerance of their community. Information, often distorted, is provided to outsiders by external forces such as the media and schools rather than through personal contacts. Homophobia, isolation, and misperceptions lead to difficulty in studying the gay population, particularly lesbians. It is difficult if not impossible for many lesbians to recognize abuse taking place within their own relationships (Island and Letellier, 1991). Females are viewed as nurturing, compassionate, compliant, and passive, so how could they be involved in aggressive behavior? Lesbians and outsiders often deny the existence of abuse in these relationships. When there are

181

"recognizable" scars such as bruises, cuts, and scratches requiring medical attention, nurses and physicians ask, How did he hurt you? and Has he hurt you before? The assumption has been made and typically is left sealed within the doctor's office. No one would or could believe that the perpetrator was the victim's female lover. Skepticism about the existence of female batterers remains.

Hoping to bring light to a subject often left in the dark, scholars began examining lesbian violence in the mid-1980s (Coleman, 1990; Kelly and Warshafsky, 1987; Renzetti, 1988). Although research is limited, its message is clear: lesbian violence is as much a problem as heterosexual violence. Therefore, lesbians should be given similar consideration as heterosexual women in crisis.

HISTORICAL RECOGNITION OF LESBIAN BATTERING

Women's organizations have assisted heterosexual women bring their plight to a national forum. Their work has enabled battered women to achieve emotional, financial, and legal support. Proponents of the women's movement, however, did little if anything to help recognize lesbian battering. Much of the women's movement is rooted in the notion that sexism prevails in the United States. How, then, could the women's movement explain males as victims and females as perpetrators? The best solution seems to have been simply to ignore the homosexual community. Advocacy groups, shelters, and other institutions understood the connection between violence and power and intimidation among battered women and their abusers. Whether out of ignorance or intention, that same connection would not be made concerning lesbian couples. As stated earlier, lesbians must share responsibility in the lack of education and concern for their own victims. A sense of denial prevails among the lesbian community. Lesbians have difficulty believing that a woman could possibly be physically and emotionally abusive, particularly to another woman. It is understood that when females are violent, it is to protect themselves from harm. Self-defense is the only acceptable explanation.

The publication of *Naming the Violence: Speaking Out about Lesbian Battering* (Lobel, 1986), in which lesbians disclose their intimate experiences, helped establish awareness among the gay community. One battered lesbian describes her battering situation as follows:

> We were together for two years. The abuse began early on, though I didn't know enough then to make such a connection. Though a Lesbian Feminist activist for years at that point, I still thought of battering as, first, a male-against-female act, and second, as being a physically violent act. I had no concept of what emotional, psychological and spiritual abuse was about.
> Like many battered people, I didn't see it coming. And if I had had a sense about what lay ahead, I was far too ignorant to call it what it was. After all, we were in love and we were intelligent women of high political consciousness (whatever that means). . . . She didn't seem to value my opinions much and had little trust in my intellect. . . . [In our] first fight (a yelling match) . . . she told me that if I was so insulted and felt that I was being treated so badly, I could leave. I took her apartment key off my key ring, left it on the bed

and headed for the door. . . . In the following two years, I tried to walk out on her many times; each time the attempt was met with physical violence or threats of suicide.

The physical abuse I endured ranged from pushing and being restrained against my will to slaps and a tackle which produced a back injury that left me in pain for several months." (Cecere, in Lobel, 1986, pp. 23–25)

DEFINITIONS OF ABUSE

Domestic violence has typically been categorized as a male-female phenomenon. Abuse may occur in any intimate relationship; it is not gender specific. This point must be made absolutely clear. Abuse cuts across all socioeconomic, racial, religious, and age groups. Although it is present in all populations, its definition remains arbitrary. As with their heterosexual counterparts, lesbians experience physical, verbal, emotional, and sexual assaults. According to the early researchers in family violence, Murray Straus and Richard Gelles, "[v]iolence is defined as an act carried out with the intention, or perceived intention, of causing physical pain or injury to another person" (1990, p. 76). Drawing from their Conflict Tactics Scale (CTS), behaviors that are considered physically abusive include:

1. Throwing something at her

2. Pushing or grabbing her

3. Slapping her

4. Kicking, biting, or hitting her

5. Beating her

6. Choking her

7. Using a knife or gun against her

Physical abuse is often preceded by other forms of abuse, particularly emotional and verbal abuse. Emotional abuse may not leave physical scars, yet its effects are just as harmful. There is a belief shared by victims and perpetrators that the initial acts of aggression are "soft forms" of abuse in that there is no real danger of injury. All forms of abuse are equally potent. It has been suggested that emotional injury will occur once physical battering has been perpetrated upon the victim (Walker, 1979). Clearly, emotional abuse is present with the onset of physical battering; yet they may exist independently. Emotional abuse is more difficult to identify than physical abuse. As a result, it appears to be "noninjurious" to the victim and perpetrator. Furthermore, due to its lack of visibility, victims, offenders, and criminal justice agencies are often unaware of the existing damage.

Emotional abuse will be defined as any form of mistreatment, including neglect: withholding money and other resources, withholding love and affection, and staying away from her lover for any unanticipated time. A common type of emotional abuse is seen in forms of threatening behavior. These include threats to leave her; hit her; cut off her funds; expose her partner's sexual orientation to family, peers, coworkers, and so forth; and kill her. Verbal abuse (e.g., insults, name calling, swearing, and screaming) also results in psychological harm. The aggressive partner uses these techniques as a method of control and intimidation.

Sexual abuse is the "most understudied topic in same-sex domestic violence" (Elliott, 1996, p. 4). One explanation for this is the sensitivity of the subject matter. It is difficult enough for heterosexual women to disclose sexual victimization, so imagine the fear lesbians face sharing similar personal information to a homophobic society or their own community in denial. Sexual abuse occurs in many forms. A lesbian forcing her partner into unwanted sexual activity (oral sex, fondling, penetration) is in fact engaging in deviate sexual conduct. Other types of sexual abuse include withholding sex as a form of punishment, making negative comments about her partner's physical appearance or sexual performance, and forcing her partner to watch or engage in pornographic materials.

Whether the assault is physical, emotional and verbal, or sexual, its roots are the same: power. The perpetrator hungers for power over her victim. But what is power? Power is the ability to coerce another person to engage in behaviors to which they object. Who are the powerful? The powerful are those who have greater social, political, and economic resources than others. Drawing on Marx's conflict theory, the powerful are those with economic means. Marx suggests that with wealth, an individual gains social and political power. In a "traditional" heterosexual household, the male is head of the household because he is either the sole economic provider or earns a higher income than his wife. Those with greater economic assets believe that they are entitled to be the primary, if not sole, decision makers. This may hold true in lesbian households as well. The female bringing forth greater resources perceives herself as dominant, head of household. Thus, in lesbian relationships, inequality may not be rooted in gender but rather in socioeconomic status.

OVERVIEW OF THE RESEARCH IN THE FIELD

There has been relatively little scholarly research conducted on the topic of lesbian battering. Only since the late 1970s have social scientists begun to examine homosexual relationships as a source of violence. Most studies on homosexual violence focus on "gay bashing." As with most scholarly research, female violence has typically been ignored, drawing on the perception that females are less violent than males. Although it is true that females engage in fewer violent acts than males, they are engaging in more serious assaults than in previous years.

Most research on lesbian battering is limited to local gay and lesbian publications. Scholars, publishing in academic journals, have had to recruit most of their subjects from these same publications. The rate of lesbian battering appears to be similar to heterosexual violence. "Preliminary studies show that 22% to 46% of all lesbians have been in a physically violent, same-sex relationship" (Elliott, 1996, p. 2). Coleman

(1990) studied ninety lesbian couples and found approximately 47% of the sample had engaged in some violence. Bologna, Waterman, and Dawson (1987) found

> about 26% of their respondents reported having been subjected to at least one act of sexual violence; 59.8% had been victims of physical violence; and 81% had experienced verbal or emotional abuse. At the same time, 68% of the respondents reported that they had both used violence against their current or most recent partner and had been victimized by a partner. (Renzetti, 1992, p. 18)

Renzetti (1988), using a twelve-page questionnaire completed by 100 lesbians, found that

> 65% of the respondents maintained their relationship with the partner who battered them for 1 to 5 years, 77% reported that the first abusive incident occurred less than 6 months after the start of the relationship. Almost all (89%) had experienced their first incident of abuse by the time the relationship was 23 months old. Slightly more than half the sample (54%) experienced more than 10 abusive incidents during the course of the relationship while 74% experienced at least 6 or more. In total, 71% stated that the battering grew progressively worse over time. (pp. 388–389)

Research on lesbian battering will help gain recognition to this neglected population as well as legitimize these intimate partnerships. As with all forms of domestic violence, lesbian abuse will be more prevalent than anticipated. Reporting practices will change in that more women will be cognizant of the problem and less fearful in finding support and guidance. Furthermore, more resources may be generated for these victims once this problem has been legitimized. As with all battered women, research helps alleviate stigma and shame placed on victims. It also reduces tolerance of violence. Thus, researchers must continue in their exploration of lesbian victimization.

CORRELATES OF ABUSE

The family is one of the most stratified institutions in the United States. Each member holds a unique position determined by age, gender, skills, and resources. Lesbian households are no different. Each partner has a distinct status resulting in a hierarchy. Although our society has declared a war on inequality, it continues to exist. The individual with power believes that she has the right to achieve and maintain authority. "Distribution of the limited resources of the family—energy, creativity, time, and economic assets to name a few—are determined by those most powerful in the hierarchy" (Lobel, 1986, p. 175). Americans have certain norms by which their lives are guided. Norms are based on one's status. Among family members, it is accepted as well as expected that the head of household doles out punishment to rule violators. Punishment is used and often tolerated, giving the dominant member a great deal of discretionary power.

So, what influences a lesbian to batter her lover? Causation is not being addressed here. Social scientists posit that an individual cannot cause certain behavior nor can any factor cause someone to behave violently. Rather, there may be a relationship between two or more variables working together that increases the probability of perpetration and victimization. Lesbians encounter various sources of conflict in their relationships, such as age differences and unique value systems. Age differences, often referred to as generation gaps, may lead to different aesthetic tastes, varying goals and aspirations, and different levels of energy. This is not to suggest that older women have less energy than younger women. Rather, age and body changes may at times restrict certain activities. Age differences also create unequal ranking in the household. The older female is viewed as the dominant figure due to her life experiences and her greater economic resources.

Another source of strain is unique value systems. Not all lesbians share similar values. Each has been socialized by separate agents of socialization: her family of orientation, peers, schools, and other agents. When there are discrepancies on decision-making issues each woman, drawing from her personal experiences, tends to believe that her way is the correct one. "If we thought that other values were better, we would change the ones we have" (Clunis and Green, 1993, p. 151).

Social class differences can also create problems in lesbian relationships. When one partner was raised in a different socioeconomic background than her lover, views on work, education, and the future may be contradictory and may result in conflict. Each woman once again views her way of life as the right way, leaving little room for tolerance. Regardless of the source of conflict, a host of other factors contribute to lesbian battering. Renzetti (1992) suggested the following as correlates of abuse: jealousy, dependency, substance abuse, and intergenerational transfer.

Jealousy

Jealousy is the resentment and envy an individual feels toward others. The jealous individual behaves in ways in which she normally would not. An individual may be jealous of her partner's friends, family, and occupation. Jealousy takes on many forms. Typically, jealousy rolls over to other dimensions of one's life. For example, a woman feeling threatened by the closeness her lover has with her parents and siblings may then feel threatened by her lover's friends as well. Jealousy is rooted in fear. Fear of losing a partner to another creates resentment, shame, and guilt. Possessiveness is often the consequence of jealousy. The fallacy that a partner who demonstrates her jealousy must truly love her because she fears losing her is in reality losing control. Her partner is then viewed as a possession, not an independent, creative, productive woman. It is also a myth to believe that a partner who attempts to control her lover's actions, appearance, thoughts, and values is able to keep her partner from straying. It becomes a self-fulfilling prophecy. The battered lesbian will resent her abuser and detach herself from her lover. The detachment may mean breaking off the relationship or separating herself emotionally from her lover while remaining in the relationship. In either scenario, she has been abandoned.

Dependency

In many intimate violent relationships, codependency exists between abuser and victim. This dependency may be aggravated in lesbian relationships due to the need to be isolated from the heterosexual community. "Research with lesbians involved in intimate relationships shows them to have a higher level of dyadic attachment or commitment to their partners than do gay men, and, in some studies, than do heterosexual partners" (Renzetti, 1992, p. 30). There is an expectation of understanding, compassion, and empathy shared among lesbians. These perceptions help alienate lesbians from other groups, but it also leaves lovers socially and emotionally isolated, enhancing vulnerability. When individuals are separated from society, resentment and anger are directed toward the source of their isolation: being a lesbian in a homophobic society.

Females are taught from childhood to be nurturing. They are socialized to identify primarily with their familial role. Little importance is placed on a woman's career. Her primary purpose for existence is to be the caregiver of the family. She identifies with her master statuses: wife, mother, or both. The problem becomes exaggerated when both partners are females, placing themselves wholly in the relationship, disregarding outside influences. The women become enmeshed, unable to concentrate on other aspects of their lives. Women have struggled for independence, self-identity, and self-worth. It is essential for women, gay or straight, to achieve these goals. One way is to acknowledge other vital statuses women possess. Not to minimize the importance of spouse and parent, there is much more to a woman than these two parts.

Substance Abuse

Scholars have suggested that substance abuse is related to domestic violence. Many batterers do consume alcohol, drugs, or both, but it is not the consumption of these narcotics which causes an individual to behave violently. Rather, alcohol and drug usage may serve as a trigger for violence. Unfortunately, such use is often given as an excuse for aggressive behavior. Regardless, substance abuse is often present in domestic violence cases. Renzetti (1992) argued that alcoholism is prevalent within the lesbian community. She offers the following explanations:

- Lesbians live in areas that are geographically surrounded by bars.
- Homophobia and the oppression of lesbians creates a sense of isolation, which is associated with alcohol consumption.
- The female anatomy attributes to greater impairment upon consumption of alcohol. "Women have less of a stomach enzyme that helps the digestion of alcohol before it passes into the bloodstream. As a result, more alcohol goes into women's bloodstreams even if women drink the same amount as men relative to body size, causing them to get drunk faster" (Renzetti, 1992, p. 63).

There is a tendency to excuse an individual from certain behaviors when alcohol or drugs are involved. It is easier to suggest that the abuser was not herself. A victim argues that the drugs took over her lover's mental capacity. An abuser argues that the alcohol or drugs caused her to behave aggressively. Regardless of the rationale, victims and offenders confuse excuses with acceptance of violence. It is imperative to change societal attitudes regarding alcohol and drug consumption. The substance does not cause the violence; it simply enhances the vulnerability to become violent.

Intergenerational Transfer

Researchers often turn to the possibility that violence is learned by children through watching their parents. Attributing factors of domestic violence to background factors is called the generational theory. This theory argues that living in a violent home increases the probability that an individual will grow up to be violent toward future family members. The family may actually serve as a breeding ground for violent behavior. The teaching of violence occurs mostly without such an intention. Children learn many lessons in relation to physical violence. Straus (1979) outlines several unintentional lessons learned:

- Those who love you the most are also those who hit you.
- Violence can be and should be used to secure positive ends; this reinforces the moral rightness of violence.
- Violence is permissible when other things do not work.

Thus, people learn to associate love with violence and to believe that violence may be necessary at times. Violence is not innate; it is learned through socialization. "Aggressive behavior is learned and is acquired through direct experience (trial and error), by observing the behavior of others (modeling) or in both ways" (Straus and Gelles, 1990, p. 441).

Research on intergenerational transfer may be applied to lesbian couples. Regardless of sexual orientation, children who grew up in violent homes are more vulnerable to violent intimate relationships than those who did not grow up in such surroundings. Homosexuals are not immune from learning aggressive behavior. Victims learn to blame themselves for their own victimization. They learn to be compliant and submissive. Perpetrators, on the other hand, learn techniques to maintain control over their partners. Each believes that this is acceptable behavior.

CHARACTERISTICS OF OFFENDERS AND VICTIMS

A woman possesses certain characteristics that increase her likelihood of perpetration and victimization. Profiling serves as a guideline; it is not definitive. Offenders and victims may share all or none of the identifiable traits. Recognizing these traits helps us identify signs of vulnerability as well as options for prevention. So, who are the offenders, and who their victims?

Abuse cuts across all racial, ethnic, socioeconomic, religious, age, and gender groups. Certain individuals, however, are more susceptible than others. Lesbian batterers may possess the following characteristics:

- Greater economic, social, and personal power. They have the ability to control their victim through threats of denying resources.
- Severe bouts of jealousy and possessiveness. The abuser, out of fear of loss of control, attempts to isolate her lover from her family and friends. A narcissist,

she craves full attention from her partner. Sharing her with others draws away from the abuser's focus.
- Experienced or observed childhood victimization. They learned that to gain compliance, physical and emotional injury may be necessary.
- Low self-esteem. Women who feel a sense of powerlessness and failure may project their own inward anger and frustration onto those they care for the most, their lovers.
- A job loss or other stressful event. Stress does not cause the actual acute battering incident, but rather serves as a stimulant. A major loss in one's life may result in anger, frustration, and futility. Hopelessness may lead to atypical behavior. The abuser wants her partner to suffer as she is suffering; this gives her a temporary feeling of control.
- Overconsumption of alcohol or drugs. Recall that substance abuse does not cause violence. It often masks as a defense against inappropriate behavior. People often engage in fantasy rather than reality. They use the alcohol and drugs as a method of escaping culpability.

Just as batterers share certain qualities, victims also possess characteristics that place them at risk. Profiling victim characteristics does not suggest that victims are to blame for their own victimization; it only serves as a method of better understanding who is in potential danger. The following traits increase the likelihood of lesbian victimization:

- A sense of powerlessness. They believe that they have no control over their lives.
- Experienced or observed childhood victimization. Childhood exposures to violence teach children that it is acceptable for the dominant members of the household to use physical and emotional sanctions to gain compliance from others.
- Low self-esteem. They believe that they deserve to be punished; if they had some value then there would be no reason for bad things to happen to them.
- Economic and social dependency on their partners. These victims rely heavily on their lovers to provide resources and companionship, which often leads to isolation and despair.

Victimization is a process. Where there is physical violence, there are events leading to the actual battering incident. In situations of emotional abuse, there is a pattern of inappropriate behavior. For example, a lover who calls her partner "stupid" will repeatedly demean and humiliate her; it is not an isolated occurrence. Lesbian victims, as with their heterosexual counterparts, suffer greatly from physical, emotional, and sexual abuse. "[B]attered lesbians experience nightmares, brief disassociative episodes, and excessive fear in situations that trigger an association to the abuse" (Hammond, 1989, p. 91). Victims also suffer from shame, helplessness, guilt, social withdrawal, sleep disorders, eating disorders, and anxiety.

Physical and psychological injury lasts for years, often a lifetime. The long-term effects can be devastating. If a victim does escape her abusive relationship, it will be extremely difficult for her to learn to trust again, which can damage potential future intimate relations. For this reason, it is essential that she receive assistance to cope with her victimization. In addition, her abuser must seek out help to understand and recognize her abusive behavior.

PREVENTION AND TREATMENT

To reduce lesbian battering, it is essential to study homosexuality. Currently, few programs are available to lesbian victims. Programs that do exist are located in large urban areas and are operated by members of the gay community. The following suggested factors may help minimize violence in these partnerships.

The most vital tool in assisting lesbian victims is to recognize their cultural needs and practices. Awareness of the gay subculture is key in identifying potential abusers and victims. Scholars must closely examine the lesbian relationship. As with their heterosexual counterparts, each lesbian relationship varies in intensity and duration. Living in a homophobic society puts unique pressures on lesbians that in turn influence their attitudes and behaviors.

Public perceptions regarding homosexuality must change. The United States encourages freedom and equality to its members. Somehow lost in this philosophy, however, are gay and lesbian communities. Americans fear homosexuality. Many fear that if they let their children play with children of gay parents, then their children will learn to accept homosexuality and maybe even become gay. These irrational fears stem from misunderstanding and lack of education.

Lesbians must also take part in helping others understand their culture. Their world is not vastly different from the heterosexual culture, and both communities must realize this situation. Gay women need to interact with heterosexual men and women. Isolation results in anger and indignation. More important is that alienation feeds into homophobia. Currently, many lesbians live in areas primarily occupied by other same-sex couples. Those who do live and work in heterosexual communities often fear disclosure. It is essential that these women feel comfortable in a heterosexual society. Each population must be tolerant and accepting of their differences. Assimilation is necessary in a healthy, productive society.

Lesbian victims stay in their relationships for many of the same reasons other battered women do. As in heterosexual violence, lesbians fear condemnation upon disclosing their secrets to family and friends. "Ironically, lesbians may be more tempted to blame other lesbians than they are heterosexual women for victimization experiences" (Hammond, 1989, p. 98). There is a sense of betrayal felt by victims from those who should best understand them and their situations. Those who do open up to friends and family are often left feeling shame and guilt. Perhaps family members were correct in judging lesbianism as an aberration. They may say that it is the victim's fault for having placed herself in such an "abnormal" environment. These negative attitudes need to be corrected. Homophobic family members only serve to distance the victim from any real assistance. When seeking help, most lesbian victims will turn to other lesbian friends for support. At times, even their friends will resist believing that there is a problem. Instead of lending support, accusations and excuses regarding aggressive behavior are made. Such behavior clearly hinders any progress.

With little support from family and friends and with love for the abuser, it is understandable that the victim remains in the relationship. Nevertheless, some victims do seek outside assistance and are able to recognize the scope of the problem. At times, these victims will eventually terminate the relationship. Exiting an abusive relationship does not occur simultaneously with the assaults. For this reason, victims and batterers must learn new acceptable techniques of conflict resolution.

Whether the victim seeks support from a therapist, psychologist, or member of the clergy, the following issues should be addressed during therapy (Rothblum and Cole, 1989, pp. 101–103):

- During intake, ask clients about the abuse. Do not, however, directly ask them whether they have been abused. Rather, ask questions such as, "Have you ever been afraid of your lover?" This type of question is not perceived as threatening.
- Assess the extent and severity of abuse. Distinguish between battering and self-defense.
- Assess violent or abusive incidents carefully if there is a question of mutual battering. Identify the batterer and the victim.
- Distinguish, to your clients, between abuse and appropriate assertive behavior.
- Help develop protection plans with clients who face future endangerment.
- Offer free or minimal cost support or networking groups for victims. Victims need to interact with other victims.
- Prior to offering couple's counseling, determine the safety of the victim.
- Be patient and nonjudgmental.
- Clearly reassure the victim that she is not to blame for the abuse.

Heterosexual therapists must be able to determine any prejudgment they have toward lesbians. Their attitudes impact the process as well as the outcome of treatment. Lesbian therapists may also carry stereotypes concerning violence in the lesbian community. They may unintentionally deny the nature and extent of the problem, which results in providing inadequate support. Thus, lesbian therapists must alleviate any stereotypes they possess so as to help women in need better.

Similar to battered wives, lesbian victims need to seek out shelter when placed in danger. Unfortunately, it is not a simple task to receive assistance from shelters. Drawing on tradition, shelters typically provide refuge only to heterosexual women. Feminists have struggled to receive support from the community and fear their work will be undermined in recognizing females as perpetrators of violence. In accepting lesbians into shelters, homophobic staff and residents are ill-equipped to cope with these clients. Moreover, staff and residents are placed in danger of outside attacks from gay bashers. Another problem shelters face is funding. Staff members may fear that resources will be reduced, if not relinquished, if a shelter is known to house lesbian victims.

For these reasons, it has been suggested that lesbians develop their own safety networks. The primary problem in obtaining lesbian shelters is funding. Finances are minimal and staff is limited, making it virtually impossible to operate shelters for lesbian victims legitimately. The first step in allocating resources and locating qualified staff is to change societal attitudes toward homosexuality. Creating separate shelters is not a simple solution, nor should it be necessary; thus, lesbians must feel comfortable in seeking support from battered women's shelters. Staff and volunteers must be trained to understand the needs of lesbian victims better. It "is not the role of abused lesbians to educate domestic violence programs about their plight, but rather the responsibility of the movement to establish consistent programs which meet the special needs of all women," Porat argues (1986, p. 82).

LEGAL ISSUES AND FUTURE TRENDS

Battered lesbians face great resistance in receiving assistance from the legal system. Many criminal justice personnel suffer from homophobia and thus do not consider lesbians' cases serious or even legitimate. It has been a long struggle for heterosexual battered women to achieve recognition, and unfortunately they still do not receive adequate support from the criminal justice system. Law enforcement officers do not take these calls as seriously as other offenses. Part of the problem lies with victims themselves. Police are often familiar with these households. They arrive at the scene and are treated as the enemy rather than ally. They are then placed in an adversarial position rather than viewed as supportive. In cases of lesbian battering, these women have increased opposition in turning to police for help. At times, police officers have harassed members of the gay community, leaving little reason to trust them.

Other agencies have also done little to help gay victims, but "a number of states have recently revised their domestic violence statutes by substituting a term such as household member for the term spouse" (Renzetti, 1992, p. 91). Although some states have made available temporary restraining orders regardless of gender, lesbians are often denied protection from their abusers. "Judges who are otherwise sympathetic to battered women may tend to see all abuse in lesbian relationships as mutual, or may actually provide the batterer with legal protection or legal sanctions over the victim" (Hammond, 1986, p. 96).

CONCLUSION

Lesbians and heterosexuals often deny the existence of lesbian battering. Much of this may be attributed to the perception that females are passive and compliant, not aggressive. Even when there are visible injuries, it is often believed that they were caused by a male perpetrator. The denial of lesbian battering may also be due in part to the women's movement, whose proponents argue that males are the elite and females the powerless group in society. This position contradicts the notion that women too can be intimidating and aggressive.

The scant research on lesbian battering does reveal its similarities to male homosexual domestic violence. Lesbians suffer from emotional, verbal, physical, and sexual abuse as do their heterosexual counterparts. The consequences of victimization do not differ based on one's sexual orientation; its effects are equally damaging. It is essential that we therefore recognize and legitimize these victims.

Battering among lesbians may be related to various factors, such as age differences and value systems. Economic inequality between partners may give one woman greater power over the other. Jealousy, dependency, and substance abuse may be factors in violent lesbian relationships. The generational theory, which posits that behavior is learned from one's family of orientation through observation, helps explain why some women batter while others remain in abusive relationships.

Recognizing certain characteristics of batterers and victims allows for early detection of potentially abusive relationships. Certain personal qualities suggest that a woman may be at greater risk of perpetrating abuse or being victimized by it. To reduce lesbian battering, it is necessary to understand homosexuality better. Public beliefs must be based on fact rather than on false assumptions. Lesbians can take some responsibility in achieving this goal. They should help educate the heterosexual society by being more visible to it. Homosexuals and heterosexuals must work together to reduce violence between intimates, regardless of their sexual orientation.

EDITORIAL SUMMARY

Lesbian battering, although new to research, is not a new phenomena. Gay women have been given little consideration and hope in addressing their intimate victimization. Through future research, society will become more tolerant of homosexuals. Accepting differences in sexual orientation will enable lesbian victims to speak freely about their plight, which in turn will legitimize their situation as well as help them gain needed control. Resources must be available to all victims, not simply to those who comply with heterosexual standards. In addition, safe houses must be provided for lesbians in danger. Within these shelters, staff members need to undergo sensitivity training and be better educated on homosexuality. Laws must change in all states to ensure that lesbian victims are able to seek support from the criminal justice system.

REFERENCES

Bologna, M. J., Waterman, C. K., and Dawson, L. J. (1987). *Violence in Gay Male and Lesbian Relationships: Implications for Practitioners and Policy Makers.* Paper presented at the Third National Conference on Family Violence Research, Durham, NH.

Cecere, D. J. (1986). The second closet: battered lesbians. In K. Lobel (Ed.), *Naming the Violence: Speaking Out about Lesbian Battering.* Seattle: Seal Press.

Clunis, D. M., and Green, G. D. (1993). *Lesbian Couples: Creating Healthy Relationships for the '90s.* Seattle: Seal Press.

Coleman, V. E. (1990). *Violence Between Lesbian Couples: A Between Groups Comparison.* Unpublished doctoral dissertation, University Microfilms International, 9109022.

Elliott, P. (1996). Shattering illusions: Same-sex domestic violence. In C. M. Renzetti and C. H. Miley (Eds.), *Violence in Gay and Lesbian Domestic Partnerships.* Newbury Park, CA: Sage.

Hammond, N. (1986). Lesbian victims and the reluctance to identify abuse. In K. Lobel (Ed.), *Naming the Violence: Speaking Out about Lesbian Battering.* Seattle: Seal Press.

Island, D., and Letellier, P. (1991). *Men Who Beat the Men Who Love Them.* New York: Harrington Park Press.

Kelly, E. E., and Warshafsky, L. (1987). *Partner Abuse in Gay Male and Lesbian Couples.* Paper presented at the Third National Conference on Family Violence Research, Durham, NH.

Lobel, K. (Ed.). (1986). *Naming the Violence: Speaking Out about Lesbian Battering.* Seattle: Seal Press.

Porat, N. (1986). Support groups for battered lesbians. In K. Lobel (Ed.), *Naming the Violence: Speaking Out about Lesbian Battering.* Seattle: Seal Press.

Renzetti, C. M. (1988). Violence in lesbian relationships: A preliminary analysis of causal factors. *Journal of Interpersonal Violence, 3,* 381–399.

Renzetti, C. M. (1992). *Violent Betrayal: Partner Abuse in Lesbian Relationships.* Newbury Park: Sage.

Renzetti, C. M., and Miley, C. H. (Eds.). (1996). *Violence in Gay and Lesbian Domestic Partnerships.* Newbury Park, CA: Sage.

Straus, M. A. (1979). Measuring intrafamily conflict and violence: The conflict tactics scale. *Journal of Marriage and the Family, 41,* 75–88.

Straus, M. A., and Gelles, R. J. (Eds.). (1990). *Physical Violence in American Families.* New Brunswick, NJ: Transaction.

Walker, L. E. (1979). *The Battered Woman.* New York: Harper and Row.

9

Understanding Elder Abuse and Neglect

Jacqueline B. Hill, MSW, MPH, ACSW
Department of Behavioral Sciences
Purdue University Calumet

Shaffdeen A. Amuwo, Ph.D.
Community Health Sciences
School of Public Health
University of Illinois at Chicago

Understanding human behavior and the social environment offers insight into the disengagement process whereby people respond to aging by gradually withdrawing from the various roles and relationships they occupied at other developmental stages during their lifetime. Disengagement theory (Cumming and Henry, 1961) refers not only to the elderly withdrawing from society but also to society withdrawing from the elderly. Disengagement is by no means universal nor inevitable and often serves as a description of relationships among the old and those younger. Societal values about the elderly, the disabled, and ageism contribute to an environment of invisibility to the problem of maltreatment of the elderly. One negative consequence of this process is the slow recognition of the problem by clinicians and other professionals. More than forty states have laws mandating that certain professionals report suspected elder abuse (Fredriksen, 1989). Various departments and units of state government are charged with enforcing of statutes intended to protect the elderly (Wolf and Pillemer, 1994). Authorities, practitioners, and researchers cannot agree on a definition of elder abuse. As a result, coordination of services falters, estimations of incidence and prevalence are unavailable, and explanations of its cause differ. Empirical investigations have been limited by sample size, inconsistent definitions of abuse and effectiveness of interventions, and other methodological issues.

HISTORICAL RECOGNITION OF ELDER ABUSE

Intergenerational conflict is not new. Admonitions to honor one's parents date back to biblical times (e.g., Deuteronomy 21:18–21). Greek mythology describes rebellious sons taking out their rage on fathers (e.g., Uranus and the Titans) in the form of competition. Parricide, the murder of either parent, set the stage for power plays in the Oedipal myth. Parricide was considered the ultimate crime because it undermined the authority of the father and destroyed the family, and was considered so unspeakable that it was not mentioned in the Bible (Foucault, 1975). Anthropologists describe cultures in which structural inequalities and conflicts with the elderly resulted in abandonment or even death (Foner, 1985). In some societies, the elderly were killed to maximize the strength of younger adults (Summner, 1906). Tensions related to property ownership can be seen in eighteenth-century documents shaped by industrialization and economic insecurities of old age. Herr and Weakland (1979) identified power struggles as the resultant dynamic of the stressors of reduced contributions and income of elderly family members.

By consensus, a culture seems to divide life informally into meaningful and useless time frames of what the future holds for certain age groups (Neugarten, 1969). Informal age norms about what people are expected to do are a part of the age structuring of our society. Formal age rules within organizations also dictate at what age people become eligible to accept the rewards of their labor and when they should cease being productive. Retirement often increases anxieties among the elderly and other family members.

As noted, abuse and neglect are phenomena that appear to have been present throughout history. Why, then, has increased interest in maltreatment of the elderly developed? First, there has been tremendous growth in the elderly population. Based on data from the National Center for Health Statistics (1989), in 1900, people over age sixty-five constituted 4% of the U.S. population. By 1988, that proportion was up to 12.4% and by the year 2000, it will be 13%. By the year 2030, it will be 22%. Population aging occurs when birthrates decline. Other reasons include improvements in life expectancy, improved standards of living, and large cohorts such as "baby boomers" who were born at a particular period in time. Such trends shift the age structure and contribute to population aging. Population aging should not be confused with the process of individual aging.

An elder is a person sixty-five years old or older. The young-old elderly, aged sixty-five to seventy-four, the old-old, aged seventy-five to eighty-four, and the oldest-old, those over age eighty-five, are commonly accepted descriptions of the elderly population. The most rapid population increase in the 1990s will be among those eighty-five years of age (Institute of Medicine, 1991). Age sixty-five does not denote uniform decline in physical and psychological functioning. People who reach the age of sixty-five can now expect to live into their eighties (National Center for Health Statistics, 1989). According to Otten (1984), "It is these 'oldest old'—often mentally or physically impaired, alone, depressed—who pose the major problems for the coming decades. It is they who will strain their families with demands for personal care and financial support. It is they who will need more of such community help as Meals on Wheels, homemaker services, special housing" (p. 1).

The reasons for considering age sixty-five as marking the start of old age are mostly social rather than biological. Aging is a subtle, gradual, lifetime process, and there are startling contrasts that mark how individuals age. The process of aging is called senescence. It affects different persons at different rates in various systems of the body.

Gains in life expectancy, or expected years of life from birth, are attributable to the elimination of disease-related premature death and to life-saving and life-preserving technology. It is not likely that these remaining years will be healthy, active, and independent ones. Many of the elderly will become victims of elder abuse.

LEGAL DEFINITIONS OF ELDER ABUSE

Abuse of the elderly gained recognition as a social policy issue in the United States in the 1980s through hearings before the House Select Committee on Aging under the sponsorship of Representatives Claude Pepper and MaryRose Oaker (1981). The hearings resulted in investigations of abuse by congressional staff members and a proposal to create a National Center on Elder Abuse funded by the U.S. Department of Health and Human Services (Quinn and Tomita, 1986). Funding was not appropriated. The center would have conducted research on incidence and prevalence of elder abuse, neglect, and exploitation. Research was already being conducted on community-based populations using retrospective case analysis, interviews with service providers, mailed questionnaires, and telephone interviews (Block and Sinnott, 1979; Lau and Kosberg, 1979; Straus, Gelles, and Steinmetz, 1980).

Elder abuse is more often a social problem than a legal one. In terms of meeting the needs of the elderly, community resources tend to be social services agencies rather than the criminal justice system when intervention is requested. Elder abuse is a sensitive subject, and the elderly person's perception of the situation as abusive or not influences whether and from what source he or she would seek help. Help-seeking patterns among the elderly are often divided into formal and informal sources. Informal sources include family members, clergy, friends, neighbors, and visitors. Formal sources include social workers, medical personnel, law enforcement, and adult protective services.

As agencies and adult protective services searched for definitions to develop intervention strategies to prevent elder abuse, earlier definitions of elder abuse were variants of the child abuse model. Protective services are for adults who are being neglected or abused or for adults whose physical or mental capacities have obviously deteriorated. The aim of protective services is to help the elderly meet their needs in their own homes, if possible. Adult protective service workers recognized the growing phenomenon of maltreatment of the elderly but were operating without consistent classifications of "abuse." Their work was often hampered by the use of subjective definitions using moderate or mild descriptors and the perceptions of the alleged victim. Other problems, including the help-seeking behaviors of the alleged victims of elder abuse, prevented clinicians from establishing procedures for assessing and managing the maltreatment. The definitions of elder abuse used by adult protective services units were generally broad enough to cover a variety of situations but were not clear in terms of degree. Thus, workers were left without clear guidelines regarding what degree of maltreatment constitutes abuse. This in turn could leave the worker with serious unanswered questions about abusive behaviors and outcomes that endanger elderly persons. Alternative placements include foster care, group home care, elderly supervised housing units, and adult day care centers.

The American Medical Association Council on Scientific Affairs estimated in 1987 that 2.5 million elders were abused or neglected. These rates may be underestimated because surveys often miss the very poor, the non–English speaking, those without telephones, and those in hospitals (American Medical Association, 1987). Although health professionals often treat victims of abuse, many in treatment situations fail to suspect abuse (Tilden and Shepherd, 1987; McLeer, Anwar, and Marquiling, 1989; Kurz, 1987; Brewer and Jones, 1989). Training programs for various medical specialties often do not include curricula on family violence (Tilden et al., 1994). Tilden's research included a slightly higher proportion of women than men and whose median year of graduation from their respective professional training was 1977. This period in time was sufficient to include gender issues and the status of women. It also calls into question the effect of mandatory reporting laws and the absence of protocols to treat and report suspected cases of abuse.

DEFINITIONS OF ABUSE AND NEGLECT

Most of the definitions of elder abuse focus on abuse that occurs between caregivers and specific elderly population groups, such as Alzheimer's patients, stroke victims, or persons with dementia (Block and Sinott, 1979; Lau and Kosberg, 1979; Ryden, 1988; Hamel et al., 1990; Paveza et al., 1992). Professionals who work with older adults tend to agree that elder abuse can be described as behavior that includes the infliction of physical and mental pain on an elderly person in an environment that exacerbates the aging process. Other forms of abuse include financial exploitation and withholding food and medical attention as well as unnecessary restraint or overmedication (O'Malley, Segars, Perez, Mitchell, and Knuepfel, 1979; Gioglio and Blakemore, 1983).

Wolf (1986) described definitions of abuse and neglect constructed to evaluate three model projects funded by the Administration on Aging in 1981. The two foci of the research effort were to investigate the nature and causes of elder abuse, its victims, and perpetrators and to compare impact, community response, case resolution, and service approaches in Worcester, Massachusetts; Syracuse, New York; and the state of Rhode Island. Findings of the research categorized elder abuse into several distinct types and established the notion that abusers are less likely than nonabusers to be caregivers under stress. The abuser's psychological state and the interdependence of the abuser and the elderly person suggest that exchange theory may explain some forms of abuse. Families that are more troubled than other families and that contain impaired members may be destabilized by the declining physical and mental health status of the elderly victim.

The categories from this research seem to be the most practical when assessing and planning intervention services for the elderly because they evolved from a case-control study (Pillemer, 1986). The same definitions were used in a stratified random sample of 2020 community-dwelling elderly persons aged sixty-five or older, in the Boston metropolitan area (Pillemer and Finkelhor, 1988).

Abuse

Abuse can be divided into three categories—physical abuse, psychological abuse, and material abuse—defined as follows (Pillemer and Finkelhor, 1988, p. 220):

Physical abuse is the infliction of physical pain or injury or physical coercion (e.g., slapped, bruised, sexually molested, cut, burned, physically restrained).

Psychological abuse is the infliction of mental anguish (e.g., called names, treated as a child, frightened, humiliated, intimidated, threatened, isolated).

Material abuse is the illegal or improper exploitation or use of funds or other resources.

Neglect

Two kinds of neglect are active neglect and passive neglect (Pillemer and Finkelhor, 1988, p. 220):

Active neglect is the refusal or failure to fulfill a caretaking obligation, including a conscious and intentional attempt to inflict physical or emotional stress on the elder (e.g., deliberate abandonment or deliberate denial of food or health-related services).

Passive neglect is the refusal or failure to fulfill a caretaking obligation, excluding a conscious and intentional attempt to inflict physical or emotional distress on the elder (e.g., abandonment or nonprovision of food or health-related services because of inadequate knowledge, laziness, infirmity, or disputes concerning the value of prescribed services).

Explanations of substantiated cases were based on the unhealthy dependence of the victim on the perpetrator and vice versa. Many of the studies previously cited identified abuse and neglect without clear and consistent definitions and degree of maltreatment.

Stress was identified as a contributing factor in most of the research. It was not determined whether or not stress was the antecedent or a consequence of maltreatment. Caregiver burden, disability, and being female were issues in the abused population.

Maltreatment of the elderly can be viewed as both acts of omission (neglect) and commission (abuse). As an intentional act, substantiation has to be made of its frequency, duration, intensity, severity, and consequences. Elder maltreatment includes physical abuse, sexual abuse, emotional abuse, neglect, willful deprivation of food and medical care, and financial exploitation. Surveys of elder abuse have reported interactive behaviors characterized by violence in cases of family members caring for physically and cognitively impaired relatives (Minuchin, Montalvo, Guerney, Rosman, and Schumer, 1967; Pepper and Oaker, 1981; Ryden, 1988; Steinmetz, 1988; Hamel et al., 1990). Any investigation and definition of "caseness" will be guided by each state's definition of behavior that is labeled abusive or neglectful. Abusers are often those in a position of trust, such as family members or other acceptable caregivers (Pillemer and Finkelhor, 1989; Podnieks and Pillemer, 1990).

The types of abuse generally agreed upon by researchers are:

1. Physical: causing or inflicting physical pain or injury
2. Emotional: causing or inflicting mental anguish
3. Sexual: touching or physically forced sexual activities with an older person without consent or understanding
4. Exploitation: the misuse of an older person's resources for financial gain

Neglect includes failure of the caregiver to provide basic necessities of life such as physical care, proper nutrition, medical attention, a safe environment, protection from harm, and freedom from exploitation or profit whereby someone other than the elderly person is enriched.

INDICATORS OF PHYSICAL ABUSE

Indicators of physical abuse include injuries, bone fractures, sexual assault, bruises from binding or restraints, burns, eating disorders, sexually transmitted diseases, spiral fractures, retinal hemorrhages, internal injuries, abrasions, or other unexplained injuries.

Failure to thrive as a phenomenon experienced by older persons appeared in the literature (Quinn and Tomita, 1986; Braun, Wykle, and Cowling, 1988) to alert practitioners to dehydration, malnutrition, and depression as a form of physical abuse and neglect. The term "failure to thrive" was first used in the pediatric literature to describe institutionalized infants who exhibited the symptom complex of "listlessness, relative immobility, quietness, indifferent appetite, failure to gain weight and the appearance of unhappiness" (Bakwin, 1949). In the elderly, cases of failure to thrive can occur in institutions as well as in independent living situations.

INDICATORS OF EMOTIONAL ABUSE

Indicators of emotional abuse include poor sleep habits or fear of sleep, being easily frightened, fears or phobias, agitation when being assisted with toileting or bathing, being overly anxious to please, having anxiety and worry, and having a caretaker who appears to intimidate the elderly person.

OVERVIEW OF OTHER RESEARCH IN THE FIELD

Many research efforts to date on elder abuse have been exploratory, descriptive studies examining specific patterns of abuse among persons sixty years of age or older who live alone, with family members, or with other relatives in the community. Data were gathered using a variety of methods, different sampling techniques, and data collection. The limited agreement on the definition of abuse and neglect makes findings less generalizable than other data. They do, however, uncover regional, cultural, and family characteristics that distinguish elder abuse from other forms of adult abuse.

Research efforts during the 1970s approached the subject from many different perspectives: the victim's, caretakers' stress, life span of the violence, agency interventions, and barriers to service. In the 1980s, research interests shifted from typologies to concepts such as relationships between the caretaker and the older person (Pillemer, 1985) and motivations and circumstances for abuse (Chen, Bell, Dolinsky, Doyle, and Dunn, 1981; Steinmetz, 1983; Giordano and Giordano, 1984; Filinson and Ingman, 1989).

O'Malley et al. (1979) conducted research in Massachusetts in an attempt to provide information on the nature of elder abuse. They defined active neglect as "the deprivation by a caretaker of services, which are necessary for the elderly person to maintain their mental and physical health" (p. 2). Their findings revealed that third-party observers, social workers, nurses, and home-care workers were the informants in cases of abuse 70% of the time. Seventy-five percent of the victims in the study had a mental or physical disability and lived with the abuser. Lau and Kosberg (1979) conducted similar research in Cleveland, Ohio, and discovered that 82% of the abusers were relatives of the victim. Particularly distressing was that one-third of the elderly determined to be abused denied any problem. Hudson and Johnson (1986) reported on the different typologies used in describing "neglect." Other conflicts within the family such as child and spousal abuse are topics of investigation by researchers and social scientists who describe violence within families along a continuum. The recognition of elder abuse has evolved as a result of documentation of the extent of violence across the life span. The life span of violence research hypothesis generated interest in the multidimensional forms of violence in the home and the positioning of vulnerable family members at greater risk of victimization by intimates (Steinmetz, 1983). These concerns and the willingness of states to intervene in family life provided the opportunity to remove maltreatment of the elderly from a family-controlled domain to activities that would investigate and substantiate alleged cases of abuse.

Like other types of family violence, abuse of the elderly is not limited to a single act. It includes acts of omission: behaviors that cause pain and physical injury, isolation, withholding food and medical care, and financial exploitation. It can occur within the privacy of a family, and it can occur in an institutional setting. No single factor has been identified as the cause of elder abuse. Most researchers agree that the family in which elder abuse is occurring is likely to be experiencing stress (Justice and Duncan, 1976; Steinmetz, 1983; Hudson, 1986).

Violence within the family can be measured using the severe violence subscale of the Conflict Tactics Scales (CTS; Straus et al., 1980). The CTS has been used extensively in research on family violence and elder abuse (Straus and Gelles, 1986; Pillemer, 1986; Finkelhor and Pillemer, 1987).

CHARACTERISTICS OF OFFENDERS AND VICTIMS

Characteristics of Offenders

The best fit for a profile of the offender can be derived from theoretical explanations of elder abuse. Several theoretical explanations for elder abuse have been suggested, but few have been subjected to empirical testing. From the earliest theoretical explanation of the "situational model" (Cantor, 1983; Zaritt, Reever, and Bach-Peterson, 1982; Finkelor and Pillemer, 1984) to the social exchange theory (Homans, 1961), and symbolic interaction (Blumer, 1969; Mead, [1934], 1962; Phillips, 1983), abuse and neglect are viewed as a consequence of the interaction of individuals.

The premise of the situational model is that a confluence of factors contribute to the stress associated with caregiving, and this confluence in turn increases the likelihood of abusive acts being directed at the individual associated with the stress. It is difficult for professionals working in the field to establish a victim/perpetrator dyad when a legally competent elder may wish to exercise self-determination and not act in his or her own best interest. Elders themselves play a part in the construction of abusive situations. The situational model received support from its effectiveness in explaining child abuse and other forms of family violence (Finkelhor and Pillemer, 1984). Elderly-related factors that create stress for caregivers include physical and emotional dependency, poor health or impairment, isolation, lack of supportive and satisfying relationships, and "difficult" personalities. Finkelhor and Pillemer noted that child abuse and elder abuse are similar to the extent that both involve longstanding relationships with emotional and often economic dependence.

The explanatory power of the situational model is weak because of the assumption that child abuse, elder abuse, and other forms of intrafamily violence share many similarities. Several types of abuse often occur simultaneously. The causes of physical abuse may be quite different from the causes of financial abuse.

The social exchange theory, first advanced by Homans (1961), includes four basic premises:

1. Individuals and groups act rationally to maximize rewards and minimize costs to themselves. These transactions are not only economic; they also include psychological satisfaction. The principle of reciprocity is implicit in these interactions; people should help those who have assisted them no matter what the cost. Individuals often choose interactions from which they can derive a sense of "profit" in the form of increased social opportunities, personal enhancement, or a sense of self-worth.

2. Individuals use their past experience to predict the outcome of anticipatory relationships, particularly as they appraise costs and benefits involved in reaching their desired goal.

3. An individual will maintain an interaction as long as it continues to be more rewarding than costly.

4. When one individual is dependent on another, the latter accrues power based on the imbalance of the exchange.

The social exchange theory is a version of interactionism that focuses on what people seem to be getting out of their interactions and what they contribute to them. In a transactional sense, both parties must be examined to determine who is benefiting more and why. A key factor in defining the elderly's status is the balance between their contributions to society, which are determined by their control of power resources, and the cost of supporting them.

Symbolic interactionism is a level of communication that gives information that is not always intentional, without speaking. People dress and use body language, gestures, and symbols that convey choices when interacting with others. These choices tell other people about an individual, what that person likes, how that person behaves in intimate groups, how social roles are learned, and how social structures are created in the course of repeated interactions among individuals and groups. Other forces shape behavior as well. Sociologists refer to all these aspects of behavior as symbolic interactionism when describing social life as a quilt of little scenes and dramas in which people indicate their actions, respond to others' actions, build identities, and construct informal rules of behavior. Symbolic interaction explains some of the dynamic interactions between older individuals and their social world. Using this approach, abuse and neglect are viewed as a consequence of the interaction within families. If an older person forgets to turn off the stove burner, he or she is likely to be labeled by relatives as senile. Yet a younger person's forgetfulness will be forgiven and explained as being busy and preoccupied. When an elderly person becomes indifferent to food choices or a once-favorite food becomes unrecognizable, the elderly person may be viewed as being difficult or noncompliant. In similar situations, young children are permitted opportunities to express their displeasure with certain foods in a nonthreatening environment as a sign of their independence.

Physical changes in aging adults have an impact on how older people view themselves and their adaptive strategies. Because people derive their self-concept from interacting with others in their social milieu, disengagement, low self-esteem, and dissatisfaction with life may result from how other people interpret the elderly's behavior. For example, when confronted with change, whether relocating to another residence or learning to adapt to a new role, older individuals are expected to try to master the changing situation while extracting from the larger environment whatever they can to retain a positive self-concept. If the adaptation to a new environment is not mutually satisfying, the tension created within the family group is blamed on the recent changes. Loss of power or the ability to control one's environment is offered as one explanation of why older people, left with only the capacity for compliance, disengage.

This perspective contributes to our understanding of how interactions shape our views and affect our perceptions of how people age. Advancing age is associated with changes to the physical appearance and functioning of the human body. Physical decline does not present many positive attributes and thus focuses on the question of how individuals adapt and respond to old age.

Caregiver Burden

"Caregiver burden" is a term often used to describe the physical, emotional, financial and other problems encountered by persons who provide services to the impaired elderly. The physical demands of providing daily personal assistance such as changing bedding, bathing, feeding, dressing, and monitoring are experienced most frequently by caregivers who live with the care recipient. Financial burdens include not only direct costs of medical or hired help but also indirect opportunity costs of lost income or missed opportunities like promotions and transfers, loss of leisure time, interrupted careers, and years of personal freedom lost along with social relationships.

Emotional burdens for caregivers include feeling alone, angry, isolated, and overwhelmed and a sense of abandonment within their own community. The demands of elder care differ from child care when the decline of the frail elderly person is contrasted with children growing up and becoming independent. Most families do not use formal services for respite care and continue to provide care even though community support services are available.

Caregivers frequently suffer from drug and alcohol abuse or are pathologically violent people (O'Malley, Everitt, and Campion, 1983). Perpetrators often engage in verbal berating, harassment, or intimidation. Threats of punishment or deprivation of essential needs and even isolation from friends and other family members are common tactics used by abusers in home situations. Some abusers have disabling conditions themselves: addiction to alcohol or other drugs, mental retardation, serious psychiatric disturbances, or the inability to make appropriate judgments when taking care of a dependent elder person. Wolf and Pillemer (1989) found that 64% of the perpetrators were male, 90% were white, and most were sons of the victim.

The norm of reciprocity has been used to explain interpersonal actions and the dynamics of relationships (Kenny and La Voie, 1982). Relatives including spouses and children account for the majority of the cases (Pillemer and Finkelhor, 1989; Pillemer, 1986). Financial problems, being socially isolated, and parent hostilities in earlier life contribute to the problem of elder abuse. In addition, widely accepted social norms concerning responsibilities of family members toward each other may set the stage for conflicted feelings, anguish, and guilt.

Characteristics of the Victims

Perpetrator/victim relationships in which violence was reported (Pillemer and Finkelhor, 1988) showed roughly equal numbers of abused men and women (52% to 48%). Abused elders are likely to be living with someone else (O'Malley et al., 1979; Wolf, Godkin, and Pillemer, 1984) and are more likely to be in poor health (Lau and Kosberg, 1979; Steinmetz, 1983) than nonabused elders.

Dependency issues arise along with a disclaimer of familial responsibilities and different expectations about intergenerational assistance when elder abuse is discovered. Extended families, fictive kin (the kinship bonds of "family" extended to include friends and neighbors), and traditional values stressing respect and honor of parents is often not enough to guarantee that older relatives will receive the treatment expected from their offspring. Generational differences may influence sources of support for families with aging members. Families disadvantaged by social class often lack the economic resources to support older relatives. These same social networks can be triggers for stress and tension. Sources of aid like Social Security and disability payments have reduced the number of older people living in poverty, but elderly blacks are affected to a much greater extent than other groups. Intergenerational conflict and problems between a parent and child are intensified when the parent is in need of care and problems from earlier periods have not been resolved.

Theoretical perspectives, particularly interactionist theory (Blumer, 1962), explain the processes of interaction between family members. Attitudes about declining worth affect the role definitions in the social groups in which the elderly are members. Physical decline is not a worthy status nor is it self-validating. How one adapts to this forced retreat from work, productivity, and economic independence influences interaction between older people and their family members. There are more older women in advanced stages of decline than any other group, and they are less likely to resist abusive behavior than others (Giordano and Giordano, 1984).

CORRELATES OF ELDER MALTREATMENT

Elder abuse has been found to be associated with physical and mental impairment (Block and Sinott, 1979). Some studies (Homer and Gilleard, 1990; Cohen et al., 1990; Paveza et al., 1992) suggested that the occurrence of violent behaviors can be linked to caregiver depression, particularly when caring for an Alzheimer's disease patient. Case reports show that when adult children become caretakers and the patient is residing with the family, the level of violence increases. Some abused elderly accept their troubles without seeking relief out of resignation or their philosophy about publicizing private troubles (Lau and Kosberg, 1979).

Power in the family and the establishment of "rules" that govern relationships and private family dynamics make it difficult for professionals working in the field to sort maltreatment from the complexities of family pathology. Intergenerational conflict and earlier problems between parent and child do not disappear with the passage of time. Because the parties involved are emancipated adults, unlike cases of child abuse, it is difficult to assess the actual onset of the alleged abuse and the resources available to them to report and resist maltreatment. The elderly are likely to have financial resources and their own property, which could be a source of conflict.

There are more abused older women than men (Giordano and Giordano, 1984), and the older the person, the higher the risk of abusive behavior (O'Malley et al., 1983). If the older person is a problem drinker, feelings of anger and other acting out behaviors will surface under the influence of alcohol (O'Malley et al., 1983; Pillemer, 1986). The older the person, the higher the risks of abusive behavior, because advanced age is associated with disabling mental and physical conditions that may lead to an inability to resist or defend himself or herself from abusive treatment.

Disease-Related Factors of Dependency

Physical and mental decline in older people is not inevitable. Some changes with age are normal, others can be avoided. A growing body of evidence shows that changing certain health behaviors, even in old age, can benefit health and quality of life. Cigarette smoking is one of these habits. Studies have shown that when older smokers quit, they increase their life expectancy, reduce their risk of heart disease, and improve respiratory function and circulation (Office of Smoking and Health, 1989). Among the most frequent chronic conditions and impairments for older people are arthritis, reduced vision, hearing impairments, heart conditions, and hypertension. Other adverse effects include complicated drug regimens and unanticipated drug interactions. Alzheimer's disease is reported to be a risk factor for increased physical aggression between caregiver and patient (Ryden, 1988; Hamel et al., 1990; Paveza et al., 1992).

The causes of apparent senility are many and include drug interactions, depression, metabolic disorders, certain tumors, nutritional deficiencies, anemia, chemical intoxications, and sensory deprivation due to social isolation. Many of these conditions are reversible. The mental confusion and other effects on physical health can be minimized if older people have access to a continuing, interested, well-informed source of medical care. Elderly persons also need social system support to monitor changes in their lives, social isolation, economic changes, disease or injury, and the stress of loss and grief.

Social and Psychological Factors of Dependency

Changes in social dynamics can create stressful environments for the elderly that may lead to serious physical illness and even premature death. Stressors include the death of a spouse, changes in status that come with retirement, and the associated financial constraints that many elderly persons fear. The fear of costs associated with old age—illness, prescription costs, and food and housing costs—prevent elderly persons from engaging in the full and active lifestyles that many are capable of doing. The absence of opportunities to choose among available options as well as participation in everyday tasks and decision making is likely to produce apathy and accelerate dependency. Role reversal may occur whereby the adult child assumes the role of parent by definition. The instrumental and expressive roles played out by the child are defined by the situation.

PREVENTION AND TREATMENT

Prevention of elder abuse is very complex given the nature of the vulnerability of the elderly and that the majority of substantiated cases are self-neglect (Shiferaw et al., 1994; Foelker, Holland, Marsh, and Simmons, 1990; Hickey and Douglass, 1981).

Primarily, the family is asked to respond when serious support needs are evident. Families provide care for any number of reasons, including a sense of reciprocity, cost sharing, filial responsibility, and the interdependence of families. The role of the family and the involvement of care institutions and their personnel have been understated. Nevertheless, prevention efforts must focus on the elderly, their families, and the intervention efforts of agencies and institutions and must address all antecedents that impact or influence the vulnerability of the elderly. The major goals of prevention are to ensure the quality of life for the elderly and, given appropriate circumstances, meet their desires for self-determination while protecting them from harm.

An acceptable strategy for the prevention of elder abuse should include the principles of public health. The context of prevention in public health focuses on primary, secondary, and tertiary intervention. Forming the basis of prevention are several laws designed to protect the elderly and punish the perpetrators. Because of the complexity surrounding substantiating many forms of abuse and the need to understand and monitor self-neglect and self-abuse, however, legal intervention still rests in the power and the sovereignty of the state. In the case of maltreatment of the elderly, the state acts through the mechanism of establishing guardianship or conservatorship. In some states, the terms are interchangeable. Investigations of elder abuse include the elderly's perception of the situation, psychological issues, and the context of the situation. This may mean that the most severe cases will lead to convictions, thus making it difficult to identify the focus of prevention and where it should begin. The lack of uniformity in how to define and identify elder abuse and neglect may result in true cases that are mislabeled and in misdirected services. The consequence of this action in borderline cases that may be interpreted as mild or moderate is that the elderly victim may not receive appropriate services, which could lead to a reluctance to ask for help in the future.

Given that Pillemer and Finkelhor (1988) reported a rate of 32 abused elders per 1,000 among those elders sixty-five and older living alone or with their families, primary prevention efforts should begin with the family of the elderly. Crucial aspects of primary prevention include:

1. Addressing the correlates of elder abuse and reducing the likelihood of abuse

2. Training personnel in institutions to address issues related to elder abuse and the barriers to establishing trusting and supportive relationships when confronted with suspected cases of elder abuse

3. Developing an understanding of the psychosocial issues involved in reporting abuse by family members

4. Training, supporting, and educating potential caregivers at home to recognize the problems of decline in old age, signs of stress, being overburdened, and when to seek help

At the secondary level of prevention or intervention is the identification of potential victims and perpetrators. Intervention should focus on the elderly with chronic conditions because 58% of disabled persons that need help with daily activities are sixty-five years of age and older and are likely to live with someone else (O'Malley et al., 1979). Other considerations include the role of psychopathology, issues of interdependence and stress, being female, and being seventy years of age or older (Wolf et al., 1984). Another approach is to reduce the dependency of the perpetrator on the victim by offering vocational counseling in an attempt to overcome the financial and emotional hardships entwined in the relationship. In some cases, it may be prudent to perform a clinical assessment of the possible abuser, particularly in cases where a family member is indifferent, expresses obvious anger toward the elderly person, and refuses to provide necessary care and assistance.

The tertiary prevention of elder abuse should focus on avoiding recidivism, imploring legislators to address the issue of elder abuse, educating the public about the nature of family violence, and using the laws and remedies currently available to reduce the incidence of elder abuse.

The 1990 U.S. census (Crispell and Frey, 1997) contained questions that requested information on three kinds of limitations that affect people in their daily lives. In the census definition, people with disabilities have a physical or mental condition lasting six months or more. "Work disabilities" simply limited or prevented one from doing a job previously held. Other limitations included self-care and mobility limitations. Some people listed all three types of limitations. Sixty-two percent of noninstitutionalized elderly Americans have no limitations that interfere with their daily lives.

Healthy life measures include quality as well as length of life. An indicator of the quality of life is an individual's ability to perform activities required for daily living such as bathing, dressing, toileting, and eating (Katz et al., 1963). When difficulties occur in performing tasks in these areas, the need for assistance threatens one's independence and the opportunity to remain in the community. Sometimes independence is suddenly lost because of an event such as a stroke or a broken hip.

Geographic isolation and self-neglect place the elderly at risk for abuse and exploitation. Even when frailty is becoming noticeable, the slow decline is difficult to accept. For example, depression and confusion may lead to failure to pay bills, then a neighbor calls to say that the utilities have been shut off and the house is dark. Sometimes an expensive prescription may mean that the elderly person cannot afford groceries. The lack of medical treatment can diminish quality of life, exacerbate the aging process, and sometimes result in an early death. Gioglio and Blakemore (1983) found that financial abuse along with other forms of abuse occurred in 50% of the cases cited. In the Forsyth County Aging Study (Shiferaw et al., 1994), the most frequently substantiated charge was exploitation of resources followed by self-neglect: "The most common allegation was self neglect, followed by neglect by others, and exploitation" (p. 124).

CASE EXAMPLE OF FINANCIAL EXPLOITATION

Lena Bryant is eighty-five years old. She lives in her own home in Georgia with regular checkups from a visiting nurse for her high blood pressure and to monitor her heart. She is able to garden, perform light housekeeping tasks, bathe, and dress herself. She exhibits some signs of depression because she has no close relatives nearby. Her vision and hearing are less than perfect, and she is ambulatory with a cane. Her only surviving kin are two sons, aged sixty-three and sixty, who live in Washington, D.C., and a favorite granddaughter in her thirties who lives in Chicago. The granddaughter has managed to monitor her care by telephone using various agencies and the support of neighbors.

The time has come either to remove Lena from her home or to provide in-home help because she is becoming malnourished, is unable to cook for herself, and refuses to eat the meals supplied by Meals on Wheels. Lena is financially able to pay for home help through her own resources and those of her family. She refuses to leave her home to live with any of her relatives. A decision is made by Lena and her family to remain in her own house with some help. A person is recommended to the family and is well received by Lena. Lena adores the lady who is hired to take care of her and is able to offer praise and a more positive outlook on life. She looks forward to her early morning visits and to having breakfast, lunch, and dinner in her own house. Lena was never declared incompetent and remained in control of her finances. She was still able to do her grocery shopping with some assistance.

After several months, Lena's bank account began to dwindle. Checks were being written for exorbitant amounts by the caretaker and her youngest daughter even though Lena's children were paying the caretaker from their funds. Upon investigation, Lena's granddaughter discovered that the caretaker was "given" $3,000 via one of Lena's checks to purchase a reliable car to transport her to the doctor's office and shopping. All bank accounts were closed and an accounting was requested prior to reporting the matter to law enforcement. Lena did not realize that the events had taken place. She could not assist in the reconciliation of the bank account, and she had signed most of the checks.

Where the elderly person ends up will depend on many things: the use of transfers like Meals on Wheels, Medicaid (for nursing home care), in-home services, and homemaker services. Whether or not elders get help and in what form will depend on where they live, their family circumstances, cash and retirement reserves, and what is available in their particular locality. At one point in history, a large family was insurance enough against becoming indigent and alone in old age. That option began to erode with the advent of smaller families, women working outside the home, smaller living quarters, more mobile families, and other cultural and economic reasons.

OLDER AMERICANS ACT OF 1965

Many elderly citizens receive services in their communities that are provided as a result of the Older Americans Act of 1965. Federal law authorizes and funds direct services such as senior centers, nutrition programs, information, and referral through the operating agency, Administration on Aging, Department of Health and Human Services. The coordination of services is carried out through a three-level administrative structure, with a national Administration on Aging, state units on aging, and local area agencies of aging. The purpose of this act was to assist elderly persons to live independently in their own homes. One attempt at promoting independence for the elderly is the protection from elder abuse. The 1987 amendments to the Older Americans Act (P.L. 100-175) created a separate provision entitled Elder Abuse Prevention Activities (Title III, Part G). Procedures for developing information and referral networks, activities to identify abuse and neglect, and interviewing techniques for responding to complaints are included in the authorization. For an example of one state's statute on elder abuse and neglect, see the appendix to this chapter. All fifty states have some form of legislation that extends protection to the elderly, such as adult protective services, mental health commitment laws, and guardianship and conservatorship provisions. Most of the case management functions are performed through state units on aging.

In-home workers and other professionals should be vigilant about the possibility of abuse and neglect. Emergency room and physician protocols should include screening for elder abuse and neglect. Stressed caregivers should receive support in the form of respite or supportive counseling. Interviewing techniques, risk profiles, victim advocacy, and sensitivity to the dynamics of family violence should be integral aspects of education programs for workers. Elder persons themselves with worrisome and demanding behaviors such as wandering, combativeness, problem drinking, and poor social habits should be encouraged to cooperate with their caregivers. When available, adult day-care centers should be used for ancillary support for the family.

Practicing clinicians should receive education on family violence to improve detection and acceptance of violence as a hidden health-care problem. Compliance with mandatory reporting laws and public education should be improved so as to establish community participation in reducing family violence. Through myths and stereotyping about the old, they are portrayed as vulnerable in the media, and consequently ageism creeps into the way the elderly are treated. Block and Sinott (1979) suggested that more research into the role of ageism is needed because the old may view themselves as less worthy than other people and deserving of abusive treatment.

LEGAL ISSUES AND FUTURE TRENDS

State reporting laws and adult protective services units should encourage other professionals to act as advocates for the vulnerable elderly. Clear categories of abuse and neglect should be agreed upon as standards for investigative purposes. Civil and criminal penalties for flagrant violations and abuses should be prescribed in cases of physical or mental impairment. Evidentiary and confidentiality issues should be considered when utterances are used as statements of record. Victim's rights should be emphasized in protection efforts with procedures installed to reduce the stigma and shame associated with abuse of the elderly. Other legal strategies that could be used in special situations include order of protection, competency hearings, and involuntary commitments.

The elderly's own judgment about a situation may conflict with the practitioner's professional assessment. If perceptions differ markedly, the process of resolving the differences and improving the well-being of the elderly client will be challenging. Workers assigned to investigate cases of elder abuse and neglect will need training in cultural diversity and help-seeking behaviors of ethnic elderly groups. When designing intervention programs, considerations of ethnicity and diverse populations become important if families reveal antisocial behavior in the context of an investigation. Interventions for at-risk families should include safeguards for the elderly person as well as better information about what constitutes elder abuse.

As in child welfare cases, substitute care arrangements should be made available to the victim during the investigative process. Domicile programs that offer alternatives to nursing home placement could be used in cases of elder abuse. In cases of physical assault, financial exploitation, and sexual abuse, vigorous prosecution should be sought. Professionals working in the area of domestic violence should acknowledge the need to serve older women in violent relationships for whom the aging process offered no relief from spousal battering.

CONCLUSION

Knowing whether or not cases of elder abuse are on the rise cannot be determined without prevalence data obtained from national community studies collected over time. In the meantime, collaboration between researchers, practitioners, legislators, professional training programs, and the general public is needed to remove the invisibility of elder abuse. To present true positive reports to authorities, more reliable measures are needed to detect elder abuse. Once the reports are in the hands of the proper agency, follow-up and monitoring should follow the case management model of intervention.

Caregivers should be monitored for high-risk characteristics such as problem drinking, drug addiction, insensitivity to problems of the elderly, mental or emotional illness, and caregiving inexperience. Family systems should be evaluated for the degree of family support for impaired members. Family characteristics to watch for include disharmony, overcrowding, economic dependence upon the elderly family member, isolation, and intrafamily conflict.

EDITORIAL SUMMARY

Maltreatment of the elderly has been present throughout history. References to intergenerational conflict date back to Biblical times and can be found in Greek mythology.

Tremendous growth in the elderly population has helped to increase recent interest in the maltreatment of older persons.

Elder maltreatment is most often a social problem rather than a legal one and includes both acts of omission (neglect) and commission (abuse). Types of maltreatment of the elderly include physical abuse, sexual abuse, emotional abuse, neglect, willful deprivation of food and medical care, and financial exploitation.

Similar to other forms of family violence, abuse of the elderly is not limited to a single act, and no single factor has been identified as the cause of elder abuse. Several theoretical explanations for elder maltreatment have been suggested (e.g., situational model, social exchange theory, symbolic interaction, and caregiver burden), but few have been subjected to empirical testing.

Abusers are often those in a position of trust, such as a family member. Offender characteristics include substance use, mental retardation, psychiatric disturbances, and the inability to make appropriate judgments when caring for a dependent elder person. Abused elders are more likely to be living with someone else (e.g., family) and are more likely to be in poor health than nonabused elders. Women and the older elderly appear to be at greater risk of maltreatment than others.

Because individuals are living longer, society will have to address the special needs of the elderly. Innovative prevention strategies directed toward the elder person and his or her family must be developed to meet the challenges that come with aging.

REFERENCES

American Medical Association Council on Scientific Affairs. (1987). Elder abuse and neglect. *Journal of the American Medical Association, 257,* 966–971.

Bakwin, H. (1949). Emotional deprivation in infants. *Journal of Pediatrics, 35,* 512–521.

Block, M. R., and Sinnott, J. D. (Eds.) (1979). *The Battered Elder Syndrome: An Exploratory Study.* College Park: University of Maryland Center on Aging.

Blumer, H. (1962). Society as symbolic interaction. In A. Rose (Ed.), *Human Behavior and Social Processes.* Boston: Houghton Mifflin.

Blumer, H. (1969). *Symbolic Interactionism.* Englewood Cliffs, NJ: Prentice Hall.

Braun, J. V., Wykle, M. H., and Cowling, W. R. (1988). Failure to thrive in older persons: A concept derived. *The Gerontologist, 28*(6), 809–812.

Brewer, R. A., and Jones, J. S. (1989). Reporting edler abuse: Limitations on statutes. *Annals of Emergency Medicine, 18,* 1217–1221.

Cantor, M. H. (1983). Strain among caregivers: A study of experience in the United States. *The Gerontologist, 23*(6), 597–604.

Chen, P. N., Bell, S., Dolinsky, D., Doyle, J., and Dunn, M. (1981). Elder abuse in domestic settings: A pilot study. *Journal of Gerontological Social Work, 4,* 3–14.

Cohen, D., Luchins, D., Eisdorfer, C., Paveza, G., Ashford, J. W., Gorelick, P., Hirschman, R., Freels, S., Levy, P., Semla, T., and Shaw, H. (1990). Caring for relatives with Alzheimer's disease: The mental health risks to spouses, adult children and other family caregivers. *Behavior, Health and Aging, 1,* 171–182.

Crispell, D., and Frey, W. H. (1997). American maturity. In Harold Cox (Ed.), *Annual Editions in Aging* (11th. ed.), (pp. 109–115). Guilford, CT: Dushkin Group/Brown and Benchmark.

Cumming, E., and Henry, W. E. (1961). *Growing Old: The Process of Disengagement.* New York: Basic Books.

Filinson, R., and Ingman, S. R. (Eds.). (1989). *Elder Abuse: Practice and Policy.* New York: Human Sciences Press.

Finkelhor, D., and Pillemer, K. (1984, July). *Elder Abuse: Its Relationship to Other Forms of Domestic Violence.* Paper presented at the Second National Conference on Family Violence Research, Durham, NH.

Finkelhor, D., and Pillemer, K. (1987, July). *Correlates of Elder Abuse: A Case Control Study.* Paper presented at the Third National Conference on Family Violence Research, Durham, NH.

Foelker, G. A., Holland, J., Marsh, M., and Simmons, B. A. (1990). A community response to elder abuse. *The Gerontologist, 30,* 560–562.

Foner, N. (1985). Caring for the elderly: A cross-cultural view. In B. B. Hess and E. W. Markson (Eds.), *Growing Old in America* (pp. 71–85). New Brunswick, NJ: Transaction.

Foucault, M. (Ed.). (1975). *I, Pierre Riviere, having slaughtered my mother, my sister, and my brother: A case of parricide in the 19th century.* New York: Pantheon Books.

Fredricksen, H. I., (1989). Adult protective services: Changes with the introduction of mandatory reporting. *Journal of Abuse and Neglect, 1,* 59–70.

Gioglio, G. R., and Blakemore, P. (1983). *Elder Abuse in New Jersey: The Knowledge and Experience of Abuse Among Older New Jerseyans.* Trenton: New Jersey Department of Human Services.

Giordano, N. H., and Giordano, J. A. (1984). Elder abuse: A review of the literature. *Social Work, 29,* 232–236.

Hamel, M., Gold, D. P., Andres, D., Reis, M., Dastoor, D., Grauer, H., and Bergman, H. (1990). Predictors and consequences of aggressive behavior by community-based dementia patients. *The Gerontologist, 30,* 206–211.

Herr, J. J., and Weakland, J. H. (1979). *Counseling Elders and Their Families.* New York: Springer.

Hickey, T., and Douglas, R. L. (1981). Mistreatment of elderly in the domestic setting: An exploratory study. *American Journal of Public Health, 71,* 500–507.

Homans, G. C., (1961). *Social Behavior: Its Elementary Forms.* New York: Harcourt, Brace and World.

Homer, A. C., and Gilleard, C. (1990). Abuse of elderly people by their carers. *British Medical Journal, 301,* 1362–1369.

Hudson, M. F. (1986). Elder mistreatment: Current research. In K. A. Pillemer and R. S. Wolf (Eds.), *Elder Abuse: Conflict in the Family* (pp. 125–166). Dover, MA: Auburn House.

Hudson, M. F., and Johnson, T. F. (1986). Elder neglect and abuse: A review of the literature. In C. Eisendorfer (Ed.), *Annual Review of Gerontology and Geriatrics* (Vol. 6) (pp. 81–134). New York: Springer.

Institute of Medicine. (1991). *The Second Fifty Years: Promoting Health and Preventing Disability.* Washington, DC: National Academy Press.

Justice, B., and Duncan, D. (1976). Life crisis as a precursor to child abuse. *Public Health Reports, 91,* 110–115.

Katz, S., Ford, A., Moskowitz, R., Jackson, B., and Jaffee, M. (1963). Studies of illness in the aged: The index of activities of daily living: A standardized measure of biological and psychosocial function. *Journal of the American Medical Association, 185,* 914–919.

Kenny, D. A., and La Voie, L. (1982). Reciprocity of interpersonal attraction: A confirmed hypothesis. *Social Psychology Quarterly, 45*(1), 54–58.

Kurz, D. (1987). Emergency department responses to battered women: Resistance to medicalization. *Social Problems, 34,* 69–81.

Lau, E., and Kosberg, J. (1979, September–October). Abuse of the elderly by informal care providers. *Aging,* pp. 10–15.

McLeer, S. V., Anwar, R. A., and Marquiling, K. (1989). Education is not enough: A systems failure in protecting battered women. *Annals of Emergency Medicine, 8,* 651–653.

Mead, G. H. ([1934], 1962). *Mind, Self and Society.* Chicago: University of Chicago Press.

Minuchin, S., Montalvo, B., Guerney, B. G., Rosman, B. L., and Schumer, F. (1967). *Families of the Slums.* New York: Basic Books.

National Center for Health Statistics. (1989). *Prevention Profile: Health, United States* (Department of Health and Human Services Publication No. PHS 90–1232). Hyattsville, MD: U.S. Department of Health and Human Services.

Neugarten, B. L. (1969). Continuities and discontinuities of psychological issues into adult life. *Human Development, 12,* 121–130.

Office of Smoking and Health. (1989). *Reducing the Health Consequences of Smoking: 25 Years of Progress. A Report of the Surgeon General* (Department of Health and Human Services Publication No. CDC 89–8411). Washington, DC: U.S. Department of Health and Human Services.

Otten, A. H. (1984, July 30). Ever more Americans live into eighties and nineties, causing big problems. *Wall Street Journal*, pp. 1–10.

O'Malley, T. A., Everitt, D. E., and Campion, E. W. (1983). Identifying and preventing family-medicated abuse and neglect of elderly persons. *Annals of Medicine, 98,* 998–1005.

O'Malley, H., Segars, H., Perez, R., Mitchell, V., and Knuepfel, G. (1979). *Elder Abuse in Massachusetts: A Survey of Professionals and Paraprofessionals.* Boston: Legal Research and Services for the Elderly.

Paveza, G. J., Cohen, D., Eisendorfer, C., Freels, S., Semla, T., Ashford, J. W., Gorelick, P., Hirshman, R., Luchins, D., and Levy, P. (1992). Violence and Alzheimer's disease: Prevalence and risk factors. *The Gerontologist, 32*(4), 493–497.

Pepper, C., and Oaker, M. R. (1981). *Elder Abuse: An Estimation of a Hidden Problem* (U.S. House of Representatives, Select Committee on Aging, Publication No. 97–277). Washington, DC: U.S. Government Printing Office.

Phillips, L. R. (1983). Abuse and neglect of the frail elderly at home: An exploration of theoretical relationships. *Journal of Advanced Nursing, 8,* 379–392.

Pillemer, K. A. (1986). Risk factors in elder abuse: Results from a case-control study. In K. A. Pillemer and R. S. Wolf (Eds.), *Elder Abuse: Conflict in the Family* (pp. 239–263). Dover, MA: Auburn House.

Pillemer, K. A., and Finkelhor, D. (1988). The prevalence of elder abuse: A random sample survey. *The Gerontologist, 28*(1), 51–57.

Pillemer, K. A., and Finkelhor, D. (1989). Causes of elder abuse: Caregiver stress versus problem relatives. *American Journal of Orthopsychiatry, 59,* 179–187.

Podenieks, E., and Pillemer, K. A. (1990). *National Survey on Abuse of the Elderly in Canada.* Toronto: Ryerson Polytechnical Institute.

Quinn, M. J., and Tomita, S. K. (1986). *Elder Abuse and Neglect: Causes, Diagnosis, and Intervention Strategies.* New York: Springer.

Ryden, M. (1988). Aggressive behavior in persons with dementia living in the community. *The Alzheimer's Disease and Associated Disorder International Journal, 2,* 342–355.

Shiferaw, B., Mittelmark, M. B., Wofford, J. L., Anderson, R. T., Walls, P., and Rohrer, B. (1994). The investigation and outcome of reported cases of elder abuse: The Forsyth County aging study. *The Gerontologist, 34*(1), 123–125.

Steinmetz, S. K. (1983). Dependency, stress, and violence between middle-aged caregivers and their elderly parents. In J. L. Kosberg (Ed.), *Abuse and Maltreatment of the Elderly.* Littleton, MA: John Wright-PSG.

Steinmetz, S. K., (1988). *Duty Bound: Elder Abuse and Family Care.* Newbury Park, CA: Sage.

Straus, M. A., and Gelles, R. J. (1986). Societal change and change in family violence from 1975 to 1985 as revealed by two national surveys. *Journal of Marriage and the Family, 48,* 465–480.

Straus, M. A., Gelles, R. J., and Steinmetz S. K. (1980). *Behind Closed Doors: Violence in the American Family.* New York: Doubleday.

Summner, W. G. (1906). *Folkways: A Study of the Sociological Importance of Usage, Manners, Customs, Mores, and Morals.* New York: Ginn.

Tilden, V. A., Schmidt, B., Limandri, B., Chiodo, G., Garland, M. J., and Loveless, P. A. (1994). Factors that influence clinicians' assessment and management of family violence. *American Journal of Public Health, 84*(4), 628–633.

Tilden, V. P., and Shepherd, P. (1987). Increasing the rate of identification of battered women in an emergency department: Use of a nursing protocol. *Research in Nursing and Health, 10,* 209–215.

Wolf, R. S. (1986). Major findings from three model projects on elderly abuse. In K. A. Pillemer and R. S. Wolf (Eds.), *Elder Abuse: Conflict in the Family* (pp. 218–238). Dover, MA: Auburn House.

Wolf, R., Godkin, M., and Pillemer, K. A. (1984). *Elder Abuse and Neglect: Report from the Model Projects.* Worcester: University of Massachusetts Medical Center.

Wolf, R. S., and Pillemer, K. A. (1989). *Helping Elderly Victims: The Reality of Elder Abuse.* New York: Columbia University Press.

Wolf, R. S., and Pillemer, K. (1994). What's new in elder abuse programming? *Gerontologist, 34*(1), 126.

Zaritt, S. H., Reever, K. E., and Bach-Peterson, J. (1982). Relatives of the impaired elderly: Correlates of feelings of burden. *The Gerontologist, 20,* 649–655.

Appendix

ACT 20. ELDER ABUSE AND NEGLECT ACT
(Chapter 320 ILCS)

Section

20/1.   Short title.

20/2.   Definitions.

20/3.   Responsibilities.

20/4.   Reports of abuse or neglect.

20/5.   Procedure.

20/6.   Time.

20/7.   Review.

20/8.   Access to records.

20/9.   Authority to consent to services.

20/10.   Rules.

20/11.   Annual reports.

20/12.   Implementation.

20/1. SHORT TITLE

§Short title. This act shall be known and may be cited as the "Elder Abuse and Neglect Act."
P.A. 85-1184, §1, eff. Aug. 13, 1988.
Formerly Ill. rev. Stat. 1991, ch. 23, ¶6601.

Title of Act:
An Act in relation to the abuse and neglect of elderly persons. P.A. 85-1184, approved and eff. Aug. 13, 1988.

20/2. DEFINITIONS

§2. Definitions. As used in this Act, unless the context requires otherwise:
(a) "Abuse" means causing any physical, mental or sexual injury to an eligible adult, including exploitation of such adult's financial resources. Nothing in this Act shall be construed to mean that an eligible adult is victim of abuse or neglect for the sole reason that he or she is being furnished with or relies upon treatment by spiritual means through prayer alone, in accordance with the tenets and practices of a recognized church or religious denominations.

(b) "Department" means the Department on Aging of the State of Illinois.

(c) "Director" means the Director of the Department.

(d) "Domestic" living situation means a residence where the eligible adult lives alone or with his or her family or a caretaker, or other, but is not:

(1) A licensed facility as defined in Section 1-113 of the Nursing Home Care Act;[1]

(2) A "life care facility" as defined in the Life Care Facilities Act;[2]

(3) A home, institution, or other place operated by the federal government or agency thereof or by the State of Illinois;

(4) A hospital, sanitarium, or other institution, the principal activity or business of which is the diagnosis, care, and treatment of human illness through the maintenance and operation of organized facilities therefor, which is required to be licensed under the Hospital Licensing Act;[3]

(5) A "community living facility" as defined in the Community Living Facilities Licensing Act;[4]

(6) A "community residential alternative" as defined in the Community Residential Alternatives Licensing Act;[5] and

(7) A "community-integrated living arrangement" as defined in the Community-Integrated Living Arrangements Licensure and Certification Act.[6]

(e) "Eligible adult" means a person 60 years of age or older who resides in a domestic setting and is abused or neglected by another individual.

(f) "Emergency" means a situation in which an eligible adult is living in conditions presenting a risk of death or physical, mental, or sexual injury and is unable to consent to services which would alleviate that risk.

(g) "Neglect" means another individual's failure to provide an eligible adult with or willful withholding from an eligible adult the necessities of life including, but not limited to, food, clothing, shelter or medical care. This subsection does not create any new affirmative duty to provide support to eligible adults.

(h) "Provider agency" means any public or nonprofit agency in a planning and service area appointed by the regional administrative agency with prior approval by the Department on Aging to receive and assess reports of alleged or suspected abuse or neglect.

(i) "Regional administrative agency" means any public or nonprofit agency in a planning and service area so designated by the Department, provided that the designated Area Agency on Aging shall be designated the regional administrative agency if it so requests.

(j) "Substantiated case" means a reported case of alleged or suspected abuse or neglect in which a provided agency, after assessment, determines that there is reason to believe abuse or neglect has occurred.

P.A. 85-1184, §2, eff. Aug. 13, 1988. Amended by P.A. 86-820, Art. III, §3–11, eff. Sept. 7, 1989, P.A. 87-264, §1, eff. Sept. 4, 1991.
Formerly Ill. Rev. Stat. 1991, ch. 23, ¶6602.

20/3. RESPONSIBILITIES

§3. Responsibilities. (a) The Department shall establish, design and manage a program of services for persons 60 years of age and older who have been victims of elder abuse or neglect. The Department shall contract with or fund regional administrative agencies or provider agencies, or both, for the provision of those services pursuant to this Act.

(b) Each regional administrative agency shall designate provider agencies within its planning and service area with prior approval by the Department on Aging, monitor the use of services, provide technical assistance to the provider agencies, and be involved in program development activities.

(c) Provider agencies shall assist eligible adults who need agency services to allow them to continue to function independently. Such assistance shall include but not be limited to receiving reports of alleged or suspected abuse or neglect, conducting face-to-face assessments of such reported cases, determination of substantiated case work, and follow-up services on substantiated cases.

P.A. 85-1184, §3 eff. Aug. 13, 1988.
Formerly Ill. Rev. Stat. 1991, ch. 23, ¶6603.

20/4. REPORTS OF ABUSE OR NEGLECT

§4. Reports of abuse or neglect. (a) Any person wishing to report a case of alleged or suspected abuse or neglect may make such a report to an agency designated to receive such reports under this Act or to the Department. A person making a report under this Act in the belief that it is in the alleged victim's best interest shall be immune from criminal or civil liability or professional disciplinary action on account of making the report, notwithstanding any requirements concerning the confidentiality of information with respect to such patient which might otherwise be applicable. Law enforcement officers shall continue to report incidents or alleged abuse pursuant to the Illinois Domestic Violence Act of 1986,[7] notwithstanding any requirements under this Act.

(b) Any person, institution or agency making a report under this Act in good faith, or taking photographs or x-rays as a result of an authorized assessment, shall have immunity from any civil, criminal or other liability in any civil, criminal or other proceeding brought in consequence of making such report or assessment or on account of submitting or otherwise disclosing such photographs or x-rays to any agency designated to receive reports of alleged or suspected abuse or neglect. Any person, institution or agency authorized by the Department to provide assessment, intervention, or administrative services under this Act shall, in the good faith performance of those services, have immunity from any civil, criminal or other liability in any civil, criminal or other proceeding brought as a consequence of the performance of those services.

(c) The identity of a person making a report of alleged or suspected abuse or neglect under this Act may be disclosed by the Department or other agency provided for in this Act only with such person's written consent or by court order.

(d) The Department shall by rule establish a system for filing and compiling reports made under this Act.

P.A. 85-1184, §4, eff. Aug. 13, 1988. Amended by P.A. 87-264, §1, eff. Sept. 4, 1991; P.A. 87-435, Art. 3, §3–5, eff. Sept. 10, 1991.
Formerly Ill. Rev. Stat. 1991, ch. 23, ¶6604.

20/5. PROCEDURE

§5. Procedure. A provider agency designated to receive reports of alleged or suspected abuse or neglect under this Act shall, upon receiving such a report, conduct a face-to-face assessment with respect to such report. The assessment shall include, but not be limited to, a visit to the residence of the eligible adult who is the subject of the report and may include interviews or consultations with service agencies or individuals who may have knowledge of the eligible adult's circumstances. If, after the assessment, the provider agency determines that the case is substantiated, it shall develop a service care plan for the eligible adult. In developing the plan, the provider agency may consult with any other appropriate provider of services, and such providers shall be immune from civil or criminal liability on account of such acts. The plan shall include alternative suggested or recommended services which are appropriate to the needs of the eligible adult and which involve the least restriction of the eligible adult's activities commensurate with his needs. Only those services to which consent is provided in accordance with Section 9 of this Act shall be provided, contingent upon the availability of such services.

P.A. 85-1184, §5, eff. Aug. 13, 1988.
Formerly Ill. Rev. Stat. 1991, ch. 23, ¶6605.

20/6. TIME

§6. Time. The Department shall by rule establish the period of time within which an assessment shall begin and within which a service care plan shall be implemented. Such rules shall provide for an expedited response to emergency situations.

P.A. 85-1184, §6, eff. Aug. 13, 1988.
Formerly Ill. Rev. Stat. 1991, ch. 23, ¶6606.

20/7. REVIEW

§7. Review. All services provided to an eligible adult shall be reviewed by the provider agency on at least a quarterly basis for not less than one year to determine whether the service care plan should be continued or modified.

P.A. 85-1184, §7, eff. Aug. 13, 1988.
Formerly Ill. Rev. Stat. 1991, ch. 23, ¶6607.

20/8. ACCESS TO RECORDS

§8. Access to records. All records concerning reports of elder abuse and neglect and all records generated as a result of such reports shall be confidential and shall not be disclosed except as specifically authorized by this Act or other applicable law. Access to such records, but not access to the identity of the person or persons making a report of alleged abuse or neglect as contained in such records, shall be allowed to the following persons and for the following persons:

(a) Department staff, provider agency staff, and regional administrative staff in the furtherance of their responsibilities under this Act;

(b) A law enforcement agency investigating known or suspected elder abuse or neglect;

(c) A physician who has before him an eligible adult whom he reasonably suspects may be abused or neglected;

(d) An eligible adult reported to be abused or neglected, or such adult's guardian unless such guardian is the alleged abuser;

(e) A court, upon its finding that access to such records may be necessary for the determination of an issue before such court. However, such access shall be limited to an in camera inspection of the records, unless the court determines that disclosure of the information contained therein is necessary for the resolution of an issue then pending before it;

(f) A grand jury, upon its determination that access to such records is necessary in the conduct of its official business;

(g) Any person authorized by the Director, in writing, for audit or bona fide research purposes;

(h) A coroner or medical examiner who has reason to believe that an eligible adult had died as the result of abuse or neglect;

(i) Department of Professional Regulation staff and members of the Social Work Examining and Disciplinary Board in the course of investigating alleged violations of the Clinical Social Work and Social Work Practice Act[8] by provider agency staff.

P.A. 85-1185, §8 , eff. Aug. 13, 1988. Amended by P.A. 89-387, §100, eff. Aug. 20, 1995.
Formerly Ill. Rev. Stat. 1991, ch. 23, ¶6608.

20/9. AUTHORITY TO CONSENT TO SERVICES

§9. Authority to consent to services. (a) If an eligible adult consents to services being provided according to the service care plan, such services shall be arranged to meet the adult's needs, based upon the availability of resources to provide such services. If an adult withdraws his consent or refuses to accept such services, the services shall not be provided.

(b) If it reasonably appears to the Department or other agency designated under this Act that a person is an eligible adult and lacks the capacity to consent to necessary services, the Department or other agency may seek the appointment of a temporary guardian as provided in Article XIa of the Probate Act of 1975[9] for the purpose of consenting to such services.

(c) A guardian of the person of an eligible adult may consent to services being provided according to the service care plan. If a guardian withdraws his consent or refuses to allow services to be provided to the eligible adult, the Department may request an order of protection under the Illinois Domestic Violence Act of 1986[10] seeking appropriate remedies, and may in addition request removal of the guardian and appointment of a successor guardian.

(d) If an emergency exists and the Department or other agency designated under this Act reasonably believes that a person is an eligible adult and lacks the capacity to consent to necessary services, the Department or other agency may request an order from the circuit court of the county in which the petitioner or respondent resides or in which the alleged abuse or neglect occurred, authorizing an assessment of a report or alleged or suspected abuse or neglect and the provision of necessary services including relief available under the Illinois Domestic Violence Act of 1986.

P.A. 85-1184, §9, eff. Aug. 13, 1988.
Formerly Ill. Rev. Stat. 1991, ch. 23, ¶6609.

20/10. RULES

§10. Rules. The Department shall adopt such rules and regulations as it deems necessary to implement this Act.

P.A. 85-1184, §10, eff. Aug. 13, 1988.
Formerly Ill. Rev. Stat. 1991, ch. 23, ¶6610.

20/11. ANNUAL REPORTS

§11. The Department shall file with the Governor and the general Assembly within 90 days after the end of each fiscal year, a report concerning its implementation of this Act during such fiscal year, together with any recommendations for future implementation.

P.A. 85-1184, §11, eff. Aug. 13, 1988.
Formerly Ill. Rev. Stat. 1991, ch. 23, ¶6611.

20/12. IMPLEMENTATION

§12. Implementation. The Department shall implement this Act Statewide, beginning in such areas of the State as it shall designate by rule, as appropriated funds become available.

P.A. 85-1184, §12, eff. Aug. 13, 1988.
Formerly Ill. Rev. Stat. 1991, ch. 23, ¶6612.

---

[1]210 ILCS 45/1-113.
[2]210 ILCS 40/1 et seq.
[3]210 ILCS 85/1 et seq.
[4]210 ILCS 35/1 et seq.
[5]210 ILCS 140/1 et seq.
[6]210 ILCS 135/1 et seq.
[7]750 ILCS 60/101 et seq.
[8]225 ILC 20/1 et seq.
[9]755 ILC 5/11a-1 et seq.
[10]750 ILC 60/101 et seq.

Cultural Perspectives on Intimate Violence

Giselé Casanova Oates, Ph.D.
Department of Behavioral Sciences
Purdue University Calumet

Throughout the history of the United States, various ethnic groups have been colonized and others have immigrated and continue to immigrate. As a result, a rapidly growing proportion of the population of the United States consists of people of color. Estimates predict that by the year 2000, ethnic minorities will constitute more than 25% of the U.S. population, and by 2080, approximately 51% of the population will be ethnic minorities (Andrews, 1992). Such predictions suggest that ethnic minorities may soon become the majority in the United States. Yet even though their numbers in the population are increasing, their status is not. Ethnic minorities earn $12,000 to $15,000 less than European Americans, and a greater proportion of their group (23% to 27% versus approximately 8%) lives below the poverty level (U.S. Bureau of the Census, 1991).

In addition to economic disadvantages, people of color have consistently encountered instances of prejudice in this country. Ethnic minorities bring with them their culture, traditions, values, and beliefs, which may be quite distinct from those of the majority culture. Hence, the experience of being a person of color in the United States is quite different than that of being a member of the majority group. Lack of understanding about the cultural heritage of ethnic minority groups can lead to negative attitudes and ideas about them. Cultural insensitivity can influence intrepretations of behavior, including instances of intimate violence.

Studies that examined the relationship between intimate violence and race have suggested that ethnicity may influence whether or not an individual is identified as being abused or as the abuser. Gil (1970) conducted the first large-scale summary of national reports and concluded that families reported for abuse were drawn disproportionately from the less educated, the poor, and ethnic minorities. Specifically, African American children were found to be overrepresented as victims of abuse. Hampton, Gelles, and Harrop (1991) concurred with this finding and suggested that African American children "have been overrepresented in the national tabulation of official child abuse and neglect reports since their inception" (p. 4). Newberger, Reed, Daniel, Hyde, and Kotelchuck (1977) suggested that children from poor and minority families are more likely to be labeled as abused than children from more affluent households. The latter group of children tended to be classified as victims of accidents. Research conducted by Gelles (1982) provided support for this suggestion. Gelles reported that when physicians made a report of child abuse, they considered the child's physical condition as well as the caregiver's education, occupation, race, and ethnicity. Further, 5% of a group of physicians surveyed (N=157) indicated that the caregiver's race and ethnicity were so important that they would file an abuse report solely on the basis of those characteristics (Gelles, 1982).

Turbett and O'Toole (1980) employed a case vignette model and found that physicians' recognition of child abuse was affected by severity of injury and by the socioeconomic status and ethnicity of the parents. When the children in the case vignettes were described as having a major injury, African American children were nearly twice as likely as white children to be recognized as victims of abuse. Physicians were 33% more likely to report African American children who were identified as suffering from a major injury than children identified as white who were described as having identical injuries (Turbett and O'Toole, 1980).

Hampton (1986) reanalyzed data from the 1981 National Study of the Incidence and Severity of Child Abuse and Neglect, focusing on child maltreatment cases seen in hospitals, and found that African American and Hispanic children were more likely than white children to be reported to child protection agencies as alleged victims of maltreatment. The researcher indicated that his data suggested that African American and Hispanic families may be victimized by a process that focuses on personal characteristics, such as ethnicity, to identify them as deviant rather than focusing on their alleged behaviors (Hampton, 1986).

After considering the results of the above-noted research, a question that comes to mind is, "Why are ethnic minorities more likely to be reported as abused or to be identified as the abuser?" A possible explanation may be that biases, prejudice, or lack of knowledge about a specific culture may subject ethnic minority families to the stigma of being labeled as abusive or neglectful. Thus, the need for cultural sensitivity in understanding intimate violence has become critical. O'Keefe's (1994) research supports this sentiment. She examined racial and ethnic differences among 121 battered women (42% white, 37% Hispanic, and 21% African American) and found no significant racial or ethnic differences in the amount of husband-to-wife or wife-to-husband violence. O'Keefe also found child abuse to be unrelated to race or ethnicity. As a result of her lack of significant findings with respect to racial or ethnic differences, O'Keefe (1994) stated, "It is time to re-examine cultural biases that have encouraged the belief that family violence occurs more frequently or with greater severity in minority families, particularly in African American families" (p. 302).

Prior to the consideration of culture, traditions, and values of ethnic minorities in the United States, it is necessary to gain a better understanding of the research that has been conducted and the data that has been presented with respect to people of color. Space does not permit a comprehensive review of research that examined intimate violence among all ethnic minorities in the United States. Therefore, this chapter focuses on the following four ethnic minority groups: African Americans, Hispanics, Asian Americans, and Native Americans.

RESEARCH ON ETHNIC MINORITIES AND INTIMATE VIOLENCE

African Americans

Research that investigated intimate violence and African Americans has produced mixed results. Some researchers have suggested that African Americans compared with whites have higher rates of child abuse (e.g., Gil, 1970) whereas others have found lower rates for African Americans (e.g., Billingsley, 1969) or have found no noteworthy differences (e.g., Young, 1963).

In a comparison of 1975 and 1985 national survey rates, Hampton et al. (1991) found that although the rates of severe violence were fairly similar in African American and white homes in 1975, the rates of severe violence toward African American children were double that toward white children in 1985. Hampton et al. indicated that no evidence was found to relate the increase in rate to unfavorable social or economic conditions or to lack of access to prevention and treatment services. They suggested that the increase in rate may be due to a change in cultural attitudes concerning acts of violence that are appropriate to use on children (Hampton et al., 1991).

Cazenave and Straus (1978) analyzed a subsample of data from a 1975 national survey that included African American and white respondents. The researchers obtained data on both normative and behavioral aspects of violence and found that after controlling for class-related variables, such as income and husband's occupation, African American respondents were less violent than their white counterparts. Further, they found that the African American respondents were less likely to report slapping or spanking a child within the past year and that African Americans were less likely than their white counterparts to engage in child abuse, sibling abuse, and parent abuse at the higher income levels (Cazenave and Straus, 1978).

Although spousal violence is considered a universal problem, researchers have suggested that it is more prevalent in African American families than in European American families (Straus, Gelles, and Steinmetz, 1980). The first large-scale investigation of family violence was conducted in 1976 by Straus et al. (1980) to examine the extent of spousal violence among Americans. Straus et al. based their estimates on the self-reports of 2,143 American couples (147 African American and 1,996 non–African American) who responded to Straus's (1979) Conflict Tactics Scales. They reported that 11% of the African American women compared with 3% of the European American women were victims of wife abuse and indicated that wife abuse was 400% more frequent among African Americans than among European Americans (Straus et al., 1980). The researchers attempted to explain their findings by suggesting that "black males could be using acts of violence on their wives to compensate for cultural deprivation of resources such as income or prestige, or else black males' violence might be a reflection of the macho image of men that condones and encourages acts of physical aggression" (Straus et al., 1980, p. 136). Following a similar line of thought, several researchers have regarded racial oppression as a factor that contributes to violent behavior among African American men who batter (Asbury, 1987; Staples, 1976; Williams, 1990; Williams and Griffin, 1991).

Husband battering tends to occur less often than wife abuse, yet studies have found that incidences of the former situation are higher among African Americans than among whites. While reviewing research on women who kill, Mann (1987) indicated that most female perpetrators of homicide are African American, that their victims tend to be men, and that long-standing abuse was frequently an important motivating factor.

DeMaris (1990) examined courtship violence, a possible precursor to marital violence, in a sample of African American and white students at four southeastern universities. He found that violence against girlfriends and violence against boyfriends were both more likely to occur among African American students than among white students.

To determine which situational and background characteristics distinguished individuals who only battered their marital partners from those who also engaged in extradomestic violence, Fagen, Stewart, and Hansen (1983) collected data from 270 domestic violence victims. Their racial comparisons of spouse abuse indicated that European Americans, compared with African Americans, were more violent both inside and outside of the home.

Lockhart (1991) compared the incidence of marital violence among African American women and European American women, from a range of social classes, who were either legally married to or cohabiting with their partners. She found no significant differences between the proportion of African American and European American women who reported being victims of husband-to-wife violence during the previous year. Further, no significant differences were found between upper-class African American women and upper-class European American women with respect to reports of being victimized by husband-to-wife violence. The same finding was also true for middle- and lower-class groups of African American and European American women.

Hispanics

Investigations of intimate violence in Hispanic families tend to be sparse compared with the data collected on African American families. Scholars have theorized that a high level of male dominance among Hispanic couples may lead to high levels of family violence (Carroll, 1980). Mirande (1977), however, indicated that there is a lack of empirical support for the theorized macho patriarch in Hispanic families, and Grebler, Moore, and Guzman (1970) described the relationship of 363 Mexican American couples as "egalitarian" with respect to division of household tasks.

Sorenson and Telles (1991) surveyed Mexican Americans and non-Hispanic whites about their experience of spousal violence and found that rates for Mexican Americans born in Mexico and non-Hispanic whites born in the United States were nearly equivalent. They also found that rates of spousal violence were highest for Mexican Americans born in the United States and interpreted this finding as the result of stress experienced from cultural conflict.

In an investigation of racial differences among shelter residents, Gondolf, Fisher, and McFerron (1991) found that, compared with African American and white women, Hispanic women tended to report the longest duration of abuse and were the least likely to engage in help-seeking behavior such as contacting a friend, minister, or social service worker.

Straus and Smith (1990) examined intimate violence in a nationally representative sample of 721 Hispanic families and 4,052 non-Hispanic white families. They found that in approximately one out of four Hispanic households, an assault occurred between married or cohabiting partners during the year of the survey and that half of these incidents involved acts such as kicking, punching, biting, and choking. Their results also indicated that one out of seven Hispanic children were severely assaulted by their parents during the year of the survey. Overall, they found the rate of violence in Hispanic families to be much greater than the rate in non-Hispanic white families and suggested that the rates presented from their study were probably underestimates. Finally, Straus and Smith (1990) theorized that "the higher rate of spouse abuse in Hispanic families reflects the economic deprivation, youthfulness, and urban residence of Hispanics. When these factors are controlled, there is no statistically significant difference between Hispanics and non-Hispanic whites" (p. 364).

Asian Americans

Although Asian Americans are described as the fastest growing ethnic minority group in the United States (LaFromboise, 1992), there is a dearth of empirical research on intimate violence and Asian Americans. Asbury (1993) suggested that non-Asians hold the mistaken assumption that Asian Americans have successfully assimilated into the dominant culture, and as a result, they experience no problems related to cultural conflict. Perhaps this assumption may account for the lack of information on Asian Americans and intimate violence because it is believed that there is no problem.

Bhaumik (1988) examined cultural issues in violent Asian American families and found that Asian American wives who experienced abuse tended to come from families characterized by adherence to rigid Asian patriarchal attitudes. These attitudes contrast sharply with the greater freedom that women have in today's American society and suggest that cultural differences in gender-role expectations are an important factor in spouse abuse.

Hong and Hong (1991) investigated perspectives on child abuse and neglect among Chinese, Hispanic, and white university students. Subjects were asked to evaluate the severity of twelve vignettes that depicted parental conduct that might or might not be considered abusive or neglectful, depending on the individual's perception. Hong and Hong found that Chinese subjects, compared with Hispanic and white subjects, tended to judge parental conduct less harshly, tended to recommend agency intervention less frequently, and appeared to be less critical of parental use of physical force to achieve a desired end. Additionally, compared with Hispanic subjects, Chinese subjects tended to give greater latitude to parents with respect to child-rearing decisions even though others may not be in agreement with their choices (Hong and Hong, 1991).

Native Americans

As with Asian Americans, very little empirical research exists with respect to Native Americans and intimate violence. Scholars have suggested that this lack of research may be due to the complexities of cultural variation in Indian communities that hamper accurate reporting of cases and gaining cooperation in a community (Gelles and Lancaster, 1987; Johnson, 1981; Kadushin and Martin, 1981; Levine and Levine, 1981; Long, 1986; May, 1982; Unger, 1977).

Among the studies that have been conducted, the incidence of child abuse and neglect has been found to vary widely from tribe to tribe (Fischler, 1985; White, 1977; Wischlacz, Lane, and Kempe, 1978). Fischler (1985) found variation among Indian groups in the United States with respect to reporting of neglect cases, and White (1977) found that among the Navajo, a large percentage of abuse (50%) and neglect (80%) cases were alcohol related. Based on the results of a case-control study with Navajo women, Oakland and Kane (1973) reported a relationship between increased cases of child neglect and increased opportunities for wage labor among the women. Wischlacz et al. (1978) found sexual abuse to be less frequent among the Cheyenne River Sioux compared with U.S. averages.

Lujan, DeBruyn, May, and Bird (1989) examined child abuse and neglect among Indian tribes (eleven Pueblo tribes and one Apache tribe) in a southwestern state. Their sample consisted of fifty-three abused or neglected children targeted by a local Indian Health Service Hospital. Information was also obtained on the children's parents, grandparents, and even great-grandparents in several instances. Lujan et al. found that in their sample, child neglect was more prevalent than child abuse. The majority of children (65%), however, were both abused and neglected. Alcohol abuse was found to be present in 85% of the neglect cases and in 63% of the abuse cases. This finding lead Lujan et al. to conclude that child maltreatment occurs within the larger context of multiproblem families and that there may be an intergenerational perpetuation of these problems.

Intervention with Native American children, compared with other ethnic minority children, is somewhat unique because it is guided by the 1978 Indian Child Welfare Act. The act is based on years of research that discovered that, based on the long-standing misapplication of middle-class norms to Native American families, social service agencies had removed these children from their homes (Tower, 1996). This federal legislation replaces normal state procedures. Specifically, the federal government has empowered some reservations to establish legislative bodies, such as courts, to handle child maltreatment cases. Wischlacz and Wechsler (1983) found variations among the way in which different tribes interpret their rights under this law. Some tribes handle cases independently of outside intervention, whereas others work in conjunction with non–Native American agencies.

CULTURAL CONSIDERATIONS

Although definitions of culture may vary in certain respects, scholars agree on some central elements. In identifying these elements, Walters, Canady, and Stein (1994) purposed the following:

> Culture is a body of learned beliefs, traditions, principles, and guides for behavior that are shared among members of a particular group. Cultural elements act as a sort of road map for individuals as they interact with others. Elements of culture such as values, language, rituals, and traditions, evolve or change slowly over time and some elements take on new shapes or meanings among subgroups of people who share a geographic origin. (p. 447)

Ethnic minorities within the United States contribute to the cultural diversity of our country. Gaining an understanding and an appreciation of cultures other than one's own is an important factor when examining intimate violence among people of color. On a cautionary note, information about the culture, beliefs, and traditions of ethnic minorities should not be converted into stereotypes. Subgroups exist within ethnic minority groups; therefore, homogeneity within these groups should not be assumed. Instead, information about the culture of people of color should be used as a guide rather than as hard and fast rules for all members of an ethnic minority group.

African Americans

African Americans have a unique history of immigration to the United States. The majority of African Americans descend from ancestors who were forcibly taken from their villages in Africa and brought to America as slaves. Yet, they have made vast contributions to every aspect of this country's development. African Americans have "a heritage built upon a strong sense of family, community, and culture as well as a will to survive and progress" (Willis, 1992, p. 144).

Despite what many individuals have suggested, slavery did not eliminate the value of kinship and kinship bonds. The family, both immediate and extended, has been and remains a source of strength, resilience, and survival for African Americans. Furthermore, in contrast to the value that mainstream culture places on the nuclear (immediate) family, African Americans value and rely on the extended family. In a study of twenty-five African American and white families, Hays and Mendel (1972) found that for African Americans, the extended family was an important support system that served to buffer individuals from an environment of racial hostility. Based on their investigation of African American extended families in the southern United States, Shimkin, Louie, and Frate (as cited in Cazenave and Straus, 1978) concluded that one of the functions of the extended family was the prevention of child abuse and neglect among lower-class African Americans. Further, McAdoo (as cited in Cazenave and Straus, 1978) suggested that the extended family serves as an important source of social support for African Americans at all socioeconomic levels.

With respect to male-female relationships, African American women are generally described as being strong but not domineering. The term "egalitarian" has been used to characterize male-female relationships within African American families (Nobles, 1980). In an attempt to explain the reason for the egalitarian nature of African American male-female relationships in the home, Landry (as cited in Ucko, 1994) suggested that because African American men have generally been denied economic power, they are not privy to the male supremacy doctrine, proposed by whites, that accompanies and supports this ideology.

Respecting and obeying elders is valued within African American families because they are seen as having wisdom and hindsight. There is also a high value placed on obeying one's parents. It is believed that children need protection and guidance and that they must be disciplined. Traditionally, African American parents, as well as responsible adults in the neighborhood, participated in the training and discipline of children. The setting of limits with children is believed to be important because it teaches children to follow rules set forth by society and to respect the rights of others (Willis, 1992).

Attainment of an education is of great significance to many African Americans. It is believed that a good education will enable an individual to better his or her life circumstances and allow him or her to "give back" to the family and community.

Language is a form of identification for many African Americans. Willis (1992) described African Americans as "high-context communicators who use shared experiences, non-verbal cues and signals, and the situation itself as a large part of the communicative process" (p. 143). Some African Americans use a dialect that has been referred to as black English or more recently as Ebonics (i.e., *ebony* phon*ics*). This dialect is influenced by some African language patterns that have been retained, by geographic region, and by socioeconomic status (Willis, 1992). Black English may serve to unite its speakers. Although some African Americans may use black English, they have also been described as having the ability to "code switch" (i.e., move back and forth between standard American English and black English) depending on their audience (Genovese, 1974).

Religion has remained a source of spiritual sustenance for African Americans (Randall-David, 1989). The church serves as an informal support network for families and has been the place to provide opportunities to develop leadership and organizational skills in addition to sponsoring various community-based activities.

In contrasting the beliefs and values of African Americans with those of mainstream culture, Willis (1992) noted that African Americans value a collective orientation rather than an individual one, value kinship and extended family ties rather than nuclear or immediate family bonds, are high-context communicators instead of low-context speakers, value a religious and spiritual orientation rather than a secular one, use more authoritarian practices to discipline children rather than permissive practices, have a great respect for the elderly instead of devaluing their role in the family, and are oriented to situation rather than to time.

Hispanics

The term "Hispanic" is used to refer to individuals who live in the United States and who trace their origins to Spain or to one of the Spanish-speaking nations of Latin America (Marin and Marin, 1991). Hispanics include people of Mexican origin, Puerto Rican origin, Central or South American origin, Cuban origin, and those who originate from Spain. Thus, the Hispanic population is characterized by its diversity. Each of the Spanish-speaking nations has its own political history and immigration patterns. Yet there are some similarities (in language and culture, for example) that exist from group to group.

The use of the Spanish language is a unifying factor for Hispanics. Depending on the country of origin, there may be slight variations in the language. Zuniga (1992) suggested that in the United States, acculturation influences the degree of fluency in Spanish. Similar to African Americans, Hispanics have the tendency to code switch or shift from one language to another, depending on the audience.

A strong sense of family loyalty is characteristic of Hispanics. Thus, they may be reluctant to involve outsiders in family conflict. Hispanics are guided by a collective orientation that emphasizes the importance of family, both immediate and extended, and the community. Consequently, the extended family serves as an important support system. Traditional Hispanic families have been described as exhibiting male supremacy and female passivity. Child rearing was identified as the exclusive domain of the mother. Ramirez and Arce (1981), however, noted that the concept of *machismo,* absolute patriarchy of the father, is much less influential on the structure of contemporary Hispanic families. Ybarra-Soriano (as cited in Zuniga, 1992) found that joint decision making and greater equality of male-female roles is often descriptive of Hispanic families, especially when the wife works outside the home.

The parent-child relationship is extremely important to Hispanics. Young children are not pushed to achieve developmental milestones as are European American children, and the expression of negative emotions, such as anger and aggression, is not acceptable. Hispanic children are taught adherence to convention and respect for authority, including their elders. Such teaching is believed to result in a child who is *una persona bien educada* or a well-educated individual who will respect others as well as society's rules (Zuniga, 1992).

A large majority of Hispanics are Roman Catholic as a result of the influence of Spanish heritage. Depending on the country of origin, however, there may be a mixture of African or Indian religions blended with Catholicism. Thus, in a Hispanic home it would not be unusual to find a variety of Catholic statues (of saints, for example) next to a food offering to an African demigod (Zuniga, 1992). Finally, with respect to religion, the influence of Catholicism and its teachings against divorce may contribute to the finding that greater numbers of Hispanic women remain in abusive marriages for longer periods of time compared with European American women (Gondolf et al., 1991).

In contrasting the beliefs and values of Hispanics with those of mainstream culture, Zuniga (1992) noted that Hispanics value a collective rather than individual orientation, value interdependence and cooperation rather than independence and competition, are more relaxed with child development rather than hold strong expectations for achievement of developmental milestones, respect their elderly rather than devalue the elderly, and value the extended family system rather than the nuclear family.

Asian Americans

Asian Americans are characterized by considerable diversity and originate from three major geographic areas: (1) East Asia, which includes China, Japan, and Korea; (2) Southeast Asia, which includes Cambodia, Laos, Vietnam, Burma, Thailand, Malaysia, Indonesia, Singapore, and the Philippines; and (3) South Asia, which includes India, Pakistan, and Sri Lanka. Asian Americans have been described as the "model ethnic minority group" and, as previously noted, non-Asians mistakenly believe that they have successfully assimilated into the dominant culture (Asbury, 1993). Their customs, traditions, values, and beliefs are rooted in political and religious foundations that are thousands of years old.

Over the past 2,000 years, many Asian cultures have been influenced by the doctrines and philosophies of Buddhism, Confucianism, and Taoism. These "three teachings" serve as the religious and philosophical foundation that underlies virtually all aspects of Asian life. "Adherence to the 'three teachings' reflects a polytheistic orientation that stresses complementarity rather than conflict among Confucianism, Taoism, and Buddhism" (Chan, 1992, p. 189).

Asian Americans value collectivism as opposed to individualism, and the family is seen as the backbone of society (Chan, 1992). There is a strong sense of loyalty and obligation to the family. As with Hispanics, this may account for Asian Americans' reluctance to involve outside agencies in family matters. Cooperation, interdependence, and reciprocity are primary aspects of the family. An individual's behavior is a reflection on one's family and one's ancestors. Therefore, Asian Americans strive to defend their family honor and to save face (i.e., protect the family's reputation). Ultimately, the value of familism dictates that the family is more important than the individual.

The parental role is seen as more important than the marital relationship (Chan, 1992). Parents readily sacrifice their needs to look after the best interest of their children. Consequently, parents assume "the right to demand unquestioning obedience and loyalty from the child. The role of the parent is to define the law, and the duty of the child is to listen and obey" (Chan, 1992, p. 216). This ideal is referred to as filial piety, and it considers parents' authority over their children to be indisputable and their judgment to be unquestionable.

Education is of great value to Asian Americans. A lifelong respect and appreciation for knowledge, intelligence, and learning are ingrained in their children. Through academic achievement, Asian American children bring honor to their family while preparing for educational and occupational successes that will enhance their future.

Within Asian American families, the husband or father is traditionally seen as the principal provider. The wife's role is to take responsibility for what occurs inside the home, including managing financial matters and rearing the children (Dung, 1984). It is the wife's duty to be a good mother. Kim (1985) suggested that a wife is basically viewed as a nonperson until she gives birth to a son, after which she gains more power as a mother and even more when she becomes a mother-in-law.

In contrasting the beliefs and values of Asian Americans with those of mainstream culture, Chan (1992) noted that Asian Americans value harmony with nature rather than mastery over nature, value a collectivist orientation rather than an individual one, view religion from a polytheistic stance rather than a monotheistic stance, value cooperation instead of competition, and believe that the family is the primary unit in society rather than the individual.

Native Americans

Individuals referred to as Native Americans include American Indians, Eskimos, and Aleuts (Johnson, 1981). Their cultural and historical roots date back thousands of years. Although Native Americans reside in every state in the United States, they are often referred to as invisible because they comprise approximately 0.75% of the country's population (Joe and Malach, 1992). There is a great deal of diversity among tribes. Despite efforts to pressure them to assimilate, many Native Americans hold onto their tribal customs while also adopting many non-Indian practices.

Native Americans value harmony with nature. As such, they believe in protecting the land rather than destroying it for economic gain. They tend to be oriented to the present time rather than holding a preoccupation with the future. Native Americans value being part of a group and place great significance on group consensus with respect to decision making (Joe and Malach, 1992).

Native Americans' definition of the family includes extended family members. They value age and life experience; thus, elders are respected. Joe and Malach (1992) indicated that grandparents often assume child-rearing responsibilities so that parents can work. Native American children are often taught to be self-sufficient at an early age. They are reared in an adult-centered world, and imitation of acceptable adult behavior is rewarded.

Central to many Native American belief systems is the notion of the interconnectedness of all things, living and nonliving. This belief suggests that humans are merely a small part of the larger universe. Native Americans also believe that good health is due to the harmony of the four elements: the physical, the mental, the emotional, and the spiritual (Bopp, Bopp, Brown, and Lane, 1984). Consequently, there are many ceremonies aimed at maintaining or regaining harmony.

Because Native Americans live in a bicultural world, institutions that serve Native American children offer bilingual education. As such, attention is given to the continuation of tribal language while also teaching English. Differing levels of acculturation may impact language usage. For example, grandparents living on a reservation may tend to use their native language predominately, whereas a grandchild living in the city may use English predominately (Hoffman, 1981).

In contrasting the beliefs and values of Native Americans with those of mainstream culture, Joe and Malach (1992) noted that Native Americans value group life rather than focusing on the individual, respect elders rather than respect youth, avoid criticism or ridicule of others if possible rather than seek criticism or confrontation, value the extended family rather than the nuclear family, and seek harmony rather than progress.

INFLUENCE OF CULTURE ON INTIMATE VIOLENCE

Culture may influence an individual's opinions and manner of interpreting information. Communication styles, both verbal and nonverbal, may be influenced by culture. It may have an impact on the language one speaks as well as on one's interactions with family, friends, and strangers. Both actions and reactions may be affected by one's culture. Consequently, consideration should be given to ways in which an individual's culture could potentially influence various aspects of intimate violence. For instance, definitions, interpretations, and reporting of abusive acts may be influenced by culture. In addition, help-seeking behavior may be affected by the beliefs and values of one's culture.

In an effort to identify relationships between culture and responses to intimate violence, researchers have suggested that a higher tolerance level for violence exists in families characterized by patriarchal male-dominated relationships (e.g., Hispanics) than in other families (Carroll, 1980; Segovia-Ashley, 1978). Communication styles and language barriers may impact the reporting (or underreporting) of abuse. Zambrano (1985) suggested that in Hispanic families where the husband speaks better English than the wife, police may not understand that she is accusing her spouse of battery and may rely on the husband's translation of the incident. Language barriers may also impede help-seeking behaviors, especially when agencies have no bilingual staff.

As noted above, many ethnic minority groups place a high value on the family. Loyalty and honor to one's family are often placed before individual interests. This particular value could present a dilemma for people of color who are victims of intimate violence. Reporting abuse or seeking assistance means that one would have to accuse a family member and that the member could be arrested. Such actions could result in a "loss of face" or bring dishonor and shame to the family. In cultures where this is not sanctioned (e.g., Asian Americans), the end result may be to decide to preserve family honor and not report the abusive incident. Furthermore, many ethnic minority groups frown upon having outsiders involved in family matters. This cultural value may also prevent individuals from reporting abuse and seeking help.

Native Americans who experience intimate violence face additional problems. While it is not acceptable to seek help outside of the community (American Indian Women Against Domestic Violence, as cited in Rasche, 1988), staff members of reservation social service agencies or law enforcement officers may be related to the victim or even to the perpetrator. Such situations could lead to the possibility of bias against the victim. More specifically, the victim may not be believed or may be advised to try to work things out on his or her own rather than seek outside assistance.

Cultural attitudes and expectations about the role of children may also influence intimate violence. Parents who are from cultures that demand unquestioning obedience and respect from children (e.g., African Americans, Hispanics, and Asian Americans) may define abuse quite differently from mainstream culture. For example, frequently beating a child with an instrument that leaves welts, cuts, and bruises on his or her body may be interpreted as a means of teaching a child discipline rather than being viewed as physically abusive.

The value placed on religious beliefs and the role that the church plays in family life might impact a victim's reactions to an incident of intimate violence. As discussed previously, religious beliefs and the church play prominent roles in the lives of some ethnic minority groups (e.g., African Americans and Hispanics). Traditionally, males have dominated the leadership positions in religious organizations. Their beliefs and biases may affect the type of assistance given to female members who are victims of intimate violence. For example, Rasche (1988) suggested that African American pastors with sexists attitudes "may quote scriptures to complaining women which perpetuate male domination and female subservience" (p. 162). Further, since slavery, the church has been viewed as a source of spiritual hope and strength for African Americans. White (1985) indicated that faith in a "higher power" helped slaves endure the "pain of losing loved ones on the auction block because they had a firm belief that their families would be reunited in another life" (p. 63). The belief in claiming your reward in the afterlife could suggest to some victims that they should endure their suffering (i.e., victimization) while on Earth rather than seeking change because they will be rewarded in heaven.

In addition, some religious teachings may influence a victim's response to intimate violence. For example, Catholicism does not sanction divorce, and as noted earlier, a majority of Hispanics are Roman Catholic. It is quite conceivable that Hispanic women who are practicing Catholics being battered by their husbands may opt to remain in abusive marriages to adhere to their religious beliefs.

Although the above discussion highlights a few ways in which an individual's culture could impact various aspects of intimate violence, the situation becomes further complicated when the person is an illegal alien. In addition to dealing with cultural differences and possibly isolation, these individuals have to hide their illegal status. Thus, many illegal aliens who are victims of intimate violence may fail to report the abuse or seek help because they fear deportation. According to Rasche (1988), many women who are in the United States illegally are not aware that they are entitled to protection under the law while in this country, even if they are not citizens.

IMPLICATIONS FOR PREVENTION AND TREATMENT

People of color have unique life experiences that may influence the way they process being a victim or perpetrator of intimate violence. Employing prevention and treatment strategies developed in the majority culture to families of color could prove to be ineffective and disastrous. Consequently, the need for cultural competency is of utmost importance when developing prevention and treatment strategies to be used with families of color. Cultural competency involves the "ability to appreciate and use knowledge about culture in order to assist in the resolution of a problem" (Walters et al., 1994, p. 449). Differences in communication styles, language barriers, religious beliefs, ideas about discipline and conflict resolution, and the role of women and children in the family are just a few of the variables that should be addressed. Mental health professionals working with families of color and issues surrounding intimate violence need to have a high level of commitment given that cultural competency is "a life-long process which includes the examination of personal attitudes, the acquisition of relevant knowledge, and the development of skills which facilitate working effectively with those who are culturally different from oneself" (Walters et al., 1994, p. 449).

Acquisition of cultural competency can enhance an individual's skills and aid in the development of prevention and treatment strategies that are ethnically sensitive. That is, prevention and treatment strategies could be designed so as to build on the use of ethnic cultural concepts, values, and so forth as a means of providing more effective interventions with people of color. For example, Williams (1990) suggested that when working with African American male batterers, it would be beneficial to help them reframe their violent behavior within a cultural context, emphasizing the inconsistency between their behavior and the traditions, customs, and codes of conduct of African Americans. Ultimately, incorporating cultural elements in intimate violence prevention and treatment strategies with people of color could help to increase the chances of the strategies being successful.

CONCLUSION

The experience of being a person of color in the United States is quite different from that of being a member of the majority group. Cultural beliefs, values, and traditions of ethnic minorities may influence the way they process being a victim or perpetrator of intimate violence. A lack of understanding of cultural differences could lead to the development of stereotypes about an ethnic minority group and to the misinterpretation of behavior. Practitioners working with families of color need to develop an appreciation for their culture. Knowledge about an ethnic minority group's culture and how it may influence aspects of intimate violence can assist in the development and implementation of effective prevention and treatment.

EDITORIAL SUMMARY

A rapidly growing proportion of the U.S. population consists of people of color. Estimates predict that by the year 2080, over half of the country's population will be ethnic minorities. Their culture and values may differ from those of the majority, and those differences could contribute to misinterpretations of behavior, including acts of intimate violence.

Studies that investigated intimate violence in families of color have produced mixed results. Some researchers have suggested the existence of higher rates of child and spouse abuse among African American families compared with white families, whereas other researchers were not able to identify any such significant differences. Similar mixed results can be found for Hispanics and intimate violence. Empirical research that investigates violence in Asian American and Native American families is sparse. From the research that has been conducted, it is suggested that Asian American women who were abused tended to come from families characterized by adherence to rigid patriarchal attitudes. Alcohol abuse has been found to coexist in over half the cases of child abuse and neglect that were identified in various Native American tribes. The 1978 Indian Child Welfare Act has empowered some reservations to establish courts to handle child maltreatment cases.

An understanding and appreciation of cultural values is an important factor to consider when examining intimate violence among people of color. Despite cultural differences between African Americans, Hispanics, Asian Americans, and Native Americans, some similarities do exist. Each ethnic group places a strong value on the family, including extended family members. Individual interest takes a backseat to the best interest of the family. Involvement of outsiders in family matters is not sanctioned. Each group tends to expect their children to be obedient and to respect elders and authority figures. Males are generally the dominant figure in the household, and religious beliefs and teachings serve as important guides for family life. Given that culture can influence one's thoughts and behavior, it is important to understand how it may impact various aspects of intimate violence including definitions, interpretations and reporting of abusive acts, and help-seeking behavior.

People of color have unique life experiences that may influence the way they process intimate violence. Consequently, prevention and treatment strategies used with ethnic minority groups need to be culturally competent and ethnically sensitive. This would increase the probability of the intervention being successful.

REFERENCES

Andrews, M. M. (1992). Cultural perspectives on nursing in the 21st century. *Journal of Professional Nursing, 8*, 7–15.

Asbury, J. (1987). African-American women in violent relationships: An exploration of cultural differences. In R. L. Hampton (Ed.), *Violence in the Black Family: Correlates and Consequences* (pp. 89–105). Lexington, MA: Lexington Books.

Asbury, J. (1993). Violence in families of color in the United States. In R. L. Hampton, G. R. Adams, E. H. Potter, and R. P. Weissberg (Eds.), *Family Violence: Prevention and Treatment* (pp. 159-178). Newbury Park, CA: Sage.

Bhaumik, M. (1988). *A Study of Wife Abuse in Two Cultures: The American and the Asian American.* Los Angeles: Micrographics Department, Doheny Library, University of Southern California.

Billingsley, A. (1969). Family functioning in the low-income black community. *Casework, 50*, 563–572.

Bopp, J., Bopp, M., Brown, L., and Lane, P. (1984). *The Sacred Tree*. Alberta, Canada: Four Worlds Development Press.

Carroll, J. C. (1980). A cultural consistency theory of family violence in Mexican American and Jewish ethnic groups. In G. T. Hotaling and M. A. Straus (Eds.), *The Social Causes of Husband-Wife Violence* (pp. 93–106). Minneapolis: University of Minnesota Press.

Cazenave, N. A., and Straus, M. A. (1978). Race, class, network embeddedness, and family violence: A search for potent support systems. *Journal of Comparative Family Studies, 10,* 281–300.

Chan, S. (1992). Families with Asian roots. In E. W. Lynch and M. J. Hanson (Eds.), *Developing Cross-Cultural Competency: A Guide for Working with Young Children and Their Families* (pp. 181–257). Baltimore: Paul H. Brookes.

DeMaris, A. (1990). The dynamics of generational transfer in courtship violence: A biracial exploration. *Journal of Marriage and the Family, 52,* 219–232.

Dung, T. N. (1984). Understanding Asian families: A Vietnamese perspective. *Children Today, 13,* 10–12.

Fagen, J., Stewart, D., and Hansen, K. (1983). Violent men or violent husbands? Background factors and situational correlates. In D. Finkelhor, R. J. Gelles, G. T. Hotaling, and M. A. Straus (Eds.), *The Dark Side of Families: Current Family Violence Research* (pp. 49–69). Beverly Hills, CA: Sage.

Fischler, R. S. (1985). Child abuse and neglect in American Indian communities. *Child Abuse and Neglect, 9,* 95–106.

Gelles, R. J.(1982). Child abuse and family violence: Implications for medical professionals. In E. H. Newberger (Ed.), *Child Abuse* (pp. 55–67). Boston: Little, Brown.

Gelles, R. J., and Lancaster, J. B. (1987). *Child Abuse and Neglect: Biosocial Dimensions.* New York: Aldine de Gruyter.

Genovese, E. D. (1974). *Roll, Jordan, Roll: The World Slaves Made.* New York: Pantheon Books.

Gil, D. G. (1970). *Violence Against Children: Physical Child Abuse in the United States.* Cambridge, MA: Harvard University Press.

Gondolf, E. W., Fisher, E., and McFerron, J. R. (1991). Racial differences among shelter residents: A comparison of Anglo, black, and Hispanic battered women. In R. L. Hampton (Ed.), *Black Family Violence* (pp. 103–113). Lexington, MA: Lexington Books.

Grebler, L., Moore, J. W., and Guzman, R. C. (1970). *The Mexican American People.* New York: Emerson Hall.

Hampton, R. L. (1986). Race, ethnicity, and child maltreatment: An analysis of cases recognized and reported by hospitals. In R. Staples (Ed.), *The Black Family: Essays and Studies* (3rd ed.) (pp. 178–191). Belmont, CA: Wadsworth.

Hampton, R. L., Gelles, R. J., and Harrop, J. (1991). Is violence in black families increasing? A comparison of 1975 and 1985 national survey rates. In R. L. Hampton (Ed.), *Black Family Violence* (pp. 3–18). Lexington, MA: Lexington Books.

Hays, W., and Mendel, C. H. (1972). Extended kinship relations in black and white families. *Journal of Marriage and the Family, 35,* 51–57.

Hoffman, F. (1981). *The American Indian Family: Strengths and Stresses.* Isleta, NM: American Indian Social Research and Development Association.

Hong, G. K., and Hong, L. K. (1991). Comparative perspectives on child abuse and neglect: Chinese versus Hispanics and whites. *Child Welfare, 70,* 463–475.

Joe, J. R., and Malach, R. S. (1992). Families with Native American roots. In E. W. Lynch and M. J. Hanson (Eds.), *Developing Cross-Cultural Competency: A Guide for Working with Young Children and Their Families* (pp. 89–119). Baltimore: Paul H. Brookes.

Johnson, D. R. (1981). The socioeconomic context of child abuse and neglect in native South America. In J. E. Korbin (Ed.), *Child Abuse and Neglect: Cross-Cultural Perspectives* (pp. 56–70). Berkeley: University of California Press.

Kadushin, A., and Martin, J. A. (1981). *Child Abuse: An Interactional Event.* New York: Columbia University Press.

Kim, S. C. (1985). Family therapy for Asian Americans: A strategic-structural framework. *Psychotherapy, 22,* 342–348.

LaFromboise, T. (1992). In obligation to our people: Giving merit to culture and individual differences. *Focus, 6,* 11–14.

Levine, S., and Levine, R. (1981). Child abuse and neglect in sub-Saharan Africa. In J. E. Korbin (Ed.), *Child Abuse and Neglect: Cross-Cultural Perspectives* (pp. 35–55). Berkeley: University of California Press.

Lockhart, L. L. (1991). Spousal violence: A cross-racial perspective. In R. L. Hampton (Ed.), *Black Family Violence* (pp. 85–101). Lexington, MA: Lexington Books.

Long, K. A. (1986). Cultural considerations in the assessment and treatment of intrafamilial abuse. *American Journal of Orthopsychiatry, 56,* 131–136.

Lujan, C., DeBruyn, L. M., May, P. A., and Bird, M. E. (1989). Profile of abused and neglected American Indian children in the southwest. *Child Abuse and Neglect, 13,* 449–461.

Mann, C. R. (1987). Black women who kill. In R. L. Hampton (Ed.), *Violence in the Black Family* (pp. 129–146). Lexington, MA: Lexington Books.

Marin, G., and Marin, B. V. (1991). *Research with Hispanic Populations.* Newbury Park, CA: Sage.

May, P. A. (1982). Substance abuse and American Indians: Prevalence and susceptibility. *International Journal of Addictions, 17,* 1185–1209.

Mirande, A. (1977). The Chicano family: A reanalysis of conflicting views. *Journal of Marriage and the Family, 39,* 747–756.

Newberger, E. H., Reed, R. B., Daniel, J. H., Hyde, J. N., and Kotelchuck, M. (1977). Pediatric social illness: Toward an etiologic classification. *Pediatrics, 60,* 178–185.

Nobles, W. (1980). Africanity: Its role in black families. *Black Scholar, 9,* 10–17.

Oakland, L., and Kane, R. L. (1973). The working mother and child neglect on the Navajo reservation. *Pediatrics, 51,* 849–853.

O'Keefe, M. (1994). Racial/ethnic differences among battered women and their children. *Journal of Child and Family Studies, 3,* 283–305.

Ramirez, O., and Arce, C. H. (1981). The contemporary Chicano family: An empirically based review. In A. Baron, Jr. (Ed.), *Explorations in Chicano Psychology* (pp. 3–28). New York: Praeger.

Randall-David, E. (1989). *Strategies for Working with Culturally Diverse Communities and Clients.* Washington, D.C.: Association for the Care of Children's Health.

Rasche, C. E. (1988). Minority women and domestic violence: The unique dilemmas of battered women of color. *Journal of Contemporary Criminal Justice, 4,* 150–171.

Segovia-Ashley. (1978). Shelters: Short-term needs. In *Battered Women: Issues of Public Policy.* Washington, DC: Commission on Civil Rights.

Sorenson, S. B., and Telles, C. A. (1991). Self-reports of spousal violence in a Mexican-American and non-Hispanic white population. *Violence and Victims, 6,* 3–15.

Staples, R. (1976). Race and family violence: The internal colonialism perspective. In L. E. Gary and L. P. Brown (Eds.), *Crime and Its Impact on the Black Community* (pp. 85–96). Washington, D. C.: Institute for Urban Development Center, Howard University.

Straus, M. A. (1979). Measuring intrafamily conflict and violence: The conflict tactics (CT) scales. *Journal of Marriage and the Family, 41,* 75–88.

Straus, M. A., Gelles, R. J., and Steinmetz, S. (1980). *Behind Closed Doors: Violence in American Families.* Garden City, NY: Doubleday.

Straus, M. A., and Smith, C. (1990). Violence in Hispanic families in the United States: Incidence rates and structural interpretations. In M. A. Straus and R. J. Gelles (Eds.), *Physical Violence in American Families: Risk Factors and Adaptations to Violence in 8,145 Families* (pp. 341–367). New Brunswick, NJ: Transaction.

Tower, C. C. (1996). *Understanding Child Abuse and Neglect.* Needham Heights, MA: Allyn and Bacon.

Turbett, J. P., and O'Toole, R. (1980). *Physician's Recognition of Child Abuse.* Paper presented at the annual meeting of the American Sociological Association, New York.

Ucko, L. G. (1994). Culture and violence: The interaction of Africa and America. *Sex Roles, 31,* 185–204.

Unger, S. (1977). *The Destruction of American Indian Families.* New York: American Association of Indian Affairs.

U.S. Bureau of the Census. (1991). *Statistical Abstract of the United States 1991* (11th ed.). Washington, DC: U.S. Department of Commerce.

Walters, J. L., Canady, R., and Stein, T. (1994). Evaluating multicultural approaches in HIV/AIDS educational material. *AIDS Education and Prevention, 6,* 446–453.

White, E. C. (1985). *Chain Chain Change: For Black Women Dealing with Physical and Emotional Abuse.* Seattle: Seal Press.

White, R. (1977). *Navajo Child Abuse and Neglect Study.* Baltimore: Department of Maternal and Child Health, Johns Hopkins University.

Williams, O. J. (1990). Spouse abuse: Social learning, attribution and intervention. *Journal of Health and Social Policy, 1,* 91–109.

Williams, O. J., and Griffin, L. W. (1991). Elder abuse in the black family. In R. L. Hampton (Ed.), *Black Family Violence* (pp. 117–127). Lexington, MA: Lexington Books.

Willis, W. (1992). Families with African-American roots. In E. W. Lynch and M. J. Hanson (Eds.), *Developing Cross-Cultural Competency: A Guide for Working with Young Children and Their Families* (pp. 121–150). Baltimore: Paul H. Brookes.

Wischlacz, C., Lane, J., and Kempe, C. H. (1978). Indian child welfare: A community team approach to protective services. *Child Abuse and Neglect, 2,* 29–35.

Wischlacz, C., and Wechsler, J. G. (1983). American Indian law on child abuse and neglect. *Child Abuse and Neglect, 7,* 347–350.

Young, L. R. (1963). *Wednesday's Children: A Study of Child Neglect and Abuse.* New York: McGraw-Hill.

Zambrano, M. M. (1985). *Mejor sola que mal acompanada.* Seattle: Seal Press. (Includes English translation.)

Zuniga, M. E. (1992). Families with Latino roots. In E. W. Lynch and M. J. Hanson (Eds.), *Developing Cross-Cultural Competency: A Guide for Working with Young Children and Their Families* (pp. 151–179). Baltimore: Paul H. Brookes.

Index

abandonment, 58, 204
  See also child neglect
abuse, definitions of
  in child abuse, 2–4
  in gay domestic violence, 165
  in elder abuse, 198, 199, 200
abusers. *See* offenders
academic deficits, as consequence of child
    physical abuse, 11
accommodation syndrome, 40
Accused, The, 89
acquaintance rape. *See* date rape
Acquaintance Rape: The Hidden Crime, 88
acquired immunodeficiency syndrome
    (AIDS), 161–162, 163, 165, 166
active neglect, 199
adaptive failure, 9
"Addictive Love" workshops, 106
Administration on Aging, 198, 210
adolescents
  beliefs about rape, 87, 95–96, 104
  as child physical abuse victims, 11
  as child sexual abuse offenders, 40
  neglect of, 68–69
  vulnerability to dating violence, 99
adoption, and child neglect, 64
Aetiology of Hysteria, 27
African Americans
  attitudes toward violence, 227
  children, overrepresentation as victims
    of abuse, 226, 227
  culture and traditions of, 232–233
  extended family, 231–232
  history of, immigration and slavery, 231
  male batterers, treatment of, 238
  rate of child neglect among, 72

and spousal violence, 227–228
Against Her Will, 89
Against Our Will: Men, Women, and Rape,
    87
age
  of child neglect victims, 72
  of child physical abuse victims, 9–11
  of child sexual abuse victims, 32, 35, 43
  and elder abuse and neglect, 206
  as lesbian battering factor, 186
  of parents, and child neglect, 66
ageism, 195
aggravated assault, 94
aggression, and child sexual abuse, 35
aggressiveness, as consequence of child
    physical abuse, 10
aggressors. *See* offenders
aging
  disengagement theory, 195
  of general population, 196, 197
  physical changes and self-concept,
    203–204
AIDS. *See* acquired immunodeficiency
    syndrome
alcohol abuse
  as child abuse and neglect factor, 66–67
  by child physical abuse perpetrators, 8
  as consequence of child physical abuse, 12
  and dating violence, 93, 101, 104
  and elder abuse and neglect, 204, 206
  and family violence, 147, 148–149
  fetal alcohol syndrome, 74
  by gay male domestic batterers, 167–168
  by lesbian batterers, 187, 189
  among Native Americans, 230
  and wife abuse, 125, 128

245

altered emotionality, as consequence of child sexual abuse, 34
Alzheimer's disease, 198, 205, 206
American Medical Association, Council on Scientific Affairs, 198
American Society for the Prevention of Cruelty to Animals (ASPCA), 1, 60
Antioch College, sexual harassment policies, 108–109
anxiety
    as child neglect factor, 66
    in child physical abuse perpetrators, 8
    as consequence of child physical abuse, 11
    as consequence of child sexual abuse, 34
Asian Americans
    child abuse and neglect among, 230
    culture and traditions of, 234–235
    origins of, 234
    wife abuse among, 229–230
ASPCA. *See* American Society for the Prevention of Cruelty to Animals
assault, definition of, 94, 164
attribution theory of dating violence, 101
avoidance, as consequence of child sexual abuse, 34

Baby Jane Doe, case of, 71
Barr, Roseanne, 29
battered child syndrome, 1–2, 28, 60–61, 95
battered husband syndrome, 95, 138, 139, 140
battered wife syndrome, 95, 131
Bohmer, Carol, 88
Brownmiller, Susan, 87
Brown University theater model on dating violence, 106
buffers, 5
bundling, 84

Caffey, J., shaken baby syndrome, 9–10
Campus Sexual Assault Victim's Bill of Rights, 108
CAPTA. *See* Child Abuse Prevention and Treatment Act

caregiver burden, 204–205
Catholicism, 233–234, 237
challengers, 5
Chicago Model for Child Abuse Prevention, 74
Child Abuse Amendment Act of 1984, 71
Child Abuse Prevention and Treatment Act (CAPTA), 30, 62–63, 71
child advocacy, 44–45
child development
    and child sexual abuse, 43
    parents understanding of, 5–6, 8, 66
    stages of, and child neglect, 67–69
    stages of, and child physical abuse, 9–11
Childhood Level of Living scale, 65–66
child molester
    characteristics of, 41–42
    definition of, 30
    extrafamilial CSA, 40
child neglect
    among Asian Americans, 230
    and child physical abuse, 3
    correlates of, 65–67
    definitions of, 57, 61–62
    integrated model of, 67–71
    legal issues, 74
    among Native Americans, 230–231
    organized efforts against, 58–60
    prevalence of, 59, 68
    prevention and treatment, 73–74
    recognition of, historical, 57–58
    recognition of, in medical community, 60–61
    research on, 64–65
    trends in, 74–75
    types of, 63
child physical abuse
    among African Americans, 227
    among Asian Americans, 230
    and child sexual abuse, 36
    cognitive-behavioral models of, 5–6
    definitions of, 2–4
    factors contributing to, 5, 7–9
    among Hispanics, 229
    models of, history, 4

among Native Americans, 230–231
organizational models of, 4–5
perpetrators of, characteristics, 6–9
prevention and treatment, 12–15
and race of victim, 226–227
recognition of, historical, 1–2
victims of, characteristics, 9–12
child-rearing. *See* parenting
child sexual abuse (CSA)
adaptation, 34
attitudes and beliefs toward, 26, 48–49
and child physical abuse, 3
definitions of, 29–33
denial of, 25–26
legal proceedings, 46–48
offenders, characteristics of, 40–42
prevalence of, 29, 33–34, 43
prevention and treatment of, 43–46
recognition of, historical, 27–29
time frame of, 34, 35
victims of, 26, 29, 43
Cincinnati Bengals, gang rape case, 89
Civil Rights Act of 1964, 122
civil rights movement, 28
close relationships research, 97
cocaine babies, 74
codependency theory of gay male domestic
abuse, 170
code switching, 232, 233
cognitive-behavioral models, of child
physical abuse, 5–6
cognitive distortions, as consequence of
child sexual abuse, 34
collectivism, 232–233, 234, 235
communication styles, and cultural
influences, 236
communication theory of gay male
domestic violence, 169
community
gay, reactions to domestic abuse, 163,
173, 175, 181–182
intervention in child neglect cases, 70
Neighbors Helping Neighbors report, 75
role of in child neglect, 70–71

compensatory factors in child physical
abuse, 5
competence, parental, 13, 14
conceptual models, of child sexual abuse,
36–37
Conflict Tactics Scales (CTS)
use of in dating violence research, 87,
102
use of in elder abuse studies, 202
use of in husband battering research,
141, 142, 144, 145
use of in lesbian battering studies, 183
control
as issue in elder abuse and neglect,
205–206
as issue in gay male domestic violence,
167
as issue in lesbian battering, 184, 188
violence as means of, 105, 124–125, 166
*Coping with Date Rape and Acquaintance
Rape,* 88
corporal punishment, 4, 14, 237
See also child physical abuse
counseling
in gay domestic abuse cases, 173–174
of lesbian battering victims, 191
in wife abuses cases, 129
courtship. *See* dating
criminal harassment, 93
criminal justice system
response to child neglect, 59, 74
response to child sexual abuse, 46–48
response to gay male domestic violence,
172, 175
response to husband battering, 152
response to lesbian battering cases, 192
response to wife abuse, 121–122, 128,
130–131
CSA. *See* child sexual abuse
CTS. *See* Conflict Tactics Scales
cultural bias, 227
culture
and child physical abuse, 4
and child sexual abuse, 37–38
and dating violence, 95, 104–105

culture *(continued)*
    definitions of, 231
    gay subculture, 190
    influence on intimate violence, 236–237
    of minority groups, 225
    non-Western, and child neglect, 61–62
    sensitivity to, in abuse prevention and
        treatment, 237–238
    and treatment of elders, 196
    and wife abuse, 125–126
cycle of child abuse, 38
    See also intergenerational transmission
cycle of violence
    and dating violence, 105
    and gay male domestic violence,
        170–171, 172

date rape
    emergence of, 87–90
    legal recognition of, 108
    preconditions model of, 88
    prevalence of, 95–96
    research on, 95
    Rohypnol, use of, 89–90
    theoretical model of causes, 97
dating
    history of, 83
    use of term in research literature, 91
dating violence
    among African Americans, 228
    beliefs and assumptions about, 96,
        107–108
    correlates of, 98–102
    definitions of, 90–94
    legal issues, 107–109
    legal status, 93–94
    prevalence of, 86, 95–96
    prevention and treatment, 105–107
    recognition of, history, 83–87
    research on, 94–98
    responses to, 101
    risk markers for, 101–102
    theories and models of, 97–98, 102
    types of, 86–87, 92
    See also date rape

Dating Violence Intervention Program, 106
Dating Violence: Young Women in Danger,
    87
death
    from child neglect, 63
    from child physical abuse, 9–10
    from domestic violence, 123
    spousal homicide, 146
    See also homicide
Declaration of the Rights of the Child, 59
dementia, 198
demographic factors, in child physical
    abuse, 7
denial
    of child sexual abuse, 25–26, 27, 45, 49
    in gay domestic violence, 167
    of wife abuse, 127
dependency
    and elder abuse, 199, 206–207
    and lesbian battering, 186–187, 189
depression
    in child physical abuse perpetrators, 8
    in child sexual abuse offenders, 42
    as consequence of child physical abuse,
        11
    as consequence of child sexual abuse,
        34
    of elder abuse victims, 206, 208
    in elders' caregivers, 205
    in gay male abuse victims, 170
    in wife abuse offenders, 124–125
detachment, as consequence of child
    physical abuse, 11
developmental theory
    of dating violence, 97–98, 102
    of gay male domestic violence, 169
disabilities
    and child physical abuse, 7
    effects of on lifestyle of elderly, 208
discrimination, wife abuse as, 123
disengagement theory, 195, 204
disturbed relatedness, as consequence of
    child sexual abuse, 34
domestic violence
    definitions of, 163–164

See also child physical abuse; child
sexual abuse; elderly abuse and
neglect; husband battering; lesbian
battering; male-to-male gay domestic
violence; wife abuse
Dotson, Gary, 89
drug abuse
as child abuse and neglect factor, 66–67,
70
and child neglect, 74
and child physical abuse, 8
and dating violence, 93, 104
and elder abuse and neglect, 204
and family violence, 147, 148
by gay male domestic batterers, 167–168
by lesbian batterers, 187, 189
and wife abuse, 125

ecological models
of child neglect, 65, 70
of child physical abuse, 4
economic conditions
and child physical abuse, 4, 13, 14
and child sexual abuse, 38–39
economic deprivation
in gay male relationships, 165
in lesbian relationships, 183
economic exploitation
in dating relationships, 92
in elder abuse, 198, 199, 200
education
African American attitudes toward, 232
Asian American attitudes toward, 235
Hispanic attitudes toward, 233
of medical personnel, about domestic
abuse, 198
Native American attitudes toward,
235–236
to prevent child neglect, 73
to prevent child physical abuse, 14, 15
to prevent child sexual abuse, 45
for preventing dating violence, 106
of support service personnel, about gay
male domestic abuse, 171, 174
educational neglect, 63, 72

elder
African American, 232
definition of, 196–197
elder abuse and neglect
abusers, characteristics of, 201, 204–205
case example of, 209
correlates of, 205–207
definitions of, 195–196, 197–200,
217–218
indicators of, 200–201
legal issues, 210–211
Older Americans Act of 1965, 210
prevalence of, 198
prevention and treatment, 207–209
recognition of, historical, 196–197
reporting of, 195, 219–220
research into, 201–202
theories of, 202–204
Elder Abuse and Neglect Act, 217–223
Elder Abuse Prevention Activities, 210
emotional abuse
as aspect of child sexual abuse, 32
and child physical abuse, 3
in dating relationships, 85, 92
of elderly, 200, 201
in lesbian relationships, 183–184
emotional neglect, 63
endangerment, child physical abuse as, 3
enduring conditions, 5
English common law, and spousal abuse,
94–95, 120
Erikson Institute for Advanced Study in
Child Development, 65
Estrich, Susan, 88
European Americans, and spousal abuse,
227–228
expert testimony, and child sexual abuse
cases, 47
extended family
African American, 231–232
and elder abuse and neglect, 205
and Native Americans, 235
and wife abuse, 125
external inhibitors, and date rape, 88
extrafamilial child sexual abuse, 31, 41

failure to thrive (FTT), 63, 200
family
    destabilization of, by aging of members,
        199
    extended, 125, 205, 231–232, 235
    lesbian households, 185
    nuclear, 125
    patriarchal, 125–126
    socialization function of, 125
family dysfunction model of family
    violence, 147–148
family systems model of child physical
    abuse, 4
fathers, and child sexual abuse, 40
FBI Uniform Crime Reports, and husband
    battering research, 146
federal approach to domestic violence,
    122–123
feminism
    antifeminist backlash, 89
    feminist model of family violence, 147,
        148
    perspective on wife abuse, 125–126, 144
    See also women's movement
Ferenczi, S., 28
fetal alcohol syndrome, 74
fetus, status of, 74
fictive kin, 205
Fields, M. D., 138–139
financial exploitation. *See* economic
    exploitation
flooding, 107
followers, and gang rape, 96
Forsyth County Aging Study, 209
Foster, Jodie, 89
Fourteenth Amendment, 171
French, Amy, 105
Freud, Sigmund, 25–26, 27–28
Freudian development theory, infant stage
    of, 68

gang rape, 89, 96
Gay and Lesbian Community Action
    Council, 161
gay bashing, 162, 184

gay domestic violence
    recognition of, historical, 162
    See also lesbian battering; male-to-male
        gay domestic violence
Gay Men's Domestic Violence Project, 174
Gelles, R. J.
    African Americans, rates of domestic
        violence among, 226, 227
    on husband battering, 139–410, 141, 153
    on intergenerational transfer, 188
    work with Suzanne K. Steinmetz, 138,
        139
    violence, definition of, 141–142, 183
gender
    of child neglect victims, 72
    role definitions, and dating violence, 98
General Hospital, 87
Great Depression, 83

Harris, Lynn, 90, 91
Harvard School of Public Health, 65
hate crimes
    rape as, 108
    wife abuse as, 123
Hate Crimes Statistics Act of 1990, 108
Hawaii Health Start, 73
health care, access to, and child neglect, 66
Health Families of America, 74
Health Families of Illinois (HFI), 74
health problems
    and child neglect, 66
    and child physical abuse, 7
    and elder abuse, 205, 206
    and wife abuse, 128
healthy life measures, 208
hearsay, in child sexual abuse cases, 46–47
heterosexist control, 165, 184
hidden nature of abuse, 119, 121, 163
high school students, and dating violence,
        94, 100
Hispanics
    child abuse among, 229
    culture and traditions of, 233–234
    definition of, 233
    male dominance theory, 229

rate of child neglect among, 72
rates of spousal violence, 229
HIV. *See* human immunodeficiency virus
home visitation programs, as child neglect
    prevention method, 73
homicide
    battered husband defense, 151–152
    and child abuse, 9–10
    and domestic violence, 123
    of gay men, 163
    spousal, 146
homophobia, 165–166, 181, 187, 190, 192
homosexuality and depression, in CSA
    victims, 35
hostility, and child physical abuse, 8
House Select Committee on Aging, 197
human immunodeficiency virus (HIV),
    165, 166
husband battering
    among African Americans, 228
    correlates of, 147–150
    definitions of, 141–143
    as diversion from wife battering, 137
    offenders and victims, characteristics of,
        150–152
    prevention and treatment, 152–153
    recognition of, historical, 138–141
    reporting of, 145
    research on, 143–146
    as self-defense, 143
    and wife abuse, debate on, 139, 140,
        143–144
hyperactivity, as consequence of child
    physical abuse, 10

impaired self-reference, as consequence of
    child sexual abuse, 34
incarceration, for wife abuse, 131
incest
    characteristics of, 31–32
    definition of, 32
    vs. extrafamilial CSA, 31, 41
    general denial of, 25–26
    intergenerational transmission of, 42
    offenders, characteristics of, 40–42

as symptom of dysfunctional family,
    39
    victims of, 43
Indian Child Welfare Act, 230–231
individual, definition of, 67
individual perspective on wife abuse,
    124–125
individual psychopathology model for
    domestic violence, 147
Industrial Revolution, 58
I Never Called It Rape, 88
infants
    as child physical abuse victims, 9–10
    as cocaine babies, 74
    neglect of, 63, 67–68
informed consent, 32
inhibitors of violence, 125
initiators, and gang rape, 96
interactionist theory, of elder abuse,
    205
intergenerational conflict, 196, 204–205,
    206
intergenerational transmission
    breaking the cycle of, 49
    and child physical abuse, 7
    and child sexual abuse, 38, 42
    and dating violence, 101
    definition of, 12
    and gay male domestic abuse,
        168–169
    and husband battering, 147–148
    and lesbian battering, 188, 189
    and wife abuse, 126–127
internal inhibitors and date rape, 88
International Convention on the Rights of
    the Child, 59
Internet
    as dating violence research source, 98
    husband battering case on, 151
interpersonal factors, and dating violence,
    101
intervention strategies for dating violence,
    106
intrapsychic factors and dating violence,
    101

isolation
  as child neglect factor, 66
  of child physical abuse victims, 12
  as child sexual abuse factor, 38, 39
  as consequence of child sexual abuse, 34
  and elder abuse, 202, 204, 206, 208
  in gay male relationships, 165, 166
  and lesbian battering, 181, 187
  as wife abuse factor, 127–128

jealousy
  and dating violence, 101
  and gay male domestic violence, 168
  and lesbian battering, 186, 188
juvenile delinquency, as consequence of
  child physical abuse, 11

Kanin, E. J.
  on attitudes of college men to rape, 87
  on male aggression in dating, 85
Kempe, Dr. Henry, battered child syndrome
  article, 1–2, 28, 60–61
Kempers Institute, 65
Kids Count Data Book, 75
Kinsey, et al. on incest, 28
Kirchner, R. M., 138–139
Kluft, R. P., personal reaction to subject of
  incest, 26
Knutson, J. F., hyperreactivity and child
  physical abuse, 7
Koss, Dr. Mary, 88

labeling, risks of, 26–27
language
  as form of identification among African
    Americans, 232
  of Native Americans, 236
  as unifying factor for Hispanics, 233
lawyers, role of in child sexual abuse cases,
  48
learned helplessness, 131
legal proceedings
  in child sexual abuse cases, 46–48
  in dating violence cases, 107–108

in elder abuse or neglect cases, 220
  evidence of child physical abuse, 3
legislation
  child abuse, mandated reporting of, 2, 62
  Child Abuse Amendment Act of 1984, 71
  Child Abuse Prevention and Treatment
    Act (CAPTA), 30, 62–63, 71
  Civil Rights Act of 1964, 122
  on dating violence, 91
  on elder abuse and neglect, 210–211
  Elder Abuse and Neglect Act, 217–223
  on gay male domestic violence, 171, 174
  Hate Crimes Statistics Act of 1990, 108
  Indian Child Welfare Act, 230–231
  Older Americans Act of 1965, 210
  revised to include gay victims, 192
  to stop child abuse, in Britain, 60
  Student Right-to-Know and Campus
    Security Act of 1990, 108
  Victims of Crime Act of 1984, 108
  Violence Against Women Act of 1993,
    122–123
lesbian battering
  attitudes and beliefs about, 181–182, 190
  batterers, characteristics of, 188–189
  correlates of, 185–188
  in dating relationship, 98, 99
  definitions of, 183–184
  effects of, 189–190
  prevalence of, 161
  prevention and treatment, 190–192
  recognition of, historical, 181, 182–183
  research on, 184–185
  victims, characteristics of, 189–191
life expectancy, 197
loneliness, and child physical abuse, 8

machismo, 233
McNeely, R. L., 140
Makepeace, J., courtship violence among
  college students study, 86, 91
  developmental theory of courtship
    violence, 97–98, 102
  on research methodology, 86

male social support model of dating
  violence, 102
male-to-male gay domestic violence
  batterers, profile of, 167–169
  and cycle of violence, 170–171
  definitions of, 164–165
  effects of, 171
  and gay community, 163, 173, 175
  myths about, 162–163
  prevalence of, 161–162, 174
  preventive strategies, 171–174
  recognition of, historical, 162–163
  victims, profile of, 169–170
marital conflict
  and child neglect, 69
  and child sexual abuse, 42
Marx's conflict theory, 184
mass media, role of in child abuse
  prevention, 14–15
mediation, as intervention in wife abuse
  cases, 128–129
medical neglect, 63–64, 72, 200
men
  aggressiveness of, *vs.* women, 142
  as child sexual abuse offenders, 40
  as dating violence offenders, 87, 95
  as murderers, characteristics of, 146
  relationship between sexual and physical
    violence, 98
  as victims of elder abuse, 205, 206
men's movement, 141
mental illness
  in child physical abuse perpetrators, 4, 8
  as consequence of child physical abuse, 12
  and elder abuse, 204
  and husband battering, 151
  and individual psychopathology model
    of family violence, 147
mental retardation
  and child neglect, 64
  and elder abuse, 204
Merrill, Greg, 161
Minneapolis Domestic Violence
  Experiment, 130, 172–173

Minnesota Coalition for Battered Women,
  106
Minnesota Mother-Child Interaction
  Project, 65
minority groups
  and child neglect, 69
  and child physical abuse, 3
  definitions of abuse, 142
  gay male victims of abuse, 165, 166
  and need for cultural competency in
    abuse prevention and treatment,
    237–238
  percentage of population, 225
  vulnerability to dating violence, 99
  See also African Americans; Asian
    Americans; Hispanics; Native
    Americans
*Morning After: Sex, Fear, and Feminism on
  Campus, The,* 88–89
mothers
  and child neglect, 69
  and child sexual abuse, 40, 42
motivation, for date rape, 88
Ms. magazine, date rape article, 88
mutual violence
  in dating relationships, 86
  in marriage, 144
  See also symmetrical violence

*Naming the Violence: Speaking Out about
  Lesbian Battering,* 182–183
National Center on Child Abuse and
  Neglect (NCCAN), 62–63, 64
National Center on Elder Abuse, 197
National Child Abuse and Neglect Data
  Systems, 63
National Clearinghouse on Family
  Violence, 93
National Committee to Prevent Child
  Abuse, 74
National Crime Victim Survey (NCVS),
  123, 144
National Domestic Violence Hotline
  number, 107

National Family Violence Resurvey, 123, 140

National Family Violence Survey, 138, 139

National Institute of Justice, 173

National Institute on Drug Abuse, 66–67

National Society for the Prevention of Cruelty to Children (Britain), 60

National Study of the Incidence and Severity of Child Abuse and Neglect, 226

Native Americans
child abuse and neglect among, 230–231
culture and traditions of, 235–236
definition of, 235
reporting abuse, special problems with, 236–237

NCCAN. *See* National Center on Child Abuse and Neglect

neglect
definition of, in elder abuse and neglect, 198, 199–200
in gay domestic situations, 164
in lesbian battering, 183

Neighbors Helping Neighbors, 75

New Hope for Women, 93

New York Society for the Prevention of Cruelty to Children, 1, 60

norm of reciprocity, 204

nuclear family, 125

Oaker, MaryRose, 197

offenders
abusers of elderly, 201, 204–205
child neglect, 69, 71–72
child physical abusers, 4, 5–7
child sexual abusers, 40–42
in dating violence, 103–104
gale male batterers, 167–169
husband batterers, 147, 150–152
identification as, and race, 226
lesbian batterers, 188–189
meaning and use of term, 27
wife abusers, 124–125, 126–128

Older Americans Act of 1965, 210

oral sex, forced, 94

organizational models of child physical abuse, 4–5

Pagelow, M. D., 139

parenting
and child neglect, 65–66
and child physical abuse, 5–6, 8–9
practices of African Americans, 227, 232, 237
practices of Asian Americans, 234–235, 237
practices of Hispanics, 233, 237
practices of Native Americans, 235
and treatment of child abuse, 13–14

parents
and child neglect, 63, 69
and child physical abuse, 4, 5
and incest, 40, 42
single, 7, 42, 69, 71
young, 7, 66, 69, 74
See also stepparents

parricide, 196

Parrot, Andrea, 88

passive neglect, 199

patriarchal culture
and child sexual abuse, 37–38
and domestic violence, 229, 236
and husband battering, 148
and male violence, 84
and wife abuse, 125–126

pedophilia, 30

people of color. *See* minority groups

People v. Walker, 151–152

Pepper, Claude, 197

perpetrators. *See* offenders

personality attributes model of child sexual abuse, 37

Phil Donahue Show, 89

physical abuse
in dating relationships, 92
of elderly, 199, 200
in gay male relationships, 165
in lesbian relationships, 183

physical handicaps, and child physical abuse, 7

physical neglect, 63
physicians
    caregiver race and abuse reporting by, 226
    child physical abuse, recognition of, 1
    role of in child sexual abuse cases, 48
Playboy magazine, date-rape hype article, 88
police
    and gay community, 172, 192
    response to lesbian battering calls, 192
    role of in child sexual abuse cases, 48
    role of in wife abuse cases, 121–122, 128, 130–131
    See also criminal justice system
posttraumatic stress disorder
    as consequence of child sexual abuse, 34, 35
    and dating violence, 107
potentiating factors, in child physical abuse, 5
poverty
    as contributing factor in child abuse, 14
    as contributing factor in child neglect, 64, 66, 69, 70, 72
    as contributing factor in child sexual abuse, 38–39
    as contributing factor in husband battering, 148
    as contributing factor in wife abuse, 125
    percentage of minority groups in, 225
power. *See* control
preadolescents, neglect of, 68
pregnancy
    and dating violence, 99
    and wife abuse, 126
prejudice
    against minorities, 225, 226
    See also homophobia
prevention
    of child physical abuse, 12–15
    of child neglect, 73–74
    of child sexual abuse, 43–46
    of elder abuse and neglect, 207–209
    of gay male domestic abuse, 171–174

of husband battering, 152–153
of lesbian battering, 190–192
of wife abuse, 128–130
primary prevention
    of child neglect, 73
    of child physical abuse, 13
    of child sexual abuse, 44–45
    of elder abuse and neglect, 207–208
prison. *See* incarceration
probation, and wife abuse, 131
promiscuity, as consequence of child sexual abuse, 34
prostitution, as consequence of child sexual abuse, 34
protective components, 5
psychiatric model of child physical abuse, 4
psychological abuse
    in dating relationships, 93
    of elderly, 199
    in gay male relationships, 165
psychosomatic illness, and child physical abuse, 7
puberty, 69

race
    of child neglect victims, 72
    See also minority groups
racism, and dating violence, 99
rape
    acceptability of, 96
    child, 41
    definition of, 94
    false allegations, 98
    laws, 89, 108
    in male-to-male gay domestic relationships, 165
    myths about, 104
    prevalence of, 95–96
    See also child sexual abuse; date rape; gang rape; sexual assault
reactive attachment disorder of infancy, 63
Real Rape: How the Legal System Victimizes Women Who Say No, 88
reckless endangerment, definition of, 94

religion
    and African Americans, 232
    and Asian Americans, 234, 235
    and Hispanics, 233–234
    and Native Americans, 235
    and victim's reaction to abuse, 237
reporting of abuse
    child abuse, 2, 62
    child sexual abuse, 48
    cultural influences on, 236
    elder abuse, 195, 219–220
    gay male domestic abuse, 163, 170
    husband battering, 145
    lesbian battering, 185, 190, 191
    Native Americans, special problems
        with, 236–237
    wife abuse, 121
research methodological design
    of child sexual abuse studies, 33, 36, 38
    of dating violence studies, 86–87
    of husband battering studies, concerns
        about, 144, 145–146
resiliency, in child sexual abuse victims,
    49–50
resilient adults, 27
    See also survivors; victims
restraining orders
    and gay male domestic violence, 172
    and husband battering, 152
retaliation, and dating violence, 101
Rideout case, 89
right to confront accuser, and child sexual
    abuse cases, 47
Robinson-Simpson, G., 140
Rohypnol, 89–90
Roiphe, Katie, 88–89
Roman Law of the Twelve Fables, 58
romanticizing, and dating violence, 99
Ronald McDonald Children's Charities,
    74
roofies. *See* Rohypnol
rule of thumb, 95, 120

safety
    of battered husbands, 152–153

of lesbian victims, 192
    steps for abused to take, 106–107, 174
salutogenic approach to study of CSA, 49
Saunders, D. G., 140–141
schools, role of in child sexual abuse cases,
    48
secondary prevention
    of child neglect, 73, 74
    of child physical abuse, 13
    of child sexual abuse, 44, 45
    of elder abuse and neglect, 208
self-concept
    and dating violence, 101
    and elder abuse and neglect, 203–204
    and wife abuse, 127
self-control, and wife abuse, 124
self-defense
    and dating violence, 101
    and husband battering, 143, 146
self-destructiveness
    as consequence of child physical abuse,
        11
    as consequence of child sexual abuse, 34
self-esteem
    of battered husbands, 150–151
    and child neglect, 63
    of child physical abuse perpetrators, 8
    of child physical abuse victims, 11, 12
    of child sexual abuse victims, 34–35
    of elder abuse victims, 204
    of gay male abuse victims, 170
    of gay male batterers, 167
    of lesbian battering victims, 189
    of wife abuse victims and batterers, 126
self-neglect, 207, 208, 209
senility. *See* dementia
sexism, and dating violence, 98–99
sexual abuse
    in dating relationships, 92, 93
    of elderly, 200
    in gay male relationships, 165
    in lesbian relationships, 184
    and physical violence, 98
    in wife abuse, 127
    See also child sexual abuse

sexual assault
and child sexual abuse, 32, 35
definition of, 94
and husband battering, 143
*Sexual Assault on Campus: The Problem
with the Solution,* 88
sexual deviancy and dysfunction, as
consequence of child sexual abuse,
34, 35
shaken baby syndrome, 9–10, 67
shelters
for gay men, 171
for lesbian victims, 191–192
for men, 152
for women, 128
Shotland, R. S., 97
situational model, of elder abuse, 202
sleep disturbance, as consequence of child
physical abuse, 11
Smith, William Kennedy, 89
social class differences, as lesbian battering
factor, 186
social exchange model, of elder abuse, 202,
202–203
social factors in child physical abuse, 7
social information processing model of
child physical abuse, 5–6
social interaction model of child sexual
abuse, 37
social learning theory
of dating violence, 102
of gay male domestic violence, 169
social services agencies
and child physical abuse, 3
and child sexual abuse cases, 47, 48
and gay male domestic abuse, 171–172,
173
societal perspective on wife abuse, 125
society
and child sexual abuse, 43–44
role of in child neglect, 71
sociobiological model of child physical
abuse, 4
sociodemographic factors and dating
violence, 102

sociological model of child physical abuse,
4
sociopolitical theory of gay male domestic
violence, 169
sodomy
definition of, 94
forced, in gay male relationships, 165
Sousa, Carol, 106
spousal abuse
and dating violence, 94
history of, 94–95
See also husband battering; wife abuse
stalking, 152
State of Florida v. Lloyd, 89
Steinmetz, Suzanne K., 138–139
stepparents, 7
stigmatization of CSA victims,
perpetrators, and families, 45
Stockholm syndrome, 107
Straus, M. A.
African Americans, rates of domestic
violence among, 227–228
on child abuse and young mothers, 69
on class and domestic violence, 148
Hispanics, rates of domestic violence
among, 229
on intergenerational transfer, 188
on male *vs.* female injuries in domestic
violence, 149
on mental illness and domestic violence,
141
on husband battering, 139–140, 141, 153
on substance abuse and domestic
violence, 125, 147
and use of Conflict Tactics Scales, 87
violence, definition of, 141–142, 183
work with Suzanne K. Steinmetz, 138,
139
See also Conflict Tactics Scales
stress
and arrival of baby in family, 67
and child physical abuse, 8
and dating violence, 101
of elder abuse victims, 205
and elders' caregivers, 199, 200, 202

stress *(continued)*
 as lesbian battering factor, 189
 as wife abuse factor, 125, 128
stroke victims, 198
structural conditions approach. *See*
 feminist model
Student Right-to-Know and Campus
 Security Act of 1990, 108
substance abuse
 as child neglect factor, 64, 66–67
 in child sexual abuse offender, 42
 See also alcohol abuse; drug abuse
suffrage, 121
suicide
 and dating violence, threats of, 103
 and victims of child physical abuse, 11
support systems
 and child neglect, 72
 and dating violence, 99
 for elderly, 197–198, 206
 and gay male domestic abuse, 173, 175
 in schools and shelters, 106
survivors
 of child sexual abuse, 26, 29, 49
 meaning and use of term, 27
 See also victims
symbolic interactionism, 203
symmetrical violence, 141, 142, 143, 145
systems theory, and child sexual abuse
 correlates, 37, 39

Tailhook Naval harassment scandal, 89
Teen Dating Violence Project, 106
television violence and aggressive
 behavior, 15
tertiary prevention
 of child neglect, 73, 74
 of child physical abuse, 12–13
 of child sexual abuse, 44, 45
 of elder abuse and neglect, 208
testosterone, levels of and wife abuse,
 125
theater model, of dating violence
 prevention, 106
therapy. *See* counseling

Thompson, Emily, 60
threats
 in dating relationships, 85, 93
 in elder abuse cases, 204
 in lesbian battering, 183, 188
transactional models of child physical
 abuse, 4, 5
transient conditions, 5
trauma
 and child sexual abuse, 32
 and dating violence, 107
Tyson, Mike, 89

United Nations
 Declaration of the Rights of the Child,
 59, 61
 International Convention on the Rights
 of the Child, 59
 International Year of the Child, 61
Unity House Families in Crisis Program,
 153
U.S. Advisory Board on Child Abuse and
 Neglect, 75
U.S. Department of Health, Education, and
 Welfare Children's Bureau, 61, 62
U.S. Senate Subcommittee on Children and
 Youth, 61

value systems, factor in lesbian battering,
 186
vandalism, 165
verbal abuse
 in dating relationships, 91
 by elders' caregivers, 204
 and legal definition of domestic
 violence, 122
 in lesbian battering, 183
Verdicchio, Nadean, 153
victim blaming, 162, 167
victim resistance to date rape, 88
victims
 bill of rights, 130
 of child neglect, 67–69, 69, 72
 of child physical abuse, 9–12
 of child sexual abuse, 26, 29, 39–40, 43

of date rape, 90
of dating violence, 103
of elder abuse, 205
of gay male domestic abuse, 169–170
of husband battering, 148–149, 150–152
of lesbian battering, 189–191
meaning and use of term, 26–27
relationship to abuser, and legal status, 122
resiliency, 49–50
treatment of, by legal and social system, 48
of wife abuse, 124, 126–128
Victims of Crime Act of 1984, 108
violence
    categories of, 138–139
    as characteristic of child sexual abuse offender, 42
    definitions of, 91, 142
    life span of, 201
    as means of control, 105
    and race, relationship between, 226
    symmetrical, 141, 142, 143
Violence Against Women Act of 1993, 122–123
Violence in Dating Relationships: Emerging Social Issues, 87
vulnerability components, 5

Walker, L.
    cycle of violence, 170–171
    See also cycle of violence
Warshaw, Robin, 88
weapons
    and dating violence, 92, 103
    and husband battering, 138, 139, 142
    and wife abuse, 123
When He's Not a Stranger, 89
wife abuse
    among African Americans, 227–228
    among Asian Americans, 229–230
    beliefs about, 127
    correlates of, 124–126
    criminal justice system, role of, 121–122, 128, 130–131
    definitions of, 122–123

among Hispanics, 229
and husband battering, debate on, 139
intervention and treatment, 128–130
offenders and victims, characteristics of, 126–128
prevalence of, 123–124
recognition of, historical, 119, 120–122
reporting of, 121
trends, 130–131
Wilson, Mary Ellen, 1, 59, 60
Winfrey, Oprah, 29
witnesses in child sexual abuse cases, 48
women
    African American, 232
    and alcohol abuse, physical susceptibility, 187
    as child sexual abuse offenders, 40
    as dating violence offenders, 86, 87, 95
    as dating violence victims, 86, 87, 105
    as domestic violence victims, 123
    forms of violence used by, as different from men, 139–140
    as husband batterers, 141
    as murderers, characteristics of, 146
    race of, and victimization, 226
    relationship between sexual and physical violence, 98
    status of, and wife abuse, 124–125, 126
    stereotypes of, and lesbian battering, 181–182, 187
    subjugation of, 95
    as victims of child sexual abuse, 34
    as victims of elder abuse, 205, 206
    violent behaviors or, 139, 142
women's movement
    and criminal justice system response to wife abuse, 130
    and lesbian battering, 182
    and recognition of child sexual abuse, 28
    and recognition of sexual violence, 89
    and recognition of spousal abuse, 95, 138
    and recognition of violence against women, 162
World War II, 83

Other Books from
Butterworth-Heinemann

Contemporary Criminal Law
David T. Skelton
1997   400pp   pb   0-7506-9811-X

Crime and Justice in America: A Human Perspective, Fifth Edition
Leonard Territo, James B. Halsted and Max L. Bromley
1998   707pp   hc   0-7506-7011-8

Criminal Investigation: Law and Practice
Michael F. Brown
1997   368pp   pb   0-7506-9665-6

Introduction to Law Enforcement: An Insider's View
William G. Doerner
1997   400pp   pb   0-7506-9812-8

Workplace Violence: Before, During, and After
Sandra L. Heskett
1996   210pp   hc   0-7506-9671-0

Detailed information on these and all other BH-Criminal Justice titles may be found in the our catalog(Item #800). To request a copy, call 1-800-366-2665. You can also visit our web site at: http://www.bh.com

These books are available from all good bookstores or in case of difficulty call: 1-800-366-2665 in the U.S. or +44-1865-310366 in Europe.

E-Mail Mailing List

An e-mail mailing list giving information on latest releases, special promotions/ offers and other news relating to Butterworth-Heinemann Criminal Justice titles is available. To subscribe, send an e-mail message to majordomo@world.std.com. Include in message body (not in subject line) subscribe bh-criminal-justice